WILLIAM AND ELEANOR GRAYSON

By Lucy Baker

IV

Library of Congress Pre-Assigned
Control Number200799934433
Copyright 2008
By Lucy Baker-Dickey
ISBN: 978-1-929440-13-9
Printed in China
Bisac: His 036030, His 036120

Nautilus Publishing Company
4807 Brighton Lakes Blvd.
Boynton Beach, FL. 33436
Since 1981
San: 299 9501

12/2010

B
GRA

William Grayson
And the
Constitution,
1788

Debates in the Commonwealth of Virginia
On the Adoption of the Constitution

In the words of the patriots

William Grayson: Patriot, Founding Father, Colonel in the Revolution, aide to Gen. Washington, Member, House of Burgess, House of Delegates, Continental Congress Senator from Virginia in the First Federal Congress

By Lucy Baker
Fourth Great Granddaughter of William Grayson

WITH GRATITUDE TO:
The Patriots of Virginia
And the members of
The Virginia Ratifying Convention of 1788
The
Library of Congress,
"Letters of Delegates to Congress,"
1784 through 1788
"American Memory"
And the
"U.S. Congressional Documents and Debates"
1765 to 1788

With special recognition for the sixty seven pen and pencil illustrations of Benson J. Lossing, from "The Pictorial Field-Book of the Revolution" Vol's 1 & 2, Published in 1850, Harper & Brothers, New York.

List of Illustrations by the Author:

Drawings of William Grayson as a teenager, as a young man, in Congress, in mid-life and at 54, the year he died and an illustration of how Belle Air Mansion might have been and all drawings of Eleanor. Six drawings.

With much gratitude for assistance with historic facts to:
Don L. Wilson: Virginiana Librarian, Ruth E. Lloyd Information Center for Genealogy and Local History Prince William Public Library System, Bull Run Regional Library, 8051 Ashton Avenue, Manassas, Virginia, 20110-2892 www.pwcgov.org/library/relic.

Editor: Lori Saunders, Phd

Graphic Art direction, cover, pictures and text
Alan Hammerschmidt

This book is lovingly

DEDICATED TO THE MEMORY
OF

WILLIAM GRAYSON

And to the People of The Old Dominion
Whose persistence & dedication
Gave us Liberty and a new
Nation with Sound Government

This text provides the speeches of the Patriots at the Virginia Ratifying Convention of 1788, according to the Library of Congress files of the Delegates to Congress, volumes 1784 through 1788 and letters from 1785 to 1789.

TABLE OF CONTENTS

PREFACE

This book is intended to re-awaken the memory of William Grayson whose depth of commitment and dedication to the cause of liberty and justice has been forgotten. May this effort help a great American regain his position as Patriot and Founding Father. Grayson should be remembered for helping to secure liberty for America under the rule of Law.

Please forgive perfections and errors in fact. Much information was found in musty, old manuscripts.

Moments on a bloody Battlefield or in a shouting rant in defense of a motion in Congress; were no less intense whether over war or ideals The passionate acts of the patriots who formed a Republic and pledged their hearts and lives to unite thirteen states into a free nation, were heroic acts of selflessness with no appropriate earthly reward.

Founding Fathers in satin trousers and powdered wigs, with elegant manners outwited, coerced, inveigled or persuaded their peers over ideologies or to win their vote.

Splitting into factions, our forefathers dueled with words to create a Constitution that for the first time in history, protected the rights of the individual while the world watched in fascination.

Virginia and Massachusetts had more than their share of patriots who helped create a new Nation under a sound government, where men were free and unencumbered.

We honor the sacrifices of our Founding Fathers and are eternally grateful for their sublime leadership.

In the copies of original letters, I left the spelling and words as I found them unless they were indecipherable. William Grayson's speeches are given in full. Other speeches may be summarized, omitted or paraphrased for meaning & content.

GOD BLESS AMERICA, AS HE BLESSED OUR PATRIOTS

Other Books by Lucy Baker

1. The Life of William Grayson, a Screenplay
    ISBN: 978-1929440-14-6
2. William Grayson and The Constitution, 1788
    ISBN: 978-1929440-13-9
3. Poppelsdorfer Allee
    ISBN: 978-1929440-11-5
4. Dark Before Dawn
    ISBN: 978-1929440-10-8
5. Secrets of Lost River
    ISBN: 978-1929440-01-6
6. Miracles
    ISBN: 978-1929440-00-9
7. Heart of Stone
    ISBN: 978-1929440-05-4
8. In Six Months You Get Bananas
    ISBN: 978-976-8056-85-6
9. Birds of the Caribbean
    ISBN: 978-976-9501-60-7
10. Second Edition ISBN: 978-1929440-17-0

11. Fish of the Caribbean
    ISBN: 978-1929440-04-7
12. Poisonous Plants of the Caribbean
    ISBN: 978-1929440-03-0
13. Treating Ailments With Plants and Herbs
    ISBN: 978-9769501-62-1
14. Journey Towards The Light
    ISBN: 978-1929440-07-3
15. Miracles, a screenplay
    ISBN: 978-1929440-08-5
16. Heart of Stone, a screenplay
    ISBN: 978-1929440-09-X

AUT LIEBER, AUT NULLUS

WILLIAM GRAYSON AND THE CONSTITUTION, 1788
INTRODUCTION

William Grayson, (1736-1790) was born in an era of America's greatest historic accomplishments, and not surprisingly found himself in the center of the eighteenth century's most stupendous events.

In William's youth Virginia was one of thirteen colonies that stretched from New England to Georgia, with a vast region amounting to thousands of acres between the northern and southern states. The early eastern coastal states were part of a mammoth land mass that stretched westward for more than three thousand miles, the nucleus of a mighty nation. Millions of forested acres west of the Atlantic ocean fired the imagination and in the era to follow, would be explored and settled. Exploration would consist of high adventure and excitement, but nothing compared with the events of monumental importance to America that were to occur first.

Spain, England and France all had holdings in America in the eighteenth century, but in the year of William's birth, 1736, no one had envisioned uniting the huge land mass into a mighty nation with a unique government that would elect their representatives to serve in a bi-cameral congress with a president elected by the people and given extraordinary powers.

Gradually, reacting to minor offenses that proliferated into major tyrannies, a few brave men came forward with a cry for freedom and independence and began to form a plan. Quickly their message spred across the land.

William Grayson was among the fortunate men, who became leaders of the new nation. They were called Patriots and Founding fathers, and their opinions on national and local affairs were greatly sought after.

Virginia was not the only colony to foster patriots and heroes. Each colony had its share, however, Virginia vied with Massachusetts to produce the most remarkable number of the new Republic's most passionate and brilliant leaders.

RALEIGH TAVERN: Willsbg, VA. When Lord Dunmore dissolved the House of Burgess on Sept 27, 1774. the patriots assembled here in the Apollo Room

In conversation with his brother Spence and their cousin James Monroe, sixteen years William's junior, a flame was lit that fanned the fire of freedom and these cousins with similar dreams began to organize what would become a struggle for liberty that would involve war with Britain, one of the mightiest nations on earth.

William had a special fondness for James, the son of his mother's brother James. Suzanna Monro Grayson loved her brother and his son while young James doted on his older cousin William who introduced James into the political scene while he was quite young.

Gathering others to their cause, their numbers grew. Soon remarkable deeds were accumulating in the name of liberty. Britain scorned the colonist's bravado, underestimating how badly the colonists wanted freedom and how fed up they were with British rule.

William Grayson rendered himself completely to the quest for freedom and the founding of a new nation, and used all the talent and strength he possessed in that quest. No one donated greater quality or variety of services than William Grayson. Young men in 1775 looked ahead and saw adventure, ultimate victory and the thrill of battle. No cause was more heady than a fight for liberty.

William Grayson was cherished in Virginia and through his work, became well known throughout the colonies. William had years of active membership in the House of Burgess, (where no list of members remains), the House of Delegates and four years in the Continental Congress. William was a national figure in American politics, yet today the name of William Grayson is scarcely mentioned in the history of the Revolution, and he remains unknown to most Americans. The causes for this anonymity are multiple and though William Grayson was not ambitious of fame he deserves to be remembered and honored for his sacrifice to Virginia and the nation he loved so well.

William was born with every advantage and brimmed with self-confidence. He was excruciatingly aware of his advantaged life, without daring to exploit circumstance or exact other than friendship and loyalty from his peers, the most famous men in America. Later in life he would experience the heartbreak and calumny that struck a spear into the very heart of loyalty and undying friendship.

William formed ideologies and dreamed in gigantic proportions, finding himself one of the best educated men among his peers with a law degree from so prestigious a place as Oxford. In those days just as now, that mattered greatly, With spectacular ideas, and supreme efforts, a new nation would be born.

No matter what happened, William would be on hand to participate in the glorious adventure and like all patriots, was prepared to lay down his life if necessary.

One of William's highest priorities was to assure equality for men of all class and race. He was not alone in this pursuit Accompanied by his close friends and allies, Patrick Henry, Richard Henry Lee, and George Mason among legions of Virginians of like minds, this overwhelming principle would be accomplished.

Early on, William showed signs of prescience and made a few predictions that could not fail to come true. One concerned lasting enmity between the north and the south, the other, the need to develop the land to the west, and last, that the Mississippi River be kept in the ownership of America and available for the sole use of Americans and not that of any other country.

William Grayson's dedication and sacrifice is recorded here, that he might receive the honor he deserves for his service to Virginia and the nation that he loved with all his heart.

William Grayson died before the history the Revolutionary era was written, and when histories were compiled, authors turned to survivors, who, after the revolution, continued to lead lives of commendable service, accruing for themselves even more fame. The lives of Marshall, Tyler, Pendleton, Monroe, Adams, Jefferson and Hamilton were equally distinguished, but since they survived and continued to hold high office, after the framing of the Constitution, they more often became the subjects of biographies. Authors are attracted to well-known entities not obscure ones, and survival became another factor in selecting worthy subjects.

William Grayson was well equipped for his role in America's fight for freedom and the aftermath of forming a solid republican government. As an elected representative, William held the Articles of the Constitution in his hands at the convention in Richmond, Virginia in June of 1788 where

187 members gathered on a warm summer day to vote for or against the new document. In the middle of that august committee stood a small mahogany table on which lay a slim sheaf of papers calle the Constitution. Each member had his own highly marked copy. They were closeted in a large, room and without prompting began to dissect every article, section and clause, knowing their duty was to vote on whether the Constitution should replace the familiar Articles of Confederation that had served in

America as the rule of Law since the tumultuous year of 1777.

Through the month of June, these men argued and debated over every nuance, agonizing that an important consideration was missing, protection for the rights of the individual. There were other divisive issues of substance that when presented, electrified the air in that hot, shuttered room. Armed with moral fiber and unquestionable integrity, Grayson's legalistic mind and superb education enabled him to pronounce judgments that brought accolades or vitriolic attack from the best minds and smartest company in Virginia, whose job it was to read and fully assess the "Paper on the table."

After years in Congress and many speeches in the convention, William would be called the greatest debator of the era. At his right hand was his close friend Patrick Henry, clearly the greatest orator of the century. The one called the second best orator was William and Henry's good friend and ally in most things, James Innis.

Most of the patriots of the Revolution were dead by the time histories of the era were compiled. By then, consideration for who were the greatest contributors, was a subjective matter. In place of formal histories, books and biographies, posthumous to Grayson, yet contemporary to distinguished actors in the drama of history, and in the absence of abundant material, authors were inspired by personal motives, to panegyrize deceased patriots. Despite the best motivations, the contributions of many great men were virtually ignored while others were exaggerated.

Grayson never had a biographer, although Hugh Blair Grigsby did an admiral study of Grayson and became an unwitting admirer. In the book, "Pictorial field book of the Revolution," Benson J. Lossing describes Grayson as eloquent, handsome and brilliant, the greatest debator of his era. Grigsby's hand drawn pictures and sketches were done one hundred and fifty years after the great battles of the American revolution. Carting his sketch-book, Lossing walked the fields, lanes and by-ways to the exact location of historic events, there to sketch and take notes, final-izing his text through available research ma-terial. With exacting efforts, Lossing learned all he could about William Grayson and then wrote about him in glowing terms. Archival documents and papers were published in which Lossing, Schroeder and other seekers of truth uncovered facts yielding partial, if tardy justice to departed patriots. Men like Robert Harmon Harrison from Maryland, a

lawyer and scholar, who succeeded Joseph Reed as Washington's Secretary in the Continental Army, was one of William Grayson's closest lifelong friends, for whom he named a son. Harrison, in like manner was not sur-passed in patriotism or ability, but dying as he did, a few months after William Grayson, serves as an example of historic bias, as little is said about Harrison's considerable contribution. George Washington would otherwise not have offered Harrison a prestigious seat on the Supreme Court, not once, but twice. Both times Harrison declined; for an unsuccessful run for the presidency, (against Washington), but mostly because of Harrison's bla-tant opposition to the Constitution as it was drafted and before any amend-ments were discussed or added. Harrison became as outspoken as Grayson on the Constitution, even though he was from Maryland.

William Grayson was the grandfather of William Grayson Carter, Kentucky State senator, and Confederate General John Breckinridge Grayson. The latter Grayson was also the grandson of Kentucky Senator John Breckinridge (1760-1806) of the Breckinridge political family, who were also related to Senators Henry Clay and Thomas Hart Benton. William Grayson's tenure in the U.S. Senate as the first United States Senator from Virginia, was limited to 1789 to 1790 due to his untimely death. He served in the first congress beside Richard Henry Lee who received the largest number of votes, while James Madison came in third and William second. Madison went on to become a member of the House of Representatives, a disappointing position, lacking the power of a senator in that decade.

William served in the Continental Congress from 1784 to 1787.

Reverend Spence Grayson

Congress first met in Carpenter's Hall, Philadelphia on september 5, 1774. The keynote speaker, Patrick Henry, said, "I am not a Virginian, but an American" to enormous cheers.

The Continental Congress' last sessions were in New York from November 3 to March 2, 1788.

After William's untimely death, his first cousin, James Monroe took William's congressional seat for the unexpired term. There was doubt that Monroe had learned his politics at Grayson's knee. Monroe would become the 5th President of the U. S. and a very fine one. William would have been so proud. The cousins were close all their lives.

WILLIAM 'S PERSONAL LIFE

William Grayson was born in 1736, the third son of Benjamin Grayson who propitiously married Susannah Monroe; a beautiful, twice widowed heiress. Susannah inherited the fortunes of two previous husbands, Charles Tyler and William Linton. She had two sons by Tyler and a son and a daughter by Linton. After her marriage to Benjamin Grayson, their children were raised together and developed lifelong relationships.

John Tyler who served with William Grayson in the Virginia Ratifying Convention in 1788, was a close friend who would father the tenth president. He was not William's step-brother of the same name.

William and Spence remained close to William Linton, their half-brother who operated an Ordinary in Colchester. They also kept company with Charles Tyler another step-brother. Their mother Susannah heir to the founder of the Monroe/ Munro family dating back to "Ocaan, Prince of Fernaugh," the chief of a Scottish clan, driven from Scotland to Ireland in the 4th century. Ocaan dwelt by Lough Foyle, on the Roe water, about 1000 AD, from whence came the name Munro (Man from Roe). Duncan I, King of Scots in 1034, was descended from the first Munro, as was William I, Duke of Normandy, King of England, who in 1066 led the Norman invasion of England.

In 1640 a sea captain, Andrew Monroe, arrived in Virginia, married and fathered a son name Andrew, who in turn fathered James Monroe. The Grayson lineage was connected to Scotland and England through John Grayson, who was born in Kent, Deal, England in 1656, and came to America as a young man.

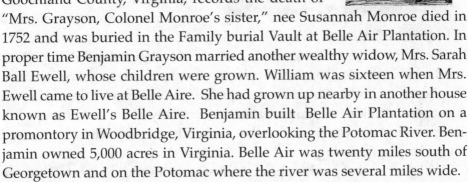

John Grayson died in 1736, the year William Grayson, son of Benjamin Grayson, was born.

The St. James Northam Parish register of Goochland County, Virginia, records the death of "Mrs. Grayson, Colonel Monroe's sister," nee Susannah Monroe died in 1752 and was buried in the Family burial Vault at Belle Air Plantation. In proper time Benjamin Grayson married another wealthy widow, Mrs. Sarah Ball Ewell, whose children were grown. William was sixteen when Mrs. Ewell came to live at Belle Aire. She had grown up nearby in another house known as Ewell's Belle Aire. Benjamin built Belle Air Plantation on a promontory in Woodbridge, Virginia, overlooking the Potomac River. Benjamin owned 5,000 acres in Virginia. Belle Air was twenty miles south of Georgetown and on the Potomac where the river was several miles wide.

Benjamin Grayson senior, was a captain in the militia, a guardian to a number of wealthy children as well as the executor of several large estates. His main occupation was planter and merchant. These labors coupled with two advantageous marriages made him a rich man. hence, the Grayson offspring enjoyed advantages reserved for the privileged who grew up in the finest society and were handsome, talented and intelligent. William's sister Susannah was described as a beautiful heiress. Before they went to school the Grayson children were tutored at home by the best teachers available.

As young men the Grayson sons learned how to duel and handle guns. They rode well and had their own horses. William's favorite pastime was racing his horses in local competitions with other horse lovers, which meant gentleman of means. Sometimes the competitions were held at Mount Vernon in the company of George Washington. Fine horses remained a lifelong passion for William.

Benjamin insisted that his sons learn how to run a plantation knowing that one day they would have their own, and must know how to plant and harvest, the importance of shade trees and orchards and how to keep financial records. They had many slaves so the children were taught from an early age to treat slaves with respect.

In William's youth, a black boy named Punch became William's companion. Punch drove William's carriage, and accompanied him to college as his valet and manservant, and attended him through the war years, the sessions in congress and was by his side on the sad day that William passed into heaven in September of 1790. William's father died in 1757. William

THE JERSEY PRISON-SHIP.‡

inherited 2,800 acres, 20 slaves and ten thousand pounds. Benjamin Grayson senior was buried in the Grayson Family Burial Vault at Belle Air, beside his beloved Susannah. The Grayson's Vault was fashioned after George Washington's vault at Mount Vernon and is in dire need of restoration.

William's brother Benjamin became his legal guardian until William reached majority. William's financial account during those years, indicated that he spent considerable money on pleasure, including betting on horses, eating and drinking at ordinaries in the company of his male friends; behavior typical of a young swain who was handsome and rich and possessed a healthy zest for living.

William cared about his appearance as most men did in the eighteenth century. His wardrobe contained fine clothes, leather shoes with silver buckles, thick woolen capes, jackets and fine linen shirts with monograms, lace neck cloths and many adornments.

William's brother Spence was two years older than William and an outstanding person whom everyone loved. Spence sailed to England to study and came back wearing the austere ministerial garments of a priest in the Church of England, (Episcopalian). Spence was a favorite of George Washington's, who asked Spence to officiate at the wedding of his nephew Augustine Washington, so named after George Washington's father.

Spence Grayson served as the rector of Cameron parish and then at Dettigen parish in Prince William, County, Virginia.

William and Spence were often guests at Mount Vernon and received Martha and George Washington at Belle Air and Grayson's Hill. Spence Grayson served as Chaplain to William's regiment during the American revolution. Spence and William's elder brother Benjamin, a merchant and judge, eagerly pursued their father's financial success, however, Benjamin's ill temper and intolerant behavior was a serious dilemma for a viable business man or a circuit court judge. Benjamin's disasterous dabbling in real estate inevitably netted enormous losses. Desperate for money, Benjamin exploited his role as guardian to his syblings, borrowing heavily from Spence and Susanna's trust funds, thereby depleting their inheritance .

Angry and bitter at his misfortune, Benjamin got into more scrapes that culminated in crude and humiliating lawsuits for battery, trespassing and assault. Public embarrassment forced Benjamin to retire from the bench and ended his misbegotten deeds, but there were legal ramifications to follow that effected his family.

In 1758 William was twenty-one when he left home to attend the College of Philadelphia, later to become the University of Pennsylvania. Punch accompanied him as servant, valet and driver.

Entertaining grandiose dreams of glory, in 1760 when he was 23, William bought himself a marvelous sword with an ornately crafted sil- ver hilt for the sum of 110 pounds. A family could live on that sum for a year. William could

MOUNT VERNON, VIRGINIA, George Washington inherited The estate from his brother Lawrence, Who named the place for Admiral Vernon

not resist the purchase to accessorize his expensive new wardrobe for his journey to London to continue his studies at the close of 1760.

Upon his arrival in London, William enrolled in the Middle Temple, an Inn of the Court, where he studied diligently to master Latin and Greek, as well as the classics and sciences. Having a feel for the law, William went on to Oxford to obtain a degree in Law. William was adept at English history and literature and became an authority on both. His Latin was excellent. He developed the habit of correcting those who spoke Latin less well.

One of William's favorite authors was Jean Louis De Lolme, who wrote the "Constitution of England," a book William often quoted.

Through a natural affinity for the law, and being an earnest student, William developed a parliamentary brilliance, along with a remarkable ability to ascertain facts and elucidate them for the benefit of others, often with a withering sarcasm that was both entertaining and scathingly effective. These tactics diligently applied proved helpful in his pursuits as diplomat, lawyer and politician, and were enhanced when accompanied by a winning smile and honest charm born of sincerity and competence. William 's extreme good looks and obvious advantages predicated success. Since childhood, William had been indoctrinated in the tenets of morality and religion and held fast to the highest principles. As an idealist, nothing was more important to him than personal integrity.

A shining opportunity was fast approaching and William was primed to to respond and in fact, had been preparing for such a time. Nothing was more heady to a young man than fighting for their country's freedom.

By 1764, William Grayson was the possessor of the finest education available in America or England. He was getting a late start after years of pursuing pleasure and fulfilling minor incentives. With new goals in place, William proved himself an excellent student and a scholar. His legal expertise would be an invaluable asset in his public life.

The only position ever desired by William Grayson, other than the military, was to be a judge of the Court of Chancery in 1787. He spoke to James Monroe about spreading the word that he would be interested in an appointment, but nothing ever came of it. Shortly thereafter William was elected to the highest post of his career; Senator from Virginia to the Federal Congress, but much would occur before that event.

In England, having caught wind of Benjamin's disgrace in 1764, William returned to Virginia earlier than planned, eager to participate in the fight for independence, but first he would marry his sweetheart Eleanor Smallwood, the daughter of a Baltimore, Maryland magistrate. Her brother William Smallwood, was Governor Of Maryland. Washington would appoint him general in the Continental Army. Their father, Bayne Smallwood, was a Charles County delegate to the Maryland Assembly and a Justice of the Maryland Superior Court.

William and Eleanor's first son, Alfred (Frederick) William, was born in 1764. another son, George Washington Grayson followed in 1767, and a daughter, Hebe in 1769. Lastly Robert Harrison Grayson arrived in 1771 if our calculations are correct.

Belle Air plantation was a short ride by horseback to Mount Vernon. William and Spence often made the trip for fox hunting, or to shoot birds and sometimes stayed overnight or for a weekend. William was five years younger than Martha Washington.

Early in life, George Washington became William's idol and mentor. One day William brought his cousin James Monroe who was sixteen-years younger, to meet George Washington, who took an immediate interest in the lad and a warm, lasting relationship began that day.(1) Washington was not disappointed in Monroe, except perhaps, on the occasion of the Virginia Ratifying Convention when James Monroe voted with William against the Constitution.

By 1788, nothing could be done about foreign debts or impending problems of national importance without a working, viable government. Knowing this, Washington was anxious to effect a working government.

William Grayson was the most handsome man in Congress. His appearance like his manners was noble and elegant. He stood well over six feet and his hair was thick and as black as a raven's wing, his large eyes deep set, black and shiny. His complexion was robust and his teeth remarkably white and well formed. His lips were full and well shaped. His head was large, his noble brow high and wide. William weighed two hundred and fifty pounds by the time he reached thirty. Many commented on how grand and well turned out he was astride a horse. Soon he would wear the brilliant uniform of a colonel and ride his horse to war and finally have an appropriate use for his grand sword.

In 1783 Washington and some of his officers were weighed at West Point. Washington weighed 209 pounds, Gen. Lincoln 224, Gen. Knox 280, Gen. Huntington 132, Col. Swift 219, Col. Henry Jackson 230, Lt. Col Huntington 232, Lt. Col Cobb 186, Lt. Col Humphreys 221 pounds.

Possessor of an exuberant personality, gifted with wit and charm, William was unaccustomed to holding his thoughts in check and was often outspoken. It was not unusual for him to be caustic or highly derisive if the occasion warranted. Likewise, his highly developed sense of humor was unbridled and William was generous in its use. While walking with Edward Carrington and Judge St. George Tucker, in New York, Grayson was so amusing that his friends could scarcely keep on their feet, for laughing, while William showed no emotion at all. William's passion and sense of honor could evoke acerbic rhetoric if confronted with injustice. Naturally, he quickly discovered the value in using his incredible wit as a tool, a well sharpened weapon against his political opponents whom he could wither with scorn or cause to blanch under a barrage of deprecating remarks.

Strong in principles, William stood with those who voted against the Constitution, the Anti-Federalists, who fought hard for amendments to the Constitution. Some historians say the Anti-Federalists best exhibited the qualities of democracy by espousing political equality.

Clearly William chose the military as his role in the cause of freedom. Politics would come later. Undoubtedly he wanted his mentor George Washington, to be proud of him. Serving in the Continental Army was a special calling with the likelihood of war with England looming near.

VIRGINIA IN THE EIGHTEENTH CENTURY

After the revolution, Virginia was divided into ten districts. One day have ninety-five Counties, by far the largest state in the union. Virginia gave the government a marvelous gift by most graciously ceding more then

CHARLES CITY COURT HOUSE, VIRGINIA
Smallest Cnty in Virginia. Birthplace of President Tyler and William Henry Harrison, the town where Jefferson married Martha Skelton, (23) a widow. They had two daughters

half its land mass for the sole benefit of the federal government. Thereby dividing the "Old Dominion" into six states: West Virginia, Ohio, Kentucky, Illinois, Indiana, and Virginia.

After the war for independence, the fledgling nation was bankrupt, unable to pay even the interest on their loans from Holland, France and Spain. Once sold, the land ceded by Virginia to the Federal Government that accounted for most of the northwest territory up too the Mississippi river, the United States would be able to settle their foreign debts and avoid a possible takeover by a foreign power, Washington's main worry. Washington was desperate that the Constitution be ratified, to begin the business of governing to secure the nation from foreign interests. As Commander in chief, Washington feared the arrival of ships from foreign nations, fighting offshore, for the newly declared nation, so poor as to beg for help from foreign nations.

Exhausted by eight years of war, America was left with the remnants of a ruined economy. Many homes and families had been shattered by war and the entire nation weakened by internal strife and dissent. Politicians were of three basic types: Progressive, reactionary or radical, all striving to form and defend a Republican government, while pursuing individual aims with a sanguine mix both personal and political.

Virginians living in the tidewater region were different from those living in the north or west sections of Virginia, and their needs varied from those of the residents of the Piedmont, the western area near the magnificent Blue Ridge Mountain, yet all were proud to be a part of Virginia.

Virginians put aside personal preferences to address the mutual problem of taxation and the role of state versus a strong central government called (Consolidation.)

Even more pressing was the implementation of the Judicial system as stipulated under the Constitution; accepting a Federal Judiciary into each state in lieu of their familiar, theretofore completely adequate State Court System and their personally known and trusted local judges. Virginians wanted courts that were accessible by foot, rather than travelling for miles to mandatorily attend Federal courts.

The new document, the Constitution, called for Federal courts to take over many of the cases formerly handled under the jurisdiction of the state courts, thereby provoking a major controversy in the state and Federal judicial system. William, with a host of supporters spoke against any diminution of the authority of the state Courts and considered any disruption in their solidarity to be a blatantly false manipulation. Most attorneys agreed on this principle or lack thereof.

Much of the arable land in Virginia's Northern Neck, from the Potomac to the Rappahannock, on towards the Blue Ridge Mountains, was controlled by a few rich families who out of fairness and a valuable source of income, leased a large portion of their holdings to tenants. Therefore, only 30% of the inhabitants of the Northern Neck owned land. The majority of owners, had farms smaller than two hundred acres, and many had less. Only land-owners could vote, so the wealthy controlled the economy and policy decisions. The Northern Neck was the area of the aristocrats,  those with money, breeding and privilege. Of the 100 richest families in Virginia, 55 lived in Northern Neck. In the southernmost part of Virginia, half the adult men owned their own land and far fewer leased. Here was Virginian's middle class. Virginians were responsible for the payment of their share of the large state debt, from the war. Certificates and paper currency issued by both sides during the revolution, were re-evaluated. Most paper money was in the northern states giving northerners an advantage in paying their taxes. A majority of Virginia's counties had insufficient funds to pay their portion of the state debt. Then there was the problem of private debts to foreign countries and personal loans from Englishmen.

Land sold for a dollar an acre. Grayson thought the price should be raised to $1.50 an acre, and eventually higher. Land was the nation's greatest commodity, one that was plentifold.

The Southside of Virginia was depressed and unable to meet their share of the taxes, consequently, they were ridiculed and called slothful. Getting states to pay their share of taxes was a nationwide problem. Regarding the law and its enforcement concerning collecting taxes was a gross inadequacy in the Articles of Confederation along with the problem of how to enforce the treaty with Britain over treatment of loyalists who remained in the colonies. Another was the money owed to British firms and the matter of slaves who had been abducted or lured away by the British under unrealistic promises.

Lastly, England had the temerity to expect to keep British military posts that they had built and operated for years in the colonies, under the aegis and ownership of England, which America was adamantly against for obvious and reasons.

In 1784, a bill was passed in Congress that dealt with conflicts in the treaty with England, demanding that all slaves be returned or the treaty would be abandoned. The Southside of Virginia was adamantine against repayment of loans or removal of restrictions against Loyalists who remained in Virginia. There was abundant rancor and bitterness on all sides and pent up anger that went unassuaged.

The British outposts north of the Ohio river, were rightly blamed for continuing Indian attacks that frightened the population and obstructed the natural movement westward where thousands of acres waited development. Indians especially, hated the military forts, and constantly attacked them and the areas surrounding them. Expansion was a neccesity. In the words of William Grayson, "Without westward expansion there will be no great nation."

An uproar erupted in Congress in response to a motion for " consolidation;" an all-powerful central government that would end any thought of self-rule throughout the colonies. How far would the factions veer from established goals? Some members preferred a strong central government, while others preferred the familiar terms of the Articles of Confederation. Virginians were basically willing that Congress remain powerful within the framework of the Confederation, but this original flawed document contained no leverage for collecting taxes; besides there were flaws in the control of commerce in the Articles of Confederation. (2)

Gentlemen planters were proud of their breeding stock, elegant horses and sturdy work animals. Planting and maintaining fruit- bearing orchards that provided jams and jellies for the table and to grace their lands was a considerable occupation for gentlemen planters who took pride in their orchards and vineyards and happily shared their root stock and seedlings with other planters. In a long letter to George Washington, March 10, 1785, William Grayson wrote, "With respect to the Aspen and Yew trees (Washington had asked for) I beg leave to acquaint you that I sent to Sprigg's ford to see if the tree which the Doct. had giv'n me had produc'd any scions, and was inform'd there were none; I then applied to Mr. Landon Carter who had several at his plantation on Bull Run; Mrs. Grayson whom I left at Mr. Orr's promis'd me to carry them behind her carriage to Dumfries & to send them from thence to Mount Vernon together with any scions of the Yew tree which she with the assistance of Doctr. Graham and Mr. R. Graham, might procure." (3)

Wealthy families sent to England or France for furnishings, wallpaper and fabrics, and competed in building fine homes and show places, furnishing them with choice items from Europe. Europe also dictated the fashions for men and women, especially the styles worn

A CALECHE

at court. Objet d' art and chinoiserie from China were in high demand, especially china, porcelains, silk fabrics and marvelously constructed designs of landscapes and nature's rapture transferred to wallpaper with gorgeous birds and flowers were the rage in America and Europe. Women waited for months for deliveries from China.

The eighteenth century was known for its grace and elegance. Men were graceful even in fighting and dueling with a proper display of English manners. Clothes were either homespun or highly fashionable and truly gorgeous. Although the colonists could not compete with the protocol established at the royal Courts of Europe, most Americans held royalty in high regard.

Men wore white neck cloths, fresh each day, and for special occasions, lace jabots, brocade waistcoats, velvet vests, satin trousers and stockings of black, gray or white silk. Men of quality, taste and wealth, wore silver or gold buckles on their shoes and belts, and handsomely pressed silver buttons on coats, vests and uniforms. Jewelry was beautifully fashioned of gold with precious stones. Men wore rings and broaches of precious or semi precious jewels. Women wore jewels in their hair and men wore jewels in the ruffled lace jabots, over their breasts, on their lapels or on ribbons that stretched across their chests.

SERIOUS CONSIDERATIONS FOR WILLIAM

On February 27,1766, Richard Henry Lee, who became William's lifelong associate, wrote the "Leedstown Resolution," otherwise called the "The Westmoreland Resolves,"(R.H. Lee was from Westmoreland). Richard had two brothers: Francis Lightfoot Lee and Arthur Henry Lighthorse Lee and his brothers, Harry Lee and Richard Bland Lee were cousins. The latter fathered Robert Edward Lee.

William Grayson signed the document, protesting repeated tyranny by the Brits against the colonies, the latest, "The Stamp Act." The "Resolve" concerned birthright privileges, Reason, Law, and Compact, declared:

"If anyone deprives a person of these rights they would become a most dangerous enemy;" this concise document was straight forward in warning the colonists not to trust the English, and recommending that the colonists stand together against their assaults and misdeeds. This was one of

VIRGINIA MARKET WAGON

the first documents to recommend dis-allegiance from England, self-rule and independence. (4)

Many colonists remained loyal to the crown, for one reason or another, and hoped the British would adjust their policies and restore peace, and prayed that the colonists determined on independence would re-align their beliefs.

The law in America was based on English Law. William was devoted to the writings of De Lolme and the Baron de Secondat, a French author, known as Montesquieu, whom the most learned of the patriots quoted to the extreme, as a mark of their knowledge.

In 1766, George Washington and William Grayson served on the vestry at Truro Episcopal Church in Fairfax County, Virginia. In 1767, William was appointed attorney for the parish: "To prosecute suits for this parish, be now appointed attorney in fact for the parish, that he receive all moneys and tobacco arising from fines and judgements, and account with the vestry annually for the same, at the laying of the parish levy."(5)

In congress on December 11, 1788, Mr, Harrison reported a bill to incorporate the Episcopal Church. On December 22, it passed the House by a vote of 47 to 38. Madison, Marshall, Grayson, Ben Harrison of Berkeley, J. Jones, Miles King, Joseph Jones of Dinwiddie, Joseph Jones of King George, Thornton, Corbin, Willis, Riddick, Eyre, Ronald, Ruffin, Edmunds of sussex, and Briggs voted Aye. Incorporating the Protestant clergy of the Episcopal church was the ultimate issue. A major religious controversy began at the first Assembly in 1776 and legislatively terminated in 1802 with an order to sell the glebe lands, infusing bitterness and anger on both sides that would be judged throughout the accumulative history of the church and remain a problem for centuries to come. On February 27, 1766, William Grayson became the leader of the "Committee of Correspondence" as the situation with England worsened. The outcry against English oppression grew, committees were formed, resolutions and pamphlets were circulated with fervor, embuing a legion of heroes, like William Grayson, with the fire of freedom.

WILLIAM'S MILITARY CAREER BEGINS

On November 11, 1774, William organized a company of Virginia Militiamen, called "The Independent Company of Cadets. "Their motto, "Aut Liber, Aut Nullus, "without liberty, there is nothing, and, "Resolved unanimously that Thomas Blackburn, Richard Graham and Phillip Richard Francis Lee, gentlemen, do wait on Col. George Washington and request him to take command of this company, as its field officer and that he will be pleased to direct the fashion of their uniform, that they also acquaint him with the motto of their company which is to be found upon their colors."(6) Washington yielded to solicitations from various companies and reviewed them at appointed rendezvous." William was elected Captain of his militiamen (7) and wrote to Washington thanking him for providing muskets.

John Page wrote to Thomas Jefferson, saying, "William Grayson is highly deserving of encouragement. Do introduce him and recommend him to your friends. He will make a figure at the head of a regiment. He displayed Spirit and Conduct at Hampton." He had seen Grayson looking magnificent on horseback at the head of a column. (8)

On December 9, 1774, William was voted one of twenty-five members of the "Committee of Safety." He was moving into a higher realm of politics and service. So outstanding was his commitment and appearance, that Major General Charles Lee wrote a letter to his Commander in Chief, George Washington:

"I have been desired to recommend William Grayson as a man of extra merit. He sets out soon to make application to the Congress for an establishment." (9) George Washington knew William Grayson and was well aware of fine qualities. William Grayson was in Washington's confidence and so was Spence. Their sister Susanna had married John Orr in 1761 when she was sixteen. John had come from Whitehaven, Scotlandas a merchant and carried his beautiful bride to his 400 acre estate at Leedstown, Virginia. John's father was the Reverend Alexander Orr of Haselside, County Ayr, Scotland and his mother was Lady Agnes Dalrymple of Waterside County, Scotland who was born in July 1720.

Lund Washington wrote: "Grayson enjoyed the intimacy and esteem of General Washington to a large extent." Washington already believed iin William's potential and agreed with Major General Charles Lee's assessment. Soon William would wear the beautiful sword and ride his finest stallion into war and the pages of history. From Washington's Diary: "Nov. 25, 1768. Mr. Bryan Fairfax as well as Messrs. Grayson, and Phil Alexander

came here by sunrise. Hunted and catched a fox with these and my Lord, his brother and Colonel Fairfax, all of whom with Mrs. Fairfax and Mr. Watson of England, dined here."(10)

In June, 1775, Washington was chosen to command the Army in the American cause and Lund Washington, to accommodate his distant cousin, arrived in Virginia to manage Mount Vernon in Washington's absence. Lund would stay at the estate from 1775 to 1785.Meanwhile, Lund Washington married Susan, Monroe, Spence Grayson's daughter and continued to gather information, letters and memoirs from Susan's family regarding their history, William and Spence Grayson's careers and personal life. Lund wrote, "It does not fall within the scope of this sketch to write a panegyric or even a biography of Col. Grayson. All that it can do is present a synopsis of the prominent events of his life. The husband of my wife's grandmother's sister, Susanna Monroe, lived during the lives of the persons in this record, and I am but relying upon copying, the papers written by him 30 or 40 years ago. I am also indebted for some data from my cousins, (by marriage), the late Col. Peter G. Washington and Mr. Frederick William, Spence Grayson of Philadelphia, and from what I have learned from older members and family friends." (11) Lund took an enormous interest in the Grayson family Spence owned Belle Air. He married Mary Waggoner and they had seventeen children. Three of Spence and Mary's children died in infancy. They were fortunate that so many survived, for so many children died at birth or in childhood during the eighteenth century. The rest of Spence and Mary's children were raised at Belle Air.

GRAYSON'S HILL

William and Eleanor needed a place to live, so William bought acreage in Dumfries, 26 miles from Georgetown, where he built a large house, stables and houses for their slaves and overseer. Here William and Eleanor created a beautiful, productive plantation. The rich, virgin soil of Virginia blessed them with a hearty harvest. William kept a stable of horses, an orchard of fruit trees and planted some lovely, large shade trees.

William and Eleanor raised their four children at "Grayson's Hill" in

Dumfries, Virginia, six miles south of Belle Air in Woodbridge, Virginia. In 1768 William Grayson was often away from home so Eleanor visited her family in Maryland. In William's absence the small estate in Dumfries flourished. They had eight slaves and an overseer on the tax roles, and a tidy, plantation, complete with a fine orchard. The rolling hills looked lovelier every spring and the town was thriving. By appealing to the town council of Dumfries, William Grayson was granted

A River Bateau.

acreage on a very hilly site on the western perimeter of the town, on which he built his estate, two sizable, brick houses, numerous outbuildings, pens and stables for farm animals and stalls for his thoroughbreds. The high hilltop was fed by a deep swift flowing stream, known as Grayson's creek, an offshoot of the fast flowing Occoquan river. The creek and all other tributaries have long since vanished, choked by rubble and debris from an enormous landfill of the 20th century, put there by Potomac Landfill owned by the Crippen family.

In 1765, William set up his Law practice in the bustling town of Dumfries, Virginia, where he represented his neighbors and friends, including George Washington, Robert Carter, a major land baron, and George Mason a gentleman of impeccable manners and education. Occasionally William represented a penurious client, pro bono, establishing a reputation for not only being smart and capable, but charitable as well.

Nearly two hundred years after William Grayson's death, on Tuesday, May 15, 1983, Donald L. Wilson, a noteworthy historian and librarian visited Grayson's Hill in Dumfries with two archaeologists from the Northern Virginia Chapter of the Archaeological Society of Virginia where they made a topographical map of the site, locating the foundation ruins of two brick houses of the period of William Grayson. This was before the site was buried under the landfill. Also discovered were remains of outbuildings and coarse red earthenware, pieces of Rhenish Stoneware, Chinese blue-white porcelain, creamware, (including royal and featheredge plate fragments), delftware, fireplace tiles and white saltglaze stoneware, dating to the period of William Grayson's residency. A Bellarmine jug was found intact, as well as rosehead nails, fragments of spurs, a boar's tusk and flat brass buttons of the Revolutionary war era. Don Wilson saw that this information was sent to the Virginia Historical Society. Other investigators have identified brick from the 18th century and roof slate rubble and expensive crockery on Grayson's Hill before it was buried under a disgusting twentieth century landfill, and mountain of trash and debris.

Famous Grayson's Hill was used as a redoubt during the Civil Way by Confederate forces. Cannons were placed strategically to lob shots at Union Army vessels as they sailed up the Occoquan. A graveyard of Confederate

THE OLD MAGAZINE
Williamsburg, Va. Site where Lord Dunmore removed the powder and Patrick Henry made him pay for it.

soldiers and many relics of the military redoubt on Grayson's Hill are lost to investigation or memorial markers and deeply buried under tons of debris.

On December 12, 1782, he and Eleanor sold a tract of land on the Occoquan to William Helm. (12) In the fall of 1788, the mansion at Grayson's Hill was destroyed by fire while William Grayson was serving in Congress. William arranged to move his family to Fredericksburg, Virginia where they owned property. In January of 1790 bought 800 acres and a grist mill in Frederick county. He also bought 124 acres and a dwelling house with more mills in Frederick County.

The Virginia census of 1787 for Prince William County indicated that there were two sons at home with the Grayson family. Perhaps they were George, born in 1766, who would be 21, and Robert Harrison Grayson who would have been sixteen. Eleanor would have preferred to live in town, had she not been so ill. William had long planned to send his eldest son, Alfred William Spence Grayson to study in France and had been seeking advice on the particulars. Alfred was very bright.

With his finances in chaos by 1788, William Grayson signed a note to Robert Bogess for 294 pounds, mentioned in an appellate court case. William Grayson was mortgaging, buying and selling much land in Prince William County by March, 1789. (13) On July 6, 1789 Bertrand Ewell and his wife Frances sold Grayson a tract of land in Dumfries of 40 acres, between Fulsom's Branch and Warehouse Branch.

In January, 1790, Grayson sold land in Dumfries to Alexander Henderson. William also bought 124 acres with a dwelling house and mills in Frederick County and again in the same year he bought 800 acres and a grist mill in Frederick County. The Grayson's most likely moved to this country house in Fredericksburg after their house in Dumfries was destroyed by a massive fire. Grayson's library and private papers were destroyed as well as all their personal belongings.

After years of sacrifice in the military, Grayson's finances were in bad shape. To add to their problems, Eleanor was ill. Neither knew they were on the brink of tragedy.

It was difficult leaving Eleanor to face so much alone, especially when she was not well, but Eleanor had often been left alone and had coped well in William's absence for she was capable and courageous and kept her condition secret so William would not worry while fulfilling his responsibilities in Congress. For men of that era duty came first.

The fire in at Grayson's Hill destroyed Grayson's personal papers and his library which contained familiar titles by his favorite authors, Jean Louis De Lolme and Baron de Montesquieu, along with his collection of books in Latin and Greek and books on the law.

Unfortunately there are not many original letters left, but there are abundant copies of letters and speeches from the eighteenth century written by or to William Grayson.

Dr. Jon Kukla discovered documents written by Grayson at the University of Virginia, which inspired "Freedom and Good Government: Anti-federalist William Grayson's Intended Amendments to the United States Constitution." (14)

A myriad of speeches and letters of William Grayson represent the manner in which Grayson expressed his ideas and philosophy and the result of his efforts in the House of Delegates and Congress, along with the Virginia Ratifying Convention where he shared the leadership with Patrick Henry, James Monroe, Richard Henry Lee and a substantial list of many other who were quite naturally sympathetic with the Anti-Federalists.

James Madison stood in heated opposition to those who were against the Constitution and finally allowed that some changes might be possible. Basically, James Madison took the criticism of the Constitution personally. William's military service is clearly defined; the battles, his courage, and the valor he displayed at Monmouth Court House.

The record of his life is remarkable and provides a portrait of William Grayson as a brave Patriot, soldier, Founding Father and being a deeply religious family man.

DUMFRIES, VIRGINIA

Dumfries, Virginia is credited with being the first chartered town in the United States in 1749, incorporated in 1961.

In the early eighteenth century, Dumfries was a well populated, prominent address, a desirable place to live and to operate a business. Merchants flocked to the small town and built brick mansions and large warehouses on or near the deep harbor on Occoquan Creek. Tall masted ships from Europe arrived regularly, bringing much needed provisions and luxury items that were not yet available in America.

Benjamin Grayson senior, William's father, manufactured hearty biscuits that were daily fare on shipboard and popular with ship's chandler's and grocers. These "crackers" sold as far up the James River as there were settlements, and there were many that extended deep into Indian country.

THE BATTLE FIELD AT MONMOUTH, June 28, 1778

People made their home in Dumfries because of the services and industries at hand and because it was in an active seaport with a large population, everything that was desirable.

William's law practice was successful and provided extra income, although his primary source of revenue was from the property he owned and leased. His reputation as a just and clever man was growing in the region, however, outside the south, he was still unknown.

In Dumfries, there were any number of men with wealth. There were also craftsmen and artisans, farmers and shoemakers. The town thrived. Then disaster struck quickly and without recall.

Due to the rapid development of farms and plantations along the various waterways and streams that fed off the Occoquan and the James river, tons of topsoil were loosened by farming or constructing buildings. This detritus flowed downstream to the harbor forming layer after layer of silt on the bottom of the creek-bed a development dangerous to deep drafted ships from Europe who arrived regularly. Remedial efforts to clear the harbor failed, as the flow of loosened soil silted onto the harbor floor. Soon, it was impossible for ocean-going ships to navigate up the creek to the port of Dumfries, and the port was quickly abandoned in lieu of nearby ports, one on the Potomac at Georgetown, and another at Baltimore, Maryland. Overnight, Dumfries sank into oblivion. A major fire in 1848 destroyed the pier, the warehouses and public buildings and the remainder of the grand houses on Main street. Today, few substantial houses remain to substantiate Dumfries' former glory, but descendants of the first inhabitants have recall and recorded legends. They revere the memory of their native son, Colonel Grayson, and are proud of the glory days in Dumfries' history.

DUTY TO HIS COUNTRY

Suspecting ill conceived plots by the colonists, in April, 1775, British Lord Dunmore confiscated the gun powder in the public magazine at Williamsburg where the house of Burgess met. Thinking fast, Patrick Henry confronted Lord Dunmore and exacted the return of the powder or its value in coin. This bold confrontation precipitated a meeting in Dumfries led by Captain Grayson who saw to it that a a resolution was passed, thanking Patrick Henry for his spirited, patriotic action.

At the same time, a proposal was sent to Captain Grayson by the Independent Company of Spotsylvania County to unite and march with them to Williamsburg to demonstrate their determination to prevent a repetition of that kind of outrage. Captain Grayson united with Mr. Lee

Washington visits a wounded officer

of his company and immediately submitted the question to the common field officer of the several Independent Companies, dated April 22, 1775, Dumfries, VA, " Sir, We have just received a letter from the officers of the Independent Company of Spotsylvania which is herewith enclosed, We immediately called together this company and the vote put whether they would march to Williamsburg for the purpose mentioned in that letter, which was carried unanimously. We have nothing more to add, but that we are well assured you may depend on them for that or any other service, which respects the liberty of America. We expect your answer and determination by Mr. Davess. We have the honor to be, Your most obedient servant, William Grayson, By order of the Company." (15) This event was sparked by eager, patriotic men, set on freedom and willing to fight for it. Patrick Henry, governor of Virginia wrote to General Washington, "Colonels Baylor and Grayson are collecting regiments,& three others are forming in Virginia." Shortly after they were formed, Grayson confided to James Monroe, that the "Articles of Confederation, "were inadequate and had to be amended or they should not be ratified.

About this time William began to suffer intensely from bouts of gout with insufferable pain in his feet and ankles, causing them to swell enormously. From then on he suffered unremitting pain and misery

Local representatives from the Virginia colonists were elected by their peers, to serve in The House of Burgess, a colonial governing system in

Williamsburg where the colonists managed local affairs. Aware that Virginians were speaking of independence in 1776, Lord Dunmore, closed and barricaded the House of Burgess.

General Charles Lee

Quickly the Colonials established the House of Delegates nearby and continued to hold meetings. Various Boards, Conventions and the Continental Congress, followed. The Board of War, would become the War Department; the Board of Finance, the Treasury. After Grayson resigned from the army he served on the Board of War at the request of Washington, who was Grayson's mentor.

One book became a bible for William Grayson, it was titled, "Wealth of Nations, "and was published in 1776 by Adam Smith, a learned Scottish economist and idealist, whose beliefs became for young William the basis of his established view on the science of political economics. William often used this simple quote from Adam's book:" Let commerce alone; it will take care of itself." (16)

The cousins, James and William were sixteen years apart but closely allied in principle and theory and acted in concert on all accounts. Obviously James held William and Spence in high regard, but it was William who introduced James to the men who opened doors for him. The cousins were close all their lives. William and James served in congress together and fought in the Continental Army, often in the same battles along with Richard Henry Lee, a friend and fellow Virginian of similar persuasion.

Grayson and Monroe fought in the battle of Trenton on December 26, 1776 and were present when Washington and his troops crossed the Delaware after dark to reach the British and Hessian troops at Trenton, a perilous and freezing crossing. During the ensuing battle James was seriously injured. The presence of a doctor saved his life. A cannon ball skimmed across his chest and lodged in his left armpit. Hastily the doctor removed the shot and James recovered. The officers in the Continental Army were not as visible to the public as those who gave speeches and wrote resolutions. Their podium would come following the war.

Thomas Jefferson wrote the Declaration of Independence in 1776, using for inspiration, the Virginia Declaration of Rights, which was written by George Mason, a brilliant Patriot. Lt. Col. Johnston carried the "Declaration of Congress of the Independence of America," from congress to Washington's army headquarters on the 4th of July, causing little stir.

On June 21, 1776 Washington appointed Grayson his assistant secretary. Two months later on August 24, 1776 he promoted him to Aide-de-camp. Grayson served in this post until January 11, 1777 when he took command of a Continental Regiment and his rank raised to Lt. Colonel. On March 29, 1777. (17) William Grayson's regiment fought at White Plains, Brandywine, Long Island, Germantown and through the action and aftermath of Valley Forge. At the battle of Monmouth Court House on June 28, 1778, Grayson showed outstanding valor. He and his regiment went to the center of battle, by-passing General Charles Lee, who stood aside and failed to join the fight. Grayson's regiment was cut to ribbons. Unscathed, Grayson was left without a command sure that Washington would re-appoint him. Why had General Charles Lee failed to join the battle and to rile at his commander when he was rebuked?

On his way to join Washington, near the end of June, 1778, General Charles Lee stopped near Morristown, PA, after sending forward 2,700 of his troops forward to the Delaware. Resting at a house near Basking Ridge, Lee wrote to General Horatio Gates about the loss of Fort Washington. "There was never so damned a stroke, entrenous, a certain great man is most damnably deficient. I have neither guides, cavalry, medicines, money, shoes or stockings. I must act with the greatest circumspection. Tories are in my front, rear and on my flanks. The mass of the people is strangely contaminated. In short unless something which I do not expect turns up, we are lost. Our counsels have been weak to the last degree." Word of General Lee's discontent and disparaging remarks about Washington got back to Henry Lauren's son John, who challenged Lee to a duel and gave him a minor wound in December, 1778.

Rather than give him a new regiment, Washington asked Grayson to represent the Army in the military trial of General Charles Lee who was Court Marshalled on August 12, 1778, for dis-obedience, misbehavior and disrespect to his commanding officer and suspended from command for one year. This onerous duty created a conflict of sorts for William because Charles Lee was an old friend, but William handled the affair in so gentlemanly a manner that Charles Lee held nothing against him, and upon his death, out of regard for William, willed him a fine thoroughbred pony.

General Lee was only furloughed from duty with the army for one year but he was so huiliated by the Court Marshall that he chose not to return to duty after the year passed, and he became consumed with bitterness for all that might have been. He was probably thinking how close he had come to being commander in chief. Thereafter bitterness and a fallow life style ruined his life. The events at Monmouth stirred enormous controversy, considering General Lee's hesitancy to commit to battle. Conjecture mounted that Lee's move was part of a failed coup to replace Washington with himself in the weeks preceding the battle, an attempted coup d'etat.

JOIN OR DIE
This woodcut was supposed to have been done by Ben Franklin When h e owned the Boston Gazette. It was a symbol used in the French & Indian Wars, but in time acquired a different meaning.

At Monmouth, Lee wanted at the very least, to see Washington humiliated by another defeat and behaved abominably if not traitorously.

Grayson was out of a job again, so Washington put him to work using his legal expertise in collaboration with British General Howe, to engage in the exchange of prisoners taken at Valley Forge in the spring of 1778. British General Gates had been recalled to England and Sir William Howe replaced him as head of his Majesty's troops.

William Grayson continued to suffer periodically from gout, an illness exacerbated by diet, environment and stress that would plague him all his life and finally cause his death once it deteriorated his kidneys and left him the pain, debilitation and misery of uncontrollable bloody diarrhea.

Grayson was anxious to negotiate an exchange for his friend Henry Laurens, the former President of the Continental Congress, but the British kept Laurens prisoner for two years. In the end, Laurens was exchanged for Lord Cornwallis on December 31,1781, after the battle of Yorktown. (18)

Grayson resigned from the army in January of 1779. Once more, Washington guided him. This time towards the Board of War, but William was exhausted from four years of fighting and went home for a long rest before assuming his new duties. By December of 1779, Grayson had taken up his appointment with the recently formed Board of War. On January 10, 1780, a letter addressed to "The honorable President of the Continental Congress, Philadelphia," signed Charles Lee was read aloud: "Ordered, That this letter be referred to the Board of Treasury." It was signed Charles Lee, "Berkeley County, Sir, I understand that it is in contemplation of Congress on the principle of economy to strike me from service. They must know very little of me, if they suppose that I would accept money since the confirmation of the wicked and infamous sentence which was passed upon me. I am, Sir, your most obedient servant. Charles Lee" Excuse my not writing in my own hand, but my hand is injured. Congress answered General Charles Lee by telling him his services would no longer be required. (19)

POLITICS

After his soldiering days, William Grayson devoted his energies to his law practice and engaged in buying and selling land. Finally there was time to organize, make improvements to his plantation and spent time with Eleanor and their growing family. Once his personal life was in order he would find a meaningful way to serve the nation again. The war ended in 1781 at the battle of Yorktown, Virginia, a year and a half after William left the army. He served six years and ten months. To defeat the British and win independence was an unbelievable victory. Never before had an upstart nation

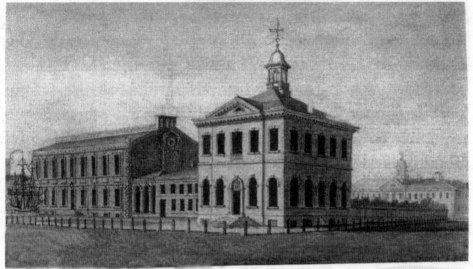

The State House and Congress Hall, James P. Malcolm
Ca. 1792-94, Collection of H. Richard Dietrich Jr. photograph
By Lynn Rosenthal, Philadelphia Museum of Art

outfought an etablished and great nation. Victorious at last, Americans were elated and anxious to form a permanent government based on law and order with liberty for all.

Word of William's valor at Monmouth spread. As a member of the Virginia House of Delegates, he was anxious express his ideas to so sophisticated a gathering. William was well spoken and graciously received and immediately garnered attention, which assured his election to the Continental Congress, which William looked on as greater opportunity to espouse the principles dearest to his heart, and perhaps make a difference in national affairs. At once he attracted nationwide attention, not just with his peer group, but the general population who viewed William as a man of substance and a leader of consequence especially when he locked horns with the leaders from the north with such skill and tact that their mutual paths were soothed. No doubt they had discussed the most important issues of the day only to find themselves on opposite sides on paths that were un-tenable.

CONGRESS HALL, Phil. The 45 feet square first floor, used by

William had formed an ideology. He saw problems that required hard won cooperation between the southern and northern states. One of William's lifelong worries was the serious inequity between the northern and southern states and the need to remedy problems where possible. The northern states were "carrying states." The southern states, "producing states." The north was more sophisticated, their buildings formidable, their mansions larger, their banks more prestigious, and they had manufacturing plants. The southern "aristocratic patriots" were gentlemen with plantations, beautiful columned mansions on the impressive silver waterways of Virginia. The south oozed with charm, and every variety of organic produce grew in the dark, rich soil to the delight of all. Tobacco and cotton were the largest agricultural resources but vegetables of every variety were grown and distributed to the northern states. The soil was so rich that farmers bragged; you could kick the soil with the heel of your boot, drop in a seed, spit on it, stomp, and a stalk of corn would grow. The south produced, but the power of government, implementation, money and manipulation, was lodged in the north where an urbane lifestyle and production was heavily concentrated. How different the north was from the ease and graciousness of the south where elegant gentlemen Planters let their slaves do the work, and rarely soiled their hands and life moved at a slower pace and many southerner's livlihood depended on what their lands produced, which was a great variety of agricultural products.

In 1784, in a speech before the VA. House of Delegates Grayson deplored the disparity between the states and warned of impending peril. Recalling his warnings 65 years later, many said Grayson predicted the "Civil War." Clearly by 1861 the north was fed up with slavery. The south attempted to arbitrate their destiny by dictating terms of cooperation with the north to no avail. Unparalleled by the northern atmosphere, in regard to the rapidly evolving sophistication and charm of her cities and manufacturing zeal. The south was undauntd and somehow managed to retain their faith and pride in all the south represented. Southern planters readily agreed on the inequity of owning slaves and clearly understood that slavery in America had to end, and were prepared to deal with the issue. Meanwhile, they had fields to harvest and slaves at hand whom they had owned all their lives. Three hundred slaves maintained Mt. Vernon and and few dared criticize General Washington. Slavery was a fixed way of life. It would take War to end slavery as well as bring an end to many fine southern traditions.

The Federal Government had the power. William Grayson didn't need a crystal ball. In the absence of change, war between the states was inevitable. No one knew how to solve the inequities and hold back the tide of hatred that fueled Civil War.

CHRONOLOGY OF WILLIAM GRAYSON'S LIFE

1736: Born in Dumfries, Virginia

1752: Mother Susannah dies and is buried at Belle Air1757: Father Benjamin dies, buried at Belle Air

1758: Goes to the College of Philadelphia

1760: Goes to England, attends Middle Temple

1761 Attends Oxford, to get Law degree

1764: Returns to Dumfries. Marries Eleanor Smallwood

1765: Sets up Law practice in Dumfries

1766: Meets Richard Henry Lee, signs the Leedstown Resolution

1767 Elected to serve on County Committee of Correspondence

1774: One of 25 members elected to the committee of Safety

1774: Becomes Captain of Virginia Minuteman Militia

1775: Serves in Virginia convention to guide Virginia to statehood

1776: Comm.Lt. Colonel, becomes Aide de Camp to Washington

1777: Distinguishes himself at the battle of Monmouth

1778: Negotiates prisoner exchange at Valley Forge

1778: Heads Court Martial of General Charles Lee

1779: Resigns from active military service

1779 Becomes Commissioner of State Board of War

1780 Practiced Law and invested in land

1784 Elected to the House of Delegates

1785 Elected to his third term in the Continental Congress, rents house in Philadelphia

1785: Works on sale & division of western lands

1787: Serves second term in Continental Congress
1788: The Ratifying Convention in Richmond
1789: Elected as a senator to the first Federal Congress, serves first term
1789: Eleanor dies in September.
1790: William dies in March

THE EVOLVING CRISES

1775 was a dramatic and exciting time in America. England was determined to bring the American colonies to heel and exact respect and profit from the costly regime. The colonists reacted unfavorably to every interference in their peaceful lives and began to react strongly to what they considered unreasonable and unfair treatment by the English, while England maintained and protected the colonies at heavy cost and wanted a return for their investment. Consequently the English levied taxes on everything, tea, paper, ink, dice, playing cards, and stamps that marked various communications. Under ever more exacting taxes, the colonists began to rebel, frowning on the excessive taxes as grossly unfair. Two organized and orderly revolts against "The Stamp Act" and "the Boston Tea Party," were in direct response to harsh British rule and unfair taxation. Clearly England had the opportunity to appease the colonists and restore peace; instead, they asserted more measures obviously underestimating the humble society they controlled so avidly. The British considered their American subjects ungrateful and unwieldy and deserving of chastisement. The colonists struggled against tyranny, insisting on a voice in their destiny; which was interpreted by England as unmitigated ingratitude from a colony of inordinately, undisciplined ruffians.

Aristocratic titles from England or Europe were disallowed in the wild and savage lands of the colonies. In this heated atmosphere the American Revolution began in earnest on April 19, 1775, when the British, seemingly in error, fired on American Minutemen at Lexington, Massachusetts, and then followed them to Concord, firing on their flanks at will. The gates of hell opened at the sound of these first shots and war in all its pain and glory descended on a colony that screamed for independence, without guns, warm clothing or uniforms, imbued with the precious ideal of liberty, equality and justice for all.

Bloody battles and a thousand skirmishes followed and war with England exploded into reality. In England the war was called, "The Revolt of the American Colonies." The British had three times more soldiers, plentiful weapons and ammunition and every advantage, including military training and expertize. None other than the brave and stubborn colonists believed Americans had a chance of winning against a great and powerfu nation that had every advantage, but they were determined to give their all in their quest for freedom.

America was hard at war and struggling beyond their mens when a miracle happened and France came to their aid. A single Frenchman led the way and no man gave more to the American cause then Marie Joseph Paul Yves Roch Gilbert du Motier, the Marquis de La Fayette, who arrived with his own ships, as well

a soldiers at his own expense, to fight beside the colonists. Lafayette stayed until the final battle. Indeed he even led a Regiment at the final battle of Yorktown. Lafayette had endured six years of the Revolution that ended in October, 1781 at Yorktown, Virginia, where 8,800 colonists and 7,000 French troops defeated 7,000 English soldiers under General Cornwallis, who surrendered on October 9, 1781 after a dramatic battle with French ships blocking the British from escape by sea, while American and French troops held the British fast on the beach, hammering them with cannon and rifle fire. It was truly remarkable that the colonists won. This remarkable feat gained the American colonies the attention and respect of the whole world who began to expect great things from Americans and waited rather impatiently for their next move.

VIRGINIA'S DECLARATION OF RIGHTS:

From the Virginia convention of Delegates, June 12, 1776 The Virginia Declaration was drafted by George Mason, and amended by Thomas Ludwell Lee and members of the convention. The Declaration contained sixteen Articles on the subject of the "Rights of the people of Virginia." This foundation affirmed by Virginians, was the basis of Government, "The inherent right to Life, Liberty, Property, and the pursuit of happiness and safety, that all men are by nature equally free and independent." The brilliance of this last statement has endured for generations and become the symbol of all that is best in America.

Virginians viewed government as a servant of the people and put restrictions on its power. Their Declaration rejected the notion of privileged political classes (the Aristocracy) or hereditary office that permitted emoluments and privileges. This declaration recommended the separation of

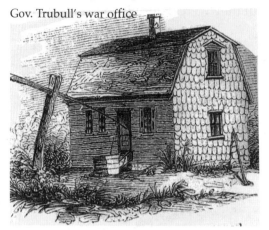

Gov. Trubull's war office

power, free and open elections, and a division between Legislative and Executive powers, distinct from the Judicial and the representatives of the first two departments. Men were to serve for a time and then return to their former occupation so men with fresh ideas could be employed. Frequent elections were held for the benefit of new delegates, who were expected to arrive with a whole set of fresh, new ideas.

The Declaration declared that no government should suspend or execute laws without consent of the people or their representatives, and defended the documented legal right of a defendant to confront his accusers and witnesses who could be called upon for supportive evidence in his defense.

Defendants had the right to a speedy trial by an impartial jury of his vicinage (peers who lived in the vicinity), and that no man be compelled to give evidence against himself. (self-incrimination). A later clause was added against "cruel and unusual punishment, baseless search and seizure, and required a trial by jury, freedom of the press, and freedom of religion;

"All men are equally entitled to the free exercise of religion." Lastly, there was "an injunction against a standing Army at times of peace, but approval for a regulated Militia."

The most important part of the "Virginia Declaration of Rights" was the protection of the individual from an all-powerful government with mutable laws; This was the first time a Constitution protected the rights of individuals. It was an inspired document, taken from European Law, (Magna Carta), and dedicated to freedom and rights under the law, a great beginning. The document representing a newly formed nation would establish a standard for individual rights that met the test of time, and established a new meaning of freedom. News of the events in America circled the globe.

HISTORY OF THE ARTICLES OF CONFEDERATION AND
PERPETUAL UNION

"The Articles of Confederation and Perpetual Union," were prepared by a committee of thirteen members of the second Continental Congress in 1776 and presented to the states for acceptance in 1777, while William Grayson was distinguishing himself at the battle of Mommouth Court House. They were **de facto** until their ratification in 1781 and then became, **de jure.** The Articles provided for making war, negoitiating agreements and treaties, resolution of the western territories, but mostly secured freedom, sovereignty and the independence of the U.S. While war raged, no one examined the inadequacies in the governing document, but there were flaws and once the light of reason shone fully on the governing principles, there were many complaints that would have to be dealt with and changed.

Early on Grayson spoke of needed changes in the Articles of Confederaion in a letter to his cousin James. He even made preparatory notes on the changes and mentioned these to George Washington. Somehow he was ignored. Washington clearly favored James Madison and John Adams as his henchmen although appearing on the surface to be still warm and friendly to William and even receptive. Perhaps William was naive a this moment and did not rise sufficeintly to the occasion.

Article two, read," Each state retains its sovereignty, freedom and independence, and every power, jurisdiction and right which is not by this Confederation expressly delegated."

The document was assembled hastily and adopted and served as the only governing document for the colonies through Revolution. The Articles began with a firm "League of Friendship,"but Soon the states dissolved into separate sovereign entities, each entitled to one vote, equal to the other states, regardless of the size of the state. (unfair).

On any issue, nine out of thirteen votes designated a majority and carried the vote. Some felt this equation too risky in dealing with treaties with foreign countries, trade taxation both internal and external and all forms of commerce, between states or countries, a necessary and compelling need.

Apparent to many was the need for a stronger document, one that would unite the south and the north under a central government, and allow the states to empower their delegates. The residents of each state mandatorily voted for delegates who journeyed to New York to represent their state in the Continental Congress. Although a stronger, more cohesive central government was needed, no one was willing to destroy the unique power held by each state with an inadequate, perhaps cumbersome replacement. Still, the Confederation document was inadequate and woud have to be altered. Statesmen were prepared to deal with this.

THE CONVENTION TO AMEND THE CONFEDERATION
Philadelphia, September, 1786.

In May, 1786, Charles Pinckney, of S.C. proposed revising the Articles but it took James Madison to invite men to the Annapolis, Convention to discuss the problem where a few representatives from only five states met and endorsed a motion for all states to assemble to discuss improving the Articles. A bill was introduced in Congress and approved, asking that the Confederation be altered in Philadephia in May, 1787. For varying reasons many leading politicians and statesman declined to attend the convention or were otherwise engaged and unable to attend.

George Mason attended but he was clearly disturbed and verbally-warned the members, "The eyes of the United States are turned upon this Assembly and their Expectations raised to a very anxious degree."

George Washington ordered secrecy and the doors and shutters drawn and the assembled group closed uncomfortably inside. Only the men inside know what transpired.

Eventually they voted!

When it was announced that rather than amend the Articles of Confederation, a whole new document would be written, George Mason rushed out in a rage, bitterly disappointed, only to become a leader in opposition to the "new paper" called the Constitution. Mason, a brilliant Virginian practically screamed: "The document has no "Declaration of rights." Ultimately George Mason's views prevailed.

Edmund Randolph, Governor of Virginia also walked out without signing.(20) Clearly at that time, Edmund Randolph stood firmly with those who would soon be tagged Anti-Federalists, an unfortunaate Nom de plume for men who loved their country and wanted the strongest, fairest government and were not at Anti anything worthy.

Washington did not want word of what transpired in the Convention to escape to the crowds outside, but the news leaked anyway and the crowd learned that the Confederation had been tossed aside.

Many were outraged that their beloved Articles of Confederation no longer existed and in its place was a new and secret document. Some were sufficiently outraged as to suggest that the government be sued for abuse of power because the Convention was to amend not replace their beloved governing document in the newly formed United

States of America. that had ruled as the Congress of the Confederation.

News of the creation of an entirely new document upon which the goverment woud base its laws and conceptions also caused an enormous uproar among politicians. Immediately it was recognized that a unique opportunity to participate in the creation of a superb bit of legislation that lay at the heart of the republic, was at hand. Bright men agonized how they could be part of the mighty plan, to create a perfect document that would make history all over the world.

Once the document was published and read, people with opposite views split into factions. The name "Federalist" was given to those who approved of the the new document, the Constitution, and those who would change or amend it were unjustly called "Anti-Federalist." Actually there was a third group who looked at the "Constitution," contemptuously for what was not included, or for its excesses. They would not bother to change it. They would trash it. Many in the last two groups believed that the president, along with his cronies in the Senate, was given too much power and that the document fostered an aristocratical view . Then the word" Consolidation;" slipped in, meaning having a powerful central government with little if any power delegated to state governments. The Constitution also favored northern states, almost neglecting the southern states who would be at a distinct disadvantage in matters of impost and commerce.

Many members assessed the newly drafted Constitution as an illegal document because the resolution to assemble was intended solely to change the "Articles of Confederation," not to form an entirely new document.

That impasse on legality of the Constitution was overcome because no one wanted to take on the onerous duty of pressing charges, feeling it was hopeless and would cause public ostracization and ridicule.

SURRENDER OF THE BRITISH AT YORKTOWN

Instead, men began to work on the wording of the Constitution with James Madison, Washington's choice to frame the document. The occasion was definitely one where William Grayson's skills could have been put to use. William could easily have felt slighted by this decision of his commander in chief and life-long friend. Grayson was better equipped by education and held a law degree. James Madison, the president's choice, had never studied law and was not an expert in jurisprudence. It is an understatement to say that all who had been left out of the writing of the Constitution were piqued.

In planning what kind of government to establish, a well thought out plan was presented by Edmund Randolph, Governor of Virginia. It was called, "The Virginia Plan," and recommended a government of three equal parts; the Executive, to lead and enforce the law, (the President), the Judicial (the courts, headed by the Supreme Court) to rule legally and interpret law, and lastly, the Legislative to include a Congress and Senate and a house of representatives from all over the nation (thirteen colonies). The House would create laws that would go to the Senate for a final vote as a double check.

Representatives of the smaller states feared their strength would be usurped by the larger states, or a too powerful Federal Government. Then, New Jersey came up with a plan and presented it, but it was not favored. Alexander Hamilton rose to present his plan, which was difficult to understand and immediately rejected. Then the "Great Compromise" was suggested by the representative from Connecticut, thoroughly discussed, voted on, and incorporated into the "Virginia Plan," the "whole" then being adopted by a majority.

Those assembled knew the limitations of the "Articles of Confederation; "under which, the government could create laws, but had no power or fiat to enforce them. A government that had no control over states that refused to cooperate had no power and was viewed as worthless.

No one had anticipated the variance in taxes, depending on where cargo landed or if it was produced in the states or from which country it was imported and the variety of taxes involved in all shipments, especially those from the northern states to those in the southern most inhabited parts.

Wealth and power were concentrated in the north while the southern states were looked on as a "mere Milch cow" in William Grayson's words, in the Continental Congress. Merchandise imported to New York, from Europe, then deported to Virginia, were mandated to pay a share of the international importation tax, along with all local taxes, from New York,

from Europe, then deported to Virginia, were mandated to pay a share of the international importation tax, along with all local taxes, from New York, called imposts. These taxes cost Virginia over twice as much as if they had imported the items directly from Europe, preferably in their own ships. Considerable taxes were involved in shipping imported goods to the south and handlers along the route added another portion to the exorbitant imposts. The south demanded fair taxation and began to import directly from Europe, to create equity in commerce, internal and foreign.

At the convention to form the Constitution, the presentation of the Federalists appeared to be based on a monarchical or aristocratical society when it became clear that only men of property and estates were eligible for high public office; because only the rich could afford to serve without a salary. This view was the antithesis of the Anti-Federalist's credo and blatantly separated the two factions, but compromises were eventually instigated to enable them to work together. This was a commendable asset considering their vast differences geographically and idealistically.

The format of the Philadelphia convention, was to deliberate in secret until the Constitution was in its final form Under the new system, only nine states out of thirteen were needed to ratify the document. This referenced future legal documents and vastly important issues that the Anti-Federalists viewed as dangerous to the principles of justice and liberty. The Confederation Articles never addressed the need to lay and collect taxes and the problem of commerce remained a major concern until the Constitutional Convention in Philadelphia discussed strengthening the government and solving problems of taxes and commerce. From the beginning, Consolidation was a problem; an all-powerful government

STATE HOUSE in N.Y. on Walnut Street. In 1776 the Continental Congress me on the first floor and Provincial Assemblies on the second. The Dec. of Ind. Was read here

ruling over states and how much independence to grant the states. Equally important was the number of senators and representatives and how to apportion the number based on the disparate populations in the states.

Before the Philadelphia Constitutional Convention ended the Constitution was signed. Each state was promised ample opportunity to meet to discuss and ratify the document. Virginians would insist on amendments. The facts were publicized. Not many had faith in the promises made.

THE CONSTITUTION OF THE UNITED STATES

The Articles of the Constitution caused a nationwide outcry of significant proportion. Far from the expected response, the citizenry reacted as if they had been duped and they were angry.

They resented being stripped of the familiar Articles of Confederation they had lived with for years, which they effected to prefer. Naivete on the part of law-makers predicted a happy disposition for the Constitution, partly because it was endorsed by George Washington, who had encouraged James Madison to draft the words and incorporate the ideas of leading, stalwart politicians who were hand picked.

Not everyone was pleased, nor could be. At first, sixty percent of the representatives were firmly against the Constitution and based their eventual acquiescence on the promise of amendments, the fear of disunion, and pressure applied by Washington. In the struggle for cohesion few would be intellectually satisfied. "Amendments" were suggested by Anti-Federalists in lieu of rejecting the document and voting against it. Instead they compromised by accepting the promise of amendments. Drawing minimal support from a few ecumenically minded northerners the Federalists struggled to gain a majority. Both sides fought to outclass their opponents.

Methods of courting ran from discussing a viewpoint to carefully prepared, often incendiary documents, that were published and distributed by hand or tacked on public buildings in the usual manner.

William Grayson was among the first to speak of the necessity of incorporating the rights of individuals in the Constitution. He had expressed this belief early and often in the Continental Congress. Others joined this rhetoric. The outcome netted them a "Bill of Rights." Much credit was attributed to William Grayson for his foresight then and now for his attention on items like emphasis on trial by jury, and rights of the individual being basic requirements before any Constitution would be acceptable to anyone in his faction. Due credit on these subjects was also given to George Mason and Patrick Henry.

Grayson's peers agreed that personal rights and personal freedom were mandatory. Equality meant equal privileges for everyone, humble or rich. No one denied this principle for it was as inalienable as life and liberty.

Since events like these had never been experienced before especially in so vast and magic a setting, patriots received a lightning education and formed decisions that would have lasting effect on the future success or

give birth to dreams and hope for glory, and to do so under a sound legalistic structure, called government.

Patrick Henry, one of the most expressive politicians, heavily invested in freedom and sound government, was passionately dedicated. He would be a leader in the Anti-Federalist movement and his speeches would be recorded in the history books for

OLD TOWER AT NEWPORT, RHODE ISLAND
Was a windmill until the British blew off its roof and four f---

he truly was the most inspired spokesman of the revolutionary era and a man who put all of his passion into his beliefs and used them well in delivering memorable speeches.

Everyone with a voice and an opinion was heavily invested in freedom and was duty bound to inform and impress their colleagues to vote for or against the challenging document, the most important piece of legislation in the United States.

From its inception, Patrick Henry was dead set against the Constitution and its flaws, and agreed with Grayson that the document should be inculcated, for its gross errors. The host of Anti-Federalists were amazed at the audacity of those who had formed such a document and supported it as if it was written on papyrus, and were appalled by the implication of pomposity in some matters and the lack of respect for state's rights that denied judicial sovereignty to state jurisdictions. These issues might not concern Washington, but would effect his role in the office of the president.

Patrick Henry was inflamed with indignation over powers delegated to a President who would answer primarily to his "cronies in the Senate," and declared that the brush of monarchy painted a clear threat of a powerful north, that exhorted unequal power over the southern states. The south was enervated unless they discovered a vehicle in which to exalt their philosophy and ideals.

Patrick Henry and William Grayson called upon the best minds in the south to unite to discuss expedient strategy to defeat the blind acceptance of a document so lacking in merit as to be judged elementary, and yet salvageable if amended. The Anti-Federalist's aim was to find a method to prevail on principle, and the issue of adopting the Constitution became the most important event in their lives because the ideals embodied at its core would rule their nation.

Neither Grayson or Henry, or their followers, were willing to throw away their principles for any reward, be it on earth or in heaven though they be pitilessly excoriated on every side, as they were.

There is no record of Washington contacting Grayson for his opinion, on the Constitution, although he contacted others. This fact must have devastated and puzzled William, who agonized over the fact, not without some degree of ambivalence and strong pique.

Did Grayson wonder if his ideas and methods had been too strong? Had he made fun of a high ranking person once too often, one whom Washington held in regard? Like many in politics, Grayson had ridiculed John Adams, for his appearance and his views, believing his tendency to lean towards monarchy to be a dangerous political thrust. Besides, William particularly disliked  Adams and took every opportunity to scorn and demean him to the delight of his companions who were often in stitches over William's caustic and cutting remarks regarding John Adams, the son of an impoverished tinker.

Neither George Mason or Patrick Henry fought in the revolutionary army but they served their country with dedication and passion first exhibited in the House of Burgess; always in the political limelight delivering passionate speeches on every phase of national relevance, wary of British dominance and the growing power of the northern states over the south.

Mason served in the House of Delegates and then the Continental Congress and Patrick Henry served in both institutions, and was a two term Governor of Virginia from 1776 to 1779 and from 1784 to1786. In Henry's late years he was elected to Congress and appeared to have changed in regard to his previous harsh sentiments regarding the Federalist's. Judge Tyler would defend him. Sadly, Patrick Henry died three months before taking his seat in the Senate. He and Washington both died in 1799, outliving Grayson by nine important years in U.S. history.

Mason and Henry's deeds and speeches, assured them posthumous fame, rightly granting them eternal recognition in Virginia's history, and a life of nationwide recognition.

With a thousand miles plus between Massachusetts and South Carolina, seldom were the champions of their regions known outside their locale. Getting votes in national elections was difficult unless a candidate had national fame or sufficient backing from established leaders meaning they were well known.

Washington held power over everyone, dwarfing the average man, yet he was not infallible and accrued the usual enemies. Loyalty meant the world to him, still he was careless of his own loyalties.

MORRIS'S HOUSE

In the frontier days, fighting the French and Indian wars was a scenario of fast changing theatre wherein Washington became a strong military leader. The incomparable Wilderness training stood him in good stead and provided him with the credentials to assume command of the Continental Forces perhaps better than anyone else at hand.

Besides being fearless. Washington was a good judge of men. His mind was sound and clear and he was possessed of a calm, thoughtful demeanor, always the gentleman. Washington culled advisors from the brightest minds available. Aware of his intellectual limitations he counted on men of genius to give him advise and this helped him rule. George Washington was the most revered man in America, then and now. Such greatness transcends time and establishes precedents.

After the American Revolution, an end was made to all things royal in America in particular inherited European titles. Citizens of the newly formed states were reminded to leave behind all thoughts of kingly endowments or any hint of royal asperations.

Aristocratic ideas did not equate with the principles of equal rights in a fledgling Republic. On the ratification of the Constitution, Grayson wrote to James Madison, who in 1776 was one of his closest friends: "Despite the government's weakness, I have not yet made up my mind on the subject. I am doubtful whether it is not better to bear those ills we have than fly to others that we know not of." (21)

Many letters were exchanged between Madison and Grayson for both respected the talents of the other.

William Grayson studied the Constitution carefully His letters reflect his receptivity to new ideas. He would not be quick to condemn or be unfair regarding an issue so important to the nation he loved. After a period of studious assimilation, William Grayson swore that the document was damned unless it was amended. Many agreed with him and the battle was on to amend the Constitution or strike it down. Anger stalked the streets, whispers became shouts and dissension ruled.

CHRONOLOGY OF IMPORTANT EVENTS IN AMERICA

1619	Opening of the House of Burgess
September 5, 1774	The first Continental Congress
May 10, 1775	The battles of Lexington and Concord
June 15, 1775	Ethan Allen takes Fort Ticonderoga
June 17, 1775	Bunker Hill
July 4, 1776	The Declaration of Independence, Pa.
September 22, 1776	British execute Nathan Hale as a spy
1776 to 1778,	Thirteen states form State Constitutions
1774 to 1778	Continental Congress, 3 sessions
October 28, 1776	Battle of White Plains
December 26, 1776	Battle of Trenton
January 3, 1777	Battle of Princeton
1777	Articles of Confederation incorporated
July 7, 1777	Battle of Hubbardton
August 16, 1777	Battle of Bennington
September 11, 1777	Battle of Brandywine
October 7, 1777	Battle of Saratoga, surrender of General Burgoyne
November 16, 1777	British take forts Mifflin and Monroe
December 18, 1777	Am. troops winter at Valley Forge
December, 1779	Am. troops winter at Morristown, N. Jersey
June 18, 1778	Americans break winter camp
June 28, 1778	Battle of Monmouth Court House
August 29,	1778 Battle of Rhode Island
March 3, 1779	Battle of Briar Creek, Georgia
July 16, 1779	Battle of Stony Point
September 23, 1779	Seige of Savannah
April 10, 1780	Seige of Charlestown, South Carolina
April 14, 1780	Battle of Monck's Creek
May 29, 1780	Massacre of Americans at Warsaw, N. C.
August 16, 1780	Battle of Camden, S.C.
October 7, 1780	Battle of King's Mountain
January 17, 1781	Battle of Cowpens, S.C.
March 15, 1781	Battle of Guildford Court House, N.C.
April 25, 1781	Battle of Hobkerk's Hill, S.C.
September 8, 1781	Battle of Eutaw Springs, S.C.
October 5, 1781	Battle of Yorktown, Virginia
July 11, 1782	British evacuate Savannah, Georgia

April 11, 1783	Congress proclaims hostilities cease
Nov. 2, 1783	Farewell to troops by Washington
	At Rocky Hill, N.J.
Dec.4, 1783	Washington bids adieu to his officers
	At Fraunces Tavern
1786	The Constitutional Convention at Philadelphia
1788	The Virginia Ratifying Convention.

William Grayson was unable to attend the Constitutional Convention in Philadelphia in 1786 although he was in Philadelphia serving in Congress. After the Constitution became a legal document, congressional representatives who had been poignantly missing from the Constitutional convention, namely William Grayson and Patrick Henry, were the first to decry the illegality of the document as a rallying base for the Anti-Federalists.

Those with foresight projected a rich future for the United States and enormous growth through expansion westward. William Grayson declared there would be no great nation without westward development, and predicted that the nation would consist of only seven states unless the nation moved westward.

Small states feared their power would be usurped by larger states, in a Constitution that favored powerful Federal Government. Differences in geographical philosophy were expressed: Anti-Federalists felt mandated by their constituents, to represent the opinions of those who elected them, while the Federalists expected Congress to educate the populace and adjudicate accordingly. One would do what the people wanted, the other would inform the people how to think, and vote. The latter view was why Federalists were labeled aristocratic and arrogant for ignoring, "of the people, by the people, and for the people. "The essence of the democratic government the patriots were struggling to establish.

There were only 74 men at the Constitutional Convention from 12 states. After writing a whole new document only 40 men signed, 12 walked out in disgust nd three refused to sign:
G. Mason, E. Randolph and Eldridge Gerry. James Madison, the architect of the Constitution was aided by Robert Morris, a merchant and delegate to the Philadelphia Convention. Robert Morris was born in 1734 in Lancashire, England, and became a very rich man in Pennsylvania. Morris' generosity during the war reduced him to poverty. Robert Morris wrote the Preamble.

Before the State Constitutional convention ended, the Anti-Federalists, fighting for amendments were told, "Sign, then amend," which many were unwilling to do.

George Washington, fearing the vulnerability of the union, got word to the representatives to sign, and worry about amendments later, but the Anti-Federalists, felt that signing previous to amendments meant that amendments would never be granted, and in that belief they were correct.

State Constitutional conventions were the last chance to attain amendments. An Articles in the Constitution explained the terms under which the constitution could be amended. Throughout subsequent years many amendments would be presented, but few would be accepted and become law.

In the Spring of 1787, William Grayson rented a house in Philadelphia so Eleanor, their three sons and only daughter Hebe could be with him while he served his third year in Congress.

William was sorely disappointed not to be able to attend the Constitutional Convention in Philadelphia, but he met with the delegates from Virginia every evening in open defiance of the secrecy mandate. It was necessary that those opposing the Constitution plan their tactics on the topics of the speeches to be delivered at the hearing.

Conspicuously absent from the Convention were Richard Henry Lee, Patrick Henry, Thomas Jefferson, John Adams, Samuel Adams and John Hancock, for one or more reasons. Patrick Henry was discouraged by the aristocratic posture of the Federalists, and said he "smelled a rat," and refused to attend. Outsiders meeting with their counterparts after daily sessions in the convention were seen whispering in the pubs to keep current.

In framing the Constitution a difficult decision was whether there should be an executive committee to advise the President.

Also under consideration was how to fill various government roles; should they be paid positions or voluntary. Only wealthy men could serve without receiving compensation and this idea led to contention. Salaried positions were mandatory, but public servants were not to be so well paid as to impede the work to be done by the governing body.

There were problems in every Article and solutions would be hard won. Federalists and Anti-Federalists parried and thrust steadfastly, convinced of the sagacity of their opinions.

Democracy was a word not frequently used in the era of the Constitution. Politicians believed they were establishing a Republic. Unknown to them, the words they used and the principles they espoused , freedom, equality and the rule of law lay were the pulsing heart of a democracy.

Leaders of policy spoke of great achievements, causing less empowered working class men to feel denied and inferior. To the delight of men such as Thomas Jefferson and William Grayson this would change. These two believed that the "Constitution" was written to protect the rights, of all men including butchers, tradesmen, carpenters, shoe makers, clothiers, stone masons and blacksmiths as well as plantation owners and bankers.

In a true democracy, humble men had as much right to the liberties of America as rich, well educated men and when underprivileged men began to run for office in open elections, and won important offices, it led the way for others to aspire to respected positions in their communities. Humble men learned to make a few personal changes, and found it was not difficult to learn manners and dress like a gentleman. These changes elevated them and thus began a change in class delineation all over America. The tenets of democracy were at work. America was on its way to greatness but the path would be steep and the efforts labored.

America in the eighteenth century was considered a great "Land of Opportunity," a place to escape from oppression of one kind or another. By 1800, "Democracy" began in earnest, regardless of whether this had been the intention of the "Founding Fathers." Their philosophy and words had enflamed the hearts of Americans as they struggled for acceptance and success, which occurred when men realized they had options and asserted their basic rights in sensible ways, and not by either force or anger. Between the Federalists and the Anti-Federalists, it was the latter who more often represented the principles of democracy. From the onset, Federalists, led by James Madison and Alexander Hamilton, showed a penchant for monarchy.

FRAUNCE'S TAVERN, New York, after a sumptuous dinner celebration, Washington took leave of his men and went into retirement at Mt. Vernon in Dec. 1783

John Adams, the son of a humble tinker, perhaps had higher pretentious than most. He had been selected by George Washington, to be at his right hand, but there was a quandary over what title to give him. It all depended on what role the president would choose for himself. John Adams suggested Washington become King, assuming he too would therefore become a member of royalty, something the public accused him of courting, perhaps unfairly, but the insults and public jeering continued.

William Grayson was livid at Adam's apparent egomania and thirst for power and spoke vehemently against America becoming a monarchy and Washington a King.

Un-necessarily but employing great wit, William openly ridiculed Adams for his hunger for power and position and spoke of his humble origin and inappropriate egotistical assumptions at every turn, verbally and in writing. William seemed to have forgotten or conveniently overlooked the fact that John Adams clearly was Washington's first choice.

As vice president, John Adams was active in supporting measures to increase presidential power and prestige. Many believed he was still looking for grandeur or monarchistic benefits to descend on him. Grossly offended, when Adams learned his salary was only $5,000, Grayson wrote Patrick Henry, "I am in great hopes the house will offend him more by reducing it further." When Adams fretted about what title would be appropriate for him, Grayson wrote that it should be, "His Limpid Highness," or "His Superfluous Excellency." (22) Grayson thought John Adams was a self seeking buffoon, draped in delusions of grandeur that he had previously been denied. Most likely every joke that William told about Adams or any other dignitary on Washington's staff was carried directly to Washington, but William was not the only one who ridiculed Adams.

By 1781, America was on the brink of bankruptcy. After so hard and long a military fight, followed by the dire consequences of having to establih a sound government, the men were exhausted. With no time to waste there was much to accomplish. Somehow they must tend to the business of selling land, America's greatest asset. an undeniable plus asset, and establish a tax system that worked. All this in order to save what the American colonists had risked so much to accomplish.

Washington knew the peril the nation faced without a governing document and pushed everyone involved to come up with a rapid ratification of the Constitution. so the new government could begin. Washington's worse fear was that state representatives would fail to produce a governing document that would allow the process of self governing could begin, an exciting, necessary function for the enfant country if they were to succeed.

Meanwhile, amidst much wrangling and shifts in public opinion, America waited for an outcome of the Virginia Ratifying Convention, fully aware of what rode on their final decision. Even the funds to invest the new government were non-existent.

Any day the fabric of the nation could crumble and the expansive new nation might fall prey to foreign nations. arriving at night offshore. By morning it coud be over. The colonists were too tired to begin a new offensive. It was imperative to appear to be solvent and protected and capable of governing a nation. Indeed Washington could scarcely sleep for fear of

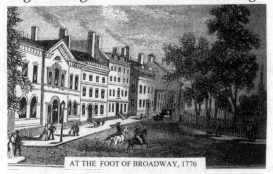

AT THE FOOT OF BROADWAY, 1776

being attacked by any number of foreign states who had long had their eye on capturing such a precious jewel as the massive lands of America. The situation was critical.

As a result, Washington wrote to the state conventions and individual men asking them to ratify the Constitution as quickly as possible, fearing the Constitution could be entangled in endless wrangling over issues for months, while men struggled over every nuance, even though Washington, through his informants, knew that certain changes were indeed necessary. Washington would not purposely mis-represent anything, especially the ease with which amendments could be obtained once the vote was confirmed, but on that score he was grossly mistaken.

Men who loved Washington and felt secure with him, unabashedly informed him of the inadequacies of the document, but, blinded by the danger of anarchy if the flimsy structure of government collapsed, Washington ignored those warnings and asked them to sign the Constitution and worry about changes later.

Linked to this acceptance of the Constitution, without change, was Washington's unspoken plea for loyalty, which meant signing regardless of principles, and this separated many in the Virginia constituency, men like Grayson, Patrick Henry, George Mason, Richard Henry Lee, Governor Randolph, Benjamin Harrison and James Monroe who were deaf to the pleas to compromize their integrity.

Many delegates were expected out of loyalty, to ratify the Constitution and they balked, even though they loved their Commander in Chief and had followed him into willingly into battle. Possibly, George Washington viewed the failure of men to rally to his command, as an act tantamount to disloyalty.

If only men could have set aside their integrity, oh what choice positions in the Federal government they might have won, rather than to swallow instead the bitter pill of dis-allegiance from their commander and friend. Perhaps it was to God's justice they answered to, not mankind or earthly fame.

To men like Grayson, Henry, Lee, Monroe, Mason and the rest, it was like consuming a bitter pill of dis-allegiance from their commander and friend. It was to God's justice they answered not that of mankind or earthly fame. To men like Grayson, Henry, Lee, Monroe, Mason and the rest, it was a matter of principle over expediency and for honor and integrity they paid a very high price!

CARPENTER'S HALL.

The prestige of the House of Representatives had always been less than the Senate, and the office began to excite notice: "Why is it that alone among modern representative assemblies the American House of Representatives tends to decline in prestige and authority?" (23 The expectation was that the House of Representatives would take a dominant position like the House of Commons, but its degradation began so soon that Fisher Ames noted it as early as 1797. Writing to Hamilton he observed: "The Heads of departments are chief clerks. Instead of being the ministry, the organs of executive power, imparting a momentum to the operation of the laws, they are precluded even from communicating with the house by reports. Com-mittees already are the Ministers and while the House indulges a jealousy of encroachment in its functions, which are properly deliberative, it does not perceive that these are impaired and nullified by the monopoly as well as the perversion of information by these committees." Justice Story, who entered Congress in 1808 as a Jeffersonian Republican, noted the process of degradation, and in his opinion, pointed out the cause: (24) "The Executive is compelled to resort to secret and unseen influences, private interviews and arrangements to accomplish its appropriate purposes, instead of proposing and sustaining its own duties and measures by a bold, manly appeal to the nation from its representatives."

The last of the organic acts of the Constitutional session was to establishing the judiciary, and here the absence of vision was most obvious. The strength and justice of the Judiciary were imperative in the development of the American constitutional system. Heated debate centered primarily on the conflict between state and federal courts.

Although Maclay's diary lent a one-sided, somewhat distorted account of the proceedings in the Senate, the debate was clear.

Ellsworth of Connecticut had principal charge of the bill. At the outset Lee and Grayson's attempted to confine the jurisdiction of federal courts to icases of Admiralty and were overwhelmed by the opposition. They then suggested that the Supreme Court allow the state courts the privilege of retaining jurisdiction over their usual cases, but Madison held that nothing less than a system of Federal Courts in every state, distinct from the state courts, would satisfy the requirements of the Constitution.

SUGAR HOUSE on Liberty Street in New York was used as a Prison by the

Both Grayson and Henry had law degrees, Madison did not. Obviously Grayson had more faith in the State courts, their lawyers and judges, than Madison. Grayson and Henry had practiced law in the local Court system and Madison had not, Grayson was indignant at the sleight and considered the comments and the final ruling an insult to the Judicial system of Viginia and its lawyers and judges.

Author's Comment: The ruling meant doubling the judiciary systems; Having both Circuit, Federal and Superior Courts, (Courts of Appeal) in every state, a superfluous measure. When the bill was taken up in the House, there was a long debate. The costly duplication of judicial establishments in all states, that began with the Constitution of 1788, remained in policy, and was a burden on the Federal and State Judicial System, and is best described worldwide, as an American peculiarity. The advocates of an unhampered state jurisdiction, unburdened by Federal overview were further dismayed to be accused of being hostile to the Constitution, which was not factually true. More-over, they were defending principle.

Decisive judicial argument hinged on the untrustworthiness of the state courts. Madison urged his view with impetus, pointing out that: "In some States, the spirits are so dependent on state legislatures, as to make the federal laws dependent on them. This would throw us back into all the embarrassments, which characterized our former situation."

Such was the low repute of the State legislatures in some minds, that the only way to argue their- view, was to state that "Congress shall have power, in its fullest extent, to correct, reverse, or affirm, any decree of a state court." This assertion of federal authority was made by Jackson of Georgia in the course of a long legal argument that affirmed Maclay's bold statement. (that rancor and contention were rampant)." (25)

The debate in the Virginia Ratifying Convention did not follow sectional lines, and in general was not unfairly described as "a lawyer's wrangle"

THE FOREIGN OFFICE
New York, on So. 6th St. 12 feet wide. Foreign Sec.
Livingston's office was on the 2nd floor in the front, with offi
in the rear and on the third Floor

by MacClay but that was not unusual.

Arguments over the location of the permanent capitol over shadowed all else, and caused arguments of enormous magnitude between the north and south each fighting for pre-eminence.

Author's Comment Continued: William worked diligently in public and behind the scenes to prevent the nation's capitol from being in a northern location, which would add to the imbalance of power between the states. Grayson had chosen Georgetown on the Potomac as the best site for the capitol and George Washington had given Grayson his approval of the site in a letter, but his selection was not yet a matter of public record.

When Congress chose Trenton New Jersey as the permanent site of the federal capitol, William Grayson got the votes to see that Congress withheld the funds to build the capitol city, effectively putting Trenton on hold. Grayson pleaded that placing the capitol in the north proliferated inequities between the states and recommended a southern location. Eight years after William Grayson's death, George Washington, once his closest friend, chose the site of the capitol.

Once the Constitution left the Philadelphia convention, it was voted on by the Senate and the House. The majority of Federalists did not believe anything could be gained by fighting for amendments, taking a stand and not budging. Once it passed to the Senate, it was rightly assumed that the House would then accept the Constitution unblemished, from the senate.

Grayson's statements reflected the relevancy of his argument regarding inequities between the Federal and State Court system; Again the all powerful Federal government, disemboweling the authority of the State." (26) Grayson lost his argument but there remained a hue and cry regarding the echelons of the Court protocol by which the Law of the Land operated. Instead of rectifying those short comings, however minor, they were passed over each year until they were absorbed into the whole cloth of a flawed judicial system.

On October 5th, 1787, three weeks after the Constitution was signed, copies went out to the states for ratification, and a political pamphlet was published, representing the Anti-Federalist view. The author of Centinel #1, was believed to be Samuel Bryan, but no name was given. The subject dealt

was Samuel Bryan. His subject dealt with checks and balances, the responsibility of the Fed. Government.

On the same day, James Madison published in the New York Packet "Federalist Paper #10, "The Union as a Safeguard Against Domestic Faction and Insurrection," in answer," and from the same New York Packet, either Alexander Hamilton or James Madison wrote Federalist Paper #51" titled "The Structure of the Government Must Furnish the Proper Checks and Balances Between the Different Departments."

On October 8, 1787 the first of the "Letters From the Federal Farmer were circulated and an intellectual "battle of pens" ensued. Federalists wrote theses, pamphlets and articles trumpeting the "Constitution," urging men to sign, while allowing the country to tend to important governmental measures. The factions drenched paper with their inked ideals and printed theories in the press, for several months. James Madison wrote 29 of the Federalist essays, Hamilton 51 and John Jay 5.

Madison's personal letters in October, 1787 were full of alarm and reflected his growing fear that opponents of the Constitution would so prejudice the public as to plummet the country into incredible danger, internally, and externally. He did not understand the patriots refusal to support the Constitution in lieu of the lack of funds to pay the overwhelming national debt without a functioning government and could not rationalize that the opposition understood the peril that rejecting the document created. (27) Both sides accused each other of fantasizing unknown horrors and dangers from foreign countries.

THE STATE HOUSE AT ANNAPOLIS, MARYLAND
Associated with glorious events. The continental Congres
Adjourned from Princeton to meet here on November 26

THE PREAMBLE: The Preamble denotes no power, and merely explains the meaning of the Constitution: Elementary school children in America learn these words: We the People of the United States, In Order to form a more perfect Union, establish Justice, insure domestic Tranquility, provide for the common defense, promote the general Welfare, and secure the Blessings of Liberty to ourselves and our Posterity, do ordain and establish this Constitution for the United States of America.

THE ARTICLES OF THE CONSTITUTION, completed on September 17,

1787, Ratified on March 4, 1789. There were seven original artiles and there-have been twenty-seven amendments:

ARTICLE ONE: **The Legislative Branch.** All legislative Powers herein granted shall be vested in a Congress of The United States, which shall consist of a Senate and House of Representatives.

ARTICLE TWO: The Legislative
Section One: Legislative Power vested
The House of Representatives shall be composed of Members chosen every second Year by the People of the several States, and the Electors in each State shall have the Qualifications requisite for Electors of the most numerous Branch of the State Legislature . No Person shall be a Representative who shall not have attained to Age of Twenty five Years, and been seven Years a Citizen of the United States, and who shall not, when elected, be an Inhabitant of the State in which he shall be chosen.

Section Two: House of Representatives
Representatives and direct Taxes shall be apportioned among the several States, which may be included within the Union, according to their respective Numbers, which shall be determined by adding to the whole Number of free Persons, including those bound to Service for a Term of Years, and excluding Indians not taxed, three fifths of all other Persons. The actual Enumeration shall be made within three Years after the first Meeting of the Congress of the United States and within every subsequent Term of ten Years, in such Manner as they shall by Law direct. The Number of Representatives shall not exceed one for every thirty thousand, but each State shall have at Least one Representative and until such enumeration shall be made, the State of New Hampshire shall be entitled to chuse three, Massachusetts eight, Rhode Island and Providence Plantations one, Conn. five, New York six, New Jersey four, Pennsylvania eight, Delaware one, Maryland six, Virginia ten, North Carolina five, South Caroline five and Georgia three. When vacancies happen in the Representation from any State, the Executive Authority thereof shall issue Writs of Election to fill Vacancies. The House of Representatives shall chuse their Speaker and other Officers; and shall have the sole Power of Impeachment.

Section Three: Senate
The Senate of the United States shall be composed of two Senators from

each State, chosen by the Legislature thereof for six Years; and each Senator shall have one Vote. Immediately after they shall be assembled in Consequence of the first election, they shall be divided as equally as may be into three Classes. The Seats of the Senators of the first Class shall be vacated at the expiration of the second Year, of the second Class at the Expiration of the fourth Year, and of the third Class at the Expiration of the sixth Year, so that one third may be chosen every second Year; and if Vacancies happen by Resignation, or otherwise. During the Recess of the Legislature of any State, the Executive thereof may make temporary Appointments until the next Meeting of the Legislature, which shall then fill such Vacancies. No Person shall be a Senator who shall not have attained to the Age of thirty Years, and been nine Years a Citizen of the United States. And who shall not, when elected be an Inhabitant of that State for which he shall be chosen. The Vice President of the United States shall be President of the Senate, but shall have no Vote, unless they be equally divided. The Senate shall chuse their other Officers, and also a President pro tempore, in the Absence of the Vice President, or when he shall exercise the Office of the President of the U.S. The Senate shall have the sole Power to try all Impeachments. When sitting for the Purpose, they shall be on Oath or Affirmation. When the Pres. of the United States is tried, the Chief Justice shall preside: And no Person shall be convicted without the concurrence of two thirds of the Members present. Judgment in Cases of Impeachment shall not extend further than to removal from Office, and disqualification to hold and enjoy any Office of honor, Trust or Profit under the United States: but the Party convicted shall nevertheless be liable and subject to Indictment, Trial, Judgment and Punishment, according to law.

Section four: Elections of Senators & Representatives

The times, Places and Manner of holding elections for Senators and Representatives, shall be prescribed in each State by the Legislature thereof; but the Congress may at any time by Law make or alter such Regulations, except as to the Places of chusing Senators. The Congress shall assemble at least once in every Year, and such Meeting shall be on the first Monday in December unless they shall by Law appoint a different Day.

THE OLD STONE HOUSE
Richmond, Virginia. The first house built in Richmond

Section Five: Rules of the House and Senate

Each House shall be the Judge of the elections, Returns and Qualification of its own Members, and a Majority of each shall constitute a Quorum to do Business, but a smaller Number may adjourn from day to day, and may be authorized to compel the Attendance of absent Members, in such Manner, and under such Penalties as each House may provide. Each House shall keep a Journal of its Proceedings, and from time to time publish the same, excepting such Parts as may in their Judgment require Secrecy; and the Yeas and nays of the Members of either House on any question shall, at the Desire of one fifth of those Present, be entered on the Journal. Neither House, during the Session of Congress, shall, without the consent of the other, adjourn for more than three days, nor to any other Place then that in which the two Houses shall be sitting.

Section 6: Compensation & Privileges of Members

The Senators and Representative shall receive a Compensation for their Services, to be ascertained by Law, and paid out of the Treasury of the United States. They shall in all Cases, except Treason, Felony and Breach of the Peace, be privileged from Arrest during their attendance at the Session of their respective Houses, and in going to and returning from the same; and for any Speech of Debate in either House, they shall not be questioned in any other Place. No Senator or Representative shall, during the Time for which he was elected, be appointed to any civil Office under the Authority of the United States, which shall have been created, or the Emoluments whereof shall have been increased during such time; and no Person holding any Office under the U. S., shall be a Member of either Houses during his Continuance in Office.

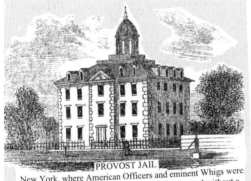

PROVOST JAIL
New York, where American Officers and eminent Whigs were
... and brutally beaten. Many were hanged without a

Section 7: Passage of Bills

All Bills for raising Revenue shall originate in the House of Representatives; but the Senate may propose or concur with Amendments as on other Bills. Every Bill which shall have passed the House of Representatives and the Senate, shall, before it become a Law, be presented to the President of the

United States: It he approve he shall sign it, but if not he shall return it, with his Objections to the House in which it shall have originated, who shall enter the Objections at large on their journal and proceed to reconsider it if after such Reconsideration two thirds of that House shall agree to pass the Bill, it shall be sent together with the Objections, to the other House, by which it shall likewise be reconsidered, and if approved by two thirds of the House, it shall become a Law. But in all Cases the Votes of both Houses shall be determined by yeas and Nays, and the Names of the Persons voting for and against the Bill shall be entered on the Journal of each House respectively. It any Bill shall not be returned by the President within ten Days after it shall have been presented to him, the Same shall be a Law. Every Order, Resolution, or Vote to which the Concurrence of the Senate and House of Representatives may be necessary (except on Adjournment) shall be presented to the President of the United States; and before Same shall take Effect. Shall be approved by him, or being disapproved by him, shall be repassed by two thirds of the Senate and Hs. of Rep., according to the Rules and Limitations prescribed in a Bill.

Section 8: Scope of Legislative Power

The Congress shall have Power To Lay and collect Taxes, Duties, Imposts and Excises, to pay the Debts and provide for the Common Defense and general Welfare of the United States; but all duties, Inputs and Excises shall be uniform throughout the United States; to borrow Money on the credit of the United States; To regulate Commerce with foreign Nations, and among the several States, and with the Indian Tribes; To estab-

RALL'S HEAD-QUARTERS.[2]

lish an uniform Rule of Naturalization, and uniform Laws on the subject of Bankruptcies throughout the United States; To coin Money, regulate the Value thereof, and of foreign Coin, and fix the standard of Weights and Measures:

To provide for the Punishment of counterfeiting the Securities and current Coin of the United States: To establish Post Offices and post Roads: To promote the Progress of Science and useful Arts, by securing for limited Times to Authors and Inventors the exclusive Right to their respective Writings and Discoveries: To constitute Tribunals inferior to the supreme Court;

To define and punish Piracies and Felonies committed on the high Seas, and Offenses against the Law of Nations; To declare War, grant Letters of Marque and Reprisal, and make Rules concerning Captures on Land and Water; To raise and support Armies, but no Appropriation of Money to that Use shall be for a longer Term than two Years;

To provide and maintain a Navy; To make Rules for the Government and Regulation of the land and naval Forces; To provide for calling forth the Militia to execute the Laws of the Union, suppress Insurrection and repel Invasions; To provide for organizing, among, and disciplining, the Militia, and for governing such Part of them as may be employed in the Service of the United States, reserving to the States respectively, the Appointment of the Offices, and the Authority of training the Militia according to the discipline prescribed by Congress.

To exercise Legislation in all Cases whatsoever, over such District (not exceeding ten Miles square) as may, by Cession of particular States, and the Acceptance of Congress, become the Seat of Government of the United States, and to exercise like Authority over all Places purchased by the Consent of the Legislature of the State in which the Same shall be, for the Erections of Forts, Magazines, Arsenals, dock-Yards, and other needful Buildings-And To make all Laws which shall be necessary and proper for carrying into Execution the foregoing Powers, and all other Powers vested by this Constitution in the Government of the United States, or in any Department or Officer thereof.

Section 9: Limits of Legislative Power

The Migration or Importation of such Persons as any of the States now existing shall think proper to admit, shall not be prohibited by the Congress prior to the Year one thousand eight hundred and eight, but a Tax or duty may be imposed on Such Importation, not exceeding ten dollars for each

Person. The Privilege of the Writ of Habeas Corpus shall not be suspended, unless when in Cases of Rebellion or Invasion the public Safety requires it.

No Bill of Attainder of ex post facto Law shall be passed. No Capitation, or other direct, Tax shall be laid, unless in Proportion to the Census or enumeration herein before directed to be taken. No Tax or Duty shall be laid on Articles exported from any State. No preference shall be given by any Regulation of Commerce or Revenue to the Ports of one State over those of another; nor shall Vessels bound to, or from, one State, be obliged to enter, clear, or pay Duties in another. No money shall be drawn from the Treasury, but in Consequence of Appropriations made by Law; and a regular Statement and Account of the Receipts and Expenditures of all public Money shall be published from time to time. No Title of Nobility shall be granted by the United States; And no Person holding any Office of Profit or Trust shall not, without the Consent of the congress, accept of any present, Emolument, Office or Title, of any kind whatever, from a King, Prince, or foreign State.

Section 10: Limits on States

No State shall enter into any Treaty, Alliance, or Confederation; grant Letters of Marque and Reprisal; coin Money' emit Bills of Credit; make any thing but gold and silver Coin a Tender in Payment of Debts; pass any Bill of Attainder, expost facto Law, or Law impairing the Obligation of Contracts, or grant any Title of Nobility. No State shall, without the Consent of the Congress, lay any Imposts or duties on Imports or Exports, except what may be absolutely necessary for executing it's inspection Laws: and the net Produce of all Duties and Imposts, laid by any State on Imports or Exports, shall be for the Use of the Treasury of the United States; and all such Laws shall be subject to the Revision and Controul of the Congress. No State shall, without the Consent of the Congress, lay any Duty of Tonnage, keep Troops, or ships of War in time of Peace, enter into any Agreement of Compact with another State, or with a foreign Power, or engage in War, unless actually invaded, or in imminent Danger as will not admit of delay.

ARTICLE TWO: The Presidency
Section 1: Election, Installation, Removal

The executive Power shall be vested in a President of the United States of America. He shall hold his Office during the Term of four Years, and, together with the Vice President, chosen for the same Term, be elected, as follows: Each State shall appoint, in such Manner as the legislature thereof may direct, a Number of Electors, equal to the whole Number of Senators and Representatives to which the State may be entitled in the congress: But no Senator or Repre

sentative or any person holding an Office of Trust of Profit under the United States, shall be appointed an Elector. The electors shall meet in their respective States, and vote by Ballot for two Persons, of whom one at least shall not be an Inhabitant of the same State with themselves. And they shall make a List of all the Persons voted for, and of the number of Votes for each; which List they shall sign and certify, and transmit sealed to the Seat of the Government of the United States, directed to the President of the Senate. The President of the Senate shall, in the Presence of the Senate and House of Representative, open all the Certificates, and the Votes shall then be counted. The Person having the greatest Number of votes shall be the President, if such Number be a Majority of the whole Number of Electors appointed; and if there be more than one who have such Majority, and have an equal Number of Votes, then the House of Representatives shall immediately chuse by Ballot one of them for President; and if no Person have a Majority, then from the five highest on the List the said House shall in like Manner chuse the President. But in chusing the President, the Votes shall be taken by States, the Representative from each State having one Vote; A quorum for this purpose shall consist of a Member or Members from two thirds of the States and a Majority of all the States shall be necessary to a Choice. In every Case, after the Choice of the President, the Person having the greatest Number of votes of the Electors shall be the Vice President. But if there should remain two or more who have equal Votes, the Senate shall chuse from them by Ballot the vice President. The Congress may determine the Time of chusing the electors, and the Day on which they shall give their Votes; which Day shall be the same through out the United States. No Person except a natural born Citizen, or a Citizen of the United States, at the time of the Adoption of this Constitution, shall be eligible to the Office of President; neither shall any Person be eligible to that Office who shall not have attained to the Age of thirty-five Years, and been fourteen Years a Resident with the United States. In case of the Removal of the President from Office, or of his Death, Resignation or Inability to discharge the Powers and Duties of the said Office, the Same shall devolve on the Vice President, and of the Congress may by Law provide for the Case of Removal, Death, Resignation or Inability, both of the President and Vice President, declaring who will then act as President, and such Officer shall act accordingly, until the Disability be removed, or a President shall be elected. The President shall, at stated Times, receive for his Services, a Compensation, which shall neither be increased nor diminished during the Period for which he shall have been elected, and he shall not receive within that Period any other Emolument from the United States, or any of them. Before he enter on the Execution of his Office, he shall take the following Oath or Affirmation:

"I do solemnly swear (or affirm) that I will faithfully execute the Office of President of the United States, and will to the best of my ability preserve, protect and defend the Constitution of the U.S."

Section 2: Presidential Power

The President shall be Commander in Chief of the Army and Navy of the United  States, and of the Militia of the several States, when called into the actual Service of the United States; he may require the Opinion, in writing, of the principal Officer in each of the executive departments, upon any subject relating to the Duties of their respective Offices, and he shall have Power to grant Reprieves and pardons for Offenses against the United States, except in Cases of Impeachment.

He shall have Power, by and with the Advice and Consent of the Senate, to make Treaties, provided two thirds of the Senators present concur; and he shall nominate, and by and with the Advice and Consent of the Senate, shall appoint ambassadors, other public Ministers and Consuls, Judges of the supreme Court and all other Officers of the United States, whose Appointments are not herein otherwise provided for, and which shall be established by Law; but the congress may by Law vest the Appt. of such inferior Officers, as they think proper, in the President alone, in the Courts of Law, or in the Heads of Departments. The President shall have Power to fill up all Vacancies that may happen during the Recess of the Senate, by granting Commissions which shall expire at the End of the next Session.

Section 3: State of the Union, Receive Ambassadors, Laws Faithfully Executed, Commissioning Officers

He shall from time to time give to the Congress Information of the State of the Union and recommend to their Consideration such Measures as he shall judge necessary and expedient; he may, on extraordinary Occasions, convene both Houses, or either of them, and in Case of Disagreement between them, with Respect to the time of Adjournment, he may adjourn them to such Time as he shall think proper; he shall receive Ambassadors and other public Ministers; he shall take Care that the Laws be faithfully executed, and shall Commission all the Officers of the U.S.

Section 4: Impeachment

The President, vice President and all civil Officers of the United States, shall be removed from Office on Impeachment for, and conviction of, Treason, Bribery, or other high Crimes and Misdemeanors.

ARTICLE THREE: The Judiciary

Section 1: Judicial Power Vested The judicial Power of the United States shall be vested in one supreme Court, and in such inferior Courts as the Congress may from time to time ordain and establish. The Judges, both of the supreme and inferior Courts, shall hold their Offices during good Behavior, and shall, at stated Times, receive for their Services a Compensation, which shall not be diminished during their Continuance in Office.

Section 2: Scope of Judicial Power

The judicial Power shall extend to all Cases in Law and Equity, arising under this Constitution, the Laws of the United States, and Treaties made, or which shall be made, under their Authority; to all Cases affecting ambassadors, other public Ministers and Consuls; to all Cases of Admiralty and maritime Jurisdiction; between a State and Citizens of another State; between Citizens of different States; between Citizens of the same State claiming Lands under Grants of different States, and between a State, or the citizens thereof, and foreign States, Citizens or subjects. In all Cases affecting Ambassadors, other public Ministers and Consuls, and those in which a State shall be Party, the supreme court shall have original Jurisdiction. In all the other Cases before mentioned, the supreme Court shall have appellate Jurisdiction, both as to Law and Fact, with such Exceptions, and under such Regulations as the Congress shall make. The trial of all Crimes, except in Cases of Impeachment, shall be by Jury; and such Trial shall be held in the State where the said Crimes shall have been committed; but when not committed within any State, the Trial shall be at such Place as the Congress may by Law direct.

Section 3: Treason

Treason against the United States, shall consist only in levying War against them, or in adhering to their Enemies, giving them Aid and Comfort. No Person shall be convicted of Treason unless on the Testimony of two Witnesses to the same overt Act, or on Confession in open Court. The Congress shall have Power to declare the Punishment of Treason, but no Attainder of Treason shall work Corruption of Blood, or Forfeiture except during the Life of the Person attainted.

ARTICLE 4: The States
Section 1: Full Faith and Credit
Full Faith and Credit shall be given in each State to the public Arts, Records and Judicial Proceedings of every other State. And the Congress may be general Laws prescribe the Manner in which such Acts, Records and Proceedings shall be proved, and the Effect thereof.

Section 2: Privileges & Immunities, Extradition, Fugitive Slaves
The Citizens of each State shall be entitled to all Privileges and Immunities of Citizens in the several States. A Person charged in any State with Treason, Felony, or other Crime, who shall flee from Justice, and be found in another State, shall on Demand of the executive Authority of the State from which he fled, be delivered up, to be removed to the State having Jurisdiction of the Crime. No Person held to Service or Labour in one State, under the Laws thereof, escaping into another, shall, in Consequence of any Law or Regulation therein, be discharged from such Service or Labour, but shall be delivered on Claim of the party to whom such Service or Labour may be due.

Section 3: Admission of States New States may be admitted by the Congress into this Union; but no new State shall be formed or erected within the Jurisdiction of any other State; nor any States be formed by the Junction of two or more States, or parts of States, without the Consent of the Legislatures of the States concerned as well as of the Congress. Congress shall have Power to dispose of and make all needful Rules and Regulations respecting the Territory or other Property belonging to the United States; and nothing in this Constitution shall be so construed as to Prejudice any Claims of the United States, or of any particular State.

Section 4: Guarantees to States
The United States shall guarantee to every State in this Union a Republican form of Government, and shall protect each of them against Invasion; and on application of the Legislature, or of the Executive (when the Legislature

cannot be convened) against domestic Violence.

ARTICLE 5 : The Amendment Process

The Congress, whenever two thirds of both Houses shall deem it necessary, shall propose Amendments to this constitution, or, on the Application of the Legislatures of two thirds of the several States, shall call a Convention for proposing Amendments, which, in either Case, shall be valid to all Intents and Purposes, as Part of this Constitution, when ratified by the Legislatures of three fourths of the several States, or by Conventions in three fourths thereof, as the one or the other Mode of Ratification may be proposed by the Congress; Provided that no Amendment which may be made prior to the Year One thousand eight hundred and eight shall in any Manner affect the first and fourth Clauses in the Ninth Section of the first Article; and that no State, without its Consent, shall be deprived of its equal Suffrage in the Senate.

ARTICLE 6: Legal Status of the Constitution

All debts contracted and Engagements entered into, before the Adoption of this Constitution, shall be as valid against the United States under this Constitution, as under the Confederation.

The Constitution, and the Laws of the United States which shall be made in Pursuance thereof, and all Treaties made, or which shall be made, under the Authority of the United States, shall be the supreme Law of the Land, and the Judges in every State shall be bound thereby, any Thing in the Constitution of Laws of any State to the Contrary notwithstanding.

The Senators and Representatives before mentioned, and the Members of the several State Legislatures, and executive and Judicial Officers, of the United States and of the several states, shall be bound by Oath or Affirmation, to support this Constitution; but no religious Test shall ever be required as a Qualification to any Office or public Trust under the United States

ARTICLE 7: Ratification:

The Ratification of the Conventions of nine States, shall be sufficient for the Establishment of this Constitution between the States so ratifying the Same. The Word, "the," being interlined between the seventh and eighth Lines of the first Page, the Word "thirty" being partly written on an erasure in the fifteenth Line of the first Page. The Words "is tried" being interlined between the thirty second and thirty- third Lines of the first page and the Word "the" being interlined between the forty third and forty fourth Lines of the second page. Attest William Jackson Secretary,

Done in convention by the Unanimous Consent of the States present the Seventeenth Day of September in the Year of our Lord one thousand seven hundred and Eighty seven and of the Independence of the United States of America the twelfth. In witness whereof We have hereunto subscribed our Names: Names followed beginning with George Washington, President, deputy from Virginia.

THE IMPACT OF THE CONSTITUTION ON THE NATION

The Constitution was adopted by a majority vote and copies sent to the states. To adopt, ten states had to ratify for the Constitution to become the Law of the Land. Nine states voted for the Constitution before it was Virginia's turn. The entire country watched in anticipation. Virginia contained some of the greatest minds and most courageous men in the Union. Men who were mostly against the Constitution in its original state. They believed with changes it would be acceptable. Sixty percent of Virginians were Anti-Federalists before the Virginia Ratifying Convention. James Madison, who was instrumental in the formation of the Constitution, was not planning to attend the Virginia convention but changed his mind at the last minute, hoping to defend any misunderstood passages. William Grayson was chosen as one of the representatives of Prince William County (28)

THE NORTHWEST ORDINANCE
OR THE LAND ORDINANCE OF 1785

Author's Comment: "Despite any defects, the Ordinance proved to be one of the wisest, most influential acts of the Revolutionary period," that inaugurated a system of land surveys which perfected by experience, were adopted by nearly every civilized country in the world. No act of the confederation government evinced a more genuine national spirit. This ordinance together with the better known Ordinance of 1787, guaranteed the American colonist against exploitation by the national government or by any of the original thirteen states, and thus formed the basis for the American Colonial system." (29) "William Grayson led this most significant legislation and saw it pass under the Articles of Confederation. The Ordinance of 1785 defined policies for admitting new states into the Union and excluded slavery from the Northwest Territory: Ohio, Indiana, Illinois, Michigan and Wisconsin. Grayson prepared and presented the 1785 Northwest Ordinance to Congress and witnessed its passage under a, majority vote. Jefferson was credited with furthering the work and finishing a Northwest Ordinance in 1787 with the assistance of William Grayson.

THE SOCIETY OF THE CINCINNATI

After the war, Major General Henry Knox, at the urging of General Washington, started a society as a means of ongoing fellowship for the Officers of the Continental Army, and to develop charitable funds to assist families of the original members along with securing pensions for Revolutionary War veterans. The society first met at a dinner in New York in 1783. George Washington was elected the first President. The name of the organization stood for Lucius Quintus Cincinnatus, a 5th C. B.C. Roman farmer who left his farm to lead Rome into battle. Their motto, "He gave up everything to serve the Republic." The first born of every member was eligible for membership. Centuries later these rules would ease a bit. Washington asked William Grayson to be a charter member and William happily joined the Society.

LETTERS BETWEEN OUTSTANDING MEN, 1785-1787
Prior to the Virginia Ratifying Convention

Letter from Richard Henry Lee to Francis Lightfoot Lee: " My dear brother, New York, July 14, 1787. I arrived this place a week ago almost destroyed with heat and fatigue. Here I found Grayson in the Chair of Congress Locum Tenens for the President who is absent. After some difficulty we passed an Ordinance for establishing a temporary Government beyond the Ohio as preparatory to the sale of the Country. And now we are considering an offer made to purchase 5 or 6 millions of Acres with public Securities. I hope we shall agree with the offer, but really the difficulty is so great to get anything done, that it is not easy for the plainest propositions to succeed. We owe much money, the pressure of Taxes." On April 14, 1785, a committee in Congress presented An Ordinance for ascertaining the mode of disposing of lands in the Western Territory, comprised of Pierce Long, Rufus King, David Howell, William Samuel Johnson, R.R. Livingston, Archibald Stewart, Joseph Gardner, John Henry, William Grayson, Hugh Williamson, John Byull, William Houstoun. Several changes were suggested and voted upon. Grayson sent two printed reports to James Madison who forwarded them to James Monroe, reporting progress.

George Washington to Grayson from Mount Vernon on June 22, 1785: Dear Sir: Since my last to you I have be our letters of the 5th, 27th, and of May, and beg your acceptance of my thanks for their enclosures, and for the communications you were pleased to make me therein. I am very glad to find you have pass'd an Ordinance of Congress respecting the sale of the Western Lands: I am too well acquainted with the local politics of individual States, not to have foreseen the difficulties you met with in this business; these things are to be regretted, but not to be altered until liberality of sentiment is more universal. Fixing the Seat of Empire at any spot on the Delaware, is in my humble opinion, demonstrably wrong: To incur an expense for what may be call'd the permanent seat of Congress, at this time, is I conceive evidently impolitic; for without the gift of prophecy, I will venture to predict that under any circumstance of confederation, it will not remain so far to the Eastward long; and that until the public is in better circumstances, it ought not to be built at all. Time, too powerful for sophistry, will point out the place and disarm localities of their power. In the meanwhile let the widow, the Orphan and the suffering Soldier, who are crying to you for their dues, receive that which can very well be rendered to them. There is nothing new in this quarter of an interesting nature, to communicate, unless you should not have been informed that the Potomac navigation proceeds under favourable auspices: At the general meeting of the subscribers in May last, it appeared that upwards of 400 of the 500 shares had been engaged; many more have been subscribed since; a Board of Directors have been chosen, proper characters and Labourers advertised for, to commence the work in the least difficult parts of the river, 'till a skillful Engineer can be engaged to undertake those which are more so; by the tenth of next month. I take the liberty of assuring the enclosed letter to your care and assure you of the resp.& esteem with which I have the honor to be, Sir, & Fr. George Washington (30)

Authors Comment: Congress adopted the Land Ordinance of 1785 on May 20, of that year. Under the Articles of Confederation, Congress did not have the power to raise revenue by direct taxation, thus set a goal to raise money through the sale of land in the largely unmapped territory west of the original colonies, acquired from England at the close of hostilities. The act called for political organization of the western territories that were to be divided into ten states, without any direction as to method or governance. The 1785 ordinance laid a foundation for land policy that was extant until the Homestead Act of 1862. The Land Ordinance established the basis for a Public Land Survey System, dividing land into townships, six miles on each side. Each town was sub-divided into 36 sections of one square mile, to be further reduced when sod to settlers and speculators. Section 16 in each township was reserved for schools. Sections 8, 11, 26 and 29 were set aside to compensate Revolutionary War veterans with gifts of land, for their service.

William Grayson wrote to George Washington on May 5, 1785, describing the details of the Land Ordinance. (31) William Grayson is credited with fathering the 1785 Ordinance. Thomas Jefferson is credited with the Ordinance of 1787. This ordinance was signed by Congress on July 13, 1787: It was, "An Ordinance for the government of the territory of the United States North West of the river Ohio, and for extending the fundamental principles of civil and religious liberty, which form the basis whereon these republics, their laws and constitutions which hereafter shall be formed in the said territory; to provide also for the establishment of States and permanent government therein, and for their admission to a share in the federal Councils on an equal footing with the original States, at as earlier periods may be consistent with the general interest. Three from Virginia voted Aye, William Grayson, Richard H. Lee and Paul Carrington. (32)

George Washington to Will Grayson, Jan.22,1785, Mt. Vernon,
Dear Sir: Your letter, with the Books, Potomac bill and other papers, did not reach this until past eleven o'clock on Monday forenoon; at which hour having set off for Alexandria, I did not receive the dispatches until my return in the evening.

The next morning I forwarded the Bill to Messrs. Fitzgerald Hartshorn to act upon, and to get a number of copies struck for promulgation, and the benefit of those who might wish to become subscribers.

For the trouble you have had with the Books and for your care of the letters and papers which accompanied them, you will please to accept my thanks. It would have given me much satisfaction if, instead of pursuing the rout thro' Frederick, you had resolved to have taken this road to the seat of congress: besides the pleasure of seeing you, I wished to have had some conversation with you on the subject of the late generosity of the Assembly towards me; for I will freely confess to you my dear sir, that no circumstance has happened to me since I quitted the walks of public life that has given me more embarrassment, than the act vesting me with 150 shares in the tolls for Potomac and James rivers.

On the one hand I consider this instance of the regard and attention of my native State as more than a mere compliment: This evidence of her good opinion and wishes to serve me is *unequivocal and substantial,* it has impressed me with sentiments of the deepest gratitude and I should be hurt, if I could think that my non-acceptance. Did you not my good sir tell me when I had the pleasure of spending an evening with you at Dumfries, that you either had or could procure me some Scions of the Aspin tree? Are there any young shoots which could be had of the Yew tree, or Hemlock (for I do not now recollect which of there it is) that grows on the Margin of Quantico Creek?

Plantations of this kind are now become my amusement and I should be glad to know where I could obtain a supply of such sorts of trees as would diversify the scene. With great esteem and regard, I am, etc. George Washington.

William Grayson to George Washington, March 10, 1785

Dear Sir, I had the honor of your favor of the 22nd of Jany. Just as I was setting off from Dumfries, and I should have answered it from Mr. (John) Orr's in Loudoun, (33) where I was detained some time on account of Mrs. Grayson's illness, if I had not wish'd for more time to reflect on the subject matter of it. It would have giv'n me great pleasure (if my particular situation would have permitted) to have waited on you at Mount Vernon & to have convers'd with you on the occasion as I could in that case have entered more fully into the different circumstances than it is practicable to do by a communication on paper.

I shall now however give you the best information in my power, as also my own sentiments with the utmost candor & sincerity; It was talk'd of by gentlemen of the House that some mark of attention and respect (not barely complimentary) should be paid you by your native Country; that the other States in the Union knew you only as an American, but that your own knew you as an American and a Virginian; the only difficulty was how to fall on any expedient that might not wound your feelings on the one hand or be unworthy of the Legislature.

While matters remain'd in a situation altogether inconclusive, a gentleman of the Assy. made a motion respecting you, which it was thought advisable to oppose on the principle of particular impropriety; however it was soon discovered from the temper of the House that if the question had been put it would have been carried without a dissentient as those in the opposition would also have voted for the measure; recourse was therefore had to entreaty & he was prevail'd on to withdraw it, on being promis'd a plan should be brought forward which should in some degree imbrace his views as well as the wishes of the House; accordingly the act which took effect was presented the next day, & immediately pass'd both Houses.

Some of the reasons which suggested it were these; It had appeared by  conversations out of doors, on the passage of the river bills, that the House were anxious (as you had patronized them and opened their importance to public view) that the credit of the undertaking should be ascribed to yourself & it was wish'd that this might appear by some public act of the legislature. In pursuing this idea, it was thought that such an act might with propriety contain a grant of a certain number of shares to yourself which at the same time would be an instance of the attention of the House might also serve in part as a reason for taking up the subject and introducing the other matter.

It was reasoned by those who countenanc'd this particular plan, that the grant when measured by the European scale (the only criterion by which it could be judged) was correlatively inconsiderable, as to exclude every idea of it's being looked upon as a reward for services; that the value of the subject was so precarious & depended on such a variety of circumstances as almost to prevent the sensation of property in the mind.

That the act would carry to Posterity an evidence of the part you had acted in this great undertaking, the remembrance of which would be kept up by the possessions which were granted by the Assembly and retained by your family; That under every view of the subject could be considered in no other light than the Act itself set forth, an honorable testimonial of the gratitude & affection of your native Country. The gentlemen who favored this particular mode, designedly contracted the number of shares in order to guard it against the objections which you now suppose it to be liable to, as the blank with equal facility might have fill'd up in such a manner as to have comprehended objects of much greater magnitude.

The idea of your being subjected to the performance of any particular service never once occurred and so far from it's being suppos'd that you are in any degree circumscribed by the act I am perfectly satisfyed you will yourself confer the obligation by the acceptance. I will not pretend to say that the House do not wish you to devote some portion of your leisure reflections to the furtherance of this great national object; this is also I verily believe the case with every man who has reflected on the matter; indeed numbers rest the success of the measure in a great degree on the event.

But then Sir this is hop'd for, not as the effect or condition of the act but merely as the result of your own inclinations; they suppose such a line of conduct will at the same time, be highly honorable to yourself & that this is one of those few great objects on which you can now with propriety fix your attention. The House I am convinc'd would feel very sensibly if they suppos'd you conceived yourself to be less independent on this account, or that any act of theirs should have a tendency to prevent you from offering your advice to your Country whenever you conceived it necessary These were the ideas  which prevail'd in general on the occasion; there was a great variety of sentiments, and a great deal said about the matter particularly witht. doors where every man spoke his mind freely; indeed candor obliges me to inform you that there were not wanting some who thought you were plac'd in a situation which call'd for assistance of a very different nature from the present. With respect to what you hint as to it's being considered in the light of a pension, I am satisfied it can never be the case under any view of the subject; indeed I cannot concieve there can be any such thing in our governments according to the ideas generally annex'd to it, and if instead of a precarious unproductive property it had been the grant of an annuity from the United States.

I think it would not have been liable to this appellation, for I look upon the uninfluenced grant of a free people in a very different light from a gift which proceeds from the caprice of Princes or Ministers and which is always supposed whether true or false to be founded on the principle of favoritism; this distinction is preserved in the Brittish constitution & is productive of sensations essentially different, the one conveying the idea of personal favor and the other that of acknowledg'd merit.

If then the grants of parliament in a Monarchy are looked upon as highly honorable to the person who recieves them, how much stronger ought the impression to be in a republican government, where the principle of action is always suppos'd to be Virtue.

Upon the whole however as you have plac'd so much confidence in me as to consult me on the occasion, and as the subject is a very delicate one, I would rather advise that you should not accept the grant at present in any other manner than that of acting under it, leaving your ultimate decision to time & future reflection. There are persons in the world interested in defeating the whole undertaking, and from motives of resentment alone might be induced to misrepresent the purity of your intenti and though I have not the least doubt myself of the propriety of your accepting the grant yet it would be a painful reflection in me to think I had recommended a measure which had the most distant tendency in lessening you in the estimation of

OLD TAVERN AT CHARLES CITY, VA
Where the militia gathered. Scene of a surprise attack by the British in which several american were killed or captured.

the world. It is certain if I had thought not it decidedly right, I never would have voted for it as a representative of the people; and I have every reason to believe that this was the case with every member of the House, who never would have offered a thing which they conciev'd it was improper in you to recieve. If you should at a future period and after the maturest consideration find yourself unalterably determined against converting it to your own use, you will always have it in your power to appropriate either the principal or profits to public purposes of essential utility; though this will contradict the desires and wishes of your fellow citizens, and counteract the purposes which gave rise to the measure I think it will be less objectionable than an absolute rejection in the first instance. It will shew a willingness on your part to comply with their request as far as your own sensations would permit you. I hope however that at some future period, and after you have thoroughly weighed all the circumstances, you will find yourself disposed as well from the propriety of the thing itself, as the impulse of your own feelings towards your parent State, to accept of the grant in the manner originally designed by the legislature, and that the same may go and descend to your representative agreeable to their intentions. The Assembly of Virginia have no doubt a regard for your interest, but I am satisfied they have a much higher one for your personal fame & honor.

I shall now leave this subject with observing that there are strong reasons to be urged against your parting with the power giv'n you by the act, and which in my opinion essentially regards the success of the undertaking, but as your own feelings are connected with the subject I find a repugnance in pressing them in point of delicacy. I shall therefore leave them & their operations to the suggestions of your own mind making no doubt they will have such an effect as the magnitude of the object and your attachment to it's success may with propriety point out. With respect to the Aspen & Yew trees, I beg leave to acquaint you, that I sent to Sprigg's ford to see if the tree which the Doctr. had giv'n me had produc'd any scions, and was inform'd there were none.

I then applied to Mr. Landon Carter who had several at his plantation on Bull run; Mrs. Grayson whom I left at Mr. Orr's promis'd me to carry them behind her carriage to Dumfries & to send them from thence to Mount Vernon together with any scions of the yew tree which she with the assis-

tance of Doctr. Graham & Mr. R. Graham, might be able to procure. We have very little news here, Mr. Marbois has informed us there will be no war between the Emperor and the Dutch, & the Minister of the latter expresses himself to the same purpose, but neither have communicated the terms of the pacification.

Congress are engaged in a plan for opening their land office on the Western waters. In recommending a plan for extending their powers in forming Commercial treaties, In regulating the post Office and in making a Peace establishment.

They have directed a treaty to be form'd if practicable with the Piratical States on the Coasts of Africa; I expect a Minister will be appointed to the Court of Spain after the arrival here of Don diego Gardoqui.

I presume an ambassador will be appointed to Holland in place of Mr. Adams who goes to the Court. of St. James.

I have the honor to be, with the highest respect, Yr Aff. Friend & Most Obedient. Servant William Grayson.

Author's Comment: The Virginia assembly vested Washington with 50 shares in the Potowmack River Co. and 100 shares in the James River Co., for his role in opening both rivers to navigation.

Washington's finest, most dramatic act was his farewell to the Continental Army and its dismissal, after which Washington turned and walked humbly away without fanfare, or demands.

Washington had served as Commander in Chief from June 14, 1775 to 1783. He was genuinely surprised to be called to serve as President and preferred to remain out of the limelight, in retirement at Mount Vernon. (34)

Any other man holding such power, might have made himself emperor, but Washington showed enormous presence and humility on that auspicious occasion, as he did on most.

This humility made him all the more revered an likely earned him the presidency.

Charles Thomson to Hannah Thomson, April 3, 1785

(Thomson was secretary to Congress, and became a controversial figure)
Dear Hannah The badness of the weather having as I suppose prevented the arrival of the post, I have not had the pleasure of a letter from you since that of the 29 of last Month, which I acknowledged the receipt of, in my last

Mrs. Falls's.¹

of the 31ˢᵗ. I mentioned in that letter that Congress had come to a decision on the business of my Office. Though I believe that this matter originated in the ambition of one and the malice and resentment of another, I determined to let it take its course without deigning to interfere or to converse with any members upon it lest I should seem to be courting favour.

The Committee indeed to whom it was referred desiring to have my Opinion on the duties of the office & the necessity of erecting a new department, I gave it freely & subscribed my name, leaving them at full liberty to make what use of it or to shew it to whom they pleased.

At the first opening of the business it appeared to be precipitated, and that though the plan of ambition might have been laid the measures of accomplishing it had not been concerted or fully arranged.

However being brought forward it gave an opportunity of sounding the dis-position of the states, but this was done with so little skill in political maneuvers as to turn the attention or at least direct their suspicions to an individual and to point out the measure as an object of ambition rather than of public utility, & the disposition of the house was shewn in such a way that whether the suspicions were well or ill founded, the feelings & pride of the individual must have been a good deal hurt. The plan and schemes of malice were deeper and better laid. Under pretence of collecting in one view the duties of the Office An Ordinance was prepared with such art that it should be rather for the purpose of establishing a new office than for ascertaining the powers of one already established.

This would give an opportunity of a new election, and provided there was any probability of gratifying resentment in that way to say nothing of the term of continuance in Office, but if that could not be obtained, then to introduce a clause for an annual election. This plan was deep laid, but much hurt by a coalition with the other, and prosececuted with that perservering cunning & malice for which the author is distinguished. Unfortunately for him what he conceived a masterly strroke displayed the author in his true colors and produced an effectm the contrary of what he desired. I shall explain myself further when we have the pleasure of meeting. For as you observe I must reserve something for conversation & not commit everything to writing.

We had last evening a violent storm of hail, snow & afterwards rain, with two or three severe claps of thunder. This I hope will prove the breaking up of the winter, which though it could not be called severe when compared with last winter yet has been long and tedious.

From what I hear, the roads are extremely bad. Indeed it cannot be otherwise. The ground being so deeply soaked, and the surface frozen all last month & to this time no warm sun or drying winds to exhale the Moisture, I hope now for clear weather and fine roads. I have been to look at the garden or rather a lot for a garden for it is altogether a waste behind the house I have taken. The Landlord has engaged a carpenter to make up the fence & make the necessary repairs about it. I do not think it will be worth while for me to do any thing towards putting it into order, till we take possession, especially as the stable is so situated that the horses are led to it through the garden. I have examined what used to be called the study and think it will answer extremely well for William and Ruth.

There is a lamp just by the front door as you mentioned. My love to Rob, Am. & Jonathan and to all friends. On Friday I recd. a letter from Gervais informing that he declines the Office of Commissioner so that there is an opening & chance for our friend G.C.

I wish with all my heart the place was filled and the board set to business. Adieu my dear Hannah, with unfeigned affection I am Your loving husband, Cha Thomson [P.S.] Monday April 4. Just as I was going to seal this I recd. your two letters. I fancy J has not seen all the fields that are sown, for Joe, acknowedged to me there was about 100 acres or rather more in full grain. (35)

I enclose an account of Scot for engraving the seal and shall be much obliged if you will pay it & get a receipt. William knows where he lives.

Author's Comment: Thomson had long been unhappy in his position as secretary to Congress, especially since Congress departed from Philadelphia in June, 1783, and he had apparently considered resigning since the breakup of the Committee of the States in Annapolis in a steamy August of 1784. The prospect of moving with Congress to Trenton and then to New York did not sit well with him, and the election November 30 of Richard Henry Lee as president of Congress, a leading member of the anti-

Thomson faction, gave added stimulus to thoughts of retirement. Charles had angered many delegates over the years, and some who thought that he had sided with their enemies, sought ways to curtail his influence.

Eldridge Gerry, for example, was leading a Massachts. attempt to require an annual election of secretary of Congress, and in December voiced optimism over the prospect that Thomson, whom he despised, would resign before moving to New York. Thomson, however, recovered his resolve to continue in office, and regained a calm demeanor since the effort "to revise the institution of the Secretary" had not resulted in any changes that would undercut his authority. This effort to remove Thomson was revived with the appointment of a committee on January 31st, consisting of David Howell, James Monroe, Charles Pinckney, Robert R. Livingston, and Joseph Gardner, who reported a draft ordinance on February 25 on which debate was scheduled for March 4th, but postponed to March 18th.

A Spanish Caravel.

An effort by Pinckney to delay a consideration to study "the propriety of creating a secretary for the home department" whose duties would be incorporated into the office of the secretary was rejected during this debate, as was a second such effort during a second reading on the 31st. Immediately after Congress proceeded to its third adoption, that same day. (36) Thomson saw Congress' efforts to reshape the duties of his office and he was exasperated at the drift in congressional policy and sensed the personal animosity, since leaving Philadelphia in June, 1783. Eldridge Gerry had also been a mover in the February 1784 attempt "to revise the regulations of the Department of The Secretary of Congress."

Arthur Lee, whom Thomson considered his most bitter enemy and one whom he apparently thought had twice attempted to poison him, was no longer a threat as he was no longer in Congress. (37)

William Grayson to George Washington, April 15, 1785, N. Y.

Dear Sir, I did myself the honor of writing to you by Post the 10th of march last in answer to your favor of the 22nd of January, & I hope my letter has before this got safe to hand. On my being appointed one of the Commee. for draughting the Ordnance for ascertaining the mode of disposing of lands in the Western territory, the President was kind enough to furnish me with an extract of your letter to him on the subject of the back Country, which now induces me to conclude it will be agreeable to you to be informed of the farther progress of this important business.

The Ordnance was reported to Congress three days ago, & ordered to be printed, & I now take the earliest opportunity of sending you a copy; The idea of a sale by public Venue, in

HASBROUCK HOUSE, Orange County N. Y.
Washington and his lady stayed overnight here in 1783
The dining room was called the room with seven doors

such large quantities, appears at first view eccentric, & objectionable; I shall therefore mention to you reasons which those who are advocates for the measure offer in it's support.

They say this cannot be avoided witht. affording an undue advantage to those whose contiguity to the territory has giv'n them an opportunity of investigating the qualities of the land.

That there certainly must be a difference in the value of the lands in different parts of the Country, and that this difference & most be ascertained witht. an actual survey in the first instance & a sale by competition in the next. That with respect to the quantity of land offered for sale in a township, it will not have the effect of injuring the poorer class of people, or of establishing monopolies in speculators & ingrossers: That experience is directly against the inference, for that the Eastern States, where lands are more equally divided than in any other part of the Continent were generally settled in that manner; That the idea of a township with the temptation of a support for religion & education holds forth an inducement for neighbourhoods of the same religious sentiments to confederate for the purpose of purchasing and settling together.

That the Southern mode would defeat this end by introducing the idea of indiscriminate locations & settlements, which have a tendency to destroy all those inducements. to emigration which are derived from friendships, religion and relative connections.

That the same consequence would result from sales in small quantities under the present plan; That the advantages of an equal representation, the effect of laying off the country in this manner; The exemption from controversy on account of bounds to the latest ages; the fertility of the lands; the facilities of communication with the Atlantic through a variety of channels, as also with the Brittish & Spaniards; the fur & pelt trade; & the right of forming free governments for themselves, must solicit emigrants from all parts of the world, & insure settlement of the country in a most rapid manner, that speculators & ingrossers, if they purchase the lands in the first instance cannot long retain them on account of the high price they will be obliged to give & the consequent loss of interest while remaining in their hands uncultivated.

That if they however should make money by ingrossing, the great design of the land office is answered which is revenue; and that this cannot affect any but European emigrants or those who were not at hand to purchase in the first instance; that if it is an evil, it will cure itself, which has been the case in Lincoln County Virginia, where the lands were first in the hands of Monopolists: but who were forced to part with them from a reguard to the general defense. That the expense & delay would be too great to divide the territory into fractional parts by actual surveys, and if this is not done sales at public venue cannot be made, as with a previous knowledge of the quality of the lands no comparative estimate can be formed between different undivided societies.

That the offering a small number of townships for sale at a time is an answer to the objection on account of delay, and at the same time it prevents the price from being diminished on acct. of the Markets being overstocked. That the present plan excludes all the formalities of warrants, entries, locations, returns & caveats, as the first & last process is a deed. That it supercedes the necessity of Courts for the determination of disputes, as well as that of creating new officers for carrying the plan into execution.

That the mode of laying out the same in squares is attended with the least possible expense, there being only two sides of the square to run in almost all cases. That the expense will be repaid to the Continent in a ten-fold ratio, by preventing fraud in the Surveyors. That the drawing for the townships and sending them on to the different States is conformable to the principles of the government, one State having an equal right to the best lands at it's market with the other: as also of disposing of it's public securities in that way. That if the Country is to be settled out of the bowels of the Atlantic States it is but fair the idea of each State's contributing it's proportion of emigrants should be countenanced by measures operating for that purpose.

That if the plan should be found by experience to be wrong, it can easily be altered by reducing the quantities & multiplying the surveys. These were the principal reasonings on the Committee in favor of the measure and on which it would give me great satisfaction to have your sentiments, as it involves consequences of the most extensive nature, and is still liable to be rejected altogether by Congress, or to be so altered as to clear it of the exceptionable parts; perhaps the present draught might have been less objectionable if we had all had the same views. Some gentlemen looked upon it as a matter of revenue only & that it was true policy to get the money witht. parting with inhabitants to populate the Country & thereby prevent the lands in the original states from depreciating. Others (I think) were afraid of an interference with the lands now at market in the individual States: part of the Eastern Gentlemen wish to have the lands sold in such a manner as to suit their own people who may chuse to emigrate, of which I believe there will be great numbers coming from Connecticut.

But others are apprehensive of the consequences which may result from the new States taking their position in the Confederacy. They perhaps wish that this event may be delayed as be raised for the purpose of protecting the settlers on the Western frontiers &

POHICK CHURCH, IN TRURO PARISH, Virginia on the road to Alexandria, VA. Where Washington worshipped

preventing unwarrantable intrusions on the public lands, & for guarding the public stores. I apologize to you for the length of this letter; the subject appeared to me of the greatest consequence & I was desirous you might have the fullest information thereon; As the communicating a report of a Commee. while under the deliberation of Congress is agt. rule, I shall thank you to retain the possession of it yourself. I have the honor to be, with the highest respect, Yr. Affect. friend & Most Obedient servant. Willm. Grayson (38)

Author's Comment: The proposed ordinance on the Northwest Territory evolved from a March 2nd broadside printing by John Dunlap until its fifth and final form on May 20th, 1785. After reading the ordinance March 4 and 16, Congress referred it to a grand congressional committee of which Grayson was the pivotal member. The committee's modified ordinance was read on April 12 and printed and distributed, but re-committed that same day. After lengthy debate from April 20 to 26, a considerably altered ordinance was entered on the journals, and recommitted. Debate continued until April 29th with only eight states attending. "The plan cannot be compleated without a fuller representation of the States." Congress re-

compleated without a fuller representation of the States." Congress resumed consideration briefly on May 2 with the whole committee attending, but it was not until nine states were present on May 18, that Congress entered into debate over the third reading, and after final amendments, the ordinance was at last passed on May 20,1785. John Dunlap prepared 500 copies for distribution. They were printed and re-distributed.

George Washington to William Grayson, Mount Vernon April 25, 1785.
Dr. Sir: I will not let your favor of the fifteenth, for which I thank you, go unacknowledged, tho' it is not in my power to give it the consideration I wish, to comply with the request you have made, being upon the eve of a journey to Richmond to a meeting of the Dismal Swamp company, which by my own appointment is to take place on Monday next; into that part of the country I am hurried by an express which is just arrived with the acct. of the deaths of the mother and Brother of Mrs. Washington, in the last of whose hands (Mr. B. Dandridge) the embarrassed affairs of Mr. Custis had been placed, and call for immediate attention.

To be candid, I have had scarce time to give the report of the Committee,

CONGRESS HALL

which you did me the honor to send me, a reading, much less to consider the force and tendency of it. If experience has proven that the most advantageous way of disposing of Land, is by whole Townships, there is no arguing against facts; therefore, if I had time I shou'd have said nothing on that head: but from the cursory reading I have given it, it strikes me that by suffering each State to dispose of a proportionate part of the whole in the State, that there may be State jobbing:

In other words that citizens of each State may be favored at the expense of the Union; whilst a reference of these matters to them has, in my opinion, a tendency to set up separate interests; And to promote the independence of individual states upon the downfall of the federal government, which in my opinion is already too feeble, much too humiliated and tottering, to be supported without props of Congress.

It is scarcely to be imagined that any man, or society of men, who may incline to possess a township, would make the purchase without viewing the Land in person or by an Agent. Wherein then lies great advantage of the sale in each State, and by State officers? for from the same parity of reasoning, there should be different places in each State for the accommodation of its Citizens. Would not all the ostensible purposes be fully answered by sufficient promulgation in each State, of the time and place of Sale to be holden at the nearest convenient place to the Land, or at the seat of Congress. Is it not highly probable that those who may incline to emigrate, or their Agents would attend at such time and place? And (there being no fixed prices to the Land) would not be the high or low sale of it depend upon the number of purchasers and the competition occasioned thereby; and are not these more likely to be greater at one time and place than at thirteen? One place might draw the world to it, if proper notice be given: but foreigners would scarcely know what to do with thirteen, to which, or when to go to them. These are first thoughts, perhaps incongruous ones, and such as I myself might reprobate upon more mature consideration: at present however, I am impressed with them, and (under the rose) a penetrating eye, and close observation, will discover thro' various disguises a disinclination to add new States to the confederation, westward of New York, the inevitable consequence of emigration to, and the population of that territory: and as to restraining the citizens of the Atlantic states from transplanting themselves to that soil, when prompted thereto by interest or inclination, you might as well attempt (while our Governmts. are free) to prevent the reflux of the tide, when you had got it into your rivers. As the report of the Committee

goes into the minutia, it is not minute enough, if I read it a right; it provides for the irregular lines, and parts of townships, occasioned by the interference with the Indian boundaries, but not for its interference with Lake Erie, the western boundary of Pennsylvania (if it is governed by the meanders of the Delaware or the Ohio river which separates the ceded Lands from Virginia, all of which involve the same consequences.

I thank you for the sentiments and information, given me in your letter of the 10th. of March, respecting the Potomac navigation. My present determination is, to hold the shares which this State has been pleased to present me, in trust for the use and benefit of it: this will subserve the plan, encrease the public revenue, and not interfere with the line of conduct I had prescribed myself. I am, etc. On April 29 Washington left Mount Vernon for Richmond, Va., which he reached on the evening of May 1. He left Richmond May 4, and arrived at Mount Vernon, May 6.

William Grayson to Timothy Pickering, N. York, April 27, 1785,

Dear Sir, Receiv'd your favor; in consequence of which I shall write to Mr. Graham for the receipt which you desire. Indeed I should have done this sooner, but I have been a little indispos'd till within these three days. Before I arrived at this place, Genl Knox was elected Secretary at war; he has since come here, and is now acting in his office; from what I can learn he has accepted of the appointment under a supposition that his house rent will be paid. Poor Carlton is in a distrest situation; he will shortly be out of pay and un-pensioned; I am striving to get something allowed him by way of compensation though I am afraid no great matter can be affected, as it is not among the vices of republicans to be prodigal in the article of rewarding for services which are past.

Since my arrival I have been busily engaged in assisting about framing an ordinance for the disposal of the Western territory; I think there has been as much said and wrote about it as would fill forty Volumes, and yet we seem far from a conclusion, so difficult is it to form any system,which will suit our complex government, & where the interests of the component parts are suppos'd to be so different. I made a motion for Amendmts. three days ago, which has nearly divided the Continent into equal moieties; the object of it was to double the quantity of surveying & to sell the lands & townships alternately; this I did under the impression that it would accommodate both the East ern & Southern States. However this has been strongly objected to, & both sides adhere to their opinion; so that here we stick, without any movement either retrograde or progressive. I inclose you the draught of the Ordnance as it stands; which you will be kind enough to keep in your hands in such a manner as to prevent it from being published, this being against the rules.

I believe it will pass ultimately in a shape very like this, at least none of the great principles except perhaps the one alluded to will be changed. By it you will observe that there is no office created by it worth your accept tance. If in the arrangement of the Post Office or any other matter any thing occurs which may be worth your notice, I have the pleasure of informing you of it.

I can assure you with great truth it will give me real satisfaction to do every thing in my power towards accomplishing any object which you may have in view. I am with my complimt. to the family, yr. Affect. frd. & most obed serv, Willm. Grayson

William Grayson to James Madison, May 1, 1785, New York
Dear Sir, I am afraid my silence since I came to this place has giv'n you some reason to suspect me to be impregnated with that vis inertia, which has been so often attributed to me: the only apology I have to make, is that I wish'd to have some thing to write to you worth your acceptance. However as there would be some danger in risquing a farther delay, I shall give you what I have in the matter. The New England delegates wish to sell the Continental lands, rough as it runs; what I miss in quality I will make up in quantity. All our attentions here have been for some time turned towards the hostile preparations between the Emperor & the Dutch; as it was thought the event might have a considerable influence on the affairs of the United States. The packet which arrived has brought different accounts of what is doing respecting this business; however I take the following to be nearly the truth of the case: That the Emperor only made the opening the Schelde a pretext for marching his troops into the low Countries while he has been underhandedly treating with the Elector of Bavaria for an exchange of his territories in the low countries for Bavaria: That France has not only been privy to the negotiations but has actually countenanc'd them; While no other power has entertain'd de Deux Ponts pre-

FREEHOLD MEETING HOUSE
New Jersey, site of the BATTLE OF MONMOUTH

sumptive heir to Bavaria, on recieving the first notice of it, made application to the King of Prussia, supposing that old Statesman would exert himself to the utmost, to prevent Bavaria from becoming part of the domains of the House of Austria. It therefore seems to be probable that all those who wish to preserve the proper balance of power in the Germanic body will unite with the Prussian Monarcagainst this accession of weight to the Austrian scale; Should this confederacy take place in its fullest extent, it will be very formidable and in all liklihood produce a bloody contest before the matter is finally decided. War therefore seems to be as probable as ever although the ground of the contest may be altered. For my own part I cannot clearly find out from any informations which. I have had, what have been the views of the Court of France; they seem to have departed from their ancient principles in assisting the Austrian family to increase their power; 'tis true they adopted this system in the last reign, but then the French Statesmen say, that nothing done during that period ought to be quoted from their history. If the Queen of France has drawn in the Ministry to countenance the measures of her brother it is an evidence of her great influence in the Government. But from what appears at present, it is no Proof of the credence of the public-councils as it is obvious if France up large standing armies, she must neglect her marine by which she will risque her foreign possessions whenever she happens to be engaged in a war with G. B. The Parliament has so lately sit, that little has yet transpired; the Minister is to bring forward. a plan for a Parliamentary "form, which it is thought will require all his interest & ability to support. The Wallachians who were so oppress'd as to be drove into a state resistance are on the point of being subjugated; they are in number about seven hundred thousand; & I heartily wish they were all here. Congress are engaged in ascertaining a mode for the disposal of the territory; I send you the first draught as reported by the Grand Commee. also a second edition with amendments in Congress. The matter is still under consideration, and other alterations will no doubt take effect. An amendment is now before the house for making the Townships 6 Miles. Square. & for dividing those townships by actual surveys into quarters of townships, marking at every interval of a mile (in running the external lines of the quarters,) comers for the sections of 640 acres; Then to sell every other township by sections: The reservation (instead of the four corner sections,) to be the central section of every quarter; that is to say the inside lot, whose corner is not ascertained: Whether this will be carried or not I cannot tell, the Eastern people being amazingly attached to their own customs, and unreasonably anxious to have every thing regulated according to their own pleasure. The construction of the deed of cession from Virga. has taken up four days, & at length 'it is agreed not to sell any land between the little Miami & Scioto

THE OLD CAPITOL
Williamsburg, Virginia. Where the House of Burgess met.
Built in the shape of an H By Queen Anne. Near the college of
William & Mary. Used As an Open Court House.

until the conditions respecting the Offs. & soldiers are complied with. Some Members of Congress think they have a right to have the land laid off for the Officers & soldiers in such manner as they please & by their own Surveyors, provided they give good land.

The requisition for the present year is before Congress; one article to wit 30,000 dollars for foederal buildings at Trenton, I objected to, & was supported by the delegates of Maryland, Delaware, & New Hampshire.N. Carolina was divided. Unfortunately for me the rest of the delegates for our State do not think as I do; (This is entre nouz). I shall notwithstanding do every thing in my power to frustrate the measure. We shall in all probability get it struck out of the requisition, because nine States will not vote for it; I understand however that it is intended to get seven states to vote for the sum out of the loans in Holland supposing that as a hundred thousand dollars were voted at Trenton by nine States, generally, that seven can direct the particular appropriation. This matter I have not yet considered, and I know how it will turn out on investigation however I hope I find means to avoid it for the present year, & I hope by the next the Southern States will understand their interests better.

Congress have refused to let the State discount any part of the monies paid for the Western territory, out of the requisitions for the present year & I believe if they don't help themselves, they will never find Congress willing to discount. In the mean time they will sell the lands. We do not intend to sell lands between the Miami and Scioto rivers until the claims of the Virginia Continental troops had been satisfied, & the Officers & soldiers chuseby sections. If the State insists on the right of surveying agreeable to their own laws I should suppose that Congress could have no objection to appointing commrs. for deciding that question as well as all oth-

PHILLIP'S MANOR HOUSE

ers that might arise respecting the Compact. Mr. King of Massachusets has a resolution ready drawn which he reserves till the Ordinance is passed for preventing slavery in the new State. Seven States might be found liberal enough to adopt it. Seven hundred men are voted for protecting the settlers on the frontiers, for guarding the public stores & for preventing unwarrantable intrusions.on the lands of the U. S. I inclose vou a plan for altering the 9th article of the confederation. (Rights granted the Federal Government). A treaty is directed to be held with the Barbary States to purchase their friendship. Treaties are also to be held with the Cherokees, Chickesaws & with the Western Indians shortly. I am sure you are surfeited; therefore conclude with great sincerity, Yr. Affect. Friend & Mo. Obed. Servt. Willm. Grayson (39)

Author's Comment: Congress resolved on December 20, 1784, that a sum not exceeding $100,000 be set aside for the construction of federal buildings in Trenton, N.J. However, the March 31 committee on requisitions recommended only $30,000 for that purpose and Grayson's April 5 effort to strike that amount was successful. The following day Congress reinstated the sum and recommitted the report for the original amount. Grayson did not want the Capitol in a northern state and chose Georgetown and conveyed this information to George Washington, who agreed.

William Grayson to Timothy Pickering, May 1, 1785, New York
Dear Sir. Since writing to you, I have received a letter from Graham, informing me, he is afraid of an execution against him on the judgments, & requests the receipts of the Plaintiff & the Assignee, may be sent to him.
I shall thank you to inclose them by the' first oppy; directing for him at Dumfries. In answer to his letter, I have desired him to send the receipt which you desire. We have nothing new since except that a negotiation is going on between the Emperor & the Elector of Bavaria, to exchange Bavaria for the low countries. This it is thought (far from producing peace) will have a direct tendency to bring on war immediately though perhaps

upon different grounds. France and the Emperor have it seems been maneuvering together; the Dutch have also had a finger in the pye. (40) I remain, yr. Affect. fd. & Most Obed. servt, Willm.Grayson.

Author's Comment: Joseph Carleton, secretary in the war office, had not been compensated for his seven years of service despite the considerable responsibility he bore, especially during the resignation of Benjamin Lincoln in November 1773, for which he received only $1,000 a year, the same as a secretary. Promising Congress to continue his duties until the newly-appointed Henry Knox could find a replacement, Carleton appealed to Congress on April 23 for "a just and reasonable compensation for his deranged finances that "prevent my returning with decency to private life." Carleton's letter and supporting documents were referred on the 26th to a committee chaired by William Grayson, which recommended on June 7th that Carleton receive $1,500 a yea, less what he had already been paid,"For some time he was engaged in service until the arrival of General Knox." On September 27th, Congress granted hm only $1,000 in consideration of his "extra services." General Knox reappointed Carleton secretary in May.

George Washington

William Grayson to George Washington, May 5, 1785 N.Y.,

Dear Sir. I have received your letter of the 25th of April, for which I am much oblig'd to you; I am sorry for the melancholy occasion which has induc'd you to leave Mount Vernon, and for the affliction which the loss of such near relations had involved Mrs. Washington..

The Ordinance for disposing of the western territory has been under consideration ever since I wrote you last & has underwent several alterations, the most considerable of which is that one half the land is to be sold by sections or lots, & the other half by entire Townships; & the dimension of each township is reduc'd to six miles; I now expect the Ordinance will be completed in a few days, it having the opinion of most gentlemen that it is better to pass it in it's present form nearly, than to delay it much longer & incur the risque of losing the country altogether.

As soon as it is finished I shall do myself the honor to inclose you a copy, and though it will be far from being the best that could be made, yet I verily believe it is the best that under present circumstances can be procured.

There have appeared so many interfering interests, most of them imaginary, so many ill founded jealousies & suspicions throughout the whole, that I am only surprised the Ordinance is not more exceptionable; indeed if the importuities of the Public Creditors & the reluctance to pay them by taxation & the direct or implied had not been so great.

I am satisfied no Land Ordinance could have been procured, except under such disadvantages as would in a great degree have excluded the idea of actual settlements within any short length of time. This is not strange when we reflect that several of the States are averse to new votes from that part of the Continent & that some of them are now disposing of their own vacant lands, & of course wish to have their particular debts paid

VAN CORTLAND'S SUGAR HOUSE

& their own countries settled in the first instance before there is any interference from any other quarter.

With respect to the different places of sale, it is certainly open to the objections you mention, but it was absolutely necessary to accede to the measure, before we could advance a single step. Since the receipt of your letter I have hinted to some of the members the propriety of altering this part, but find that the idea of allowing the Citizens of each State an equal chance of trying the good lands at their own doors, was one of the strongest reasons with them for consenting to the ordinance.

As to the individual states interfering in the sale, it is guarded against; and in case the loan Officer who is responsible only to Congress cannot dispose of the land in a limited time, it is to be return'd to the Treasury board: With respect to the fractional parts of Townships the Ordinance has now provided for all cases which can occur, except with respect to the Pennsylvania line. The Course of the new State from the Ohio will be due North, and the dispute with Pennsylvania will be open to discussion hereafter. I am sorry to observe that throughout this measure, there has been a necessity for sacrificing one's opinion to that of others to move forward.

There has never been above ten States on the floor & nine of these were necessary to concur in one Sentiment, least they should refuse to vote for the Ordinance on it's passage. The price is fix'd at a dollar the acre liquidated certificates, that is the land is not to be sold under that.

The reason for establishing this sum was that a part of the house were for half a dollar, and another part for two dollars & others for intermediate sums between the two extremes, so that ultimately this was agreed upon as a central ground. If it is too high (which I am afraid is the case) it may hereafter be corrected by a resolution. I still mean to move for some amendments which I think will not only advance the sale, but increase the facility of purchasing to foreigners, though from present appearances I own I have but little hopes of success. After this affair is over, the requisition for the current year will be brought forward with but little hope of success.

Sums between the two extremes were suggested, so that ultimately this was agreed upon as a central ground. If it is too high (which I am afraid is the case) it may hereafter be corrected by a resolution. I still mean to move for some amendments which I think will not only advance the sale, but increase the facility of purchasing to foreigners, though from present appearances I own I have little hopes of success. After this affair is over, the requisition for the current year will be brought forward.

The article of 30,000 dollars for the erection of foederal buildings at Trenton I have already objected to, & shall continue to oppose by every means in my power, as I look upon the measure to be fundamentally wrong, & I am in hopes nine States cannot be found to vote for it; should those in opposition to the measure be able to put off the execution for the present year it is to be expected that the Southern States will open their eyes to their true interests & view this subject in a different light.

What I at present fear is, that failing to get this article allowed in the requisition they will attempt to draw the money from Holland by a vote of seven States in as much as a hundred thousand dollars were voted at Trenton for that purpose although no particular fund was assigned, I own this matter has giv'n me some disgust, as I see an intemperate ardor to carry it into execution before the sense of the Union is known.

I have no doubt that some gentlemen have come into Congress expressly for that purpose. I take the liberty of introducing Mr. St. Greave a delegate from North Carolina a gentleman of great worth who is travelling through the State to his own Country. He will he very happy to communicate to you the news of this place. I inclose you the report of a Comme. for altering the first paragraph of the 9th article of the confederation & which embraces objects of great magnitude, & about which there is a great difference of sentiment. I have the honor to be, with the highest respect, Yr. Affect. frd. & Most Obed. sert., Willm. Grayson

William Grayson to James Madison, May 28, 1785, N. Y.

Dear Sir, I did myself the pleasure some time since of writing to you; and I expect by this time you have recieved my letter; since which nothing has happened of any consequence except the passage of the

Land Ordinance & the arrival Don Diego de Gardoqui at Philadelphia. I inclose a copy of the Ordinance & if it is not the best in the world, it is I am confident the best that could be procured for the present. There was such a variety of interests most of them imaginary, that I am only surprised it is not more defective.

The Eastern people who before the revolution never had an idea of any quantity of Earth above a hundred acres, were for selling in large tracts of 30,000 acres while the Southern people who formerly could scarce bring their imaginations down so low as to comprehended the meaning of a hundred Acres of ground were for selling the whole territory in lots of a mile square. In this situation we remained for eight days, with great obstinacy on both sides, until a kind of compromise took effect.

As to foreign news we are entirely uninformed: neither can [any] body here say with certainty what will be the event of the present hostile preparations in Europe. You have heard of the arrival of an American vessel at this place in four months from Canton in China laden with the commodities of that country It seems our Countrymen were treated with as much respect as the Subjects of any other nation: i,e. the whole are looked upon by the Chinese as Barbarians: & they have too much Asiatic hauteur to descend to any discrimination. Most of the mercantile people here are of the opinion, this commerce can be carried on better for America than to smuggle a very considerable quantity to the West Indies. I could wish to see the merchants of our State engaged in this business. Don't you think an exemption from duty on all goods imported immediately from India to our State might have a good effect? (41) In Grayson's hand with the signature clipped.

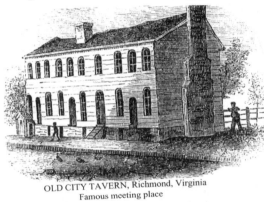

OLD CITY TAVERN, Richmond, Virginia
Famous meeting place

William Grayson to Unknown Person, June 4, 1785, New York

Dr. Sir. Your letter of May 20th has duly come to hand, but previous to this, Major Parker was appointed, on a supposition that such an office would interfere with Maj. Anderson's appointment under the State of Virginia; there is a doubt subsisting in Congress about the right of surveying, and I presume that the nomination of Anderson might have giv'n some uneasiness; With respect to Ludeman, I will whenever he applies do every thing in my power in his behalf   A few weeks since we made recommendation to the States to raise 700 Men, for the purpose of protecting the frontiers & of preventing unwarrantable intrusions on the lands of the Continent: some gentlemen are of opinion though the number of troops are small, that they ought to be commanded by an Officer of rank. I should therefore be glad to know (if this opinion should indeed gain proselytes) whether you would accept of the command: it is probable the number of troops, may be increased, especially if by this  summer's negotiation we can get possession of the British Posts.   Should you be disposed that way, let me know without loss of time; & please write a letter to Monroe, on the subject; I shall be very happy to see you here & remain with great sincerity, Yr. Affectionate friend & Most Obedient Servant, Willm. Grayson.

William Grayson to William Short, June 15, 1785, N.Y.

Dear Sir, Your favor by the packett has been duly recieved for which I am much obliged to you, and I make use of this opportunity by Mr. Mazzei to answer it. I arrived at this place early in March, since which nothing of any great importance has taken effect except the land ordinance which is herewith inclosed.

A difference of sentiment between the Eastern & Southern part of the Continent & an imaginary difference of interests has made the Ordinance less perfect than it might have been. Congress are about directing a treaty to be held with the Western Indians at Post Vincent on the Wabash this summer for extinguishing their rights to the territory between the Miami & Mississippi; should this be effected, I expect the Ordinance will be made to apply to that country, immediately as the paying the domestic debt in this way seems to be an object which every one has very much at heart.

Indeed the necessity of the measure is glaring, for while the Taxes continue high, we shall have no emigrants from beyond seas, & the want of inhabitants is perhaps our only calamity. A very considerable part of No. Carolina has revolted; They have assumed the powers of governmt. & a Capt. Cocke was here the other day with authority from them to solicit admission. Georgia has laid off a county on the Mississippi called Bourbon & settlers are gathering fast about the Natches. There is a report that the province of Maine begin to make speeches respecting independence; Vermont remains as it did when you left this. Inclosed is the report of a Commee. for altering the 9th article of the confederation. 8 States will be for it, but whether or not it will suit the 5 Southern States, is a point very questionable: perhaps some modification may be found out that will make it palatable. As the sending this report is against rule, I hope you will take good care that it is not made public indeed I think it would be best to keep it a secret. It seems to be a doubt in Congress whether the instructions to the Commrs. ought not to be changed. The principle of making treaties & granting to all the right of the most favored nations, begins to be disputed. This though entre nouz, & what I would not chuse should be mentioned to any one. Congress have had two ineffectual tryals for the election of a Minister to the Hague vice John Adams Rutledge of So. C., Governor Livingston & R. H. Harrison of Md. were nominated. The Dutch Minister grows uneasy I think that Rutledge will be elected very soon, & in all probability today. Don diego de Gardoqui, charge des affaires from the Court of Spain is arrived at Philada.; & is expected here every day; what are the objects of his mission, we are at a loss to determine.

I have the pleasure to inform you the subscriptions to the Potowmac Co. goes on well: At a meeting the other day, it was found that forty three thousand pounds were subscribed: They are therefore by the Act established a company. Genl. Washington is elected President & there is a good prospect of success. I imagine you must have heard before this, that an American vessel had arrived here in four months from Canton in China laden with the manufactures of that Country: & that our countrymen at

VIEW OF THE PLACE WHERE THE BRITISH LAID DOWN THEIR ARMS

that place had as much respect & civility shewn them as those of any other nation. The opinion here is that this trade can be carried on to great advantage, I remain yr. Affec. frd & most Obed Serv, W.Grayson. I inclose the journals of Congress.

Author's Comment: Colonial men graciously sent newspapers and the important papers of the day to those who could not easily obtain them, i.e. those serving abroad. England, France and the Netherlands usually had an American representative serving at their Courts.

Thomas Jefferson to James Monroe on June 17, 1785:
"This will be handed you by Mr. Otto who comes to America as Charge des affaires in the room of Mr. Marbois promoted to the Intendancy of Hispaniola, which office is next to that of Governor. He becomes the head of the civil as the Governor is of the military department. I am much pleased with Otto's appointment. He is good humoured, affectionate to America, will see things in a friendly light when they admit of it, in a rational one always, and will not pique himself on writing every trifling circumstance of irritation to his court. I wish you to be acquainted with him, as a friendly intercourse between individuals who do business together produces a mutual spirit of accommodation useful to both parties. It is in our interest to keep the affection of this country for us, which is considerable. A court has no affections. But those of the people whom they govern influence their decisions even in the most arbitrary governments."

William Grayson to George Washington, July 25, 1785, N.Y.
Dear Sir, The inclosed letters were handed to me the other day by young Mr. Adams, son of Mr. John Adams, who has arrived in the last packett, and no private opportunity offering, I do myself the honor of transmitting them by Post. Congress are informed by a letter from Mr. Adams, that he has been introduced to the King of G. B. in due form, and received as a public Minister from the U. S. of America. They have also received from the Commrs. for forming commercial treaties projects of two treaties; the one with the King of Prussia, the other with the Grand Duke of Tuscany; the former it is expected is signed before this by the American Ministers. Don Diego de Gardoqui (who has plenipotentiary powers) has been received and Congress have passed a commission to Mr. Jay. Secretary for foreign affairs to negotiate with them. Congress have lately paid great attention to the proposed alteration of the 9th Article of the Confederation, and it has been debated several times.

Don Diego de Gardoqui (who has plenipotentiary powers) has been received and Congress have passed a commission to Mr. Jay. Secretary for foreign affairs to negotiate with them. Congress have lately paid great attention to the proposed alteration of the 9th Article of the Confederation, and it has been debated several times.

I did myself the honor of inclosing this paper some time ago; there seems to be three opinions; some are for the alteration as reported provided Eleven & not nine States have the exercise of the powers, others are for forming a navigation act, & submitting the same to the States; a third opinion is

against any change whatever. I expect after the subject has been thoroughly investigated, it will by consent be put off till the members have had an opportunity of consulting the legislatures.

The requisition for the current year is nearly finished; By this the states are called upon to pay three Millions of dollars, i.e. one Million in specie, and two Millions in Interest on liquidated certificates; The whole containing a provision as well for the purposes of Government for Interest on the foreign & domestic debt. I beg leave to inclose propositions respecting the coinage of Gold, Silver & Copper, presently before Congress. I have the honor to be, with the highest respect Your Affectionate friend & Most. Obedient servant. Willm. Grayson.

George Washington to Will'm Grayson, August 22, 1785 Mt. Vernon

Dear Sir: During my tour up the Potomac River, with the directors to examine and to form a plan for opening and extending the navigation of it Agreeably to the acts of the Virginia and Maryland Assemblies, your favor of the 25th came to this place, with the letters brought by the son of Mr. Adams from France; for your care of which I thank you.

Appropos John Quincy Adams, did you hear him say anything of Hounds which, the Marqs. De la Fayette has written to me, were committed to his care? If he really brought them (and if he did not I am unable to account for the information.

It would have been civil in the young Gentleman to have dropped me a line respecting the disposal of them, especially as war is declared against the canine species in New York, and they being strangers, and not having formed any alliances for self-defense, but on the contrary, distressed and friendless may have been exposed not only to war, but to pestilence and famine also. If you can say anything on this subject pray do so.

Author's Commentary: John Quincy Adams had apparently found it distasteful or inconvenient to accompany the Hounds, a gift from the Marq. De la Fayette, across the Atlantic Ocean, and Washington was slightly miffed and worried about what had happened to the hounds.

William Grayson to George Washington, Sept 5, 1785, N.Y. (42)

Dear Sir, I had the honor of your favor by Post. The hounds you allude to arrived here in the midst of a hot war against their fraternity: they were however not friendless.

Your Acquaintance Doctor Cochran took very good care of them while they remained at their place & has sent them by Capt. Packard's Sloop to Mount Vernon. I make no doubt that they have got there safe. We have little news from Europe or elsewhere. Mr. Otto came over in the last packett as charge des affaires in the room of Mr. Marbois who goes to the West Indies. We are informed the Chevalier de La Luzerne is to be here shortly as Minister.

The demand of the body of Longchamps is withdrawn. For some time past there has been very few States on the floor, of course very little has been done. I am happy to hear that after inspection, you are of opinion the obstructions on the Potowmac, are not greater than you had supposed them to be. I have the honor to be, with the highest respect, Yr. Affect. frd. & Most Obed servt, Willm. Grayson

Author's Comment:

Louis-Guillaume Otto had been introduced officially by the Comte de Vergennes in a letter of June 20, to the secretary for foreign affairs, John Jay, and more importantly by Thomas Jefferson, who had known him in Paris before his departure for America.

This is how and why Thomas Jefferson wrote a letter to James Monroe and handed it to Otto in Paris for him to deliver once he reached America, namely New York. (43)

William Grayson to George Washington, October 3, 1785

Dear Sir, "The requisition is at length finished; I have now the honor of inclosing; the Article of 30,000 dollars for Foederal buildings at Trenton is expunged; & I think the opposition to that measure is gaining strength.

Some of the southern States begin to view it in a different light. Congress have passed a resolution authorizing the Post Master general under the direction of the Board of Treasury to contract with the owners of the Stage coaches for the transportation of the Mail; it is expected the contracts will be formed in the course of the next month; after which there will be three mails a week through the southern States. A new Ordinance for the Post Office is ready to be reported in which there are clauses for cross posts from Alexandria to Fort Pitt, & from Albany to the limits of Canada, but it is doubtful in this present Congress if either will take effect.

Mr. Payne has a memorial before Congress. To be allowed a sum of money for his services, to which there is a favorable report from a Commee. I am fearful that nothing of consequence will take effect. I have the honor to be, With the highest respect, Your Affectionate Friend. & Most Obed. Serv. Willm. Grayson

Author's Comment: On Sept 22, 1785, Eldridge Gerry moved to increase the sum appropriated for federal buildings to $100,000, the motion was defeated with Mass.& N.J. voting in favor. Md., VA and S.C oppos.

"William Grayson suggested Georgetown as the site for the capitol and worked hard to make that choice a reality.

Regarding Thomas Paine's request for compensation for service to the United States. Thomas Paine submitted a series of appeals to Congress beginning in 1785, asking to be paid for eleven years of service. One letter went to a committee chaired by Eldridge Gerry. Congress agreed that Paine was due "liberal Gratification" for "explaining & informing the principles of the late revolution, by ingenious, & timely publications, upon the nature of Liberty & civic Government, "but ordered no specific compensation.

In Sept. Paine appealed again. William Grayson chaired the new committee and recommended that Paine receive $4,000, but that sum was struck. Paine wrote again for his expenses for eleven years, not less than six thousand dollars. "Grayson's committee reported to Eldridge Gerry. They moved to compensate Paine but were defeated. Paine wrote again, requesting settlement of $948 for depreciation of his salary as Sec. to the Comm. for Foreign Affairs through January 1779. All previous information was referred to Eldridge Gerry who got a resolution for payment of $3,000. Congress ordered treasury to pay. (Grayson wrote this letter to Washington before Congress had taken action.) The comm. referred Paine's letter on salary depreciation to Comptroller James Milligan who wrote to Gerry that Paine's request was inappropriate because Congress had extended to the list its resolve of April 10, 1780, limiting depreciation only to those in service on that date. Paine had resigned fifteen months earlier. Congress took no further action. Paine got nothing. (44)

William Grayson to James Madison, Nov. 22, 1785, New York

Dear Sir, I wrote you by the last Post, since which other letters have arrived from the gentleman therein mentioned. They came by the last packett; and one is dated as late as the 15th of September last. In it however there is no mention of the Algerine War. Mr. Jefferson also wrote by the French packett, but his letter is of an old date. There has been a conference with Mr. Pitt. That gentleman thinks the war could make no change in the nature of the debts due by or to the citizens or subjects of either country; that the interest is as much due as principal; that the Brittish lawyers hold this opinion.

In answer Mr. A. observes the lawyers in America hold a very different opinion respecting the War, and that no jury from New Hampshire to Georgia would allow interest during the war. That the war put an end to all laws and government, consequently to all contracts made under those laws.

That it is a maxim of law that a personal right or obligation once destroyed is lost forever: that the treaty & new laws were necessary for the restoration of the contracts or obligations; that the contracts could not be said to have had any existence during the War. Mr. Pitt replied, that if these were the ideas in America, it was necessary there should be some new stipulation respecting the subject.

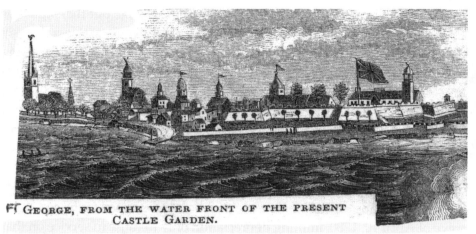

FT GEORGE, FROM THE WATER FRONT OF THE PRESENT CASTLE GARDEN.

With respect to the Negroes he acknowledged that this was so clear a case, as that satisfaction ought to be made therefor, as soon as the number carried off could be made appear. To this Mr. A. replied, that Colo. Smith who had transacted the business with Sir Guy Carleton could evince it by documents then ready to be produced. He acknowledged also with respect to Mr. A's construction of the Armistice there could be no great difficulty: that with regard to the Posts it was so connected with other matters as not to be decided on singly. As to the commercial treaty there seems to have been a great difference of sentiment; Mr. A. is of opinion that nothing will be done shortly. Mr. Pitt however has promised that during the recess of parliament he will turn his thoughts to those subjects.

Mr. A. thinks that the reason why the elector of Hanover came into the Confederation against the Emperor, was to preserve peace, in Europe, on our accounts. I need not observe he is a strong advocate for restrictions on their commerce.

 I have been detained here longer than 1 expected, waiting to forward some documents which 1 conceived might be of advantage to our State; which I have had more difficulty in procuring than I at first expected.

1 have by this post sent the aggregate amounts in specie value of the advances to each State; by which it will appear that our State has had but little comparatively.

The Union in fact owe her a million of dollars & upwards on this account provided she has made equal exertions in other respects; that is to say she has received a million less than her foederal proportion.

 It is said however that no advantage can be immediately derived from this circumstance, as it is contended that the interest on all these sums is suspended till the final settlement of accounts by the resolution of the 3rd of June 1784. This same resolution then holds out an additional temptation prolongating the settlement.

Rhode Island has had a million of dollars; is it likely then to suppose the wishes for the arrival of a period when she is to account? The same observation will apply to those who are similarly circumstanced.

It will be difficult then when Virginia meets with embarrassments to get them removed by Congress. Virginia has a demand (in opposing Lord Dunmore) of £400,000 Virga. money incurred from Sept. 1775 to December 1776: which I do not know is supported by any resolution of Congress.

It is true she has the same reason to have it allowed as Massachusets. Besides there are resolutions of Congress which direct assistance which assistance Congress says shall be paid: however it is said here that all this goes for nothing. This subject of our public accounts deserves great consideration. I hope you consider this letter confidential, & remain, Yr. Affect. friend & Most Obedt. Servt., Willm. Grayson (45)

Author's Comment: William Grayson does not agree with most of Mr. A's conclusions. Interesting though how much he confides in James Madison who is to become almost an arch enemy in his estranged political views.

William Grayson to Patrick Henry. Nov. 22, 1785, New York
Sir, Since writing by the last post, I have procured from the board of treasury, a schedule of the aggregate amounts of advances to different States in the Union; the component articles which form these amounts are about being printed, & will then be forwarded, as the charges were very numerous, and as it was necessary that every one however insignificant should be reduced to specie value by the scale of depreciation, I am not surprised that the work has taken up so much time. The advances to the State of Virginia are relatively small as your Excellency will observe by ascertaining the proportions: but from this circumstance it does not appear that any immediate advantage is to be derived to the State, as it is contended that the resolution of the 3rd of June 1784 suspends the payment of interest until the general settlement of the public accounts. I do the honor of inclosing the general account of receipts & expenditures from the first  **(HOWE'S QUARTERS)** of Nov.,1784 to the first of Nov., 1785. Mr. Morris' book of receipts & expenditures has not been authenticated by Congress, there is no other

immediate means of shewing them, I shall forward them by the first oppor-

tunity the same being too bulky for a conveyance by Post; When the Grand Commee. were sitting, they directed the Commrs. of the Treasury to furnish extracts of the correspondence of the different Commrs. of public accounts with the late financier & the present board; copies of these Extracts & etc. I beg leave to inclose, which shew the difficulties of the State of Virginia to settle accounts, as well as those of other states. An official letter from Adams dated the 15th of September makes no mention of the Algerine War; an older letter from Jefferson mentions it as common report. I have the honor to be, with the highest respect, Yr. Excys. Most Obed. & very hmble Servant, Willm.Grayson (46)

William Grayson to Patrick Henry, Nov. 22, 1785, New York

Dr Sir, Inclosed is a letter from the late President and myself respecting the funeral expenses of our worthy friend Mr. Hardy.

After writing, we had agreed it should be inclosed to your Excellency in a private letter with a request that it might not be laid before the legislature provided the connections of the deceased were disposed themselves to make the remittance in time to answer the payment of the money here.

We supposed it might be in the power of your Excellency to get information, either through the means of our friend Mr. Tyler or the parties themselves, in a short time.

I hope you will excuse the trouble I give you on this occasion; indeed I should not have taken the liberty had I not been acquainted with the friendship which subsisted between yourself, and the gentleman to whom it unfortunately relates. It is a point of delicacy in us not to give offence to the relations of a person whom we so highly valued by an immediate application to the legislature, at the same time it is to be observed that it is essentially necessary the money should be remitted in time in order that the contracts for taking up the money may be duly complied with.

William Grayson to James Madison, Nov. 23, 1785, New York

Dear Sir, I am very busy preparing to decamp for Virginia, of course I shall not lay you under the trouble of reading a long letter from me this Post. There is one thing very singular in Adam's correspondense, he is always pressing the necessity of commercial restrictions; says no treaty can be had without them, and yet he decidedly acknowledges, that in the prosecution of this commercial war there is every reason to suppose we shall incur a real war; for says he nothing but the opinion they have of our strength & their weakness prevents it at present: for the nation is against us. There are still pro's & con's here respecting the Algerine war: & not a word from Europe officially.

The new Congress have chos'n Hancock Presidt. And Doct. Ramsay Chairman until his arrival. The business immediately before them is whether Temple shall be recieved as Consul Genl. from G. Brittain. I presume it will be decided ultimately in the affirmative as Congress have passed a resolution that Ministers & Charges des Affaires at foreign courts shall be Consuls general ex Officio. Temple has come out in great State, &

has taken the best house in the City. The inconvenience which Members of Congress have experienced here this last year from living at common boarding houses, & mixing with the landlady, her Aunts, cousins & acquaintances & with all other sorts of company has been complained of loudly; We have not, I confess suffered in this way, though we have purchased the exemption dear rate to our purses; we have had a house though a small one, & yet that same house has gone deep into our allowances, so that our dignity has almost eaten up our finances.

I understand some of the States mean to relieve their delegates from the weight of this inconvenience by establishing a kind of State house at the expense of such State. Although I cannot help admiring the idea of doing something yet I think the plan of jumbling all together whether Grave or gay, married or single, like Falstaff in the buck baskett, heel (47) altogether improper. I suppose (if the legislature gets into a merry mood,) that it would be better to allow each delegate a certain sum of money, provided he disburses the same in House rent. It is also supposed hard that a Member of Congress when he goes home to see his family should be put upon stoppages. I should hope no person would be appointed but would conscientiously discharge his duty to the State to the best of his judgment. I remain Yr. Affect. fd, & Most Obed Servt., Willm. Grayson.

P.S. You will please to consider what relates to Adams as altogether confidential. The Affair of the Negroes which has made so much noise in our house is rather trifling. Negroes carried off from N.Y. Men 1,386, Women 954, Children 657, Total 2,997. The Va. Hs. of Delegates were agitated over Britain's evacuation of Virginia slaves in violation of the Treaty of Paris and were angry and wanted redress. (48)

William Grayson to James Monroe, Nov. 28, 1785, New York

Dr Sir, I imagine long before this you have heard of the death of our worthy friend Mr. Hardy; he was hardly ever well after you left us, having been much troubled with fevers, till going to Harlem heights on a party, he broke a blood vessel in coughing, & dyed the 17th of October.

His death has giv'n me the greatest concern on account of the sincere friendship I had for him; and I have been much embarrassed with his affairs since his death; his funeral has cost 385 dolls. for which I am liable; his friends being not equal to the paymt. of his private debts.

FRASER S BURIAL-PLACE

I have wrote particularly to the Governor thereon to which I refer you, & request your assistance thereon, provided this finds you at Richmond; I shall be much pinched to pay the money if I am not relieved in time.

With respect to your affairs, I have done the best that it was in my power to do; by paying the importunate, & giving fair words to the others, I have managed so that your credit has not suffered in the smallest degree.

I inclosed you by last post, all the letters which have come to hand directed to you since your departure to the care of Genl Weedon; a book referred to (I expect) in one of Mr. Jefferson's letters is now in my possession having been delivered to me by Mr. Otto.

I now inclose you the journals of Congress complete by which you will see what we have been about since you left us; since the new Congress met, nothing has been done of any consequence, except the appointing of Hancock President, and Doctor Ramsay, Chairman until his arrival; some people think he will not come forward. The business immedy. Before them is whether Temple shall be received as Consul General from G. Britain or not. I am inclined to think it will be carried in the affirmative, when the States come forward (there being but 7 at present on the floor). As Congress have committed themselves by resolving that all Ministers, Charges, &c, at for-eign Courts shall be Consuls genl. Ex Of-ficio: of course Adams is Consul genl. at the Court of G,B. There is some important foreign in-telligence but which I cannot communicate without a cypher.

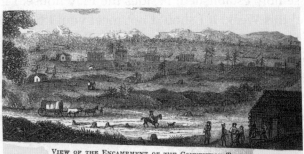

VIEW OF THE ENCAMPMENT OF THE CONVENTION TROOPS.
(From a picture in Anburey's *Travels*.)

Whether there is actually an Algerine War or not, is more than I can tell with certainty; the news comes authenticated from individuals in different parts but we have no official accts. of the matter.

They talk much about a new requisition already: & I hope you will inform yourself well about the State of our public accounts, also of the sentiments. of the legislature respecting the last request as well as of the foederal buildings at Trenton. The latter is asleep for the present.

Pray do not forget the situation of your colleagues: & yourself, it is rather unworthy the State to deduct for absent time.

The Members ought to be allowed a hundred pounds a piece for house rent if the delegate expends so much. As to stowing them all to-gether in a State house, I think it highly improper, though this I under-stand is the idea in Pensylvany. I think it would be right that we should be paid our house rent for this year: You know it was very heavy upon us.

Your friend Gerry is on the point of being united to the elder Miss Thomson; in consequence of this, I have been able to sell the black horses yesterday for 160 dollars. They were put up before this at the Coffee house, & only one hundred & eight dollars was bid for them: this I should have been obliged to have taken, if I had been under the necessity of setting off for Virginia when I expected, by keeping them I have done better for you; though bad is the best. Had it not been for the death of Mr. Hardy I would have taken them myself at the price: but circumstanced as I was I did not think it right to be concerned with them at all.

Your friends at the Sycamore are all well, & very frequently inquire after you; Rufus, the Capt.& myself were at the play with them the other evening when they made so brilliant & lovely an appearance as to depopulate all the other boxes of all the genteel males therein.

The town is likely to be very gay this winter. There is a regular Concert & assembly established; besides the Play house. I intend to decamp from [here] this Week; if I should not meet you, I beg leave to inform You that you will find our house tolerably well finished for people in our circumstances as to funds.

You may take possession of my bed & sheets till I return. I advise you to take back the black Cook again, she has left us in a fret on account of a difference between her & my Irishman that nearly proceeded to hostilities. Wishing you health & happiness, I remain yr, Affect. frd, Willm. Grayson

Author's Comment : Grayson did not leave N.Y. until Dec. 6 and wrote a note to Virginia's treasurer Jacquelin Ambler on Nov. 29: "At five days sight, of this my first bill of exchange, (the second of the same tenor and date not being paid,) pay to William Duer Esqr. on order the sum of four hundred dollars, & place the same to account of, Sir, yr. hmble servt, Willm, Grayson." Account Voucher. William was often short of cash.

William Grayson to Richard Henry Lee, Nov. 30, 1785 N. Y.
Dear Sir, I have little news to communicate. Mr. Hancock is appt. President but it is much doubted whether he will accept of this high Office. It was

VIEW FROM THE TOP OF MOUNT DEFIANCE.

surely improper to play the risquing game on such an occasion.

The business immediately before Congress is whether Mr. Temple shall be received as Consul Genl. from G.B. or not; there are on this occasion far different sentiments, though I presume when the States are fully represented (there being but seven at present) that it will be decided in the affirmative as Congress seem to have committed themselves as they have resolved that the Ministers & Charges des affaires of the U.S. are Consuls genl. Ex Officio, Of course Adams is Consul Genl. at the Court of G.B; as soon as the dispatches from the Secy. for foreign affairs arrives.

Temple himself is in a peck of troubles about it; it seems a very good salary depends on the decision.

Since your departure Adams has givn us another fire, to the old tune of commercial restrictions. Jay & Thompson have thought his last advices of so much importance as to send official (49) letters to the States to require the immediate attendance of the Members.

It is a little extraordinary that Mr. Adams should recommend a commercial war, when in the same letter he agrees that in the prosecution of this commercial war it is highly probable we shall incur a real war. We are no doubt in a good situation for war. I inclose you a schedule of the advances to the States, by which you will see that Virginia has had less by a million of dollars than her proportion.

Advantage it seems can however be taken of this circumstance in the next requisition as the resolution of the 3rd of June, 1784 suspends the payment of interest till the final settlement of the accounts, that is, till the day of Judgment. I read some part of your letter at the Sycamore alias the Virginia Hotel, which gave no small satisfaction, & like an able negotiator I drew some small advantages from it myself.

Perhaps it may still be productive. I had the honor of escorting them to the play the other evening, when they made so beautiful & elegant an appearance as to depopulate all the other boxes of the Beaux & Philanders.

They beg me to present their regards to you. If it was not for the intervention of Mrs. Lee, perhaps the expression might be more animating.

I am on the point of leaving this place. Should however anything new cast before I go I will write. Affect frd a most obed servt., Willm. Grayson

LETTERS BETWEEN OUTSTANDING MEN, 1786-1787

William Grayson to James Madison, May 28, 1786, New York

Dear Sir, Your letter has come safely to hand; I should have wrote to you sooner but could not find a thing to communicate worth your acceptance.

Till lately Congress have been perfectly inactive: for about a fortnight past we have had a tolerably full representation; however Delaware has grown uneasy & left us, and Connecticut having prevailed on Congress to accept her cession moves off tomorrow.

It is a practice with many States in the Union to come forward & be very assiduous till they have carried some State job & then decamp with precipitation leaving the public business to shift for itself. The delegation of our

State was very much embarrassed with the Connecticut business, as it was said it was but neighbors fare that Connecticut should be treated, as we had been before with respect to our cession; & that cessions of claims conveyed no right by implication to the territory not ceded.

We however after some consideration took a hostile position towards her & voted against the acceptance in every stage of it: it appeared to the delegation that the only proper claim was already vested in Congress by the cession of our State: & that their cession' was nothing but a state juggle contrived by old Roger Sherman to get a side wind confirmation to a thing they had no right to. Some of the States particularly Pennsylvany voted for them on the same principle that the powers of Europe give money to the Algerines. The advocates for the acceptance have however some plausible reasons for their opinion such as The tranquility, of the Union: The procuring a clear title to the residue of the Continental lands: the forming a barrier agt. the British as well as the Indians: appreciating the value of the adjacent territory & facilitating the settlement thereof.

The Assembly of Connecticut now sitting mean immediately to open a land Office for the 120 Miles Westwd. of the Pennsylvany line which they have reserved: & I don't see what is to prevent them from keeping it always, as the foederal constitution does not give a Court in this instance, & a war with them would cost more than the six million of acres is worth.

Mr. Adams has just informed congress that he has made a demand of the Posts & has been refused; the M. of Caermarthen states in substance as a reason for the refusal, that several of the States in the Union have violated the treaty with respect to the debts. That whenever the States shew a disposition to fulfill the treaty on their part, the King will perform his engagements according to good faith. The States which are not included in the accusation are R. Island, Connecticut, N. Hampshire, N. Jersey & Delaware.

The charge agt. Massachusetz is that she has passed a law preventing executions from issuing for interest until the judgment of May 28, 1786. The only charge agt. Maryland that I recollect, is her having received large sums of money (the property of British subjects) during the war, from their debtors. The charges against New York are heavy & numerous. With respect to Virginia I think she may at least be speciously justified for what has past; the proclamation of Governor Harrison is not imputable to her as it was not done by any authority from the legislature, & if I am rightly informed it was disapproved of as soon as they met.

As to the installment act it never did pass into law, & the British Commee. of merchants had no right to mention it in their report; but the State of Virginia has not repealed her prohibitory laws on that subject.

To this it may be answered that no such repeal was necessary for that the definitive treaty as soon as it was ratified by the contracting parties became the law of the land in every State: if it became the law of the land it of course by repealing anterior obstructions) opened the Courts of Justice to all the creditors who came within it's description.

This principle no doubt will subject the debtor who has paid into the public treasury; but where is the hardship of this if the public are liable to the debtor for such payment. From this must result that the British have no right to complain, until the Courts of Justice refuse to take cognizance of their claims on the principle of prohibitory laws.

Should the legislature view this business in as serious a light as I do, & wish to preserve the honor of the State with as much decency as the nature of the case will admit of, I submit it to your consideration whether it would not be proper for them to enact, that the late treaty of peace now is & ever has been since it's ratification by the contracting parties the law of the land in each State & of course has repealed all lawful impediments to the recovery of any British debts therein described, any law, custom or usage to the contrary notwithstanding. I am not certain I am right in my positions on the ground of the law of nations as applying to foederal governments of separate sovereignties; though I have understood this was the opinion of Count de Vergennes, as it respected the treaty with France.

At all events if it is doubtful ground it is plausible ground; & I know of no other principle that will save the honor of the State. If it is said the British have first violated the treaty with respect to the Negroes, they acknowledge the fact & agree to make satisfaction. What more can be desired? As to the Interest it is a subject of negotiation; if the point is gained, it will conduce to the benefit of Virga. as well as every other State; & in the mean time where is the danger of submitting the point to a Jury, composed of American citizens.

There is no doubt one great difficulty in the matter: if the State of Virginia adopts this or some other system confirmatory of the treaty, she then complies on her part; while at the same time if the other States adhere to their refusal, she leaves Great Britain at liberty to act as she pleases with respect to the Negroes & the Posts:

Perhaps a proper attention to this difficulty may lead to the striking impropriety of the interference of States as to the construction of a treaty in any case whatever. Your sentiments on this matter will greatly oblige me. The treaty with. the King of Prussia has been confirmed in Congress: it is in my opinion as far as it respects commercial objects, of no great importance.

Mr. Monroe I know has informed you that a day is assigned for Congress to go into a Committee of the whole on the State of the Nation; also for what purposes this is intended.

I am apprehensive this will produce nothing & that Congress will never be able to agree on the proper amendments even among themselves; **the Eastern people mean nothing more than to carry the Commercial point. There they intend to stop & would not agree if it rested with them that Congress should have the power of preventing the States from cheating one another as well as their own citizens by means of paper money.**

Mr. Pinkney who brought forward the motion, will be astounded when he meets with a proposition to prevent the States from importing any more of the seed of Cain; N. York & Pensylvany will feel themselves indisposed when they hear it proposed that it shall become a national compact that the sessions shall always be held in the centre of the Empire; how will Delaware, R. Island, Jersey & some others like to vote (with respect to new powers granted to Congress) according to their real & not their supposed importance in the Union?

I am of opinion our affairs are not arrived at such a crisis as to insure success to a reformation on proper principles; a partial reformation will be fatal; things had better remain as they are than not to probe them to the bottom. The State of Virginia having gone thus far, it is matter of great doubt with me whether she had not better go farther & propose to the other States to augment the powers of the delegates so as to comprehend all the grievances of the Union, & to combine the commercial arrangements with them, & make them dependant on each other; in this case her own objects ought not to be permitted; among which a proper and liberal mode of settling the public accounts ought not to be forgotten.

Some alterations have lately been made in the land Ordinance; the Surveyors are liberated from all kind of connection with the stars, and are now allowed to survey by the magnetic Meridian, & are limited to the territory lying Southward of the East & West line as described in the said Ordinance. The navigable waters & the carrying places between them are made common highways for ever & free to the citizens of the Atlantic States as well as those of the new States without any tax or impost whatever.

An attempt was made to change the system altogether and was

negatived; indeed the Eastern & some other States are so much attached to it, that I am satisfied no material alteration can be effected; the Geographer and surveyors will set out it is supposed immediately to carry the Ordinance into execution, provided the Indians will permit them, of which however I have very great doubts. I beg leave to inform you confidentially, that there does not appear at present the most distant prospect of forming treaties with Spain or G. Britain: That Mr. Jefferson has lately informed Congress that he has applied to the Court of France to destroy the Monopoly of the farmers general respecting Tobacco. His reasoning & calculations on this subject does him the highest honor: he has proved incontestably that it is the undoubted interest of both nations that this injurious monopoly should be destroyed. I shall not make any observations on this Subject, as I am satisfied you must have long since fully considered it, in all its relations.

I only beg leave to submit to you the propriety of the State of Virginia & Maryland through Congress representing to the Court of France in strong but affectionate language the fatal consequences of an adherence to this measure. This representation when added to the Commercial Interests of France & joined by the natural enemies of the Farmers general, will possibly shake this ruinous system.

The delegation have lately recieved a letter from the Governor stating the depredations and murders of the Wabash Indians on the Kentucki Settlements; these Indians refused to come to the treaty last year i e, they gave no answer and are now at war with the Citizens of the United States; they have therefore left no alternative to them but hostilities; the delegation intend to move tomorrow that Colo. Hannar with 400 Continental troops and such a number of Kentucki Militia as may be necessary, to march on their towns & destroy them if they do not make concessions & deliver hostages as security for their good behaviour in future. They will also press for the arrangement of a standing Indian department, In all this however they expect opposition, from the circumscribed States who being themselves in no danger, will reluctantly yield assistance to those who are exposed. I have with pleasure understood from Colonel Munro, that you intend paying this place a visit in the course of the summer. I hope you will do it in such a seasonable manner as to preclude the necessity of an immediate return, as was the case last year. I remain with great sincerity, Yr. Affect. frd. & Most Obed Servt. Willm. Grayson. (50)

Richard Henry Lee to James Madison, Oct. 25, 1786, New York,
Dear sir, You now have the report from the secretary of war mentioned in

my last letter & omitted. The opinions I conveyed then relative to the eastern commotions are daily supported by additional intelligence. The eastern gentlemen here are confirmed in sentiments on this matter and believe that the discontents will never be settled but by the sword. Perhaps their apprehensions may have some operation in their judgement: but whether so or not is irrational, for it is unquestionably true that present appearances portend extensive national calamity.

The contagion will spread and may reach Virginia. The objects of the malcontents are alluring to the vulgar and the impotency of government is rather an encouragement to, than a restraint on, the licentious.

Carrington left us a few days past to visit Colonel Grayson, whose situation is truely lamentable but will yield I trust to relaxation from business and company of friends. Yours affec., H. Lee In July, 1786 Grayson's health declined dramatically. Monroe took him to Philadelphia in Sept. to rest at home. Monroe wrote Madison of an 'extraordinary disease," Physicians diagnoses: often delirious, afflicted with strange fancies and odd apprehensions, better in A.M., with raging infirmity by night. May be "floating gout." Shippen called it a bilious affliction of the nerves and blamed laborious mental labors for want of attention to the body. It was not until Nov. that Grayson could return to Congress. (51)

William Grayson to James Monroe, Nov. 22, 1786, New York,
Dear Sir. I have received your favors, for which I am very much obliged to you. I am sorry to inform you I have continued ill ever since you left me in Philadelphia & I cannot say I am much better at this time.

I look forward to a regular fit of the gout as an event greatly to be wished for. We have no news here; Congress have not yet elected a President owing to their being too few States on the floor. Mr. Nash of N. Carolina, who lies dangerously ill, is talked of generally & nothing but his death or extreme ill health will I am persuaded prevent his election.

Colo. Lee has heard of his being left out of the delegation and is far from being pleased at the circumstance. I own I am surprised at R. H. Lee's being continued when he did not serve a day last year. Had Colo. Lee been continued instead of him, all would have been right: he is preparing to return to Virginia I wish that R. H. may resign, and he elected in his room.

The disturbances in Massachusetz bay have been considerable, and absolutely threaten the most serious consequences. It is supposed the gents are encouraged by emissaries of a certain Nation & that Vermont is in the association: how it will end God only knows, the present prospects are no doubt extremely alarming.

I wish to know when Mr. Jones and Madison mean to come forward. It will be necessary for one to set out soon, as my attendance in Congress will be extremely precarious; of course the State will in all probability be often unrepresented until one of them appears.

Mr. Kortright has got quite well; and so is all the family: they are uneasy at not having letters lately from you and Mrs. Monroe. I believe they have not heard yet from the Captain.

The Massachusetz delegation have been much more friendly I have understood since the late insurrection in their State: they look upon the foederal assistance as a matter of the greatest importance of course they wish for a continuance of the Confederation. Their General Court is now sitting, but I believe are fearful of taking any vigorous steps against the insurgents.

Mr. King sets out from this next week to meet the New York and the Massachusetz Commrs. to effect a compromise respecting the latter agt. the former: it seems they have got unlimited powers on both sides. I remain with great sincerity.

Yr. Affect. frd. and Most Obed serv. Willm. Grayson

William Grayson to James Monroe, New York, May 29, 1787
Dear Sir, Your favor has duly come to hand and for which I am much obliged. Since my last I have very little news to acquaint you with.

The draught made from Congress of members for the Constitutional Convention has made them very thin & no business of course is going on here. I believe that this will be the case until that body shall be dissolved, which I hardly think will be the case these three Months.

What will be the result of their meeting I cannot with any certainty determine, but I hardly think much good can come of it. The people of America don't appear to me to be ripe for any great innovations & it seems theyare ultimately to ratify or reject.

The weight of Genl. Washington as you justly observe is very great in America, but I hardly think it is sufficient to induce the people to pay money or part with power.

The delegates from the Eastwd. are for a very strong government, & wish to be whole; but I don't learn that the people are with them, on the contrary in Massachuzets they think that government too strong, & are about rebelling to make it more democratical. In Connecticut they have rejected the requisition for the present year & no man there would be elected to the office of a constable if he was to declare that he meant to pay a copper towards the domestic debt. R. Island has refused to send members.

The cry there is for a good government after they have paid their debts in depreciated paper: first demolish the Philistines (i.e, their Creditors) & then for propriety. N. Hampshire has not paid a shilling, since peace, & does not ever mean to pay one to all eternity: if it was attempted to tax the people for the domestic debt 500 Shays would arise in a fortnight.

In New York they pay well because they can do it by plundering N.J. & Connecticut. Jersey will go to great lengths, from motives of revenge and interest. Pennsylvany will join provided you let the sessions of the Executive of America be fixed in Philadelphia & give her other advantages in trade to compensate for the loss of State power.

I shall make no observations on the southern States, but I think they will be (perhaps from different motives) as little disposed to part with efficient power as any in the Union.

I have lately been at the Sycamore. They are all perfectly well at present, though the Captain had a severe attack last week; he was seized with a fit suddenly & alarmed the family extremely.

Mrs. Heiliger is really a fine woman, and I think after she gets over the death of her husband a little will be of great service to the family; She I hope will have influence enough to drag Esther into the World, which at the same time will be of no small service to Maria her sister. They have been totally buried since your departure.

AUTHOR'S COMMENT:
The following was an important admission on the part of William Grayson, for perhaps due to his illness he knew there would be far less stress being a judge than in his present occupation. Too bad this did not become a reality, but then he would have missed so much excitement and challenge.

I understand a vacancy is expected in the Court of Chancery & perhaps in the Genl. Court. You know best. I wish you to speak to Mr. Jones on the subject and any other of your friends on my behalf, as from yourself if you approve my being appointed witht. mentioning my having said a word to you on the matter.

I would prefer being in the Chancery by a great deal of odds.

My best respects to my worthy friend Mrs, Monroe. I hope you are well and I heartily wish you may thrive in the pursuit of the Law; when I come into the State I think I can help you amongst my old clients.

I remain your Affectionate friend. & Most Obed sert, Willm. Grayson. NB. I got your last letter open: it was sealed with a bad Wafer. (52)

George Washington to Patrick Henry, Sept. 24, 1787 Mt. Vernon,
Dear Sir, In the first moment after my return I take the liberty of sending you a copy of the Constitution which the foedral convention has submitted to the people of these states.

I accompany it with no observations; your own judgement will at one discover the good and the exceptional parts of it, and your experience of the difficulties, which have ever risen then attempts have been made to reconcile such variety of interests and loyal prejudices as pervade the several states will render explanation unnecessary.

I wish the Constitution which is offered had been made more perfect, but I sincerely believe it is the best that could be obtained at this time; and, as a constitutional door is opened for amendments hereafter the adoption of it under the present circumstances on the Union is in my opinion desirable.

From a variety of concurring accounts it appears to me that the political concerns of this country are, in a manner, suspended by a thread.

That the convention has been locked up by the reflective part of the community with a solicitude which is hardly to be conceived, and that if nothing has been on by that body, anarchy would soon have ensued, the seeds being richly sown in every soil. I am &.......George Washington

William Pierce to St. George Tucker, September 28, 1787
You ask me for such information as I can, with propriety, give you, respect to the proceedings of the Convention:

In my letter from Philadelphia, in July last, I informed you that everything was covered with the veil of se-crecy. It is now taken off, and the great work is presented to the public for their consideration. I enclose you a copy with the letter which accompanies the Constitution.

You will probably be surprised at not finding my name affixed to it; and will, no doubt, be desirous of having a reason for it. Know then, Sir, that I was absent in New York on a piece of business so necessary that it become unavoidable. I approve of its principles, and woud have signed it with all my heart had I been present.

To say, however, that I consider it as perfect, would be to make an acknowledgment immediately opposed to my judgment. Perhaps it is the only one to suit our present situation. The wisdom of the Convention was equal to something greater; but a variety of local circumstances, the inequality of states, and the dissonant interests of the different parts of the Union, made it impossible to give it any other shape or form. The great object of this new government is to consolidate the Union, and give us the appearance & power of a nation.

The inconvenience of the different states meeting on the footing of compleat equality, and as so many sovereign powers confederated, has been severely felt by the Union at large; and it is to remedy this evil that something like a national institution has become necessary. The condition of America demands a change; we must sooner or later be convulsed if we do not have some other government than the one under which we at present live. The old Federal Constitution is like a ship bearing under the weight of a tempest; it is trembling, and just on the point of sinking. If we have not another bark to take us up we shall all go down together. There are periods in the existence of a political society that require prompt and decisive measures; I mean that point of time between a people's running into anarchy and an anxious state of the public mind to be rescued from its approaching mischiefs by the intervention of some good and efficient government.

That is precisely the situation in which we seemed to be placed.

A question then arises, shall we have this government, or shall we run into confusion? It is with the people to decide the alternative. I am well aware that objections will be made to this new government when examined in the different states; some will oppose it from pride, some from self-interest, some from ignorance, but the greater number will be of that class who will oppose it from a dread of its swallowing up the individuality of the states.

Local circumstances will weigh against the general interest, and no amount of respect will be paid to all the parts aggregated which compose the Confederacy.

Good as well as bad men will probably unite their interest to oppose it, and some small convulsions may possibly happen in some of the states before it is adopted, but I am certain it is the ark that is to save us. I therefore hope and trust it will be accepted.

It is a difficult point to concentrate thirteen different interests so as to give general and compleat satisfaction. But as individuals in society (to use an old hackneyed and well known principle) give up a part of their national rights to secure the rest, so the different states should render a portion of their interests to secure the good of the whole.

Was this question proposed to each of the states separately, "What kind of government is best calculated for the people of the United States?" there would be as many different opinions as there are different interests. It would be like the decisions of the seven wise men of Greece, who were called at the Court of Periander, to give their sentiment on the nature of a perfect commonwealth; they all judged differently, but they all judged right, in the view each man had.

Many objections have been already started to the Constitution because it was not founded on a Bill of Rights; but I ask how such a thing could have been effected; I believe it would have been difficult in the extreme to have brought the different states to agree in what probably would have been proposed as the very first principle, and that is, "that all men are born equal, free and independent."

Would a Virginian have accepted it in this form? Would he not have modified some of the expressions in such a manner as to have injured the strong sense of them, if not to have buried them altogether in ambiguity and uncertainty. In my judgment, when there are restraints on power, to prevent its invading the positive rights of a people, there is no necessity for any such thing as a Bill of Rights.

I conceive civil liberty is sufficiently guarded when personal security, personal liberty, and private property, are made the peculiar care of government. Now the defined powers of each department of the government, and the restraints that naturally follow, will be sufficient to prevent the invasion of either of those rights.

Where then can be the necessity for a Bill of Rights? It is with diffidence I start this question; I confess I cannot help doubting the negative quality which it conveys, as some of the greatest men I ever knew have objected to the government for no other reason but because it was not buttoned with a Bill of Rights; men whose experience and wisdom are sufficient to give authority and support to any opinion they may choose to advance.

I set this down as a truth founded in nature, that a nation habituated to freedom will never remain quiet under an invasion of its liberties. The English history presents us with a proof of this. At the Conquest that nation lost their freedom, but they never were easy or quiet until the true balance between liberty and prerogative was established in the reign of Charles the second. The absolute rights of Englishmen are founded in nature and reason, and are coeval with the English Constitution itself.

They were always understood and insisted on by them as well without as with a Bill of Rights. This same spirit was breathed into the Americans, and they still retain it, nor will they, I flatter myself, ever resign it to any power, however plausible it may seem.

The Bill of Rights was not introduced into England until the Revolution of 1688, (upwards of 600 years after the Conquest) when the Lords and Commons presented it to the Prince and Princess of Orange.

And afterwards the same rights were asserted in the Act of Settlement at the commencement of the present century, when the crown was limited to the House of Hanover. It was deemed necessary to introduce such an instrument to satisfy the public mind in England, not as a bottom to the Constitution, but as a prop to it; and hereafter, if the same necessity should exist in America, it may be done by an act of the Legislature here, so that the Constitution not being founded on a Bill of Rights I conceive will not deprive it at any future time of being propt by one, should it become necessary.

A defect is found by some people in this new Constitution, because it has not provided, except in criminal cases, for Trial by Jury. I ask if the trial by jury in civil cases is really and substantially of any security to the liberties of a people.

In my idea the opinion of its utility is founded more in prejudice than in reason. I cannot but think that an able Judge is better qualified to decide between man and man than any twelve men possibly can be. The trial by jury appears to me to have been introduced originally to soften some of the rigors of the feudal system, as in all the countries where that strange policy prevailed, they had, according to Blackstone, "a tribunal composed of twelve good men, true boni homines, usually the vassals or tenants of the Lord, being the equals or peers of the parties litigant." This style of trial was evidently meant to give the tenants a check upon the enormous power and influence of their respective Lords; and, considered in that point of view, it may be said to be a wise scheme of juridical polity; but applied to us in America, where every man stands upon a footing of independence,and where there is not, and I trust never will be, such an odious inequality between Lord and tenant as marked the times of a Regner or an Egbert, is useless, and I think altogether unnecessary; and, if I was not in the habit of respecting the prejudices of very sensible men, I should declare it ridiculous. An Englishman to be sure will talk of it in raptures; it is a virtue in him to do so, because it is insisted on in Magna Charta (that favorite instrument of English liberty) as the great bulwark of the nation's happiness. But we in America never were in a situation to feel the same benefits from it that the English nation have.

We never had anything like the Norman trial by battle, nor great Lords presiding at the heads of numerous tribes of tenants whose influence and power we wished to set bounds to. As to trial by jury in criminal cases, it is right, it is just, perhaps it is indispensable, the life of a citizen ought not to depend on the fiat of a single person.

Prejudice, resentment, and partiality, are among the weaknesses of human nature, and are apt to pervert the judgment of the greatest and best of men. The solemnity of the trial by jury is suited to the nature of criminal cases, because, before a man is brought to answer the indictment, the fact or truth of every accusation is inquired into by the Grand Jury, composed of his fellow citizens, and the same truth or fact afterwards (should the Grand Jury find the accusation well founded is to be confirmed by the unanimous suffrage of twelve good men, "superior to all suspicion." I do not think there can be a greater guard to the liberties of a people than such a mode of trial on the affairs of life and death. But here let it rest. The most solid objection I think that can be made to any part of the new government is the power which is given to the Executive Department; it appears rather too highly mounted to preserve the equilibrium.

The authority which the President holds is as great as that possessed by the King of England. Fleets and armies must support him in it. I confess however that I am at a loss to know whether any government can have sufficient energy to effect its own ends without the aid of a military power. Some of the greatest men differ in opinion about this point, I will not pretend to decide it. It requires very little wisdom or fore thought to see into the consequences of the government when put compleatly in motion. You will observe that one branch of the Legislature is to come from the People, the other from the several State Legislatures; one is to sympathize with the people at large, the other with the sovereignty of the states, but the suffrages of the two are unequal; the House of Commons will have sixty-five votes, while the Senate has only twenty- six. Some of the states will have eight citizens of different states, and between a state and the citizens thereof, and foreign states, citizens, or subjects."

The President is to be Commander in Chief of the Fleets and Armies of the United States, and the Militia of the states when called into service of the Union. This taken collectively forms a power independent of the states as must eventually draw from them their remaining sovereignty. Whether such a thing is desirable or not let every man form his own determination.

It is clearly my opinion that we had better be consolidated than to re-main any longer a confederated republic. I would say something about the Article of Commerce, but it involves in it so much inquiry and calculation that I will reserve it for another letter.

I know the most popular opposition in Virginia will be founded on this head, but I think it can be proven beyond a doubt that a uniform regulation of its principles will secure lasting and equal advantages to every part of the empire. If this right had at first been lodged in the hands of Congress we should not at this day be in the condition we are. While a delegate at the Philadelphia Convention, or perhaps at some time after his return to Congress, Pierce entered in a volume, his notes on convention proceedings, a brief anecdote about Washington's concern about secrecy in the Constitutional convention.

James Madison to Tench Coxe Oct.1,1787, N.Y.

Dear Sir, I have received & perused with much pleasure the remarks on the proposed Constitution for the U.S, which you have been so good as to favor me with. They cannot fail I think to satisfy the most scrupulous & jealous citizens, that the Act of the Convention, whatever faults it may have in other respects is not chargeable with a dangerous similitude to real monarchy or Aristocracy. Col. Hamilton happens not to be in the City at present. As soon as he returns your commands with respect to him shall be executed. I grant that the Printers here will republish these.

Richard Henry Lee to George Mason, Oct. 1, 1787 New York

Sir, I have waited until now to answer your favor of Septr. 18th from Philadelphia, that I might inform you how the Convention plan of Government was entertained by Congress.

Your prediction of what would happen in Congress was exactly verified.

It was with us, as with you, this or nothing; & this urged with a most ex-treme intemperance. The greatness of the powers given, & the multitude of Places to be created, produces a coalition of Monarchy men, Military Men, Aristocrats, and Drones whose noise, imprudence & zeal exceeds all belief; Whilst the Commercial plunder of the South stimulates the rapacious

In this state of things, the Patriot voice is raised in vain for such changes and securities as Reason and Experience prove to be necessary against the encroachments of power upon the indispensable rights of human nature.

Some of us were clearly of opinion that the 13th article of the Confederation precluded us from giving an opinion concerning a plan subversive of the present system and eventually forming a New Confederacy of Nine instead of 13 States. (minus the southern states).

The contrary doctrine was asserted with great violence in expectation of the strong majority with which they might send it forward under terms of much approbation. Having procured an opinion that Congress was qualified to consider, to amend, to approve or disapprove; the next game was to determine that tho a right to amend existed, it would be highly inexpedient to exercise that right; but surely to transmit it with respectful marks of approbation. In this state of things I availed myself of the Right to amend, & moved the Proceedings of the Am. Antiquarian Society, Amendments copy of which I send herewith & called the ayes & nays to fix them on the journal.

This greatly alarmed the Majority & vexed them extremely; for *the plan is, to push the business on with great dispatch, & with as little opposition as possible: that it may be adopted before it has stood the test of Reflection & due examination.*
They found it most eligible at last to transmit it merely, without approving or disapproving; provided nothing but the transmission should appear on the Journal.
This compromise was settled *and they took the opportunity of inserting the word Unanimously, which applied only to simple transmission, hoping to have it mistaken for an Unanimous approbation* .
It states that Congress having Received the Constitution unanimously transmit it &c. It is certain that no Approbation was given.

This Constitution has a great many excellent Regulations in it, and if it could be reasonably amended would be a fine System. As it is, I think 'tis past doubt, that if it should be established, either a tyranny will result from it, or it will be prevented by a Civil war.
I am clearly of opinion with you that it should be sent back with amendments and Reasonable Assent to it withheld until such amendments are admitted.

You are well acquainted with Mr. Stone & others of influence in Maryland. I think it will be a great point to get Maryland & Virginia to join in the plan of Amendments & return it with them.

If you are in correspondence with our Chancelor Pendelton, it will be of much use to furnish him with the objections, and if he approves our plan, his opinion will have great weight with our Convention, and I am told that his relation Judge Pendleton of South Carolina has decided weight in the State, & that he is sensible & independent. How important will it be then to procure his union with our plan, which might probably be the case. If our Chancelor was to write largely & pressingly to him on the subject; that if possible it may be amended there also. **It is certainly the most rash and violent proceeding in the world to cram thus suddenly into Men a business of such infinite Moment to the happiness of Millions.**

One of your letters will go by the Packet, and one by a Merchant Ship. My compliments if you please to Your Lady & to the young Ladies & Gentlemen. I am dear Sir affectionately Yours, Richard Henry Lee

P.S. Suppose when the Assembly recommended a Convention to consider the new Constitution they were to use some words like these; It is earnestly recommended to the good people of Virginia to send their most wise & honest Men to this Convention that it may undergo the most intense consideration before a plan shall be without amendments adopted that admits of abuses being practiced by which the best interests of this Country may be injured and Civil Liberty greatly endanger'd. This might perhaps give a decided Tone to the business. Please send my Son Ludwell a Copy of the Amendments proposed by me to the new Constitution sent herewith.

Robert Harmon Harrison to George Washington, October 4, 1787. (From a so-called Federalist. No wonder he was one of William Grayson's best friends, as he makes such sense. Harrison was approached as Patrick Henry was, by Washington. and offered the post of Attorney General.) This is his answer, paraphrased:

I feel myself deeply interested in everything that you have had a hand in, or that comes from you, and am so well assured of the solidity of your judgment, and the rectitude of your intentions, that I shall never stick at trifles to conform myself to your opinion; in the present instance.

I am So totally uninform'd as to the general situation of America, that I can form no judgment of the necessity the convention was under to give us such a constitution as it has done; If our condition is not very desperate, I have my fears that the remedy will prove worse then the disease.

Age makes men often over cautious; I am willing to attribute my fears to that cause, but from whatever source they spring, I cannot divest myself of an opinion, that the seeds of civil discord are plentifully sown in many of the powers given both to the President and Congress, and that if the Constitution is carried into effect, the States south of the Potowmac, will be little more than appendages to those of the northward.

I shall only say, that my objections chiefly lay agst the unlimited powers of taxation and the regulations of trade, and the jurisdictions that are to be established in every State altogether independent of their laws. The sword and such powers will; nay in the nature of things they must sooner or later, establish a tyranny, not inferior to triumvirate or centum viri of Rome.

Melancton Smith to Andrew Craigie. Oct. 4, 1787, New York

Dear Craigie, I thank you most daily, for the few Lines you wrote announcing your safe arrival in twenty three days. I hope you had an agreeable passage to London, and that you found our Friend well.

I suppose you are by this time plunged, head and ears in speculation, you must only take care that you do not pursue the plan of a famous financier in France. I recommend to your consideration the scheme called the Mississippi scheme; apropos, now I have mentioned, the Mississippi scheme, could you not contrive one to dispose of Lands in the western Country?

I think it an object worth while to sound the people on your side of the water. If they should be inclined to adventure in such a speculation, I think we could do something handsome in the business. The new Constitution is reported, I would have sent you a copy of it, with the objections I have to it, but I do not think it best to put you to cost of postage. 1 will do it by the Betsy for London, which sails in about ten days.

You will remember, if any plan should offer, in which you would make more money than you want, that I am perfectly willing to take part of the burden off your shoulders. I am, Yours sincerely, Melancton Smith, (53)

Richard Henry Lee to Samuel Adams, October 5, 1787, N. York Having

long toiled with you my dear friend in the Vineyard of liberty,

I do with great pleasure submit to your wisdom and patriotism, the objections that prevail in my mind against the new Constitution proposed

for the federal government; Which objections I did propose to Congress in the form of amendments to be discussed, and that such as were approved might be forwarded to the States with the Convention system. You will have been informed by other hands why these amendments were not considered and do not appear on the Journal, and the reasons that influenced a bare transmission of the Convention plan without a syllable of approbation or disapprobation on the part of Congress.

I suppose my dear Sir, that *the good people of the United States in their late generous contest, contended for free government in the fullest, clearest, and strongest sense. That they had no idea of being brought under despotic rule under the notion of "Strong government," or in   the form of elective despotism: Chains being still Chains, whether made of gold or iron.*
The corrupting nature of power, and its insatiable appetite for increase, hath proved the necessity, and procured the adoption of the strongest and most express declarations of that Residium of natural rights, which is not intended to be given up to Society; and which indeed is not necessary to be given for any good social purpose.

In a government therefore, where the power of judging what shall be for the general welfare, which goes to every object of human legislation; and where the laws of such Judges shall be the supreme Law of the Land: It seems to be of the last consequence to declare in most explicit terms the reservations above alluded to. So much Legislature created by it.

The remedy, as it may, so it may not be applied; and if it should, a subsequent Assembly may repeal the Acts of its predecessors for the parliamentary doctrine is "quod legis posteriores priores contrarias abrogant."
Surely this it not a ground upon which a wise and good man would choose to rest the dearest rights of human nature. Indeed, some capitol defects are not within the compass of legislative redress.
The Oligarchic tendency from the combination of President, V. President, & Senate, is a ruin not within the legislative remedy.
Nor is the partial right of voting in the Senate, or the defective numbers in the house of representatives. It is of little consequence to say that the numbers in the last mentioned Assembly will increase with the population of these States, because what may happen in twenty five or twenty years hence is poor alleviation of evil, that the intermediate time is big with; for it often happens that abuse under the name of Use is riveted upon Mankind.

Nor can a good reason be assigned, for establishing a bad, instead of a good government, in the first instance, because time may amend the bad. Men do not choose to be sick because it may happen that physic may cure them. Suppose that good men came first to the administration of this government; and that they should see, or *think they see, a necessity for trying criminally a Man without giving him his Jury of the Vicinage; or that the freedom of the Press should be restrained because it disturbed the operations of the new government;* the mutilation of the jury trial, and the restraint of the Press would then follow for good purposes as it should seem, and by good men.

But these precedents will be followed by bad men to sacrifice honest and innocent men; and to suppress the exertions of the Press for wicked and tyrannic purposes; it being certainly true that:

"Omnia mala exempla exbonis orta sunt: sed ubimperium ad ignaros out minus bonos pervinit, novum illud exemplurn ab dignis et idoneis ad indignos et non idoneos fertur." Translation:

"All bad examples are derived from good ones; but when power comes to the ignorant or the less good, the new example is transferred from the worthy and fit to the unworthy and unfit."

In proof of this, we know that the wise and good Lord Holt, to support King William and revolution principles, produced doctrines in a case of Libel (King against Bear) subversive both of law and sound sense; which his Successor Lord Mannsfield (in the case of Woodfall) would have availed himself of for the restraint of the Press and the ruin of liberty.

It would appear therefore, that the consideration of human perversity renders it necessary for human safety, that in the first place, power not requisite should not be given, and in the next place that necessary powers should be carefully guarded. How far this is done in the New Constitution I submit to your wise and attentive consideration.

Whether, for the present, it may not be sufficient so to alter the Confederation as to allow Congress full liberty to make Treaties by removing the restraining clauses; by giving the Impost for a limited time, and the power of regulating trade; is a question that deserves to be considered.

But I think the new Constitution if properly amended contains many good regulations, may be admitted; And why may not such indispensable amendments be proposed by the Conventions and referred, with the new plan to Congress, that a new general Convention may so weave them into the proffer'd system that a Web may be produced fit for free men to weave?

If such amendments were proposed by a capitol state or two, & a willing-ness expressed to agree with the plan so amended;

I cannot see why it may not be effected. It is a mere begging the question to suppose, as some do, that only this Moment and this Measure will do deliberation on this most momentous business.

The public papers will inform you what violence has been practiced by the Agitators of this new System in Philadelphia to drive on its immediate adoption, As if the subject of Government were a business or passion, instead of cool, sober, and intense consideration.

I shall not leave this place before the 4th of November; in the meantime, I shall be happy to hear from you. My best compliments are presented to Mrs. Adams, and I pray to be remembered to Gen. Warren, Mr. Lovell & the good Doctor Holten when you see him.

I am, with sentiments of the truest esteem & regard, dear Sir your affectionate friend, Richard Henry Lee. (54)

James Madison to Edmund Randolph, Oct. 7, 1787, N.Y.

My dear friend, I was yesterday favored with yours of the 30th Ult. And heard with particular pleasure the favorable influence of your journey on Mrs. Randolph's health. I wrote to you shortly after my arrival here, and rehearsed the proceedings of Congress on the subject of the new federal Constitution. I have since forwarded by Mr. Hopkins a large foreign letter for you with some others for the friends of Mr. Jefferson which you will be kind enough to dispose of.

I have also delivered to Mr. Constable of this City to be forwarded by water to your care, several volumes in sheets addressed to the University of Wm. & Mary. They came in a box of books which I received by the last packet, but without a single memorandum on the subject from any quarter. They were addressed to the two Universities of Virga. & Penna. & duplicate sheets being contained in each packet. I know not how the duty in Virga. will be settled. The difficulty was avoided here, by the precaution of entering them for re-exportation. As they are a free gift, are of little value, and are destined for a public institution, I should suppose that no facility consistent with law will be withheld. Congs. are at present deliberating on the requisition

The Treasury Board have reported one in Specie alone, alleging the mischiefs produced by "Indents." It is proposed by a Committee that indents be recd. from the States, but that the conditions tying down the States to a particular mode of procuring them, be abolished, and that the indents for one year be receivable in the quotas of any year.

Sinclair is appointed Govr. of the Western Territory, & a Majr. Sergeant of Masts. the Secretary of that Establishment. A Treaty with the Indians is on the anvil as a supplemental provision for the West Country. It is not certain however that any thing will be done, as it involves money, and we shall have on the floors nine States for one day more only. We hear nothing decisive as yet concerning the general reception given to the Act of the Convention. The Advocates for it come forward more promptly than the Adversaries. The Sea Coast seems every where fond of it.

The party in Boston which was thought most likely to make opposition, are warm in espousing it. It is said that Mr. S. Adams, objects to one point only, viz the prohibition of a Religious test. Mr. Bowdoin's objections are said to lie agst. The great number of members composing the legislature, and the intricate election of the President. You will no doubt have heard of the fermentation in the Assembly of Penna. Mr. Adams is permitted to return home after Feby. Next, with thanks for the zeal & fidelity of his services as the Commission of Smith expires at that time and no provision is made for Continuing him, or appointing a Successor, the representation of the U.S. at the Court of London will cease at that period.

With every wish for your happiness, and with the sincerest affection I remain Mr. Dear Sir, Your Friend, James Madison Jr.

Richard H. Lee to George Washington, Oct. 11, 1787, N.Y.

Dear Sir, I was unwilling to interrupt your attention to more important affairs at Phila. by sending there an acknowledgement of the letter that you were pleased to honor me with from that City; especially as this place afforded nothing worthy of your notice.

We have the pleasure to see the first Act of Congress for selling federal lands N.W of Ohio becoming productive very fast. A large sum of public securities being already paid in upon the first sales: and a new Contract is ordered to be made with a company in N. Jersey for the lands between the two Miamis that will rid us of at least 2 millions more of the public debt.

There is good reason to suppose that by next spring we shall have reduced the domestic debt near six millions of dollars. And it seems clear that the lands yet to be disposed of, if well managed, will sink the whole 30 Millions that are due.

The assiduity with which the Court of London is soliciting that of Spain for the conclusion of a Commercial treaty between those powers, renders it a signal misfortune that we have not been able to get a sufficient number of the States together to produce a conclusion of the Spanish Treaty. Europe, with respect to the continuance of peace, still hangs in doubtful balance. The financial weakness of France and Great Britain most strongly opposes war, yet the state of things is such as renders it very questionable, whether even that difficulty, great as it is, will secure the continuance of peace.

It is under the strongest impressions of your goodness and candor that I venture to make the observations that follow in this letter, assuring you that I feel it among the first distresses that have happen'd to me in my life, 'that I find myself compelled by irresistible conviction of mind to doubt about the new System for federal government recommended by the late Convention.

It is Sir, in consequence of long reflection upon the nature of Man and of government, that I am led to fear the danger that will ensue to Civil Liberty from the adoption of the new system in its present form. I am fully sensible of the propriety of change in the plan of confederation, and altho there may be difficulties not inconsiderable, in procuring an adoption of such amendments to the Convention System as will give security to the just rights of human nature, and better secure from injury the discordant interests of the different parts of this Union; yet I hope these difficulties are not insurmountable.

Because we are happily uninterrupted by external war, or by such internal discords as can prevent peaceable and fair discussion, in another Convention, of those objections that are fundamentally strong against the new Constitution which abounds with useful regulations. As there is so great a part of the business well done already,

I think that such alterations as must give very general content, could not long employ another Convention when provided with the sense of the different States upon those alterations.

I am much inclined to believe that the amendments generally thought to be necessary, will be found to be of such a nature, as tho they do not oppose the exercise of a very competent federal power; are yet such as the best Theories on Government, and the best practice upon those theories have found necessary.

At the same time they are such as the opinions of our people have for ages been fixed on. It would be unnecessary for me here to enumerate particulars as I expect the honor of waiting on you at Mount Vernon on my way home in November.

Mean while I request that my respects be presented to your Lady and remembered by the rest of the good family of Mount Vernon. I have the honor to be dear Sir, with the most unfeigned respect, esteem, and affection, Your most obedient and very humble servant, R.H. Lee. P.S.

If the next Packets bring any important advices from Europe I will communicate them to you immediately. (57)

James Madison to George Washington, Oct. 14, 1787, New York, Dear Sir, The letter herewith inclosed was put into my hands yesterday by Mr. de Croevecuoer who belongs to the Consular establishment of France in this Country. I add to it a pamphlet which Mr. Pinkney has submitted to the public, or rather as he professes, to the perusal of his friends; and a printed sheet containing his ideas on a very delicate subject; too delicate in my opinion to have been properly confided to the press. He conceives that his precautions against any farther circulation of the piece than he himself authorizes, are so effectual as to justify the step. I wish he may not be disappointed. In communicating a copy to you I fulfil his wishes only.

No decisive indications of the public mind in the Northern & Middle States can yet be collected. The Reports continue to be rather favorable to the Act of the Convention from every quarter; but its adversaries will nat- dreaded by the other side. Rhode Island will be divided on this subject in the same manner as it has been on the question of paper money.

The Newspapers here have contained sundry publications animadverting on the proposed Constitution & it is known that the Government party are hostile to it. There are on the other side so many able & weighty advocates, and the conduct of the Eastern States if favorable, will add so much force to their arguments, that there is at least as much ground for hope as for apprehension.

I do not learn that any opposition is likely to be made in N. Jersey. The temper of Pennsylvania will be best known to you from the direct information which you cannot fail to receive through the Newspapers & other channels. Congress have been of late employed chiefly in settling the requisition, and in making some arrangements for the Western Country. The latter consist of the appointment of a Govr. & Secretary, and the allotment of a sum of money for Indian Treaties if they should be found necessary.

The Requisition so far as it varies our fiscal system, makes the proportion of indents receivable independently of specie, & those of different years indiscriminately receivable for any year, and does not as heretofore tie down the States to a particular mode of obtaining them.

Mr. Adams is permitted to return home after Feby. & Mr. Jeffersons appointment continued for three years longer. With the most perfect esteem & most affectionate regard, I remain Dr. Sir, Your Obedt. friend & servant, Js. Madison Jr. (58)

The shocking enclosure was Charles Pinckney's four page broadside, "Observations on the Plan of Government Submitted to the Federal Convention, In Philadelphia, on the 28th of May, 1787,"

There was presumably a speech that Charles Pinckney had intended to deliver at the Federal Convention that met in Philadelphia that ended by producing a new document called the Constitution and foregoing any alteration of the problems with the articles of Confederation.

When Charles Pinckney presented his own plan of government (which has never turned up in the years following that event), that prepared statement that Pinckney delivered to the convention was later heavily quoted by Madison many years later to refute Pinckney's claim for the primacy of his plan in shaping the final version of the Constitution.

Pinckney was out of line. He had a lot of nerve making such a claim, but perhaps he believed that was true and he had only an allusion to claim credit for forming the framework of the Constitution. **All clues to the source and content of the document created by Pinckney were supposedly were either i the imagination of Pinckney or perhaps surfeited away by someone who opposed him, or had Pinckney gotten hold of a draft carelessly left behind and discovered and delivered to Pinckney. Such a thing was impossible to imagine. No light has been shed on this incident.**

Pinckney had given his speech in Congress on August 10, 1786,. The opportunity arose when he stood to give rebuttal to John Jay's request to cede to Spain the right of the United States to navigate the Mississippi River. **(A most heated subject).**

George Washington felt it necessary to make a comment and responded on October 22, 1786, that the appearance of the broadside was inappropriate, observing that Pinckney was unwilling "to lose any fame that can be acquired by the publication of his sentiments" even though it violated

motive for printing the speech to his "appetite for expected praise: for the subject to which it relates has been dormant a considerable time and will remain so."

Author's comment: Charles Pinckney would run for president against V.P. John Adams. He lost to Adams who became president after Washington.

Richard Henry Lee to Edmund Randolph, Oct. 16, 1787, N. Y., Dear Sir, I was duly honoured with your favour of September 17th, from Philadelphia, which should have been acknowledged long before now, if the nature of the business it related to had not required time.

The establishment of the new plan of government, in its present form, is a question that involves such immense consequences, to the present times and to posterity, that it calls for the deepest attention of the best and wisest friends of their country and mankind. If it be found right, after mature deliberation, adopt it; if wrong, amend it at all events: for to say that a bad government must be established for fear of anarchy, is really saying that we should kill ourselves for fear of dying!

Experience, and the actual state of things, show that there is no difficulty in procuring a general convention, the late one having been collected without any obstruction; nor does external war, or internal discord, prevent the most cool, collected, full, and fair discussion of this all-important subject. If, with infinite ease, a convention was obtained to prepare a system, why may not another convention, with equal ease be obtained to make proper and necessary amendments? Good government is not the work of short time, or of sudden thought. From Moses to Montesquieu the greatest geniuses have been employed on this difficult subject, and yet experience has shown capitol defects in the systems produced for the government of mankind.

Since it is neither prudent nor easy to make frequent changes in government, and as bad governments have been generally found the most mixed, so it becomes of the last importance to frame the first establishment upon grounds the most unexceptionable, and such as the best theories with experience justify; not trusting, as our new constitution does, and as many approve of doing, with time and future events to correct errors that both reason and experience, in similar cases, now prove to exist in the new system. It has hitherto been supposed a fundamental truth that, in governments rightly balanced, the different branches of legislature should be unconnected, and the legislative and executive powers should be separate.

In the new constitution, the president and senate have all the executive and two-thirds of the legislative; and in some weighty instances (as making all kinds of treaties which are to be the laws of the land) they have the whole legislative and executive powers. They jointly appoint all officers, civil and military, and they (the senate) try all impeachments, either of their own members or of the officers appointed by themselves. Is there not a most formidable combination of power thus created in a few? And can the most critical eye, if a candid one, discover responsibility in this potent corps or will any sensible man say that great power, without responsibility, can be given to rulers with safety to liberty? It is most clear that the parade of impeachment is nothing to them, or any of them, as little restraint is found, I presume, from the fear of offending constituents.

The president is of four years duration, and Virginia has one vote, out of thirteen, in the choice of him. The senate is a body of six years duration, and as, in the choice of president, the largest state has but a thirteenth part, so is it in the choice of senators; and this thirteenth vote, not of the people, but of electors, two removes from the people.

This latter statement is adduced to show that responsibility is as little to be apprehended from amenability to constituents, as from the terror of impeachment. You are, therefore, sir, well warranted in saying that either a monarchy or aristocracy will be generated; perhaps the most grievous system of government may arise!

It cannot be denied, with truth, that this new constitution is, in its first principles, most highly and dangerously oligarchic; and it is a point agreed that a government of the few is, of all governments, the worst.

The only check to be found in favour of the democratic principle, in this system, is the House of Representatives, which, I believe, may justly be called a mere shred or rag of representation, it being obvious, to the least examination, that smallness of number, and great comparative disparity of power, renders that house of little effect to promote good, or restrain bad government.

But what is the power given to this ill constructed body? To judge of what may be for the general welfare, and such judgment, when made that of Congress, is to be the supreme law of the land.

This seems to be a power co-extensive with every possible object of human legislation. Yet there is no restraint, in form of bill of rights, to secure (what Dr. Blackstone calls) that residuum of human rights which is not meant to be given up to society, and which, indeed, is not necessary to be given for any good social purpose.

The rights of conscience, the freedom of the press, and the trial by jury, are at mercy. It is, indeed, stated that, in criminal cases, the trial shall be by jury; but how? In the state? What then becomes of the jury of the vicinage, or, at least, from the county in the first instance: for the states being from fifty to seven hundred miles in extent, this mode of trial, even in criminal cases, may be greatly impaired; and in civil cases the inference is strong, that it may be altogether omitted, as the Constitution positively assumes it in criminal, and is silent about civil causes. Nay, it is more strongly discountenanced in civil cases, by giving the supreme court, in case of appeal, jurisdiction, both as to law and fact. Judge Blackstone, in his learned commentaries, (article, Jury Trial,) says, it is the most transcendent privilege which any subject can enjoy, or wish for, that he cannot be affected either in his property, his liberty, or his person, but by the unanimous consent of twelve of his neighbors and equals.

A constitution, that I may venture to affirm, has, under providence, secured the just liberties of this nation for a long succession of ages; the impartial administration of justice, which secures both our persons and our properties, is the great end of civil society. But if that be entirely trusted to the magistracy, a select body of men, and those generally selected by the prince, or such as enjoy the highest offices of the state, their decisions, in spite of their own natural integrity, will have frequently an involuntary bias towards those of their own rank and dignity.

It is not to be expected, from human nature, that the few should be always attentive to the good of the many. The learned judge further says, that "every new tribunal, erected for the decision of facts, is a step towards establishing aristocracy, the most oppressive of all governments."

The answer to these objections is, that the new legislature may provide remedies! But as they may, so they may not, and if they did, a succeeding assembly may repeal the provisions.

The evil is found resting upon constitutional bottom, and the remedy upon the mutable ground of legislation, revocable at every annual meeting. It is the more unfortunate that this great security of human rights, the trial by jury, should be weakened in this system, as power is unnecessarily given, in the second section of the third article, to call people from their own country, in all cases of controversy about property between citizens of different states and foreigners, to be tried in a distant court where the Congress may sit; for although inferior congressional courts may, for the above purpose, be instituted in the different states, yet this is a matter altogether in the pleasure of the new legislature; so that if they please not to institute them, or if they do not regulate the right of appeal, the people will be exposed to endless oppression, and the necessity of submitting to pay unjust demands rather than follow suitors, through great expense, to far distant tribunals, and to be determined upon there, as it may be, without a jury.

In this congressional legislature a bare majority can enact commercial laws, so that the representatives of the seven northern states, as they will have a majority, can, by law, create the most oppressive monopolies upon the five southern states, whose circumstances and productions are essentially different from theirs, although not a single man of their voters are the representatives of, or amenable to, the people of the southern states.

Can such a set of men be, with the least colour of truth, called representatives of those they make laws for? It is supposed that the policy of the northern states will prevent such abuses! but how feeble, sir, is policy when opposed to interest among trading people, and what is the restraint arising from policy.

It is said that we may be forced, by abuse, to become ship-builders; but how long will it be before a people of agriculture can produce ships sufficient to export such bulky and such extensive commodities as ours; and if we had the ships, from whence are the seamen to come? four thousand of whom, at least, we shall want in Virginia.

In questions so Liable to abuses, why was not the necessary vote put to two-thirds of the members of the legislature? When the constitution came from the convention, so many members of that body to Congress, and those who were among the most fiery zealots for their system, that the votes of three states being of them, two states divided by them, and many others mixed with them, it is easy to see that Congress could have little opinion upon the subject.

Some denied our right to make amendments, whilst others more moderate agreed to the right, but denied the expediency of amending; but it was plain that a majority was ready to send it on in terms of approbation; my judgment and conscience forbid the last, and therefore I moved the amendments that I have the honor to send you inclosed herewith, and demanded the yeas and nays that they might appear on the journal.

This seemed to alarm and to prevent such appearance on the journal, it was agreed to transmit the constitution without a syllable of approbation or disapprobation; so that the term unanimously only applied to the transmission, as you will observe by attending to the resolve for transmitting.

Upon the whole, sir, my opinion is, that, as this constitution abounds useful regulations, at the same time that it is liable to strong and fundamental objections, the plan for us to pursue will be to propose the necessary amendments, and express our willingness to adopt it with the amendments; and to suggest the calling a new convention for the purpose of considering them. To this I see no well-founded objection, but great safety and much good to be the probable result. I am perfectly satisfied that you make such use of this letter as you shall think to be for the public good. And now, after begging your pardon for so great a trespass on your patience, and presenting my best respects to your lady, I will conclude with assuring you that, I am, with the sincerest esteem and regard, dear sir, Your most affectionate and obedient servant, Richard Henry Lee. (60) Additional:

"Every new tribunal, erected for the decision of facts, without the intervention of a jury, (whether [the tribunal is] composed of justices of the peace, commissioners of the revenue, judges of a court of conscience, or any other standing magistrates) is a step towards establishing aristocracy, the most oppressive of absolute governments. These lines were removed from the Memoir book written by the grandson of Richard Henry Lee.

He was afraid they would be mis-understood in terms of his involvement in the wrangling over the Constitution.)

Only ten of the thirty-three delegates who were present in Congress for the constitutional debate were delegates to the Philadelphia Convention that got rid of the Confederation and voted for the Constitution under a veil of secrecy according to instructions from Washington.

James Madison to George Washington, Oct. 18, 1787, New York,

Dear Sir, I have this day been honored with your favor of the 10th instant, under the same cover with which is a copy of Col. Mason's objections to the Work of the Convention. As he persists in the temper which produced his dissent it is no small satisfaction to find him reduced to such distress for a proper gloss on it; for no other consideration surely could have led him to dwell on an objection which he acknowledged to have been in some degree removed by the Convention themselves (61) on the paltry right of the Senate to propose alterations in money bills; on the appointment of the vice President, of the Senate instead of making the President of the Senate the vice President, which seemed to be the alternative; and on the possibility, that the Congress may misconstrue their powers & betray their trust so far as to grant monopolies in trade &c. If I do not forget some of his other reasons were either not at all or very faintly urged at the time when alone they ought to have been urged; such as the power of the Senate in the case of treaties, & of impeachments; and the duration in office.

With respect to the latter point I recollect well that he more than once disclaimed opposition to it. My memory fails me also if he did not acquiesce in if not vote for, the term allowed for the further importation of slaves; and the prohibition of duties on exports by the States. What he means by the dangerous tendency of the Judiciary I am at some loss to comprehend. It never was intended, nor can it be supposed that in ordinary cases the inferior tribunals will not have final jurisdiction in order to prevent the evils of which he complains. The mass of suits in every State lie between the Citizens and relate to matters not of federal cognizance.

Notwithstanding the stress laid on the necessity of a Council of the President, I strongly suspect, tho I was a friend to the thing, that if such as what Col. Mason proposed, had been established, and the power of the Senate in appointments to offices transferred, that a great clamour would have been heard from some quarters which in general echo his Objections.

What can he mean by saying that the Common law is not secured by the new Constitution, though it has been adopted by the State Constitutions. The common law is nothing more than the unwritten law, and is left by all the constitutions equally liable to legislative alterations.

I am not sure that any notice is particularly taken of it in the Constitutions of the States. If there is, nothing more is provided than a general declaration that it shall continue along with other branches of law to be in force till legally changed. The Constitution of Virga. drawn up by Col. Mason himself, is absolutely silent on the subject. An ordinance passed during that Session, declared Common law as heretofore & all Statutes prior to the 4th, of James I to be still the law of the land, merely to obviate pretexts that the separation from G. Britain threw us into a State of nature, and abolished civil rights and obligations.

Since the Revolution every State has made great inroads & with great propriety in many instances on this monarchical code. The "revisal of the laws" by a Committee of which Col. Mason was a member, though not an acting one, abounds with such innovations.

The abolition of the right of primogeniture, which I am sure Col. Mason does not disapprove, falls under this head. What could the Convention have done? If they had in general terms declared the Common law to be in force, they would have broken in upon the legal Code of every State in the most material points: they wd. have done more, they would have brought over from G.B. a thousand heterogeneous & Anti-republican doctrines, and even the ecclesiastical Hierarchy itself, for that is a art of the Common law.

If they had undertaken a discrimination, they must have formed a digest of laws, instead of a Constitution. This objection surely was not brought forward in the Convention, or it wd. have been placed in such a light that a repetition of it out of doors would scarcely have been hazarded.

Were it allowed the weight which Col. M. may suppose it deserves, it would remain to be decided whether it be candid to arraign the Convention for omissions which were never suggested to them; or prudent to vindicate the dissent by reasons which either were not previously thought of, or must have been wilfully concealed. But I am running into a comment as prolix, as it is out of place. I find by a letter from the Chancellor (Mr. Pendleton) that he views the act of the Convention in its true light, and gives it his un-equivocal approbation. His support will have great effect. The accounts we have here of some other respectable characters vary considerably. Much will depend on Mr. Henry. I am glad to find by your letter that his favorable decision on the subject may yet be hoped for. The Newspapers here begin to teem with vehement & virulent calumniations of the proposed Govt. As they are chiefly borrowed from the Pensylvania papers, you see them of course. The reports however from different quarters continue to be rather flattering. With the highest respect & sincerest attachment I remain Dear Sir Yr. Obedt. & Affecte. Servant, Js. Madison Jr.

James Madison to Edmund Randolph, Oct.21, 1787. New York

My dear friend, I mentioned in a late letter that I had addressed to your care a small box of books for the University. I now inclose the Bill of lading. Inclosed also is a bill of lading for another Box destined for Mr. W. Hay. Will you be so good as to have it handed to him?

I paid two dollars for its freight from France to this port, which he may repay to you. The money you remitted by me to Col. Carrington having somewhat exceeded the amount of his demand, the two dollars may the more properly pass into your hands. I have recd. no letter from you since your halt at the Bolling-Green. We hear that opinions are various in Virginia on the plan of the Convention. I have recd. within a few days a letter from the Chancellor by which I find that he gives it his approbation; and another from the President of William & Mary which, though it does not absolutely reject the Constitution, criticizes it pretty freely.

The Newspapers in the middle & Northern States begin to teem with controversial publications. The attacks seem to be principally levelled against the organization of the Government, and the omission of he provisions contended for in favor of the Press, & Juries &c. A new Combatant however with considerable address & plausibility, strikes at the foundation. He represents the situation of the U.S. to be such as to render any Government improper & impracticable which forms the States into one nation & is to operate directly on the people. Judging from the Newspapers one word, suppose the adversaries were the most numerous & the most in earnest. But there is no other evidence that it is the fact. On the contrary we learn that the Assembly of N. Hampshire which recieved the constitution on the point of their adjournment, were extremely pleased with it.

The information from Massachusetts denotes a favorable impression there. The Legislature of Connecticut have unanimously recommended the choice of a Convention in that State. And Mr. Baldwin who is just from the spot tells me that from present appearances the opposition will be inconsiderable; that the Assembly if it depended on them would adopt the System almost unanimously; and that the Clergy and all the literary men are exerting themselves in its favor Rhode Island is divided; The majority being violently against it. The temper of this State cannot yet be fully discerned.

A strong party is in favor of it. But they will probably be outnumbered if those whose sentiments are not yet known, should take the opposite side. N. Jersey appears to be zealous. Meetings of the people in different counties are declaring: their approbation & instructing their representatives. There will be strong opposition in Pennsylvania. The other side continues to be sanguine. Docr. Carroll came hither lately from Maryland tells me, that the public appears at present to be in favor of the Constitution, Notwithstanding these circumstances, I am far from considering the public mind as finally settled on the subject. They mount only to a strong presumption that the general sentiment in the Eastern & middle States is friendly to the proposed System at this time. Present me respectfully to Mrs. R. and accept fervent wishes for your happiness from your Affec. friend, Js. Madison.

Patrick Henry to George Washington, October 19, 1787

I have to lament that I cannot bring my Mind to accord with the proposed Constitution. The Concern I feel on this Account, is really greater than I am able to express. Perhaps mature Reflection may furnish me Reasons to change my present Sentiments into a Conformity with the Opinions of those personages For whom I have the highest Reverence.

William Grayson to James Monroe, Oct. 22, 1787 New York

Dear Sir, I have received your favor and delivered the enclosure to Miss Kortright; the Capt. being on a trip to the township. Congress four days since made a contract with Royal Flint & Associates of N. York for three millions of acres on the Wabash on nearly the same terms as that of Cutler & Serjeant, I believe I informed you that Judge Symms of Jersey had contracted for two millions between the Great & the little Miami; the whole of the Contracts will when fully complied with, amount to an extinguishment of six Millions Dollars of the domestic debt: & Congress now looking upon the Western country in its true light, i.e., as a most valuable fund for the total extinguishment of the domestic debt, have directed the treasury board to continue the sales on nearly the same terms & principles as those already made. A very considerable emigration will take effect from the five Easternmost States. A Brigade files off from Massachuzets immedy., & which is to be followed by much more considerable ones next spring & fall.

A doctor Gano a Baptist preacher in this town will carry out (it is said) his whole congregation amounting to five hundred.

Symms is beating up for volunteers in the Jerseys, as is the case with Parsons in Connecticut, & Varnum in Rhode Island; these two last are appointed Judges in the Western country. Congress have authorized St. Clair now governor of the Western territory to hold a treaty with the Indians next spring if necessary & 14,000 dollars are appropriated for this purpose.

A Treaty is also directed with the Cherokees & Creeks & 6,000 dollars are appropriated for it. The new Constitution is favorably received in Connecticut, Massachuzets & N. Jersey; in this state it is thought there is a majority against it, in Pensylvany that the Pro's and Con's are nearly equal: from Rh.Is.& New Hampshire I hear nothing. The British packett arrived last night: but we have not yet-received the dispatches from the Secy. For foreign affairs. The news of the day is that the affairs of Holland are in as bad a train as ever. I shall set out for this in about ten days and it is possible I may have the pleasure of seeing you in Richmond. I recommended you to Mr. Meade in Philada, as a lawyer to do his business, also to Lambert Cadwallader. I expect you have been employed in both cases.

I saw the family at the Sycamore last night. They are well. Mrs. Heileger goes to Santa Cruz in December Next. My best complimts. To Mrs. Munro, I remain yr. Affect.frd. & hmbl & Obedient servant, William Grayson.

Lambert Cadwalader to Edward Lloyd, October 23, 1787, N.Y.

Dear Sir, Mr Gough having mentioned your Proposal to meet the Executors of my Brother at Shrewsbury, but not recollecting that the Time was fixed by you, they now propose to meet you there on the first Day of December. As it will be inconvenient to them at any other Time to make a Journey thither they wish it may suit you to attend.

I am happy to inform you that the Sales of Land in the Western Territory beyond the Ohio exceed the Expectations of Congress; a Company from N. England have purchased about 5 Millions of Acres in that Country, Another Company is treating for a second Tract containing a Million & half or Two Millions more & a third Company came forward a few Days since with Proposals for three Millions.

The Reservations in said Tracts for public Uses amount to about 117th of the whole. The Price is a portion of a Dollar per acre and will be paid in public Securities. The Geographer of the U. States told me a few Days since that if we managed well the whole of the domestick Debt may be easily extinguished. I sincerely congratulate you on the fair Prospect there is of our soon becoming happy at Home & respectable abroad under the Operation of the new Government which from everything I can learn will very probably take Place in the Course of the ensuing Year.

New Hampshire & Massachusetts have as far as private Conversation goes, discovered a Disposition to adopt it. The Legislature of Connecticut have agreed to call a Convention—Seven eighths of the House agreed to the Measure. The Scales tis said hang pretty even in New York State. In Jersey I believe there is scarcely a dissenting Voice.

It is believed that Pa. will adopt it & of Course Delaware. You best know how Md. will act. We have favorable Intelligence from Virginia & it is believed that the three southernmost States will certainly accede. With Compts to Mrs Lloyd I remain, Dr Sir, Your very hble Servt, Lambert Cadwalader. P.S. Write to Genl Dickinson & myself at Trenton. I leave this Day.

Edward Carrington To Thomas Jefferson Oct.23, 1787 N.Y. (Edited)

Dear Sir, I have been honoured with your favor of the 4th of August. Inclosed you will receive a Copy of the report of our late Convention, which presents, not amendments to the old Confederation, but an entire new Constitution.

This work is short of the ideas I had the honor to communicate to you in June, in no other instance than an absolute negative upon the State laws.

When the report was before Congress, it was not without its direct opponents, but a great majority were for giving it a warm approbation; it was thought best, however, by its friends, barely to recommend to the several Legislatures, the holding of Conventions for its consideration, rather than send it forth with, even, a single negative to an approbatory act.

The people do not scrutinize terms; the unanimity of Congress in recommending a measure to their consideration, naturally implies approbation: but any negative to a direct approbation, would have discovered a dissention, which would have been used to favor divisions in the States.

It certainly behooved Congress to give a measure of such importance, and respectable birth, a fair chance in the deliberations of the people, and I think the step taken in that body well adapted to this idea. The project is warmly received in the Eastern States, and has become pretty generally a subject of consideration in Town-meetings, and other Assemblies of the people, the usual result whereof, are declarations for its adoption.

In the Middle States, appearances are generally for it, but not being in habits of assembling for public objects, as is the case to the Eastward, the people have given but few instances of collective declarations. Some symptoms of opposition have appeared in New York and Pensylvania; in the former, only in individual publications, which are attended with no circumstances evidencing the popular regard; the Governor holds himself in perfect silence, wishing, it is himself in an open opposition: in the latter the opposition has assumed a form somewhat more serious, but under circumstances which leave it doubtful whether it is founded in objections to the project, or the intemperance of its more zealous friends.

The Legislature was in session in Philada. when the Convention adjourned; 42 Members were for immediately calling a Convention before the measure had received the consideration of Congress, and were about to press a vote for that purpose; 19 Seceded and broke up the House, and although they, afterwards, added to their protest against the intemperance of the majority, some objections against the report, yet it is to be doubted whether they would have set themselves in opposition to it, had more moderation been used.

The next morning the resolution of Congress arrived, upon which the 42 wanting to compleat a House for business, sent their Sergeant for so many of the Seceders, who were brought by force, whereupon an Act was passed for calling a Convention in November

Seceders are from the upper counties, have carried their discontents home with them, and some of them being men of influence, will occasion an inconvenience, but Gentlemen well acquaintance with the Country are of the opinion, that their opposition will have no extensive effect, as there is, in general, a Coalescence of the two parties which have divided that State ever since the birth of her own Constitution, in support of the new Government. From the Southern States we are but imperfectly informed; every member from the Carolina's and Georgia, as well in Convention, as Congress, are warm for the new Constitution; and when we consider the ascendancy possessed by Men of this description over the people in those States, it may well be concluded, that the reception will be favorable.

*In Virginia, there may be some difficulty; two of her members in Convention, whose characters entitle them to the public confidence, refused to sign the report; these were Colo. Mason and Gov. Randolph, nor was that State without its dissentients, **of the same** description, in Congress; these were Mr. R. Lee & Mr. Grayson, but upon very opposite principles; the former because it is to strong, the latter because it is too weak and Colo. H. Lee is by no means an advocate. The Governor has declared that his refusal to sign, shall not be followed by hostility against the measure; that his wish is to get the exceptionable parts altered if practicable, but if not, that he will join in its support from the necessity of the Case.*

Mr. Madison writes you fully upon the objections from Virginia, and therefore I will not impose on your patience by repeating them; however, being merely local, and an old source of jealousy, I will present to your consideration my opinion upon one. There is the ability of a bare majority in the federal Government to regulate Commerce. It is supposed that a Majority of the Union are carriers, and that it will be for the interest, and in the power, of that majority to form regulations oppressing, by high freights, the agricultural State.

It does not appear to me that this objection is well founded. In the first place it is not true that the Majority are carriers, for Jersey and Connecticut who fall into the division, are by no means such; and New York & Pennsylvania, who also are within that division, are as much agriculture as the carrying states; but, admitting the first position to be true, I do not see that the supposed consequences would follow. No regulation could be made on other, than general and uniform principles. In that case every evil would effect its own cure.

The Southern States possess more materials for shipping than the Eastern, and if they do not follow the carrying business, it is because they are occupied in more lucrative pursuits. (A indeed they were.)

Competition amongst the Eastern States themselves, would be sufficient to correct every abusive. Laws ought doubtless to be passed for giving exclusive benefits to American ships, This would serve the eastern States, and in justice ought to be the case, as no other advantage can result from having a Navy for the security wealth derived from their agriculture. My determination to join in the adoption results from a Compound consideration of the measure itself, and the critical state of our affairs.

It has in my mind great faults; but those who met under powers and dispositions, promised greater accommodations in their deliberations than can be expected of any future Convention. The particular interests of States are exposed, and future deputations, would be clogged with instructions and biased by the presentiments of their constituents. Hence, it is fair to conclude that this is a better scheme than can be looked for from another experiment on the same considerations, I would clearly be for closing and relying upon the correction of its faults, as experience may dictate.

But when I extend my view to that approaching anarchy which nothing but the timely interposition of a new Government can avert, I am doubly urged in my wishes for the adoption. Some Gentlemen apprehend that this project is the foundation of a Monarchy or at least an oppressive Aristocracy; but my apprehensions are otherwise.

It is true there is a preposterous combination of powers in the President and Senate, which may be used improperly, but time will discover whether the tendency to abuse, will be to strengthen or relax; at all events this part of the constitution must be exceptional.

The Western Territory belonging to the united States has more effectually received the attention of Congress during this session than it ever did before. Inclosed you will receive the ordinance for establishing a Temporary Government there, and providing for its more easy passage into permanent State Governments. Under the old arrangement the country might upon the whole have become very populous, & yet inadmissable to the rights of State government, which would have been disgusting to them & ultimately inconvenient for the Empire. The new arrangement depends on the accession of Virginia which there can be no doubt of obtaining.

The Offices of the Government are filled up as follows. Genl. St. Clair Govr. Winthrop Sargent Secretary, Genl. Parsons, Genl. Armstrong junr. & Genl. Varnum, Judges. Seven Ranges of Townships are surveyed; they extend nearly to Muskingum and contain about 12 or 15 Millions of Acres. The Treasury Board in August contracted with a large Company of New

Englanders, for all the Country from the seventh Range, to Sioto, This Tract contains about 5 Millions of Acres with one of the sections for the purposes of religion, and two compleat Townships granted for a University in or near the Middle of the Tract. This contract is now actually closed. Another offer is made by judge Symes and his associates from Jersey, for about 2 Millions between the Miamis upon the same terms; sundry other propositions are forming, whereupon Congress have authorized the Treasury Board, to sell by Contract any quantity not less than a Million. The sales promise to be sufficiently rapid to give our people early relief from the pressure of the domestic debt.

I am inclined to believe that some successful experiment might be made for the sale of a part of this territory in Europe, and have suggested a trial with a few Ranges of the surveyed Townships. It did not strike Congress as eligible and of course no step was taken. I do not suppose it would be worth while to try the project on any but lands actually surveyed and well described. We have received no accounts from Europe since your August dispatches, of course the state of things there are in considerable obscurity as to us. Your remarks upon the French loan have occasioned some discussion in Congress, but many reasons operate to prevent an assent to your proposition. By some it is supposed it would be found inconvenient to shift from Creditors that will not complain of our delinquency, to those that will, by others that we have reason to rely upon the indulgence of France in the case of a debt which was contracted for the common benefit of the two nations.

My own opinion is that the transfer ought to be made if practicable. I have the Honor to be, with sincere regard, dr. Sir, Your Most Obedient. Servant., Ed. Carrington. For the October 20 adoption of this "representation," on the recommendation of a committee which was referred a motion by William Grayson on October 16, (62) The case of North Carolina's cession involved the additional problem that the state had previously made such a cession in 1784 but had repealed it the following year when Congress delayed accepting it and settlers in the affected region attempted to set up the independent state of Franklin. (63) Most likely William Grayson heard about the cession and its withdrawal and encouraged the governors of N. C. and Georgia in a motion in Congress, to repeat their generous cession of land "to benefit the country."

Nicholas Gilman to John Langdon, Oct. 23, 1787, New York
Dear Sir, I am honored with your very obliging favor of the 13th instant, which affords me great pleasure & relief; for your little boys had hardly

scrambled over the dreary district of horseeck, before I was dun'd in all Companies, for news from Mr. Langdon, and became quite disgusted with the necessary repetition of a negative answer.

I am happy your journey was so very agreeable, and believe you will not suspect me of insincerity, when I assure you it gives me great pleasure to hear of your domestic happiness. Not being in the full enjoyment of those delectable pleasures myself I always participate in some degree with those I respect & Esteem. Madison, Irvine, Carrington, Few and Baldwin desire to be remembered.

Mrs. Ellsworth and Niece are much pleased with your kind notice and desire their best respects. Gorham & King are in Boston but I assure you Mrs. King and her father will be greatly disappointed if you do not introduce them to Mrs. Langdon in the Course of the fall or winter.

If you come on I think there will soon be a Congress and I have no doubt you will be unanimously elected Presidt. As I am often questioned on the subject and believe they will think of no other member. Some matters of importance have passed Congress since you left us, in which it was disagreeable to be deprived of a vote, such as selling lands; Subject of Indian Treatys & c. From all accounts there is the greatest probability that the new Constitution will be generally adopted.

Accounts from General Washington and other eminent characters in Virginia are much in favor of it; and all reports agree that the conduct of Mason and Randolph has made them very unpopular in their state.
The conduct of the Seceders in Pennsylvania has met the pointed disapprobation of their constituents, though it is agreed the intemperence of the friends to government in that state has been the cause of considerable opposition. Sales of the Western lands are going on very well; there are applications (including what is sold) for about ten Million acres; a very considerable part of the domestic debt will be sunk in this way; yet I really wish the Citizens of New Hampshire would be so far awake to a sense of their interest as to buy their quota as an appreciation of these securities must in time take place. Pennsylvania & New York are in possession of their Quotas and Massachusetts has purchased a very considerable sum. I really hope our Legislature will assemble without loss of time; a federal spirit and a speedy adoption of the new plan is generally expected of New Hampshire and certainly no State suffers more through the inefficiency of the present or has more to hope from the adoption of the proposed Constitution. I must beg of you to write me soon and to let me know your

determination about coming on and whether there is a Vessel coming from Portsmouth to this place. Please present my most respectful Compliments to Mrs. Langdon. I have a fine warm lower parlour which I shall be very happy to relinquish for her Accommodation previous to your taking the large house in Cherry Street. With the greatest respect & Esteem, I am, Dear sir, Your Most Obedt. & Humble servant, N. Gilman.

Edward Carrington to William Short, (Jefferson's secretary in Paris), October 25, 1787, New York

My Dear Sir, I have been honoured with your favor of the 1st of August, and thank you most sincerely for this additional evidence of your friendly remembrance. There perhaps never was a period of time at which reforms and revolutions in government, were so general as now, and it is much for the honor of America, that While the more Antient Nations in Europe, are shaken to their very Centre in the operation, ours is taking thorough effect, by peaceable Convention, without interrupting for a moment the existing administration.

The Governors and Governed act in Concert for producing the Change, and the former look forward to not act with more desire, than the surrender of the old, upon the Maturity of the new Government.

You will see in the hands of Mr. Jefferson, to whom *I have inclosed it, the constitution reported by our Convention for the United States. It is far from perfection, but we should be the wisest, as well as the most fortunate, people under the Sun, could we concert a perfect system of government, and afterwards obtain an universal consent to its adoption:* **(64)**

In as much as Men differ in point of understanding, there must be proportionate defects in their joint deliberations: but the reconcilement of the various circumstances and interests an extensive and enterprizing Country comprehends, forbids that perfection should be our indispensible pursuit.

The project is warmly received in the Eastern States, and has become pretty generally a subject of consideration in Town-meetings and other Assemblies of the people, the usual result whereof are declarations for its adoption, in the Middle States appearances are generally for it, but not being in the habits of assembling for public objects, the people have given but few instances of collective declarations.

Some symptoms of opposition have appeared in New York & Pensylvania, in the latter it was, as probably, occasioned by the intemperance of those most zealous for the measure, as, objections against the plan. Of this circumstance I have given Mr. Jefferson a particular detail to which permit me to refer you. In the former some individual publications are exhibited in view, with great reluctance, the diminution of state emoluments and consequence; they hold their politics.

The Governor is perfectly silent, but it is suspected, wishes the miscarriage of the measure, taking his usual guard against being committed in a fruitless opposition. From the Southern States our information is very imperfect, but from the zeal and unanimity of the Members from the Carolina's and Georgia, as well in Convention as Congress, and from the known influence of Men of this description in those States, it is well [sic] understood that the proposed scheme will be favorably received in that quarter.

In Virginia we learn from superficial accounts from the Assembly upon their first meeting, that a great Majority of the members declare in its favor; but it has met with the dissent of two of her members in Convention & was disapproved by the same number of those who represented her in Congress.

These dissidents were Colo. Mason & Govr. Randolph in Convention who refused to sign the report. Mr. R.H. Lee & Mr. Grayson in Congress, who were actually agt. An approbatory Act, although they agreed to join in the *bare recommendation of conventions for its consid*eration in the States.

From characters of this description being opposed, we are naturally to apprehend some difficulty in that State, but I am led to believe that the generality of the adoption which is probable in the other States, will have much influence in bringing her into the measure.

We have not yet been informed what part Mr. Henry will take much will depend on him.

Mr. Madison has forwarded to Mr. Jefferson several pamphlets and pieces whish have been written for and against the Constitution from which you will have a view of the train of discussion it is undergoing; and having by this same opportunity written very fully to Mr. Jefferson, a repetition of the same to you will be needless, and to find new materials is not at present within my political scope; my plan in future will be to write you alternately, by the packets.

Richmond does not stand where it did when you left having crept up and over Shockoe Hill; it met with a severe stroke last Winter in the Burning of about 70 Houses in the heart of Commercial business, including Byrds Warehouse; in this Calamity our old and worthy friend Foushee lost nearly his all, having crowded most of his property in buildings upon the ill fated spot, the whole of which were consumed.

That poor man Curry also suffered in the loss of the greatest private house ever built perhaps in Virga; It was brick & for the first year in the occupancy of Mr. Robt. Anderson as a Tavern.

I have had so little connection with that Metropolis for sometime that I am almost as great a stranger to the changes which have taken place in its domestic arrangements as yourself.

Miss Ambler shortly after your departure sacrificed at the alter of Hymen at the tender solicitation of Colo. Brent, whose death in a very few months afterwards left her to bless some other fortunate man with the possession of her charms; she is however still single having dismissed the suits of several worthy & valuable characters.

Miss Marshal has also surrendered herself absolute to the discretion of Mr. Raleigh Colston whose retirement at Winchester is solaced by her partaking in it with him. Miss Lucy Randolph whom you knew at Wilton, has contracted a foreign alliance with Mr. Latil a French Gentleman who is in Virga. as Agent for Mr. de Baumarchais, and will probably figure in Paris before you leave it. Be good enough to let me hear from you often; your information upon European politics are not only extremely agreeable but useful to me. I am my dr Sir, with great Sincerity, Your Friend & very Humble Servt., Ed. Carrington.

P.S. The disapprobation of Mr. R. H. L. and Mr. G. are founded on very opposite principles; the former thinks the Constitution too strong, the latter is of opinion that it is too weak.

Author's Comment: Rumors were circulating that Richard.H. Lee and William Grayson failed to see things on the same terms, and both were opinionated and egotistical. This put a strain on their relationship but they were such gentlemen, they pretended to be aligned and friendly. They knew little of what the immediate future held for them. A big surprise awaited them after their stance against the Constitution.

For all the controversy and opposition stirred by the imperfect Constitution, Madison never showed the slightest doubt that he might have erred and mis-judged certain items in the Constitution., that in his assessment, it was perfect, and so was its author. His steady defense, without any understanding of the weaknesses in the Constitution or flaws in his character, stand him in odd company. Adding to the tension, George Washington, must have found it exceedingly disappointing and worrisome to find opposition among his closest friends, of the caliber of Patrick Henry, George Mason, James Monroe, William Grayson, Robert H. Harrison, etc. No doubt he and his Federalist minions had successfully reached Gov. Edmund Randolph who was once an anti-Federalist, and emerged a Federalist.

Under any other circumstance, the situation would have been tolerable, but the nation was in crises and the need to establish a working government was imperative. Former soldiers, under his command, or fellow patriots, working towards the same goals, suddenly cast in opposing roles, was a shattering concept to Washington. There would be a cushioned retaliation in the lack of appointments to high federal positions and only Federalists would be amply rewarded as the record proved.

James Madison kept his emotions in check, although he was furious over the defection of several of the Anti-federalists who had once been his closest allies, and exhibited their right to oppose the Constitution, with a jaundiced glance. While a mean spirited, bellicose mood plunged George Mason to despair, and signaled a complete loss of self control, once he realized that his faction had haplessly capitulated to the Federalists. From the middle of this letter of Madison's: "There is at present a very strong probability that nine States at least will speedily concur in establishing the Constitution. What will become of the tardy remainder? "They must be either left as outcasts from the Society, to shift for themselves, or be compelled to come in, or must come in of themselves where they will be allowed no credit for it. Can either of these situations be as eligible as a prompt and manly determination to support the union, and share its common fortunes? "He goes on to say: **"Mr. P's (Charles Pinckney)** character is as you observe well marked by the publications which I enclose. His printing the secret paper at this time could have no motive but an appetite for expected praise: for the subject to which it relates has been dormant a considerable time, and seems likely to remain so." Madison's closing absolutely drips with syrup. "With sentiments of the most perfect esteem & the most Affecte. Regard, I remain Dear Sir, Your Obedt, friend & hmbl servt., Js. Madison

Author's Comment: Madison's ambition and egotistical fancies fairly fly off the page and his shallow, self-serving statements are pure vanity without cause. His efforts and his unseemly behavior was uncalled for especialy in regard to the men of his home state that would not be tolerated by his fellow Virginians. He was angry and in a pique. He lashes out at everyone and is likely disappointed in his perceptions.

James Madison to Edmund Pendleton, October 28, 1787, N.Y.

In a kinder tone Madison says, "It would be truly mortifying if any thing should occur to prevent or retard the concurrence of a State which has generally taken the lead on great occasions. And it would be the more so in this case as it is generally believed that nine of the States at least will embrace the plan, and consequently that the tardy remainder must be reduced to the dilemma of either shifting for themselves, or coming in without any credit for it."

"Connecticut has unanimously called a Convention, and left no room to doubt her favorable disposition."

This State (Virga) has long had the character of being Anti-federal. Whether she will purge herself of it on this occasion, or not, is yet to be ascertained. Most of the respectable characters are zealous on the right side. However, the party in power is suspected on good grounds to be on the wrong side. New Jersey adopts eagerly the Constitution. Penna. is considerably divided but the majority are as yet clearly with the Convention. I have no very late information from Maryland. The reports are that the op

Not a word has been heard from the States south of Virginia, except from the lower parts of N. Carola. Where the Constitution was well received. There can be little doubt that the three southern States will go right unless the conduct of Virginia misleads them."

James Madison to his brother Ambrose Madison, (Edited)

"We have no public news. The Act of the Convention has in general been pretty well recd. As yet in the Middle & Northern States Opposition however begins to shew itself. It is not possible to say now on which side the Majority will finally lie.

The present appearance is in favor of the new constitution. The adversaries differ as much in their objections as they do for the thing itself." Remember me affectionately to my sister & all others of the family, Yrs, Js Madison

James Madison to Archibald Stuart, Oct. 30, 1787

Among other things, Madison wrote: Nothing is more common here than to see companies of intelligent people equally divided, and equally earnest, in maintaining on one side that the General Government will overwhelm the State Governments, and on the other that it will be a prey to their encroachments; on the one side that the structure of the Government is too firm and too strong, and on the other that it partakes too much of the weakness & instability of the governments of the particular States.

William Grayson to William Short, Nov. 10, 1787, New York

Dear Sir, I have received your favor, for which I am much obliged; the Convention, at Philada, about which I wrote you, have at length produced (contrary to expectation) an entire new constitution; This has put us all in an uproar. Our public papers are full of attacks and justifications of the new system: And if you go into private companies, you hear scarcely any thing else. In the Eastern States the thing is well received; the enemies to the Constitution say that this is no wonder, as they have overreached the Southern people so much in its formation.

In this State, I believe there is a great majority against it; the reason assigned by its favours is that she derives great advantages by imposing duties on the imports of Jersey & Connecticut. In Jersey, nothing is more popular. There was something singular in the affair which is that the one was determined to adopt & the other to reject the new constitution before it had made its appearance. In Pensylvany matters are warmly contested by the Republicans and Constitutionalists, but from what I have heard lately I think the former will carry their point; by that I mean that there will be a majority in favor of the new constitution. In Delaware & Maryland I hear of little or no opposition, though in the latter some was expected from Chase & Paca.

In Virginia there is a very considerable opposition from Ben. Harrison, Genl. Nelson, Patrick Henry, Thruston, Zane, Rich. H. Lee, & Co., George Mason, most of the Judges of the Genl. Court-cum multis alis of the inferior flanking parties are inlisted as opponents.

Genl. Washington however who is a host within himself is strongly in favor of it, & I am at a loss to determine how the matter will be ultimately closed. As to the two Carolinas & Georgia, I have not yet heard much about them; the general supposition is that it will go down very smoothly in those regions; as to the latter it is highly probable, as she is at present very much embarrassed with an Indian war, and in great distress; and as she will pay nothing under any government it is immaterial to her how many changes are effected; this latter observation will apply in a great degree to some of her neighbors.

With respect to my own sentiments I own I have important objections. In the first place,

I think liberty a thing of too much importance to be trusted on the

ground of implication: it should rest on principles expressed in the clearest & most unequivocal manner.

A bill of rights ought then to have preceded. Tryals by jury should have been expressly reserved in Civil as well as Criminal cases. The press ought to have been declared free.

I think the foederal Courts in the different states wrong. One Court at the session of Congress with appellative jurisdiction in the cases mentioned in the proposed constitution would have been sufficient. The representation in the Senate ought to have been in the same proportion as the lower house, except in a few cases merely of a foederal nature where the little States should be armed with a repulsive quality to preserve their own existence. And *the proposed method of making treaties, ie, by two thirds of the Senators present will be the means of losing the Mississippi for ever. Indeed we have had great difficulty to prevent it from destruction for two years past. In these & several other instances which I could enumerate, I think the generality [sic] will have too much power, but there are points where I don't think they have power enough.* **In order to face foreign powers properly & to preserve their treaties & their faith with them, they should have had a negative upon the State laws with sevl other incidental powers.**

Witht. this I am satisfied the new government if adopted will in a year or two be as contemptible as the present: It seems upon the whole I look upon the new system as a most ridiculous piece of business; something (entre nous) like the legs of Nebuchadnezar's image have been formed by jumbling or compressing a number of ideas together, **something like the legs of Nebuchadnezar's image have been formed by jumbling or compressing a number of ideas together, something like the manner in which poems were made in Swift's flying island. (65) However bad as it is, I believe it will be crammed down our throats rough & smooth with all it's imperfections:**

The temper of America is changed beyond conception since you were here. I believe they were ready to swallow almost any thing.

Mr. Adams has lately been recalled according to his request, and no provision is made for a successor: according to present appearance not even a Charge or agent will be left there.

The indisposition of some States to thank him had for the moment an injurious effect on the reappointment of Mr. Jefferson: however the thing was got over, & Mr. Adams returns with the intire approbation of Congress.

In general I think (between you & me) he and his book are thought of nearly in the same manner in this country. Nobody is yet appointed to Holland; though Mr. V. B. feels very uncomfortable on that head.

Mr. Gardoqui continues here, but has done nothing, and matters appear at a greater distance than ever. Since the Convention rose Congress have attended a little to business; & have done something for the credit of the Nation. They have either made or are about making contracts for Western territory which if complied with will have for their object the extinguishment of near six Millions of dollars of the domestic debt. I heartily wish the rage for terra firma may continue here, & that it may also extend itself to Europe.

I have often thought something might be done in that quarter; & have frequently thought in vain suggested the idea to that caput mortiuum of vitriol Congress. (devoid of vital energy).

They have also done something relative to the settlemt. of the accounts of the different States: an Ordnance is passed constituting a kind of high Court of Chancy. with considerable powers to decide on them in the last resort: The Commrs. however are not yet appointed. I am now on the point of leaving this, my time by the prest. Constitution being expired, but shall continue to write you from Virga. The delegates for our State for the next year are already appointed. They are Madison, Carrington, Harry Lee, Brown of the Senate & Cyrus Griffin: though I dont expect there will be a Congress till April or May next if then: as It is supposed the States who are for the new Constitution will be very slow in sending on their members. I remain, yr. Affect. frd & hble serv, Willm, Grayson.

P.S. Yesterday We had information that Kentucki had a Convention which adopted the idea. Will forward copies, as soon as I discover which of my correspondents will be the most willing agents in a communication with our printers. At present I am a stranger to their sentiments on the merits of the new System, and have reason to believe that a direct application to the printer from the Convention, would be used to disparage the Publication.

James White to Richard Caswell, Nov. 13, 1787, Gov. of N.C.

As White waited for the delegates to gather so Congress could convene. (Second half of letter): "I am writing to your Excellency at the time that all minds, all conversations are turned towards the interesting question of changing the foederal system it may be expected from every one who is honored with the public confidence to shew some attention to that subject.

But the gentlemen of the late delegation are so lately returned, as are also those who assisted at the convention, that I conceive it unnecessary to be very particular. Yet, as those who have been the most conversant with the subject appear to me to be the most convinced of the necessity of an efficient foederal government; I feel myself disposed to remark, that "no system could be framed which a spirit of doubt, & jealousy, might not conceive to be fraught with danger: that this over-cautious temper may be pushed to excess, I think I may be excused if I cite our present confederation in evidence, " I must in candor confess, *with the most patriotic & virtuous intentions. I am persuaded that it is pregnant with consequences which they fail to bring into view. The vote of Virga. On that subject, will either dismember the Union, or reduce her to a dilemma as mortifying to her pride, as it will be injurious to her foresight.*

I verily believe that if the patrons of this scheme, were to enter into an explicit & particular communication, they would find themselves as much at variance in detail as they are agreed in the general plan of amendments. Or if they could agree at all it would be only on a few points of very little substance, and which would not comprehend the objections of most weight in other states.

It is impossible indeed to trace the progress and tendency of this fond experiment without perceiving difficulty and danger in every Stage of it.

We never received either confirmation nor contradiction of the Reports concerning war between G.B. and France. The Dutch are prostrate before the Prussian arms. The follies and misfortunes on the other side of the Atlantic ought to be lessons of wisdom to this side. I fear we shall not derive from them profit of any sort, which they are calculated to afford us.

We have no Congs. as yet; nor any increase of the materials for one. If one were formed, it would only perhaps make the nakedness of the federal situation more conspicuous. The contributions to the treasury are failing.

Massachusetts. I am told has lately taken some resolution which effectually diverts the stream to some of her internal purposes. I perceive by the Newspapers that Delaware has decided unanimously in favor of the new Constitution. Penna. Has not yet decided. No delay however will diminish the great majority which are on the affirmative Side. The Convention of New Jersey, is meeting or actually met. The vote there will be nearly if not quite unanimous. That of Connecticut will succeed, and will pretty certainly make four ninths of the requisite number. The same cause which has instituted & countenanced the opposition in Virga. excites it in Massts. In one respect there is a remarkable difference.

In Virginia we see men equally respectable in every point of character &

marshalled in opposition to each other.

In Massts. almost all the intelligent & considerable people are on the side of the new Government. The Governor & the late Govr. though rivals & enemies, the Judges and the Bar; the men of letters; the Clergy and all the other learned professions, with that part of the Society which has the greatest interest in Good Government, are with but few exceptions in favor of the plan as it stands. The weight of this description of friends, seems to countenance the assurance which that side professes, of success. I am Dear Sir Yr. friend & sevt, James Madison

Author's Comment: The Virginia Assembly voted for an appropriation for the delegates to the conventions lodging expenses. This measure was much needed and long overdue as many who served in congress were not rich .

Samuel A. Otis to Theodore Sedgwick, June 6, 1788, New York
Samuel Otis was the father of Mercy Otis Warren, who may have been the author of the "Federal Farmer's Letters to the Republican.
" Dear Sir, After my congratulations upon the respectable elections of the present year, Give me leave to add them upon the favorable appearances from the South. Virginia is now in Convention, And must be influenced by the unanimity of Maryland, and the more recent accession of So. Carolina by a majority of two to one. The Gentlemen here, most acquainted with the affairs of Virginia, entertain the strongest hopes, but so great is the object, not without a degree of anxiety for the event. No.Carolina looks well at present, and will certainly join the list unless Virginia should be so unfortunate as to stand out, In which case N. C. may waver. In NY the opposition is powerful, but I think they will play the politician, procrastinate until the determination of Virginia & N Hampshire is known. If they assent, Join them. Congress have been pressed with an application from Kentucky that the question cannot be parryed much longer. It is of great importance to the Eastern states to bring Vermont forward; But this cannot be done without the agency of that State, Which for reasons of which I am not apprised is quite passive. No objection could operate against these measures if they went hand in hand; And really the arguments in favor of Kentucky are powerful. They have near one hundred thousand inhabitants at the immense distance of 800 miles from the seat of Government. They are courted by other powers to reject their allegiance to the USA.

Their darling hope of opening the Mississippi is cherished by those who wish ill to the Union. And Virginia, however extraordinary it may

appear, not only willing but sanguine for the measure.

The other business of Congress is detailed to the Legislature in our official letter directed to the Governour. And some few matters not proper for a public communication are made to confidential friends in the hands of my old & tried friend Mr Davis; To whom, and to the numerous list in both Houses that 1 have the felicity of putting in the same class, you will present me very respectfully. In expectation of seeing you here upon the recess of the Gen. Court I am, Sir, your most Huml Sev, Sam A Otis (66)

Alexander Hamilton to James Madison, June 8, 1788, New York,
My Dear Sir, In my last I think I informed you that the elections had turned out, beyond expectation, favourable to the Anti-Foedoral party. They have a majority of two thirds in the Convention and according to the best estimate I can form of about four sevenths in the community.

The views of the leaders in this City are pretty well ascertained to be turned towards a long adjournment say till next spring or summer.

Their incautious ones observe that this will give an opportunity to the state to see how government works and to act according to circumstances.

My reasonings on the fact are to this effect. The leaders of the party hostile to the constitution are equally hostile to the Union.

They are however afraid to reject the constitution at once because that step would bring matters to a crisis between this state and the states which had adopted the Constitution and between the parties in the state.

A separation of the Southern district from the other part of the state it is perceived would become the object of the Foederalists and of the two neighbouring states. They therefore resolve upon a long adjournment as the safest and most artful course to effect their purpose. They suppose that when the Government gets into operation it will take some steps in respect to revenue & c. which will furnish topics of declamation to its enemies in the several states and will strengthen the minorities. If any considerable discontent should show itself they will stand ready to head the opposition. If on the contrary the thing should go on smoothly and the sentiments of our own people should change they can then elect to come into the Union. They at all events take the chances, of time and the chapter of accidents. How far their friends in the Country will go with them I am not able to say, but as they have always been found very obsequious we have little reason to calculate upon an uncompliant temper in the present Instance.

For my own part the more I can penetrate the views of the Anti-foederal party in this state, the more I dread the consequences of the non adoption of the Constitution by any of the other states, the more I fear an eventual disunion and civil war.

God grant that Virginia may accede. Her example will have a vast influence on our politics. New Hampshire, all accounts give us to expect, will be an assenting state. The number of the volumes the foederalist which you desired have been forwarded, as well the second as the first, to the care of Governor Randolph. It was impossible to correct a certain error in a former letter. I requested you communicate to me by express, any decisive question in favour of the Constitution authorizing changes of horses &c with an assurance to the person sent that he will be liberally paid for his diligence.

Edward Carrington to Thomas Jefferson, June 9, 1788
My dear Sir, I had the honor to write you by the last packet by Mr. Barlow and Master G. W. Greene, since which South Carolina has acceded to the new Constitution by a great Majority.

The inclosed papers contain the act, and some of the debates of the convention. Virginia is now sitting, having met last Monday, but we have not yet received any intelligence as to the probable turn the business will take there. I am inclined to think the critical stage in which this convention meets the affair, will have much influence upon the opinions of many who sat in the opposition In adopting they will certainly avoid Commotion, and, at worst, accept a constitution upon which eight States have already agreed to hazard their happiness, and which may be amended, should it be found to operate badly; in rejecting they may produce commotion, with but little prospect of preventing the adoption.

The five States who have not yet acceded, would never agree in their objects, and could even this be brought about, they must at last rather yield to the 8, than these to the five; and it appears that the submission on either side must be intire, for should the 8 think of a compromise with the 5, there would be difficulty in gageing what points to yield.

These considerations will, I apprehend, have their effect in the convention of Virginia, & produce an issue different from that which might have taken place under other circumstances.

I am happy to find that the five are so separated that there cannot be a possible effort, to Unite in an attempt to dismember the union.

Had the southern States joined in opinion as to the Constitution, I verily believe such a desperate step would have been tried, but it would have ended in their destruction, and perhaps that of all the others. Mr. Madison

154

& I have sent you sundry Phlets written by the Friends of the Constitution I have endeavoured to select the best of those written by the other side, that you may fairly judge the arguments pro & Con.

The two books enclosed contain a number of letters under the signature of the Federal Farmer , the best, and unknown author. **I hope to send you the 2ⁿᵈ vol. Of the Fed. Farmer soon.** I have the Honor to be, my dear. Sir, with great esteem your. Sincere Friend & Humble servant, Ed. Carrington

THE DEBATES IN THE CONVENTION OF THE COMMONWEALTH OF VIRGINIA ON THE ADOPTION OF THE FEDERAL CONSTITUTION

Also Called: The Virginia Ratifying Convention of 1788, June 2 to June 27, 1788, Richmond, Virginia

By the time 170 Virginians met in Convention to decide how to vote on the Constitution, nine states had already ratified. Now it was up to Virginia. Ten ratifying votes would secure the Constitution. Virginia could choose secession from the thirteen colonies and form their own country.

Considering how large the "Old Dominion" was, Virginia would be a formidable enemy to the north one they would never want to deal with, so there was fear and a definite threat of losing the south over an incident of some minor issue that could arise at any time. The Civil war that would ensue over a plethora of reasons gave Virginians cause to think very carefully whether they wanted to remain in the union or to seriously consider what was called treason; to procede with plans to secede from the union.

Patriotic Virginians found it difficult to accept the blow the Constitution delivered to liberty in America with its many doubts and flaws. An anxious nation watched, anxious for the outcome and praying for cohesion.

They knew that Patrick Henry was against the Constitution as were William Grayson, George Mason, Ben Harrison, James Monroe and Governor Randolph all of whom were leaders in the Anti-Federalist party.

At the first session, on June 2, 1788, Edmund Pendleton, a greatly admired patriot was elected president of the Virginia Ratifying Convention. by unanimous consent.

There had been rough moments once the news hit the streets. Riots exploded in the streets of Philadelphia, when the public learned there would be a new governing document. People were loyal to the Articles of Confederacy. In that incendiary atmosphere, both sides were adamantine. In June Virginia delegates assembled at St. John's church in Richmond to ratify or reject the Federal Constitution. The location was the site of Patrick Henry's most famous speech, ending with, "Give me liberty, or give me death."

Patrick Henry was filled with apprehension lest the new Constitution destroy state sovereignty and concentrate fearful power in the hands of the chief magistrate, namely the president.

He was prepared to lift his voice eloquently against the travesty and he was sorry to reject Washington's request to sign, but Patrick found the document, rife with inequities and difficult to repair without true partisanship, which did not exist, so in complete honesty he answered Washington, saying with fervor,

"It is too flawed and inequitable," and said that he could not lend his support. Washington must have been surprised and disappointed.

So without due cause and to their eternal shame, the Federalists labelled their opponents, the Anti-Federalists, "enemies of the union, an insult and degradation. In attendance was Chancellor Wythe, a brilliant authority on jurisprudence and a signer of the Declaration of Independence. Wythe paid close attention as did John Marshall,, the brilliant and eminent chief justice, Edward Pendleton, one of Virginia's noblest sons and president of the Constitutional Convention

THE ARTICLES OF THE CONSTITUTION
Article 1 The Legislative Branch
 Section 1 The Legislature
   Section 2 The House of Representatives
   Section 3 The Senate
   Section 4 Elections, Meetings
   Section 5 Membership, rules, Journals, Adjournment
   Section 6 Compensation
   Section 7 Revenue Bills, Legislative Process, Presidential Veto
   Section 8 Powers of Congress
   Section 9 Limits of Congress
   Section 10 Powers Prohibited of States
   Article II The Executive Branch
   Section 1 The President
  Section 2 Civilian Power over Military, Cabinet, Pardon Power, Appts.
   Section 3 State of the Union, Convening Congress
   Section 4 Disqualification
   Article III The Judicial Branch
   Section 1 Judicial Powers
   Section 2 Trial by Jury, Original Jurisdiction, Jury Trials

156

THE COMMITTEE OF PRIVILEGE AND ELECTIONS

On June 2, 1788, the Committee of Privilege and Elections was appointed and comprised of:

Benjamin Harrison
George Mason
Edmund Randolph
George Nicholas
John Marshall
Edward Carrington
John Tyler
Alexander White
John Blair
Theodorick Blan
William Grayson
Daniel Fisher
Thomas Matthews
John Jones
George Wyth
William Cabell
James Taylor (Caroline)
Gabriel Jones
Francis Corbin
James Innis
James Monroe
Richard H. L
Edward Pendleton. Pendleton was elected president.

JUNE 3, 1788, The second day the convention met at the New Academy on Schocktoe Hill in Richmond, Virginia. An attempt was made to establish rules for deliberating. George Mason remarked, "Fear what will justly fall upon us, if from any sinister views we obstruct the fullest inquiry."

Mason wished measured debate, but after a dramatic speech by Patrick Henry that went on for hours, all thoughts of structure disappeared and those rising thereafter, spoke with a similar abandon, expressing their view of the Constitution and hoping for everlasting fame for themselves and their beloved Virginia and it eternal Union that seemed to hinge on the deliberations.

The air was riddled with anxiety as the members argued over clauses. If they were denied in their quest would Virginia secede from America?

SPEECHES IN THE CONVENTION

JUNE 4, 1788, Wednesday: Benjamin Harrison gave a cursory report for the committee of Privileges and Elections.

Patrick Henry said they were out of order even meeting as they had exceeded the established mandate for altering the Confederation.

Edmund Pendleton ruled Patrick Henry out of order.

THE PREAMBLE & ARTICLE 1, SECTIONS 1 & 2
Section 1: The Legislative Branch, Section 2: Legislative Power Vested

George Nicholas rose to defend the Constitution.

Patrick Henry expressed alarm and stressed the dangers inherent in the new document.

Gov. Edmund Randolph explained why he did not sign in Philadelphia and why he walked out. He stressed that failure to ratify at that point would justify disunion.

George Mason aligned himself with Henry saying they were recommending a National government not a Confederation, and that the number of congressional representatives was far too small for the population of the nation, and that there must be protection "for the dearest rights of the people." He suggested amendments to correct inequities.

James Madison defended every issue and suggested they concentrate on taxation and representation and keep to the order of the articles.

JUNE 5, 1788,

THE PREAMBLE & ARTICLES 1, SECTIONS 1 & 2, are read
the Legislative Branch. Sect. 1 The Legislature, Sect. 2 The House

George Pendleton: Defended and argued that direct taxation was a right of Congress and reminded the gathering of the inadequacies of the Confederation.
   (Already there is heated bickering and anger in the air).

PATRICK HENRY. Mr. Chairman, I am much obliged to the very worthy gentleman for his encomium. I wish I was possessed with talents, or possessed of any thing that might enable me to elucidate this great subject.

I am not free from suspicion: I am apt to entertain doubts. I rose yesterday to ask a question which arose in my own mind. When I asked that question, I thought the meaning of my interrogation was obvious.

The fate of this question and of America may depend on this. Have they said, We, the states? Have they made a proposal of a compact between states? If they had, this would be a confederation. It is otherwise most clearly a consolidated government.

The question turns, sir, on that poor little expression, We, the people, instead of the states, of America. I need not take pains to show that the principles of this system are extremely pernicious, impolitic, and dangerous.

Is this a monarchy, like England, a compact between prince and people, with checks on the former to secure the liberty of the latter? Is this a confederacy, like Holland-an association of a number of independent states, each of which retains its individual sovereignty?

It is not a democracy, wherein the people retain all their rights securely. Had these principles been adhered to, we should not have been brought to this alarming transition, from a confederacy to a consolidated government. We have no detail of how great the consideration, which, in my opinion, ought to have abounded before we recur to a government of this kind.

Here is a resolution as radical as that which separated us from Great Britain. It is radical in this transition; our rights and privileges are endangered, and the sovereignty of the states will be relinquished: and cannot we plainly see that this is actually the case?

The rights of conscience, trial by jury, Liberty of the press, all your immunities and franchises, all pretensions to human rights and privileges, are rendered insecure, if not lost, by this change, so loudly talked of by some, and inconsiderately by others. Is this tame relinquishment of rights worthy of freemen? Is it worthy of manly fortitude that ought to characterize republicans? It is said eight states have adopted this plan. I declare that if twelve states and a half had adopted it, I would, with manly firmness, and in spite of an erring world, reject it.

You are not to inquire how your trade may be increased, nor how you are to become a great and powerful people, but how your liberties can be secured; for liberty ought to be the direct end of your government.

Having premised these things, I shall, with the aid of my judgment and information, which, I confess, are not extensive, go into the discussion of this system more minutely.

Is it necessary for your liberty that you should abandon those great rights by the adoption of this system? Is the relinquishment of the trial by jury and the liberty of the press necessary for your liberty? Will the abandonment of your most sacred rights tend to the security of your liberty?

Liberty, the greatest of all earthly blessing - give us that precious jewel, and you may take every thing else! But I am fearful I have lived long enough to become an old-fashioned fellow. Perhaps an invincible attachment to the dearest rights of man may, in these refined, enlightened days, be deemed old-fashioned; if so, I am contented to be so.

I say, the time has been when every pulse of my heart beats for American liberty, and which, I believe, had a counterpart in the breast of every true American; but suspicions have gone forth-suspicions of my integrity - publicly reported that my professions are not real.

Twenty-three years ago was I supposed a traitor to my country? I was then said to be the bane of sedition, because I supported the rights of my country. I may be thought suspicious when I say our privileges and rights are in danger. But, sir, a number of the people of this country are weak enough to think these things are too true. I am happy to find that the gentleman on the other side declares they are groundless. But, sir, suspicion is a virtue as long as its object is the preservation of the public good, and as long as it stays within proper bounds: should it fall on me, I am contented: conscious rectitude is a powerful consolation.

I trust there are many who think my professions for the public good to be real. Let your suspicion look to both sides. There are many on the other side, who possibly may have been persuaded to the necessity of these measures, which I conceive to be dangerous to your liberty.

Guard with jealous attention the public liberty. Suspect every one who approaches that jewel. Unfortunately, nothing will preserve it but downright force. Whenever you give up that force, you are inevitably ruined. I am answered by gentlemen, that, though I might speak of terrors, yet the fact was, that we were surrounded by none of the dangers I apprehended. I conceive this new government to be one of those dangers: it has produced those horrors which distress many of our best citizens. We are come hither to preserve the commonwealth of Virginia, if it can be done: something must be done to preserve your liberty and mine.

The Confederation, this same despised government, merits, in my opinion, the highest encomium: it carried us through a long and dangerous

war; it rendered us victorious in that bloody conflict with a powerful nation; it has secured us a territory greater than any European monarch possesses: and shall a government which has been thus strong and vigorous, be accused of imbecility, and abandoned for want of energy?

Consider what you are about to do before you part with the government. Take longer time in reckoning things; revolutions like this have happened in almost every country in Europe; similar examples are found in ancient Greece and ancient Rome, instances of the people losing their liberty by their own carelessness and the ambition of a few.

We are cautioned by the honorable gentleman, who presides, against faction and turbulence. I acknowledge that licentiousness is dangerous, and that it ought to be provided against: I acknowledge, also, the new form of government may effectually prevent it: yet there is another thing it will as effectually do it will oppress and ruin the people.

There are sufficient guards placed against sedition and licentiousness; for, when power is given to this government to suppress these, or for any other purpose, the language it assumes is clear, express, and unequivocal; but when this Constitution speaks of privileges, there is an ambiguity, sir, a fatal ambiguity, an ambiguity which is astonishing. In the clause under consideration, there is the strangest language that I can conceive.

I mean, when it says that there shall not be more representatives than one for every thirty thousand.

How easy is it to evade this privilege! This may be satisfied by one representative from each state. Let our numbers be ever so great, this immense continent may, by this artful expression, be reduced to have but thirteen representatives. I confess this construction is not natural; but the ambiguity of the expression lays a good ground for a quarrel. Why was it not clearly and unequivocally expressed, that they should be entitled to have one for every thirty thousand? This would have obviated all disputes; and was this difficult to be done? What is the inference? When population increases, and a state shall send representatives in this proportion, Congress may remand them, because the right of having one for every thirty thousand is not clearly expressed. This possibility of reducing the number to one for each state approximates to probability by that other expression - "but each state shall at least have one representative." Now, is it not clear that, from the first expression, the number might be reduced so much that some states should have no representatives at all, were it not for the insertion of this last expression? And as this is the only restriction upon them, we may fairly conclude that they may restrain the number to one from each state.

Perhaps the same horrors may hang over my mind. I shall be told I am continually afraid: but, sir, I have strong cause of apprehension.

In some parts of the plan before you, the great rights of freemen are endangered; in other parts, absolutely taken away. How does your trial by jury stand? In civil cases gone - not sufficiently secured in criminal- this best privilege is gone.

But we are told that we need not fear; because those in power, being our representatives, will not abuse the powers we put in their hands. I am not well versed in history, **but I will submit to your recollection, whether liberty has been destroyed most often by the licentiousness of the people, or by the tyranny of rulers. I imagine, sir, you will find the balance on the side of the rulers.** Happy will you be if you miss the fate of those nations, who, omitting to resist their oppressors, or negligently suffering their liberty to be wrested from them, have groaned under intolerable nepotism!

Most of the human race are now in this deplorable condition; and those nations who have gone in search of grandeur, power, and splendor, have *also fallen a sacrifice, and been the victims of their own folly. While they acquired those visionary blessings, they lost their freedom.

My great objection to this government is, that it does not leave us the means of defending our rights, or of waging war against tyrants.

It is urged by some gentlemen, that this new plan will bring us an acquisition of strength–an army, and the militia of the states. This is an idea extremely ridiculous: gentlemen cannot be earnest. This acquisition will trample on our fallen liberty. Let my beloved Americans guard against that fatal lethargy that has pervaded the universe.

Have we the means of resisting disciplined armies, when our only defense, the militia, is put into the hands of Congress?

The honorable gentleman said that great danger would ensue if the Convention rose without adopting this system. I ask, Where is that danger? I see none. Other gentlemen have told us, within these walls, that the union is gone, or will be gone. Is not this trifling with the judgment of their fellow-citizens? Till they tell us the grounds of their fears, I will consider them as imaginary.

I rose to make inquiry where those dangers were; they could make no answer: I believe I never shall have that answer. Is there a disposition in the people of this country to revolt against the dominion of laws?

Has there been a single tumult in Virginia? Have not the people of Virginia, when laboring under the severest pressure of accumulated distresses, manifested the most cordial acquiescence in the execution of the laws? What could be more awful than their unanimous acquiescence under general distresses? Is there any revolution in Virginia?

Whither is the spirit of America gone? Whither is the genius of America fled? It was but yesterday, when our enemies marched in triumph through our country. Yet the people of this country could not be appalled by their pompous armaments: they stopped their career, and victoriously captured them. Where is the peril, now, compared to that? Some minds are agitated by foreign alarms. Happily for us, there is no real danger from Europe; that country is engaged in more arduous business: from that quarter there is no cause of fear: you may sleep in safety forever for them.

Where is the danger? If, sir, there was any, I would recur to the American spirit to defend us; that spirit which has enabled us to surmount the greatest difficulties: to that illustrious spirit I address my most fervent prayer to prevent our adopting a system destructive to liberty.

Let not gentlemen be told that it is not safe to reject this government. Wherefore is it not safe? We are told there are dangers, but those dangers are ideal; they cannot be demonstrated. To encourage us to adopt it, they tell us that there is a plain, easy way of getting amendments.

When I come to contemplate this part, I suppose that I am mad, or that my countrymen are so. **The way to amendment is, in my conception, shut**.

Let us consider this plain, way. "The Congress, whenever two thirds of both houses shall deem it necessary, shall propose amendments to this Constitution, or, on the application of the legislatures of two thirds of the several states, shall call a Convention for proposing amendments, which, in either case, shall be valid to all intents and purposes, as part of this Constitution, when ratified by the legislatures of three fourths of the several states, or by the Conventions in three fourths thereof, as the one or the other mode of ratification may be proposed by the Congress. Provided, that no amendment which may be made prior to the year 1808, shall in any manner affect the 1st and 4th clauses in the 9th section of the 1st article; and that no state, without it s consent, shall be deprived of equal suffrage in the Senate."

Hence it appears that three fourths of the states must ultimately agree to any amendments that may be necessary. Let us consider the consequence of this. However uncharitable it may appear, yet I must tell my

opinion that the most unworthy characters may get into power, and prevent the introduction of amendments.

Let us suppose for the case is supposable, possible, and probable that you happen to deal those powers to unworthy hands; will they relinquish powers already in their possession, or agree to amendments? Two thirds of the Congress, or of the state legislatures, are necessary even to propose amendments. If one third of these be unworthy men, they may prevent the application for amendments; but what is destructive and mischievous, is, that three fourths of the state legislatures, or of the state conventions, must concur in the amendments when proposed! In such numerous bodies, there must necessarily be some designing, bad men.

To suppose that so large a number as three fourths of the states will concur, is to suppose that they will possess genius, intelligence, and integrity, approaching to miraculous.

It would indeed be miraculous that they should concur in the same amendments, or even in such as would bear some likeness to one another; for four of the smallest states, that do not collectively contain one tenth part of the population of the United States, may obstruct the most salutary and necessary amendments. Nay, in these four states, six tenths of the people may reject these amendments; and suppose amendments shall be opposed to amendments, which is highly probable.

Is it possible that three-fourths can ever agree to the same amendments? A bare majority in these four small states may hinder the adoption of amendments; so that we may fairly and justly conclude that **one twentieth part of-the American people may prevent the removal of the most grievous inconveniences and oppression, by refusing to accede to amendments. A trifling minority may reject the most salutary amendments.**

Is this an easy mode of securing the public liberty? It is, sir, a most fearful situation, when the most contemptible minority can prevent the alteration of the most oppressive government; for it may, in many respects, prove as such. Is this the spirit of republicanism? What, sir, is the genius of democracy? Let me read that clause of the bill of rights of Virginia which relates to this: 3rd clause:

That government is, or ought to be, instituted for the common benefit, protection, and security of the people, nation, or community. Of all the various modes and forms of government, that is best, which is capable of producing the greatest degree of happiness and safety, and is most effectually secured against the danger of mal-administration; and that

whenever any government shall be found inadequate, or contrary to those purposes, a majority of the community hath an indubitable, unalienable, and indefeasible right to reform, alter, or abolish it, in such manner as shall be judged most conducive to the public weal. This, sir, is the language of democracy that a majority of the community have a right to alter government when found to be oppressive.

But how different is the genius of your new Constitution from this! How different from the sentiments of freemen, that a contemptible minority can prevent the good of the majority!

If, then, gentlemen, standing on this ground, are come to that point, that they are willing to bind themselves and their posterity to be oppressed, I am amazed and inexpressibly astonished.

If this be the opinion of the majority, I must submit; but to me, sir, it appears perilous and destructive.

I cannot help thinking so. Perhaps it may be the result of my age. These may be feelings natural to a man of my years, when the American spirit has left him, and his mental powers, like the members of the body, are decayed. **If, sir, amendments are left to the twentieth, or tenth part of the people of America, your liberty is gone forever.**

We have heard that there is a bribery practiced in the House of Commons, in England, and that many of the members raise themselves to preferments by selling the rights of the whole of the people. But, sir, the tenth part of that body cannot continue oppression on the rest of the people. **English liberty is, in this case, on a firmer foundation than American liberty.** It will be easily contrived to procure the opposition of one tenth of the people to any alteration, however judicious.

The honorable gentleman who presides told us that, to prevent abuses in our government, we will assemble in Convention, recall our delegated powers, and punish our servants for abusing the trust reposed in them.

Sir, we should have fine times, indeed, if, to punish tyrants, it were only sufficient to assemble the people!

Your arms, wherewith you could defend yourselves, are gone; and you have no longer an aristocratical, no longer a democratical spirit.

Did you ever read of any revolution in a nation, brought about by the punishment of those in power, inflicted by those who had no power? You read of a riot act in a country which is called one of the freest in the world, where a few neighbors cannot assemble without the risk of being shot by a hired soldiery, the engines of despotism. We may see this act in America.

A standing army we shall have, also, to execute the execrable commands of tyranny; and how are you to punish them? Will you order them to be punished? Who shall obey these orders? Will your mace-bearer be a match for a disciplined regiment? In what situation are we to be?

The clause before you gives a power of direct taxation, unbounded and unlimited, exclusive power of legislation, in all cases whatsoever, for ten miles square, and over all places purchased for the erection of forts, magazines, arsenals, dockyards, &c. What resistance could be made? The attempt would be madness. You will find the strength of this country in the hands of your enemies; their garrisons will naturally be the strongest places in the country. Your militia is given up to Congress, also, in another part of this plan: they will therefore act as they think proper: all power will be in their own possession.

You cannot force them to receive their punishment: of what service would militia be to you, when, most probably, you will not have a single musket in the state?

For, as arms are to be provided by Congress, they may or may not furnish them. Let me call your attention to that part which gives the Congress power "to provide for organizing, arming, and disciplining the militia, and for governing such part of them as may be employed in the service of the United States reserving to the states, respectively, the appointment of the officers, and the authority of training the militia according to the discipline prescribed by Congress." By this, sir, you see that their control over our last and best defense is unlimited.

If they neglect or refuse to discipline or arm our militia, they will be useless: the states can do neither - this power being exclusively given to Congress.

The power of appointing officers over men not disciplined or armed is ridiculous; **so that this pretended Little remains of power left to the states may, at the pleasure of Congress, be rendered nugatory.**

Our situation will be deplorable indeed: nor can we ever expect to get this government amended, since I have already shown that a very small minority may prevent it, and that small minority interested in the continuance of the oppression. Will the oppressor let go the oppressed? Was there ever an instance? Can the annals of mankind exhibit one single example where rulers overcharged with power willingly Let go the oppressed, though solicited and requested most earnestly?

The application for amendments will therefore be fruitless. Sometimes, the oppressed have got loose by one of those bloody struggles that desolate a country; **but a willing relinquishment of power is one of those things which human nature never was, nor ever will be, capable of.**

The honorable gentleman's observations, respecting the people's right of being the agents in the formation of this government, are not accurate, in my humble conception.

The distinction between a national government and a confederacy is not sufficiently discerned. Had the delegates, who were sent to Philadelphia, a power to propose a consolidated government instead of a confederacy. **Were they not deputed by states, and not by the people?**

The assent of the people, in their collective capacity, is not necessary to the formation of a federal government. The people have no right to enter into leagues, alliances, or confederations; States and foreign powers are the only proper agents for this kind of government.

Show me an instance where the people have exercised this business. Has it not always gone through the legislatures?

I refer you to the treaties with France, Holland, and other nations. How were they made? Were they not made by the states? Are the people, therefore, in their aggregate capacity, the proper persons to form a confederacy? This, therefore, ought to depend on the consent of the legislatures, the people having never sent delegates to make any proposition for changing the government.

Yet I must say, at the same time, that it was made on grounds the most pure; and perhaps I might have been brought to consent to it so far as to the change of government. But there is one thing in it which I never would acquiesce in. I mean, the changing it into a consolidated government, which is so abhorrent to my mind.

The honorable gentleman then went on to the figure we make with foreign nations; the contemptible one we made in France and Holland; which, according to the substance of the notes, he attributes to the present feeble government.

An opinion has gone forth, we find, that we are contemptible people: the time has been when we were thought otherwise.

Under the same despised government, we commanded the respect of all Europe: wherefore are we now reckoned otherwise?

The American spirit has fled from hence: it has gone to regions where it has never been expected; it has gone to the people of France, in search of a splendid government, a strong, energetic government. Shall we imitate the example of those nations who have gone from a simple to a splendid government? Are those nations worthy of our imitation? What can make an adequate satisfaction to them for the loss they have suffered in attaining such a government for the loss of their liberty? If we admit this consolidated government, it will be because we like a great, splendid one.

Some way or other we must be a great and mighty empire; we must have an army, and a navy, and a number of things.

When the American spirit was in its youth, the language of America was different: liberty, sir, was then the primary object.

We are descended from a people whose government was founded on liberty: our glorious forefathers of Great Britain made liberty the foundation of every thing. That country has become a great, mighty, and splendid nation; not because their government is strong and energetic, but, sir, because liberty is its direct end and foundation.

We drew the spirit of liberty from our British ancestors: by that spirit we have triumphed over every difficulty.

Now, sir, the American spirit, assisted by the ropes and chains of consolidation, is about to convert this country into a powerful and mighty empire. If you make the citizens of this country agree to become the subjects of one great consolidated empire of America, your government will not have sufficient energy to keep them together.

Such a government is incompatible with the genius of republicanism. There will be no checks, no real balances, in this government.

What can avail your specious, imaginary balances, your rope-dancing, chain-rattling, ridiculous ideal checks and contrivances? But, sir, we are not feared by foreigners; we do not make nations tremble. Would this constitute happiness, or secure liberty? I trust, sir, our political hemisphere will ever direct their operations to the security of those objects. Consider our situation, sir: go to the poor man, and ask him what he does. He will inform you that he enjoys the fruits of his labor, under his own fig-tree, with his wife and children around him, in peace and security.

Go to every other member of society, - you will find the same tranquil ease and content; you will find no alarms or disturbances. Why, then, tell us of danger, to terrify us into an adoption of this new form of government?

And yet who knows the dangers that this new system may produce when out of sight of the common people: they cannot foresee latent consequences.

I dread the operation of it on the middling and lower classes of people: it is for them I fear the adoption of this system.

I fear I tire the patience of the committee; but I beg to be indulged with a few more observations. When I thus profess myself an advocate for the liberty of the people, I shall be told I am a designing man, that I am to be a great man, that I am to be a demagogue; and many similar illiberal insinuations will be thrown out: but, sir, conscious rectitude outweighs those things with me. I see great jeopardy in this new government. I see none from our present one. I hope some gentleman or other will bring forth, in full array, those dangers, if there be any, that we may see and touch them. I have said that I thought this a consolidated government: I will now prove it. Will the great rights of the people be secured by this government? Suppose it should prove oppressive, how can it be altered?

Our bill of rights declares, "that a majority of the community hath an indubitable, unalienable, and indefeasible right to reform, alter, or abolish it, in such manner as shall be judged most conducive to the public weal."

I have just proved that one tenth, or less, of the people of America a most despicable minority, may prevent this reform or alteration. Suppose the people of Virginia wish to alter their government; can a majority of them do it? No; because they are connected with other men, or, in other words, consolidated with other states. When the people of Virginia, at a future day, wish to alter their government, though they should be unanimous in this desire, yet they may be prevented therefrom by a despicable minority at the extremity of the U.S.

The founders of your Constitution made your government changeable: but the power of changing it is gone from you. Whither is it gone? It is placed in the same hands that hold the rights of twelve other states; and those who hold those rights have the power to keep them. It is not the particular government of Virginia: one of the leading features of that government is, that a majority can alter it, when necessary for the public good.

This government is not a Virginian, but an American government. Is it not, therefore, a consolidated government?

The sixth clause of your bill of rights tells you, **"that elections of members to serve as representatives of the people in Assembly ought to be free, and that all men having sufficient evidence of permanent common interest with, and attachment to, the community, have the right of suffrage, and cannot be taxed, or deprived of their property for public uses, without their own consent, or that of their representatives so elected, nor** bound by any law to which they have not in like manner assented for the public good."

But what does this Constitution say? The clause under consideration gives an unlimited and unbounded power of taxation. Suppose every delegate from Virginia opposes a law laying a tax; what will it avail? They are opposed by a majority; eleven members can destroy their efforts: those feeble ten cannot prevent the passing the most oppressive tax law; so that, in direct opposition to the spirit and express language of your declaration of rights, **you are taxed, not by your own consent, but by people who have no connection with you.**

The next clause of the bill of rights tells you, "that all power of suspending law, or the execution of laws, by any authority, without the consent of the representatives of the people, is injurious to their rights, and ought not to be exercised." This tells us that there can be no suspension of government or laws without our own consent; yet this Constitution can counteract and suspend any of our laws that contravene its oppressive operation; for they have the power of direct taxation, which suspends our bill of rights; and it is expressly provided that they can make laws necessary for carrying their powers into execution; and it is declared paramount to the laws and constitutions of the states.

Consider how the only remaining defense we have left is destroyed in this manner.

Besides the expenses of maintaining the Senate and other house in as much splendor as they please, **there is to be a great and mighty President, with very extensive powers-the powers of a king. He is to be supported in extravagant magnificence; so that the whole of our property may be taken by this American government, by laying what taxes they please,** giving themselves what salaries they please, and suspending our laws at their pleasure. I might be thought too inquisitive, but I believe I should take up very little of your time in enumerating **the little power that is left to the government of Virginia; for this power is reduced to little or nothing:** Their garrisons, magazines, arsenals, and forts, which will be situated in the strongest places within the states.; their ten miles square, with all the fine ornaments of human life, added to their powers, and taken from the states, will reduce the power of the latter to nothing.

The voice of tradition, I trust, will inform posterity of our struggles for freedom. If our descendants be worthy of the name of Americans, they will preserve, and hand down to their latest posterity, the transactions of the present times; and, though I confess my exclamations are not worthy the hearing, they will see that I have done my utmost to preserve their liberty; for I never will give up the power of direct taxation but for a scourge.

I am willing to give it conditionally; that is, after non-compliance with requisitions. I will do more, sir, and what I hope will convince the most skeptical man that I am a lover of the American Union - that, in case Virginia shall not make punctual payment, the control of our custom-houses, and the whole regulation of trade, shall be given to Congress, and that Virginia shall depend on Congress even for passports, till Virginia shall have paid the last farthing, and furnished the last soldier. Nay, sir, there is another alternative to which I would consent;- even that they should strike us out of the Union, and take away from us all federal privileges, till we comply with federal requisitions: **but let it depend upon our own pleasure to pay our money in the most easy manner for our people.**

Were all the states, more terrible than the mother country, to join against us, I hope Virginia could defend herself; **but, sir, the dissolution of the Union is most abhorrent to my mind. The first thing I have at heart is American liberty: the second thing is American union;** and I hope the people of Virginia will endeavor to preserve that union. The increasing population of the Southern States is far greater than that of New England; consequently, in a short time, they will be far more numerous than the people of that country.

Consider this, and you will find this state more particularly interested to support American liberty, and not bind our posterity by an improvident relinquishment of our rights.

I would give the best security for a punctual compliance with requisitions; but I beseech gentlemen, at all hazards, not to give up this unlimited power of taxation.

The honorable gentleman has told us that these powers, given to Congress, are accompanied by a judiciary which will correct all. **On examination, you will find this very judiciary oppressively constructed; your jury trial destroyed, and the judges dependent on Congress.**

In this scheme of energetic government, the people will find two sets of tax-gatherers - the state and the federal sheriffs. This, it seems to me, will produce such dreadful oppression as the people cannot possibly bear.

The federal sheriff may commit what oppression, make what distresses he pleases, and ruin you with impunity; for how are you to tie his hands?

Have you any sufficiently decided means of preventing him from sucking your blood by speculations, commissions, and fees? Thus thousands of your people will be most shamefully robbed: our state sheriffs, those unfeeling blood-suckers have, under the watchful eye of our legislature, committed the most horrid and barbarous ravages on our people.

It has required the most constant vigilance of the legislature to keep them from totally ruining the people; a repeated succession of laws has been made to suppress their iniquitous speculations and cruel extortions; and as often has their nefarious ingenuity devised methods of evading the force of those laws: in the struggle they have generally triumphed over the legislature. It is a fact that lands have been sold for five shillings, which were worth one hundred pounds: if sheriffs, thus immediately under the eye of our state legislature and judiciary, have dared to commit these outrages, what would they not have done if their masters had been at Philadelphia or New York? If they perpetrate the most unwarrantable outrage on your person or property, you cannot get redress on this side of Philadelphia or New York; and how can you get it there If your domestic avocations could permit you to go thither, there you must appeal to judges sworn to support this Constitution, in opposition to that of any state, and who may also be inclined to favor their own officers. When these harpies are aided by excisemen, who may search, at any time, your houses, and most secret recesses, will the people bear it? If you think so, you differ from me. Where I thought there was a possibility of such mischiefs, I would grant power with a niggardly hand; and here there is a strong probability that these oppressions shall actually happen. I may be told that it is safe to err on that side, because such regulations may be made by Congress as shall restrain these officers, and because laws are made by our representatives, and judged by righteous judges: but, sir, as these regulations may be made, so they may not; and many reasons there are to induce a belief that they will not.

I shall therefore be an infidel on that point till the day of my death. **This Constitution is said to have beautiful features; but when I come to examine these features, sir, they appear to me horribly frightful. Among other deformities, it has an awful squinting; it squints towards monarchy; and does not this raise indignation in the breast of every true American?**

Your President may easily become king. Your Senate is so imperfectly constructed that your dearest rights may be sacrificed by what may be a small minority; and a very small minority may continue forever unchangeably this government, although horridly defective. Where are your checks in this government?

Your strongholds will be in the hands of your enemies.

It is on a supposition that your American governors shall be honest, that all the good qualities of this government are founded; but its defective and imperfect construction puts it in their power to perpetrate the worst of mischiefs, should they be bad men; and, sir, would not all the world, from the eastern to the western hemisphere, blame our distracted folly in resting our rights upon the contingency of our rulers being good or bad?

Show me that age and country where the rights and liberties of the people were placed on the sole chance of their rulers being good men, without a consequent loss of liberty! I say that the loss of that dear privilege has ever followed, with absolute certainty, every mad attempt.

If your American chief be a man of ambition and abilities, how easy is it for him to render himself absolute! The army is in his hands, and if he be a man of address, it will be attached to him, and it will be the subject of long meditation with him to seize the first auspicious moment to accomplish his design; and will the American spirit solely relieve you when this happens?

I would rather infinitely-and I am sure most of this Convention are of the same opinion-have a king, lords, and commons, than a government so replete with such insupportable evils. If we make a king, we may prescribe the rules by which he shall rule his people, and interpose such checks as shall prevent him from infringing them; but the President, in the field, at the head of his army, can prescribe the terms on which he shall reign so that any American can ever get his neck from under the galling yoke.

I cannot with patience think of this idea. If ever he violates the laws, one of two things will happen: he will come at the head of his army, to carry every thing before him; or he will give bail, or do what Mr. Chief Justice will order him. If he be guilty, will not the recollection of his crimes teach him to make one bold push for the American throne? Will not the immense difference between being master of every thing, and being ignominiously tried and punished, powerfully excite him to make this bold push?

But, sir, where is the existing force to punish him? Can he not, at the head of his army, beat down every opposition? Away with your President! we shall have a king: the army will salute him monarch: your militia will leave you, and assist in making him king, and fight against you: and what have you to oppose this force?

What will then become of you and your rights? Will not absolute despotism ensue?

The history of Switzerland clearly proves that we might be in amicable alliance with those states without adopting this Constitution. Switzerland is a confederacy, consisting of dissimilar governments. This is an example which proves that governments of dissimilar structures may be confederated. **That confederate republic has stood upwards of four hundred years; and, although several of the individual republics are democratic, and the rest aristocratic, no evil has resulted from this dissimilarity; for they have braved all the power of France and Germany during that long period.**

The Swiss spirit, sir, has kept them together; they have encountered and overcome immense difficulties with patience and fortitude. In the vicinity of powerful and ambitious monarchs, they have retained their independence, republican simplicity, and valor. [Here he makes a comparison of the people of that country and those of France, and makes a quotation from Addison illustrating the subject.]

Look at the peasants of that country and of France; and mark the difference. You will find the condition of the former far more desirable and comfortable. No matter whether the people be great, splendid, and powerful, if they enjoy freedom.

The Turkish Grand Signior, alongside of our President, would put us to disgrace; but we should be as abundantly consoled for this disgrace, when our citizens have been put in contrast with the Turkish slave.

The most valuable end of government is the liberty of the inhabitants. No possible advantages can compensate for the loss of this privilege. Show me the reason why the American Union is to be dissolved. Who are those eight adopting states? Are they averse to give us time to consider, before we conclude?

Would such a disposition render a junction with them eligible; or is it the genius of that kind of government to precipitate people hastily into measures of the utmost importance, and grant no indulgence?

If it be, sir, is it for us to accede to such a government? We have a right to have time to consider; we shall therefore insist upon it.

Unless the government be amended, we can never accept it.

The adopting states will doubtless accept our money and our regiments; and what is to be the consequence, if we are disunited? I believe it is yet doubtful, whether it is not proper to stand by a while, and see the effect of its adoption in other states.

In forming a government, the utmost care should be taken to prevent its becoming oppressive; and this government is of such an intricate and complicated nature, that no man on this earth can know its real operation.

The other states have no reason to think, from the antecedent conduct of Virginia, that she has any intention of seceding from the Union, or of being less active to support the general welfare. Would they not, therefore, acquiesce in our taking time to deliberate whether the measure be not perilously for us, and for the adopting states?

Permit me, sir, to say, that a great majority of the people, even in the adopting states, are averse to this government. I believe I would be right to say, that they have been egregiously misled. Pennsylvania has been tricked into it. If the other states who have adopted it have not been tricked, still they were too much hurried into its adoption. There were very respectable minorities in several of them; **and if reports be true, a clear majority of the people are averse to it.**

If we also accede, and it should prove grievous, the peace and prosperity of our country, which we all love, will be destroyed.

This government has not the affection of the people at present. Should it be oppressive, their affections will be totally estranged from it; and, sir, you know that a government, without their affections, can neither be durable nor happy.

I speak as one poor individual; but when I speak, I speak the language of thousands. But, sir, I mean not to breathe the spirit, nor utter the Language, of secession. I have trespassed so long on your patience, I am really concerned that I have something yet to say.

The honorable member has said, we shall be properly represented. Remember, sir, that the number of our representatives is but ten, whereof six is a majority. Will those men be possessed of sufficient information? A particular knowledge of particular districts will not suffice.

They must be well acquainted with agriculture, commerce, and a great variety of other matters throughout the continent; they must know not only the actual state of nations in Europe and America, the situations of their farmers, cottagers, and mechanics, but also the relative situations and intercourse of those nations. Our proportion of representatives is but ten men. **In England they have five hundred and fifty-eight.**

The House of Commons, in England, numerous as they are, we are told, are bribed, and have bartered away the rights of their constituents: what, then, shall become of us? Will these few protect our rights? Will they be incorruptible? You say they will be better men than the English commoners. I say they will be infinitely worse men, because they are to be chosen blindfolded: their election (the term, as applied to their appointment, is inaccurate) will be an involuntary nomination, and not a choice. I have, I fear, fatigued the committee; yet I have not said the one hundred thousandth part of what I have on my mind, and wish to impart.

On this occasion, I conceived myself bound to attend strictly to the interest of the state, and I thought her dearest rights at stake.

Having lived so long - been so much honored -my efforts, though small, are due to my country. I have found my mind hurried on, from subject to subject, on this very great occasion. We have been all out of order, from the beginning by some abler advocate than I!"

Edmund Randolph: If we go on at this great length it will take six months to decide this question.

Author's Comment: Patrick Henry's remarks were a common sentiment among Virginians, who were familiar with their State Constitution and Declaration of rights. To them, Patrick Henry was an American hero.

The words he uttered in St. John's church in Richmond, "Give me Liberty or Give me Death," set hearts ablaze with national pride and provided the strength to start a revolution in the name of freedom.

The convention would split into factions and men would be emotionally and vitriolic. The president often had to intervene. The opposing party was just beginning to organize. Many felt that a great blunder had been committed by allowing a voting state to be reached; that its formation exceeded the powers of those who formed it. By submitting it to the people for a vote, all objections were removed and the document had unfortunately become legitimized. William Grayson, Benjamin Harrison, John Tyler, Paul Carrington, James Monroe, St. George Tucker, John Blair, Henry Tazewell and Alexander White were stalwart friends of Patrick Henry who valued him and his dedication. The nation loved him and considered him the champion of the Revolution. People respected his decisions, and were effected by his ideologies and grand statements. Even the Federalists waited anxiously for his speech, wondering how much damage he would do.

June 6, 1788, Friday, Edmund Randolph, In a very long speech Randolph says he intends to vote for the Constitution because it best defends the liberties of America. He defends the right of Congress to tax directly in place of requisitions and defends every clause vehemently. He said that if the union is divided he fears it will always be so.

James Madison, In a long speech, Madison refutes every statement made by Henry and suggests that he is too fraught with fear of hidden or known dangers and tells him to stick to the facts. While Henry feels it is a positive sign that Virginia leaves the union, Madison disagrees. **(Even Jefferson in a letter from France suggested that nine states ratify and four decline and that would trigger amendments immediately)**. He says that the general government will not absorb the state governments and that the right number of representatives for Congress have been chosen.

George Nicholas, stands to refute Henry's statement's, mindful of avoiding the clause by clause routine that was desired.

DISCUSSION OF THE ARTICLES OF THE CONSTITUTION
June 7, 1788, Saturday, ARTICLE 1, SECTIONS 1 & 2 The Legislative & Legislative Power Vested, & The House
Francis Corbin, also refutes what Patrick Henry has said.
Patrick Henry, stands and asks Gov. Edmund Randolph to continue in his critique of Henry's remarks.

Edmund Randolph, addresses remarks made by Henry and Mason, speaking for a strong central government and direct taxation by Congress, and says the number of representatives is correct.

James Madison, adds little that is new, condemns the Articles of Confederation and supports taxation by the general government.

Patrick Henry, speaks until the session ends, saying where the dangers lie and refuting Randolph. He asks again like others before him for a Bill of Rights, the first, most important consideration.

June 9, Monday, ARTICLE 1, SECTION 1 & 2
Patrick Henry, uses words like lunatic and absurd for adopting prior to amending and accuses Randolph of inventing dangers.

Henry makes fun of Randolph for rushing out of the Philadelphia Convention, refusing to sign and now wanting to sign.

Henry asks for "checks" on the government before he approves and get over-heated on the subject of the government keeping secrets and ends by calling the plan a consolidated government (centralized).

June 9, 1788, Richard Henry Lee, criticizes Henry for not proceeding through the paper clause by clause, and attacking Henry's "dramatic Lightning bolts "that suggest over emoting and condemning Henry on figurative ideas rather than actual principles.

Governor Randolph, concludes the days session by accusing Henry of casting personal aspersions and insinuations of no merit. He declares that he has extracted Henry's concession to the Constitution and indicates that he has inflammatory information regarding Henry which would make people's hair stand on end. Randolph ridicules Henry's comments in reference to the history of certain other countries. Lastly he concludes that although the document be flawed, it's acceptance will prevent disunion and that is his priority.

June 10, 1788, Tuesday,
ARTICLE 1, SECTIONS 1 & 2
Governor Randolph, resumed with a long digression and ended where he started, that union is all that matters, adding that the document could be adjusted after ratification.

James Monroe, was anxious about the government and quoted Latin phrases in discussing histories of other societies, their success or failure. He admits to flaws in the Articles of Confederation but says that the new document (The Constitution) goes far to far over the top.

John Marshall, refutes Monroe and Henry's statements and claims that the Constitution's power is proper and guarded, a very long speech.

Benjamin Harrison, speaks of rejecting the Constitution as it does not protect the rights and liberties of its people.

June 10, 1788, George Nicholas, is heated and attacks Henry for his statements, accusing him of thinking only of his ideas and unwillingness to accept the ideas of others. The selfishness is over-played and could backfire on Nicholas for Henry is loved and believed to be the one true patriot.

June 11, 1788, Wednesday, ARTICLE 1, SECTION 1 & 2

William Grayson's speeches at the Ratifying Convention are given in full, others may be paraphrased or omitted.

William Grayson, Mr. Chairman, I make a few observations on this subject. If my arguments are desultory, I hope I stand justified by the bad example which has been set for me, and the necessity I am under of following my opponents through their various recesses.

I do not in the smallest degree blame the conduct of the gentlemen who represented this state in the general Convention,(in Philadelphia).

I believe that they endeavored to do all the good to this commonwealth which was in their power, and that all the members who formed that Convention did every thing within the compass of their abilities to procure the best terms for their particular states.

That they did not do more for the general good of America, is perhaps a misfortune. They are entitled however, to our thanks and those of the people.

Although I do not approve of the result of their deliberations, I do not criminate or suspect the principles on which they acted.

I desire that what I may say may not be improperly applied. I make no allusions to any gentleman whatever.

I do not pretend to say that the present Confederation is not defective. Its defects have been actually experienced. But I am afraid that they cannot be removed. It has defects arising from reasons which are inseparable from the nature of such government. If I am right, the states, with respect to their internal affairs, are left precisely as before, except in a few instances

Of course, the judiciary, should this government be adopted, would not be improved; the state government would be in this respect be nearly the same; and the Assembly may, without judge or jury, hang as many men as they may think proper to sacrifice to the good of the public. Our judiciary has been certainly improved in some respects since the revolution. The proceedings of our courts are not, at least, as rapid as they were under the royal government.

Here Grayson mentioned a particular cause, which had been thirty-one years on the docket.} The adoption of this government will not meliorate our own particular system.

I beg leave to consider the circumstances of the union antecedent to the meeting of the Convention at Philadelphia. We have been, told of phantoms and ideal dangers to lead us into measures which will, in my opinion, be the ruin of our country.

If the existence of those dangers cannot be proved, if there be no apprehension of wars, if there be no rumors of wars, it will place the subject

in a different light, and plainly evince to the world that there cannot be any reason for adopting measures which we apprehend be ruinous and destructive.

When this state proposed that the general government should be improved, Massachusetts was just recovered from a rebellion which had brought the republic to the brink of destruction….from a rebellion which was crushed by that federal government which is now so much contemned and abhorred: a vote of the august body for fifteen hundred men, aided by the exertions of the states, silenced all opposition, and shortly restored the public tranquility.

Massachusetts was satisfied that these internal commotion's were so happily settled, and was unwilling to risk any similar distresses by theoretic experiments. Were the Eastern States willing to enter into this measure? Were they willing to accede to the proposal of Virginia? In what manner was it received? Connecticut revolted at the idea. The Eastern States, were unwilling to recommend a meeting of a convention. They were well aware of the dangers of revolutions and changes. Why was every effort used, and such uncommon pains taken, to bring it about? This would have been unnecessary. Has it been approved of by the people?

Was Pennsylvania disposed to the reception of this project of reformation? No sir. She was even unwilling to amend her revenue laws, so as to make the five per centum operative. She was satisfied with things as they were. There was no complaint, that ever I heard of, from any other part of the union, except Virginia. This being the case among ourselves what dangers were there to be apprehended from foreign nations? It will be easily shown that dangers from that quarter were absolutely imaginary.

Was not France friendly? Unequivocally so. She has devised new regulations of commerce for our advantage. Did she harass us with applications for her money? Is it likely that France will quarrel with us? Is it not reasonable to suppose that she will be more desirous than ever to cling, after, losing the Dutch republic, to her best ally? How are the Dutch? We owe them money, it is true; and are they not willing that we should owe them more? Mr. Adams applied to them for a new loan to the poor despised Confederation. They readily granted it. The Dutch have a fellow-feeling for us. They were in the same situation with ourselves. I believe that the money which the Dutch borrowed of Henry IV is not yet repaid. How did they pass Queen Elizabeth's loan? At a very considerable discount. They took advantage of the weaknesses and necessities of James I, and made their own terms with that contemptible monarch. (The ungrateful ingrate, the son of Mary Queen of Scots). who never defended his mother but enjoyed every benefit from the blood line.

Loans from nations are not like loans from private men. Nations lend money, and grant assistance to one another from views of national interest.

France was willing to pluck the fairest feather out of the British Crown. This was her object in aiding us. She will not quarrel with us on pecuniary considerations. Congress considered it in this point of view; for when a proposition was made to make it a debt of private persons, it was rejected without hesitation. That respectable body wisely considered, that, while we remained their debtors in so considerable a degree, they would not be inattentive to our interest.

With respect to Spain, she is friendly in a high degree. I wish to know by whose interposition was the treaty with Morocco made. Was it not that of the king of Spain? Several predatory nations disturbed us, on going into the Mediterranean" the influence of Charles III, at the Barbary court, and four thousand pounds, procured as good a treaty with Morocco as could be expected.

But I acknowledge it is not of any consequence, since the Algerines and people of Tunis have not entered into similar measures. We have nothing to fear from Spain; and were she hostile, she could never be formidable to this country. Her strength is so scattered, that she cannot be dangerous to us in peace or war. As to Portugal, we have a treaty with her, which may be very advantageous, though it be not yet ratified.

The domestic debt is diminished by considerable sales of western lands to Cutler, Sergeant and Company; to Simms; and to Royal, Flint, and Company. The bd. of treasury is authorized to sell in Europe, or anywhere, the residue of those lands. An act of Congress has passed, to adjust the public debts between the individual states and the U.S.

Was our trade in a despicable situation? I shall say nothing of what did not come under my own observation.

When I was in Congress, sixteen vessels had sea letters in the East India trade, and two hundred vessels entered and cleared out, in the French West India Islands, in one year. I confess that public credit has suffered, and that our public creditors have been ill used. This was owing to a fault at the headquarters, to Congress in not apportioning the debts on the different states, and in not selling the western lands at an earlier period.

If requisitions have not been complied with, it must be owing to Congress, who might have put the unpopular debts on the back lands. Commutation is abhorrent to New England ideas. Speculation is abhorrent to the Eastern States. Those inconveniences have resulted from the bad policy of Congress. There are certain modes of governing the people which will succeed. There are others which will not.

The idea of consolidation is abhorrent to the people of this country. How were the sentiments of the people before the meeting of the Convention at Philadelphia? They had only one object in view.

Their ideas reached no father than to give the general government the five per centum impost, and the regulation of trade. When it was agitated in Congress, in a committee of the whole, this was all that was asked, or was deemed necessary. Since that period, their views extended farther.

Horrors have been greatly magnified since the rising of the Convention. We are now told by the honorable gentleman (Governor Randolph) that we shall have wars and rumors of wars, that every calamity is to attend us, and that we shall be ruined and disunited forever, unless we adopt this Constitution. Pennsylvania and Maryland are to fall upon us from the north, like Goths and Vandals of old; the Algerines, whose flat-sided vessels never came farther than Madeira, are to fill the Chesapeake with mighty fleets, and to attack us on our front; the Indians are to invade us with numerous armies on our rear, in order to convert our cleared lands into hunting-grounds; and the Carolinians, from the south, (mounted on alligators, I presume,) are to come and destroy our corn-fields, and eat up our little children!

These sir, are the mighty dangers which await us if we reject – dangers which are merely imaginary, and ludicrous in the extreme!

Are we to be destroyed by Maryland and Pennsylvania? What 11 democratic states make war for, and how long since have they imbibed a hostile spirit? But the generality are to attack us. Will they attack us after violating their faith in the first Union? Will they violate their faith if they do not take us into their confederacy? Have they not agreed, by the old Confederation, that the Union shall be perpetual, and that no alteration should take place without the consent of Congress, and the confirmation of the legislatures of every state?

I cannot think that there is such depravity in mankind as that, after violating public faith so flagrantly, they should make war upon us, also, for not following their example. The large states have divided the back lands among themselves, and have given as much as they thought proper to the generality. For the fear of disunion, we are told that we ought to take measures which we otherwise should not. Disunion is impossible.

The Eastern states hold the fisheries, which are their cornfields, by a hair.

They have a dispute with the British government about their limits at this moment. Is not a general and strong government necessary for their interest? If ever nations had inducements to peace, the Eastern States now have. New York and Pennsylvania anxiously look forward to the fur trade. How can they obtain it but by union?

Can the western posts be got or retained without union? How are the little states inclined? They are not likely to disunite. Their weakness will prevent them from quarrelling. Little men are seldom fond of quarrelling among giants. Is there not a strong inducement to union, while the British are on one side and the Spaniards on the other?

Thank Heaven, we have a Carthage of our own. But we are told that, if we do not embrace the present moment, we are lost forever.

Is there no difference between productive states and carrying states? If we hold out, will not the tobacco trade enable us to make terms with the carrying states? Is there nothing in a similarity of laws, religion, language and manners? Do these and the intercourse and intermarriage between people of the different states, invite them in the strongest manner to union? What would I do in the present occasion to remedy the existing defects of the present Confederation?

There are two opinions prevailing in the world, one, that mankind can only be governed by force; the other, that they are capable of freedom and a good government.

Under a supposition that mankind can govern themselves, I would recommend that the present Confederation should be amended.

Give Congress the regulation of commerce, Infuse new strength and spirit into the state governments; for when the component parts are strong, it will give energy into the state governments; although it be otherwise weak. This is proved by the union of Utrecht. **Apportion the public debts in such a manner as to throw the unpopular ones on the back lands. We are yet too young to know what we are fit for.**

Call only for requisitions for the foreign interest, and aid them by loans. The continual migration of people from Europe, and the settlement of new countries on our western frontiers are strong arguments against making new experiments in government. When these things are removed, we can, with greater prospect of success, devise changes. We ought to consider, as Montesquieu says, **whether the construction of the government be** suitable to the genius and disposition of the people, as well as a variety of other circumstances.

But if this position be not true, and men can only be governed by force, then be as gentle as possible. What, then, would I do? I would not take the British monarchy for my model. We have not materials for such a government in this country, although:

I will be bold to say, that this is one of the governments in the world where liberty and property are best secured.

But I would adopt the following government.

I would have a President for life, choosing his successor at the same time; a Senate for life, with the powers of the House of Lords; and a triennial House of Representative, with the powers of the House of Commons in England. By having such a President, we should have more independence and energy in the executive, and not be encumbered with the expense, & c. of a court and an hereditary prince and family.

By such a Senate, we should have more stability in the laws, without having an odious hereditary aristocracy. By the other branch, we should be fully and fairly represented. If sir, we are to be consolidated at all, we ought to be fully represented, and governed with sufficient energy, according to numbers in both houses.

I admit that coercion is necessary in every government in some degree; that it is manifestly wanting in our present government, and that the want of it has ruined many nations. But I should be glad to know what great degree of coercion is in this Constitution, more than in the old government, if the states still refuse to comply with requisition, and they can only be compelled by means of an army.

Suppose the people will not pay the taxes; is not the sword to be then employed? The difference is this – that, by this Constitution, the sword is employed against individuals; by the other, it is employed against the states, which is more honorable. Suppose a general resistance to pay taxes in such a state as Massachusetts; will it not be precisely the same thing as a non-compliance with requisitions?

Will this Constitution remedy the fatal inconveniences of the clashing state interests? Will not every member that goes from Virginia be actuated by state influence? So they will, also from every monarchy, with the three estates. Is it like the model of Tacitus or Montesquieu? Are there checks in it, as in the British monarchy?

There is an executive fetter in some parts, and as unlimited in another as a Roman dictator. A democratic branch marked with the strong features of aristocracy, and an aristocratic branch with all the impurities and imperfections of the British House of Commons, arising from the inequality of representation and want of responsibility.

There will be plenty of Old Sarums, (ancient Britain) if the new Constitution should be adopted. Do we love the British so well as to imitate their imperfections? We could not effect it more than in that particular instance. Are not all defects and corruption founded on inequality of representation and want of responsibility? How is the executive fashioned?

We have asked for bread, and they have given us a stone. I am willing to give the government the regulation of trade, It will be serviceable in regulating the trade among the states. But I believe that it will not be attended with the advantages generally expected.

As to direct taxation give up this, and you give up every thing, as it is the highest act of sovereignty: surrender up this inestimable jewel, and you throw away a pearl richer than all your tribe.

But it has been said by an honorable gentleman, (Mr. Pendleton,) as well as I recollect, that there could be no such thing as an interference between the two legislatures, either in point of direct taxation, or in any other case whatsoever. An honorable gentleman (Mr. Mason,) has replied that they might interfere in the case of a poll tax. I will go farther and say, that the case may happen in the judiciary.

Suppose a state execution and a federal execution issued against the same man, and the state officer and federal officer seize him at the same moment; would they divide the man in two, as Solomon directed the child to be divided who was claimed by two women? I suppose the general government, as being paramount, would prevail.

How are two legislatures to coincide, with powers transcendent, supreme, and omnipotent? For such is the definition of a legislature. There must be an external interference, not only in the collection of taxes, but in the judiciary. Was there ever such a thing in any country before? Great Britain never went so of the Irish never went so far. **I never heard of two supreme coordinate powers in one and the same country before.** I cannot conceive how it can happen. It surpasses every thing that I have read concerning other governments, or that I can conceive by the utmost of my faculties. But, sir, as a surety for every thing, the democratic branch is elected by the people. What security is there in what has already been demanded? Their number is too small. Is not a small number more easy to be corrupted than a large one?

Were not the tribunes at Rome the choice of the people? Were not the decemviri chosen by them? Was not Caesar himself the choice of the people? Did this secure them from oppression and slavery? Did this render those agents chosen by the people upright?

If five hundred and sixty members are corrupted from the same cause that our representatives will be: I mean, from Old Sarums among them , from the inequality of the representation.

How many are legislating in this country yearly? It is thought necessary to have fifteen hundred representatives, for the great purposes of legislation, throughout the union, exclusive of one hundred and sixty senators, which form a proportion of about one for every fifteen hundred persons. By the present constitution, these extensive pow-ers are to be exercised by the small number of ninety–one persons a proportion almost twenty times less than the other. **It must be degrading indeed to think that so small a number should be equal to so many!**

Such a preferential distinction must presuppose the happiest selection. They must have something divine in their composition, to merit such a preeminence.

But my greatest objection is, that it will, in its operation, be found unequal, grievous and oppressive. If it have any efficacy at all, it must be by a faction, a faction of one part of the Union against the other.

I think that it has a great natural imbecility within itself, too weak for a consolidated and too strong for a confederate government. But if it be called into action by a combination of seven states, it will be terrible indeed.

We need be at no loss to determine how this combination will be formed. There is a great difference of circumstances between the states. The interest of the carrying states is strikingly different from that of the productive states. I mean not to give offence to any part of America, but mankind are governed by interest.

The carrying states will assuredly unite, and our situation will the be wretched indeed. Our commodities will be transported on their own terms, and every measure will have for its object their particular interest:

Let ill fated Ireland be ever present to our view. We ought to be wise enough to guard against the abuse of such a government. Republics, in fact, oppress more than monarchies. If we advert to the page of history, we shall find this disposition too often manifested in republican governments.

The Romans, in ancient, and the Dutch, in modern times, oppressed their provinces in a remarkable degree.

I hope my fears are groundless; but I believe it as I do my creed, that this government will operate as a faction of seven states to oppress the rest of the union. But it may be said that we are represented, and cannot therefore be injured. A poor representation it will be! The British would have been glad to take America into the union, like the Scotch, by giving us a small representation. The Irish might be indulged with the same favor by asking for it. Will that lessen our misfortunes? A small representation gives a pretense to injure and destroy. But sir, the Scotch union is introduced by an honorable gentleman as an argument in favor of adoption. Would he wish his country to be on the same foundation as Scotland? They have but forty-five members in the House of Commons, and sixteen in the House of Lords. These go up regularly in order to be bribed. The smallness of their number puts it out of their power to carry any measure.

And this unhappy nation exhibits the only instance, perhaps, in the world, where corruption becomes a virtue. I devoutly pray that this description of Scotland may not be picturesque of the southern States, in three years! The committee being tired, as well as myself, I will take another time to give my opinion more fully on this great and important subject. Mr. Monroe, seconded by Mr. Henry, moved that the committee should rise, that Mr. Grayson might have an opportunity of continuing his argument next day. Mr. Madison insisted on doing business regularly, according to the resolution of the house.

June 12, 1788: William Grayson Continues

Mr. Chairman, I asserted yesterday that there were two opinions in the world – the one that mankind were capable of governing themselves, the other that it require actual force to govern them. On the principle that the first position was true, and which is consonant to the rights of humanity, **the house will recollect that it was my opinion to amend the present Confederation, and infuse a new portion of health and strength into the state governments; to apportion the public debts in such a manner as to throw the unpopular ones on the back lands; to divide the rest of the domestic debt among the different states; and to call for requisitions only for the interest of the foreign debt.** If, contrary to this maxim, force is necessary to govern men, I then did propose, as an alternative, not a monarchy like that of Great Britain, but a milder government as gentle as possible.

I showed, in as strong a manner as I could, some of the principal defects in the Constitution. The greatest defect is the opposition of the component parts to the interests of the whole; for, let gentlemen ascribe its defects to as many causes as their imagination may suggest, this is the principal and radical one.

I urged that, to remedy the evils which must result from this government, a more equal representation in the legislature, and proper checks against abuse, were indispensably necessary.

I do not pretend to propose for your adoption the plan of government which I mentioned as an alternative to a monarchy, in case mankind were incapable of governing themselves. I only meant, if it were once established that force was necessary to govern men, that such a plan would be more eligible to free people than the introduction of crowned heads and nobles.

Having premised this much, to obviate misconstruction, I shall proceed to the clause before us with this observation – that I prefer a complete consolidation to a partial one, but a federal government to either.

In my opinion, the states which give up the power of taxation have nothing more to give. The people of that state which suffer any power but her own immediate government to interfere with the sovereign right of taxation are gone forever. Giving the right of taxation is giving a right to increase the miseries of the people.

Is it not a political absurdity to suppose that there can be two concurrent legislatures, each possessing the supreme power of direct taxation? If two powers come in contact, must not one prevail ? Must it not strike every man's mind, that two unlimited, coequal, coordinate authorities, over the same objects, cannot exist together? But we are told that there is one instance of coexisting powers, in cases of propriety or possibility of two coequal, transcendent powers over the same object. Although these have the power of taxation, it only extends to certain degrees and for certain purposes. The powers of corporations are defined, and operate on limited objects. Their power originates by the authority of the legislature, and can be destroyed by that authority.

Persons carrying on the powers of a petty corporation may be punished for interfering with the power of the legislature. Their acts are entirely nugatory, if they contravene those of the legislature.

Scotland is also introduced to show that two different bodies may, with convenience, exercise power of taxation in the same country. How is the land tax there? There is a fixed apportionment. When England pays four shillings in the pound, Scotland only pays forty-five thousand pounds. This proportion cannot be departed from whatever augmentation may take place. There are stannary courts, and a variety of other inferior private courts in England. But when they pass the bounds of their jurisdiction, the supreme courts in Westminster Hall may on appeal, correct the abuse of their power. Is there any authority to terminate disputes between two contending powers? An observation came from an honorable gentleman, (Mr. Mason,) when speaking of the propriety of the general government's exercising this power, that, according to the rules and doctrine of representation, the thing was entirely impracticable. I agreed with him in sentiment. I waited to hear the answer from the admirers of the new Constitution. What was the answer? Gentlemen were obliged to give up the point with respect to general, uniform taxes.

They have the candor to acknowledge that taxes on slaves would not affect the Eastern States, and that taxes on fish or potash would not affect the Southern States. They are then reduced to a thin dilemma.

In order to support this part of the system, they are obliged to controvert the first maxims of representation. The best writers on this subject lay it down as a fundamental principle, that he who lays a tax should bear his proportion of paying it. A tax that might with propriety be laid, and with ease collected, in Delaware, might be highly improper in Virginia.

The taxes cannot be uniform throughout the states without being oppressive to some. If they are not uniform, some of the members will lay taxes, in the payment of which they will bear no proportion.

The members of Delaware do not return to Virginia, to give an account of their conduct. This total want of responsibility and fellow-feeling will destroy the benefits of representation. In order to obviate this objection, the gentleman has said that the same evil exists, in some degree, in the present Confederation: to which I answer, that the present Confederation had nothing to do but to say how much money is necessary, and to fix the proportion to be paid by each state. They cannot say in what manner the money shall be raised. This is left to the state legislatures. But, says the honorable gentleman, (Mr. Madison,) if we were in danger, we should be convinced of the necessity of the clause.

Are we to be terrified into a belief of its necessity? It is proposed by the opposition to amend it in the following manner – **that requisitions shall be first made, and if not paid, that direct taxes shall be laid by way of punishment.** If this ultimate right be in Congress, will it not be in their power to raise money on any emergency? Will not their credit be competent to procure any sum they may want?

Gentlemen agree that it would be proper to imitate the conduct of other countries, and great Britain particularly, in borrowing money, and establishing funds for the payment of the interest on the loans; that, when the government is properly organized, and its competency to raise money made known, public and private confidence will be the result, and men will readily lend it any sums it may need.

If this should be a fact, and the reasoning well founded, it will clearly follow that it will be practicable to borrow money in cases of great difficulty and danger, on the principles contended for by the opposition; and this observation must supersede the necessity of granting them the powers of direct taxation in the first instance, provided the right is secured in the second.

As to the idea of making extensive loans for extinguishing the present domestic debt, it is what I have not by any means in contemplation. I think it would be unnecessary, unjust and impolitic.

This country is differently situated and circumstanced from all other countries in the world. It is now thinly inhabited, but daily increasing in numbers. It would not be politic to lay grievous taxes and burdens at present. If our numbers double in twenty-five years, as is generally believed, we ought to spare the present race, because there will be double the number of persons to pay in that period of time; so that, were our matters so arranged, that the interest could bepaid regularly, and that any one might get his money when he thought proper, as is the case now in England. It would be all the public faith would require. Place the subject, however, in every point of view -whether as it related to raising money for the immediate exigencies of the state, or for the extinction of the foreign or the domestic debt – still it must be obvious, that a proper confidence is placed in the acknowledgment of the right of taxation in the second instance, that every purpose can be answered. However, sir, if the states are not blameless, why has not Congress used that coercion which is vested in their government? It is an unquestionable fact that the Belgic republic, on a similar occasion, by an exertion of force, delivered a proper justice to a delinquent province.

The gentleman said that, in case of a partial compliance with requisitions, the alternative proposed will operate unequally, by taxing those who may have already paid, as well as those who have not, and involving the innocent in the crimes of the guilty. Suppose the new government fully vested with authority to raise taxes; will also operate unequally.

To make up antecedent deficiencies, they will lay more taxes the succeeding year. By this means, those persons from whom a full proportion shall have been extracted will be saddled with a share of the deficiencies, as well as those who shall not have discharged their full portion. This mode, then, will have precisely the same unequal and unjust operation as the other. I said yesterday, that there were one thousand five hundred representatives, and one hundred and sixty senators, who transacted the affairs of the different states. But we are told that this great number is unnecessary, and that in the multitude of counselors there is folly instead of wisdom. They are dead weight on the public business, does that observation extend to Congress?

May not five men do the public business of the Union? But there is a great difference between the objects of legislation in Congress and those of the state legislatures. If the former be more complicated, there is a greater necessity of a full and adequate representation. It must be confessed that it is highly improper to trust our liberty and property in the hands of so few persons, if they were any thing less than divine. But it seems that, in this contest of power, the state government have the advantage. I am of opinion that it will be directly the reverse. What influence can the state governments be supposed to have, after the loss of their power and influence be an augmentation of those of the general government? Will not the officers of the general government receive higher compensation for their services than those of the state governments? Will not the most influential men be employed by Congress? I think the state governments, will be condemned and despised as soon as they give up the power of direct taxation; **and a state, says Montesquieu, should lose her existence sooner than her importance.**

But, sir, we are told that, if we do not give up this power to Congress, the impost will be stretched to the utmost extent. I do suppose this might follow, if the thing did not correct itself. But we know that it is the nature of this kind of taxation, that a small duty will bring more real money than a large one.

The experience of the English nation proves the truth of this assertion. There has been much said of the necessity of the five per cent, impost. I have been ever of opinion, that two and a half percent, would produce more real money into the treasury. But we need not be alarmed on this account, because, when smugglers will be induced, by heavy imposts, to elude the laws, the general government will find it their interest again to reduce them within reasonable and moderate limits.

But it is suggested that, if, direct taxation be inflicted by way of punishment, it will create great disturbances in the country. This is an assertion without argument. If a man is a reasonable being, he will submit to punishment, and acquiesce in the justice of its infliction, when he deserves it. The states will comply with the requisitions of Congress more readily when they know that this power may be ultimately used; and if they do not comply, they will have no reasons to complain of its exercise.

We are then told of the armed neutrality of the empress of Russia, the opposition to it by Great Britain, and the acquiescence of other powers. We are told that, in order to become the carriers of contending nations, it will be necessary to be formidable at sea – that we must have a fleet in case of a war between Great Britain and France. I think that the powers who formed that threat will be able to support it. But if we were certain that this would not be the case, still I think that the profits that might arise from such a transient commerce could not compensate for the expenses of rendering ourselves formidable at sea, or the dangers that would probably result from the attempt to have a fleet, in the present limited population of America, is, in my opinion, impracticable and inexpedient. Is America in a situation to have a fleet? I take it to be a rule founded on common sense, that manufacturers, as well as sailors, proceed from a redundancy of inhabitants.

Our numbers, compared to our territory, are very small indeed. I think, therefore, that all attempts to have a fleet, till our western lands are fully settled, are nugatory and vain. How will you induce your people to go to sea?

Is it not more agreeable to follow agriculture than to encounter the dangers and hardships of the ocean? The same reasoning will apply in a greater degree to manufacturers. Both are the result of necessity. It would, besides, be dangerous to have a fleet in our present weak, dispersed, and defenseless situation. The powers of Europe, who have West India possessions, would be alarmed at any extraordinary maritime exertions, and, knowing the danger of our arrival at manhood, would crush us in our infancy.

In my opinion, the great objects most necessary to be promoted and handed to, in America, are agriculture and population.

First take care that you are sufficiently strong, by land, to guard against European partition; secure your own house before you attack that of other people. I think that the sailors who would be prevailed on to go to sea would be a real loss to the community; neglect of agriculture and loss of labor would be the certain consequence of such irregular policy. I hope that, when these objections are thoroughly considered, all ideas of having a fleet, in our infant situation, will be given over.

When the American character is better known, and the government established on permanent principles when we shall be sufficiently populous, and our situation secure then come forward with a fleet; not with a small one, but with one sufficient to meet any of the maritime powers.

The honorable gentleman (Mr. Madison) said that the imposts will be less productive hereafter, on account of the increase of population. I shall not controvent manufactures sufficient, this may be the case.

In islands and thickly settled countries, where they have manufactures, the principle will hold good, but will not apply in any degree to our country. I apprehend that, among us, as the people in the lower country find themselves straitened, they will move to the frontiers, which, for a considerable period, will prevent the lower country from being very populous, or having recourse to manufactures. I cannot, therefore, but conclude that the amount of the imposts will continue to increase, at least for a great number of years. Holland, we are informed, is not happy, because she has not a Constitution like this. This is but an unsupported assertion. Do we not know the cause of her misfortunes? The evil is coeval with her existence-there are always opposite parties in that republic. There are now two parties—the aristocratic party, supporting the Prince of Orange, and the Lovestein party, supporting the rights of the people. France foments the one, and Great Britain the other, as we know, if Holland had begun with such a government as this, that the violence faction would not produce the same evils which they experience at this moment?

It is said that all our evils result from requisitions on the states. I did not expect to hear of complaints for noncompliance during the war. Do not gentlemen recollect our situation during the war? Our ports were blocked, and all means of getting money, destroyed, and almost every article taken from the farmer for the public service-as, in many instances, not to leave him enough to support his own family with tolerable decency and it cannot be forgot that another resort of government was applied to, and that press-warrants were made to answer for noncompliance of requisitions. **Every person must recollect our miserable situation during the arduous contest' therefore, I shall make no further apology for the states, during war.**

Since the peace, there have been various causes for not furnishing the necessary quotas to the general government. In some of the flourishing states, the requisitions have been attended to; in others, their non-compliance is to be attributed more to the inability of the people than to their unwillingness to advance the general interests.

Massachusetts attempted to correct the nature of things by extracting more from the people than they were able to part with. What did it produce? A revolution which shook that state to its centre. (the Shay revolt).

Paper money has been introduced. What did we do a few years ago? Struck off many millions, and by the charms of magic made the value of the emissions diminish by forty-fold ration. However unjust or unreasonable this might be, I suppose it was warranted by the inevitable laws of necessity. But, sir, there is no disposition now of having paper money; this engine of iniquity I universally reprobated. But conventions give power, and conventions can take it away. This observation does not appear to me well founded. It is not so easy to dissolve a government like this. Its dissolution may be prevented by a trifling minority of the American people.

The consent of so many states is necessary to introduce amendments, that I fear they will with great difficulty be obtained.

It is said that a strong government will increase our population by the addition of immigrants. From what quarter is immigration to proceed? From the arbitrary monarchies of Europe?

I fear this kind of population would not add much to our happiness or improvement. It is supposed that, from the prevalence of the Orange faction, numbers will come hither from Holland, although it is not imagined the strength of the government will form the inducement.

The exclusive power of legislation over the ten miles square is introduced by many gentlemen. I would not deny the utility of vesting the general government. with a power of this kind, were it properly guarded.

Perhaps I am mistaken, but it occurs to me that Congress may give exclusive privileges to merchants residing within the ten miles square, and that the same exclusive power of legislation will enable them to grant similar privileges to merchants in similar strongholds within the states.

I wish to know if there be any thing in the Constitution to prevent it. If there be, I have not been able to discover it. I may, perhaps, not thoroughly comprehend this part of the Constitution; but it strikes my mind that there is a possibility that, in process of time, and from the simple operation of effects from causes, the whole commerce of the United States may be exclusively carried on by merchants residing within the seat of government, and those places of arms which may be purchased of the state legislatures. How detrimental and injurious to the community, and how repugnant to the equal rights of mankind, such exclusive emoluments are. I submit to the consideration of the committee.

Things of a similar nature have happened in other countries; or else from whence have issued the Hanse Towns, Cinque Ports, and other places in Europe, which have peculiar privileges in commerce as well as in other matters? I do not offer this sentiment as an opinion, but a conjecture, and in the doubtful agitation of mind on a point of such infinite magnitude, only ask for information from the framers of the Constitution, whose superior opportunities must have furnished them with more ample lights on the subject than I am possessed of. Something is said on the other side with respect to the Mississippi. An honorable gentleman has mentioned that he was satisfied that no member of Congress had any idea of giving up that river. Sir, I am not at liberty, from my situation, to enter into any investigation on the subject. I am free however, to acknowledge that I have frequently heard the honorable member declare, that he conceived the object then in contemplation was the only method by which the right of that river could be ultimately secured. I have heard similar declarations from other members.

Author's Comment: William Grayson knew that Rufus King, of Mass., along with Geary, wanted to relinguish the Mississippi to Spain for twenty-five years. This kind of thinking would create a natural antipathy between Grayson and King and make it difficult for them to work together on this and subsequent matters. Surprisingly Grayson and King complimented each other on other issues and made an interesting pair.

June 12, 1788, Grayson continues: I must beg leave to observe, at the same time, that I most decidedly differed with them in sentiment.

With respect to the citizens of the Eastern and some of the Middle States, perhaps the best and surest means of discovering their general dispositions may be by having recourse to their interests.

This seems to be the pole-star to which the policy of nations is directed. If this supposition should be well founded, I think they must have reasons of considerable magnitude for wishing the exclusion of that river. If the Mississippi was yielded to Spain, the migration to the western country would be stopped, and the Northern States would not only retain their inhabitants, but preserve their superiority and influence over those of the

South. If matters go on in their present direction, there will be a number of new states to the westward–population may become greater in the southern States–the ten miles square may approach us! This they must naturally wish to prevent. I think gentlemen may know the disposition of the different states, from the geography of the country, and, from the reason and nature of thugs. Is it not highly imprudent to vest a power in the generality, which will enable those states to relinquish that river? There are but feeble restrictions at present to prevent it.

By the old Confederation, nine states are necessary to form any treaty. By this Constitution, the President, with two thirds of the members present in the Senate, can make any treaty Ten members are two thirds of a quorum. Ten members are the representative of five states. The northern States may then easily make a treaty relinquishing this river.

In my opinion, the power of making treaties, by which the territory guarded against every possibility of abuse; and the precarious situation to which those rights will be exposed is one reason, with me, among many others, for voting against its adoption."

Author's Comment: Having heard exhaustive testimony by Patrick Henry, Edmund Randolph, James Madison, Corbin, Richard Henry Lee, James Monroe and others, William Grayson rose to speak in a moment when personal animosity permeated the chamber and though surface politeness prevailed, the underlying current was charged with emotion and blatant intolerance.

Friday, June 12

**Edmund Pendleton spoke, followed by Patrick Henry. James Madison.
Friday, June 12, 1788,
ARTICLE 1 SECTIONS 1 & 2**

Mr. Nicholas: Urged that the Convention should either proceed according to the original determination, clause by clause, or to rescind that order, and go into the Constitution at large.

Patrick Henry: Opposed the motion of taking the subject clause by clause and wanted it considered at large. He observed that the subject of the Mississippi had taken a great eal of time. He wished that before they took leave of the subject that the transactions of Congress relative to the navigation of that river should be communicated to the Convention, in order that they might draw their conclusions from the best source. For this purpose, he hoped that those gentlemen who were in Congress then as well as the present members of Congress who were in Convention, would communicate what they knew on the subject. He declared that he did not wish to hurt the feelings of the gentlemen who had been in Congress, or to reflect on any private character; but that, for the information of the Convention, he was desirous of having the most authentic and faithful facts.

George Nicholas: Had no objection to Mr. Henry's proposal.

James Madison: Declared that, if the honorable gentleman thought that he had given an incorrect account of the transactions relative to the Mississippi, he would on a thorough and complete investigation, find himself mistaken; that he had his information from his own knowledge; and from a perusal of the documents and papers which related to those transactions; that it had always been his opinion that the policy which had for its object the relinquishment of that river was unwise, and the mode of conducting it was, still more exceptionable. He added, that he had no objection to light on the subject that could tend to elucidate it.

George Nicholas: hoped that, after the information should be given respecting that river, they would confine themselves to the order of the house and proceed to discuss the articles of the Constitution.

Richard Henry Lee (of Westmoreland) gave a speech, relating congressional transactions respecting that river, and strongly asserted that it was the inflexible and determined resolution of Congress never to give it up. He was followed by Henry, Monroe, and Madison.

ARTICLE 1, SECTION 1 & 2,
William Grayson: June 13, Friday, 1788:
Mr. Chairman, the honorable gentleman was mistaken when he supposed that I said seven states had absolutely voted to surrender the navigation of the Mississippi. I spoke of the general disposition of the states, which I alleged to be actuated by interest; that consequently the Carrying states were necessarily inclined against the extension of the interest and influence of the productive states; and that, therefore, they would not favor any measure to extend the settlements to the westward.

to extend the settlements to the westward.

I wished not to enter into this discussion, for the reasons mentioned by my honorable friend, (His cousin, James Monroe) Secrecy was required on this subject. I told Congress that imposing secrecy, on such a great occasion, was unwarrantable. However, as it was not given up, I conceived myself under some restraint. But since it has come before the committee, and they desire to develop the subject. I shall stand excused for mentioning what I know.

My honorable friend gave a very just account of it, when he said that the Southern States were on their guard and opposed every measure tending to relinquish or waive that valuable right. They would not agree to negotiate, but on condition that no proposition whatever should be made to surrender that great right.

There was a dispute between this country and Spain, who claimed one half of Georgia, and one half of Kentucky, or, if not that proportion, a very considerable part, as well as the absolute and exclusive navigation of the Mississippi.

The southern States thought that the navigation of the Mississippi should not be trusted to any hands but those in which the Confederation had placed the right of making treaties. That system required the consent of nine states for that purpose.

The secretary for foreign affairs was empowered to adjust the interfering claims of Spain and the United States with the Spanish minister; but as my honorable friend said, with an express prohibition of entering into any negotiation that would lead to the surrender of that river. Affairs continued in this state for some time. At length a proposition was made to Congress, not directly, but by a side wind. The first proposal was, to take off the fetters of the secretary.

When the whole came out, it was found to be a proposal to cede the Mississippi to Spain for twenty- five or thirty years, (for it was in the disjunctive), in consideration of certain commercial stipulations.

In support of this proposal, it was urged that the right was in him who surrendered; and that their acceptance of a temporary relinquishment was an acknowledge of our right (which would revert to us at the expiration), **that we could not take by war; that the thing was useless to us, and that it would be wise and politic to give it up,** as we were to receive a beneficial compensation for that temporary cession.

Congress, after a great deal of animosity, came to a resolution which, in my opinion, violated the Confederation. It was resolved, by seven states, that the prohibition in the secretary's instruction should be repealed; whereby the un-repealed part of his instructions authorized him to make a treaty, yielding that inestimable navigation, although, by the Confederation, nine states were necessary to concur in the formation of a treaty!

How, then, could seven states constitutionally adopt any measure, to which, by the Constitution, nine states alone were competent? It was entered on the journals and transmitted to the secretary of foreign affairs, for his direction in his negotiation with the Spanish minister. If I recollect rightly, by the law of nations, if a negotiator makes a treaty, in consequence of a power received from a sovereign authority, non-compliance with his stipulations is a just cause of war.

The opposition suggested (whether wrong or not let this house determine) that this was the case; that the proceedings were repugnant to the principles and express letter of the Constitution; and that, if the compact which the secretary might form with the Spanish minister should not be complied with, it would be giving Spain a just cause of quarrel; so that we should be reduced to the dilemma of either violating the Constitution by a compliance, or involving us in a war by a non-compliance. The opposition remonstrated against these transactions, (and their remonstrance was entered on the journal,) and took every step for securing this great national right. In the course of the debates in Congress on this subject, which were warm and animated, it was urged that Congress by the law of nations, had no right, even with the consent of nine states, to dismember the empire, or relinquish any part of the territory, appertaining to the aggregate society, to any foreign power. Territorial dismemberment, or the relinquishment of any other privilege, is the highest act of a sovereign power.

The right of territory has ever been considered as most sacred, and ought to be guarded in the most particular and cautious manner. Whether that navigation be secure on this principle, by the new constitution, I will not pretend to determine.

I will, however, say one thing. It is not guarded under the old system. A majority of seven states are disposed to yield it. I speak not of any particular characters. I have the charity to suppose that all mankind act on the best motives.

Suffice it for me to tell direct and plain facts, and leave the conclusion with this honorable house. It has been urged, by my honorable friend on the other side, (Mr. Madison) that the Eastern States were adverse to surrender it during the war, and that the Southern States proposed it themselves, and wished to yield it.

My honorable friend last up has well accounted for this disgraceful offer, and I will account for the refusal of the Eastern States to surrender it. Mr. Chairman, it is no new thing to you to discover these reasons. It is well known that the Newfoundland fisheries and the Mississippi are balances for one another; that the possession of one tends to the preservation of the other. This accounts for the eastern policy.

The Mississippi is not secured under the old Confederation; but it is better secured by that system than by the new Constitution. By the existing system, nine states are necessary to yield it. Nine states can give it away by the paper on your table. **I hope is will never be put in the power of a lesser number than nine states.**

Jersey is not giving up the right of the Mississippi, and Maryland is giving it up. Whatever be their object, each departed from her natural disposition. It is with great reluctance I have said any thing on the subject, and if I have misrepresented facts, I wish to be corrected. (After Monroe and Madison had their say), Grayson rose again. He was obviously ill with gout. He continued: Jersey, we are told, changed her temper on that great occasion. I believe that mutability depended on characters. But we have lost another state, Maryland. For, from fortuitous circumstances, those states deviated from their natural character, Jersey in not giving up the right of the Mississippi, and Maryland in giving it up. Whatever be their object, each departed from her natural disposition.

William Grayson: Mr. Chairman, the honorable gentleman last up, (James Madison,) concluded by leaving impressions that there were some circumstances which, were he at liberty to communicate, would induce this house to believe that the matter would never be revived. When I was in congress last, there was a resolution to apologize to his Catholic Majesty for not making the treaty, and intimating that, when the situation of things was altered, it might be done. Had it not been for one particular circumstance, it would have been concluded on the terms my honorable friend mentioned.

With respect to the Mississippi and back lands, the Eastern States are willing to relinquish that great and essential right; for they consider the

consequences of governing the Union as of more importance than those considerations which he mentioned should induce them to favor it.

But, says the honorable gentleman, there is a great difference between actually giving it up altogether, and a temporary cession. If the right was given up for twenty-five years, would this country be able to avail herself of her right, and resume it at the expiration of that period?

If ever the house of Bourbon should be at war with all Europe, that would be the golden opportunity of regaining it. Without this, we never could wrest it from the House of Bourbon, the branches of which always support each other. If things continue as they are now, emigrations will continue to that country. The hope that this great national right will be retained, will induce them to go thither.

But take away that hope, by giving up the Mississippi for twenty-five years, and emigrations will cease.

As interest actuated mankind, will they go thither when they know they cannot enjoy the privilege of navigating that river, or find a ready market for their produce?

There is a majority of states which look forward with anxiety to the benefits of the commercial project with Spain. In the course of the Spanish negotiation, our delegation thought of a project which would be accommodated to their particular interest. It was proposed, by way of compromise, as being suitable to the interest of all states, that the Spanish crown should make New Orleans a general depository. And the growth of the American states should be sent down for the use of the Spanish troops; Spain being obliged to foreign nations for provisions. This was throwing out a lure to the Eastern States to carry the produce of that whole country. But this temptation did not succeed. It was thought no object in their view, when greater objects presented themselves.

It was alleged that the emigration from the Eastern States will have the same effect as emigration from this country. I know every step will be taken to prevent emigration from thence, as it will be transferring their population to the Southern States. They will coincide in no measure that will tend to increase the weight or influence of the Southern States.

There is, therefore, a wide line of distinction between migrations from thence and from hence. But we are told, in order to make that paper acceptable to the Kentucky people, that this high act of authority cannot, by the law of nations, be warrantable, and that this great right cannot be given up. I think so also. But how will the doctrine apply to America? After it is actually given away, can it be reclaimed? If nine states give it away, what will the Kentucky people do? Will Grotius and Puffendorf relieve them? (Confiscation of enemy property after a declaration of war). If we reason what was done, if seven states attempted to do what nine states ought to have done, you may judge of the attention which will be paid to the law of nations.

Should congress make a treaty to yield Mississippi, they will find no redress in the law of nations. But, says he, Massachusetts is willing to protect emigration. When the act of Congress passed respecting the settlement of the western country, establishing a state there, it passed in a lucky moment.

I was told that state was extremely uneasy and in order to retain her inhabitants, lands in the province of Maine were lowered to the price of one dollar per acre.

As to the tract of country conveyed by New York to Massachusetts, neither of them had a right to it. Perhaps that great line of policy, of keeping the population on that side of the continent, in contra-distinction to the emigration to the westward of us, actuated Massachusetts in that transaction. There is no communication between that country and the Mississippi. The two great northern communications are by the North Rivers and by the River St. Lawrence, to the Mississippi. But there is no communication between that country, where the people of Massachusetts emigrate, and the Mississippi; nor do I believe that there ever will be one traveler from it thither. I have a great regard for the secretary of foreign affairs. In my opinion, all American is under great obligations to him. But I differed in opinion

But the Mississippi is said to be more secure under the new than the old government. It is infinitely more secure under the latter than the former. How is that fact? Seven states wished to pass an affirmative their own delicacy will lead them to be satisfied with moderate salaries. There is no restraint on corruption. They may be appointed to offices without any material restrictions and the principal source of curruption in representatives is the hope for offices and the usual rich emoluments.

James Madison speaks followed by George Nicholas, Edmund Randolph Francis Corbin: Mr. Chairman, All attempts made to bias the opinion of any gentleman on this great occasion, are, in my opinion, very reprehensible. There must be no restraint, no corruption. Men may be appointed to offices without any material restriction. The principal source of corruption in representatives is the hope for offices with the usual rich emoluments.

James Madison: Wishing to give a proper explanation suggested that the right of ascertaining their own pay, if practicable, should be fixed in the Constitution itself.

George Nicholas:
Thought it sufficiently guarded, as it prevented the members of the general government from holding offices which they created themselves, or in which they increased the emoluments; and as they could not enjoy any office during their continuance in Congress, to admit them to old offices when they left Congress, was giving them no exclusive privilege but such as every citizen had an equal right to.

John Tyler:
Was afraid that as their compensations were not fixed in the Constitution, Congress might fix them so low that none but rich men could go (to Congress); by which government might terminate in an aristocracy. The states might choose men noted for their wealth and influence and state influence could govern the senate. He thought Madison's account not satisfactory.

Saturday, June 14, 1788 , A letter from the honorable president to the Convention was read, stating his inability to attend to his duty in the house that day, whereupon the honorable John Tyler was unanimously elected vice-president, to preside during the inability of the president.

Francis Corbin: thought the Mississippi subject had been amply discussed. He hoped that the committee would enter into the discussion of the proposed Constitution regularly; but that if any gentleman would continue the inquiry relative to that river, he would answer him. He moved that they should debate clause by clause. violent storm arose causing the session to end abruptly.

ARTICLE 1, Section 3, The Senate (this section was read)

William Grayson: Mr. Chairman, I conceive the investigation of this subject, which materially concerns the welfare of this country, ought not to wound the feelings of any gentleman. I look upon this as a contest of empire. Our country is equally affected with Kentucky. The southern States are deeply interested in this subject.

If the Mississippi be shut up, emigrations will be stopped entirely. There will be no new states formed on the western waters. This will be a government of seven states.

This contest of the Mississippi involves this great national contest; that is whether one part of the continent shall govern the other.

Alexander White: Wished further discussion of that subject to be postponed till they came to that part which enables the Senate to make treaties. He seconded Mr. Corbin's motion, to proceed clause by clause.

John Tyler: Hoped that, when amendments should be brought forward, they should be at liberty to take a general view of the whole Constitution. He thought that the power of trying impeachments, added to that of making treaties, was some thing enormous, and rendered the Senate far too danger ous, and he desired changes in the Constitution.

ARTICLE 1, SECTION 6, (The 6th section of Art 1, was read) **Compensation and Privileges of Members**

James Madison answered, that it was not possible to have a system to which objections might not be made; that the junction of these powers might be in some degree objectionable, but that could not be mended. He agreed with the gentleman, that, when amendments were brought, a collective view of the whole system might be taken.

James Monroe: Wished that the honorable gentleman who had been in the federal Convention, would give information regarding the clause concerning elections. He wished to know why Congress had ultimate control over the time, place and manner of electing representatives, and the time and manner of that of senators, and also why there was an exception as to the place of electing senators.

June 14, 1788
James Maison: explained the reason being that if Congress could fix the place of choosing senators it might compel the state legislatures to elect them in a different place from their usual sessions which would produce some inconvenience not for the object of regulating the elections, but necessary to give the general government control over the time and manner of choosing senators to prevent its own dissolution.

Gov. Edmund Randolph, spoke next, followed by Henry.

Patrick Henry: Mr. Chairman, the pay of members is, by the Constitution, to be fixed by themselves, without limitation or restraint. They may therfore indulge themselves in the fullest extent. I suppose if they be good men...

The Northern States have the majority, and will endeavor to retain it. This is therefore. A contest for dominion-for empire. I apprehend that God and nature have intended, from the extent of territory and fertility of soil, that the weight of population should be on this side of the continent. At present, for various reason, it is on the other side. This dispute concerns every part of Kentucky. An investigation ought not offend any gentleman. Mr. Grayson declared the subject would be continued.

(The 4ᵗʰ and 5ᵗʰ sections of Article 1, were then read)
Section 4, Elections, Meetings
Section 5, Membership, Rules, Journals, Adjournment.

It was thought improper to leave it to the state legislatures, because it is improper that one government should be dependent on another, and the great inconveniences experienced under the old Confederation show the states would be operated upon by local considerations, as contra distinguished from general and national interests being influenced on them.

ARTICLE 1, SECTION 7, Revenue Bills, Legislative Process,
Presidential Veto:

William Grayson: June 14, 1788,
Mr. Chairman, it strikes me that they may fix wages very low. From what has happened in Great Britain, I am warranted to draw this conclusion. I think every member of the House of Commons formerly had a right to receive twenty shilling, or a guinea a day. I believe that this salary is taken away since the days of corruption. The members of the House of Comm., if I recollect rightly, get nothing for their services as such. But there are some noble emoluments to be derived from the minister, and some other advantages to be obtained.

Those who go to Parliament form an idea of emoluments. They expect something besides wages. They go in with the wishes and expectation of getting offices. This sir, may be the case with this government.

My fears are increased from the inconveniences experienced under the Confederation.

Most of the great offices have been taken out of Congress such as ambassadors to foreign courts, & c. A number of offices have been unnecessarily created and ambassadors have been sent to foreign countries with which we have nothing to do.

If the present Congress exceeded the limits of propriety though extremely limited with respect to power in the creation of offices, what may not the future Congress do, when they have, by this system, a full scope of creating what offices and annexing what salaries they please?

There are but few members in the Senate and lower house. They may all get offices at different times, as they are not excluded from being appointed to existing offices for the time for which they shall have been elected. Considering the corruption of human nature, and the general tendency of mankind to promote their own interest, I think there is great danger. I am confirmed in my opinion from what I have seen already in Congress, and among other nations.

I wish this part, therefore, to be amended, by prohibiting any senator or representative from being appointed to any office during the time for which he was elected, and by fixing their emoluments; I would not object to the Constitution on this account solely, were there no other defect.

James Madison: Mr. Chairman, let me ask those who oppose this part of the system, whether any alteration would not make it equally, or more liable to objections. Would it be better to fix their compensations? Will the value of coins always be the same? Congress will fix their wages so low that only the rich can fill the offices of senators and representatives. Who are to appoint them? The rich? No sir; the people are to choose them, They can choose those who have the most merit and least wealth.

If Congress reduce their wages to a trifle, what shall prevent the states from giving a man of merit an adequate compensation. The remedy is in our hands.

William Grayson: June 14, 1788,

Mr. Chairman, I acknowledge that the honorable gentleman has represented the clause rightly as to their exclusion from new offices; but is there any clause to hinder them from giving office to uncles, nephews, brothers, and other relations and friends? I imagine most of the offices will be created the first year, and then gentlemen will be tempted to carry on this accommodation. A worthy member has said what has been often said before that, suppose a war took place, and the most experienced and able man was unfortunately in either house, he could not be made general, if the proposed amendment was adopted. Had he read the clause, he would have discovered that it did not extend to military offices, and the restriction extends to civil officers only. No case can exist, with respect to civil offices, that would occasion a loss to the public, if the members of both houses were precluded from holding any office during the time for which they were elected.

The old confederation is so defective in point of power, that no danger can result from creating offices under it; because those who hold them cannot be paid, the power of making paper money will not be exercised. This country is so thoroughly sensible of the impropriety of it, that no attempt will be made to make any more.

So that no danger can arise, as they have not power to pay, if they appoint officers. Why not make this system as secure as that, in this respect? A great number of offices will be created, to satisfy the wants of those who shall be elected. The worthy members says, the electors can alter them. But have the people the power of making honest men be elected? If he be an honest man, and his wages so low that he could not pay his expenses, he could not serve them if elected. But there are many thirsting after office more than public good. Political adventurers go up to Congress solely to advance their own particular emoluments.

It is so in the British House of Commons. There are two sets always in that house- one the landed interest, the most patriotic and respectable; the other, a set of dependants and fortune-hunters, who are elected for their own interests, and are willing to sell the interest of their constituents to the crown. The same division may happen among our representative. This clause should not be guarded at all, as in this flimsy manner. They cannot be elected to offices for the terms for which they were elected, and continue to be members of Congress. But as they can create as many offices as they please for the particular accommodation of their friends, it might as well not be guarded. **Upon the whole, I consider it entirely imperfect.**

William Grayson, June 14, 1788, objected to the powers of the Senate to propose or concur with amendments to money bills.

He looked upon the power of proposing amendments to be equal, in principle, to that of originating, and that they were, in fact, the same. As this was his opinion, a departure from that great principle which required that the immediate representatives of the people only should interfere with

the immediate representatives of the people only should interfere with money bills, he wished to know the reasons on which it was founded.

The Lords in England had never been allowed to intermeddle with money bills. He knew not why the Senate should. In the lower house, said he, the people are represented according to their numbers. In the upper house, the states are represented in their political capacities. Delaware, or Rhode Island, has representation that is neither equal nor just? (to larger states.)

James Madison: Mr. Chairman, the criticism made by the honorable member is, that there is an ambiguity in the words, and that it is not clearly ascertained where the origination of money bills may take place. I suppose the first part of the clause is sufficiently expressed to exclude all doubts. The gentlemen who composed the Convention divided opinion concerning the utility of confining this to any particular branch. Whatever it be in Great Britain, there is a sufficient difference between us and them to render it inapplicable to this country. It has always appeared to me to be a matter of no great consequence, whether the Senate had a right of originating or proposing amendments to money bills.

William Grayson: Still, considered the power of proposing amendments to be the same, in effect, as that of originating. The Senate could strike out every word of the bill, except the word whereas, or any other introductory word, and might substitute their words. As the state of Delaware was not so large as the county of Augusta, and Rhode Island was still less, and yet had an equal suffrage in the Senate, he could not see the propriety of giving them this power, but referred it to the judgment of the house.

The 8th section of Art 1, is read) Scope of Congressional Power

Charles Clay: wondered why the Congress were to have power to provide for calling forth the militia to put the laws of the Union into execution.

James Madison, June 14, 1788 Supposed this power to be so obvious that they would occur to most gentlemen. If resistance be made to the execution of the laws, it ought to be overcome in two ways- by force or by the people, but it must be done. If insurrections arise, or invasions take place, the people ought to suppress and repel them, rather than a standing army. The best way to do these things was to put the militia on a sure footing, and enable the government to make use of their services when necessary.

George Mason: Mr. Chairman, unless there be some restrictions on the power of calling forth the militia to execute the laws of the Union, suppress insurrections, and repel invasions, we may very easily see that it will produce dreadful oppressions. It is extremely unsafe, without alterations. It would use the militia to a bad purpose, if any disturbance happened in New Hampshire, to call them from Georgia. This would harass the people so that they would agree to abolish the use of the militia, and establish a standing army. When a bill is sent with proposed amendments to the house of Representative, if they find the alterations defective, they are not conclusive. The House of Rep. are the judges of their propriety, and the recommendation of the Senate is nothing. The experience of this state justifies this clause. The House of Delegates has employed weeks in forming a money bill; and because the Senate had no power of proposing amendments, the bill was lost and a new bill obliged to be again introduced, when the insertion of one line by the Senate would have done.

June 14, 1788, ARTICLE 1, SECTION 8, Power of Congress

James Madison: cordially agreed that a standing army was one of the greatest mischiefs that can possibly happen, and said: It is a great recommendation for this system, that it provides against this evil more than any other system known to us, and, particularly, more than the old system of confederation. The most effective way to guard against a standing army, is to render it unnecessary. The most effectual way to render it unnecessary is to give the general government full power to call forth the militia, and exert the natural strength of the Union, when necessary.

Charles Clay: apprehended that, by this power, our militia might be sent to the Mississippi. He observed that the sheriff might raise the *posse comitatus* to execute the laws. He feared it would lead to the establishment of a military government, as the militia were to be called forth to put the laws into execution. He asked why this mode was preferred to the old, established custom of executing the laws.

James Madison: answered that the power existed in all countries; to call forth militia, that public force must be used when resistance to laws required it, otherwise society itself must be destroyed.

Patrick Henry: warned that the opposition should act cautiously and make a firm stand before deciding. "The sword and the purse are the two greatest instruments of government." When it came to national defense, he was persuaded to be cautious and was reluctant to surrender what he considered the most valuable of rights.

George Nicholas: said the object of government is security and public defense and they must determine the best mode to enable the general government to protect the nation, and suggested three ways, employ a standing army, depend on a militia, allow a choice between the two.

James Madison: said that the stress on the maxim, that the purse and sword ought not to be put in the same hands was the impropriety of vesting that power in the general government, adding that there would never be an efficient government in which both are not vested.

June 14, 1788, ARTICLE 1, SECTION 8 Scope of Congress' Power

Patrick Henry: Mr. Chairman, it is now confessed that this is a national government. There is not a single federal feature in it. It has been alleged within these walls, during the debates, to be national and federal, as it suited the arguments of gentlemen, checks and barriers?

The sword and purse are essentially necessary for the government. Every essential requisite must be in Congress. Where are the sword and purse of Virginia? They must go to Congress. What is become of your country? The Virginia government is but a name, It clearly results, from his last argument, that we are to be consolidated. We should be thought unwise indeed to keep two hundred legislators in Virginia, when the government is, in fact, gone to Philadelphia or New York. We are, as a state, to form no part of the government. Where are your checks?

The most essential objects of government are to be administered by government, it will be consolidated, not confederated, (a nuance: centralized or combined) The honorable gentleman wished to try the experiment. Loving this country as he does, he would surely not wish to trust his happiness to an experiment, from which much harm, but no good, may result. I will speak another time and will not fatigue the committee now. I think the friends of the opposition ought to make a pause here; for I can see no safety to my country, if you give up this power.

James Madison: Mr. Chairman, The honorable member expresses surprise that I wished to see an experiment made of a republican government, or that I would risk the happiness of my country on an experiment. What is the situation of this country at this moment? Is it not rapidly approaching anarchy? Are not the bands of the Union so absolutely relaxed as almost to amount to a dissolution? What produced despotism and tyranny in other parts of the world? Is it not agreed, upon all hands, that a reform is necessary? If any takes place, will it not be an experiment as well as this system? He acknowledges the existing system to be defective. He admits the necessity of some change. Would not the change he would choose himself be also an experiment? He has repeated objections which have already been clearly refuted, and which therefore, I will pass over. We are enlightened and vigil & I should be happy to see the people paying respect to the laws and magistracy. But is respect paid to our laws? Every man's experience will tell him more, perhaps, than any thing I could say. Public and private confidence daily and rapidly decrease. Experiments must be made, and in that form which we must find most to the interest of our country.

Gov. Edmund Randolph, June 14, 1788

Mr. Chairman, our attention is summoned to this clause respecting the militia, and alarms are thrown out to persuade us that it involves a multiplicity of danger. It is supposed by the honorable gentleman lately up, and another gentleman, that the clause for calling forth the militia to suppress insurrection instead of using civil force in the first instance, the militia are to be called forth to arrest petty offenders against the laws.

Ought not common sense to be the rule of interpreting this Constitution? Is there an exclusion of the civil power? Does it provide that the laws are to be enforced by military coercion in all cases? No, sir. All that we are to infer is, that when the civil power is not sufficient, the militia must be drawn out. Who are they? He says (and I cheerfully acquiesce in the rectitude of the assertion) that they are the bulwark of our liberties.

Shall we be afraid that the people, this bulwark of freedom, will turn instruments of slavery? The officers are to be appointed by the states. Will you admit that they will act so criminally as to turn against their country? The officers of the general government are attached to it, because they derive their appointment from it. Admitting the militia officers to be corrupt, what is to make them be in favor of the general government?

Will not the same reason attach them to the state governments? But it is feared that the militia are to be subjected to martial law when not in service. They are only to be called out in three cases, and only to be governed by the authority of Congress when actual service to the United States; so that their articles of war no longer operate when in actual service to the Union. Can it be presumed that you can vest the supreme power of the United States with the power of defense, and yet take away this natural defense from them? You risk the general defense by withholding this power. The honorable gentleman, speaking of responsibility, has mistaken facts. He says the king cannot pardon offenders found guilty on impeachment. The king can pardon after impeachment, though not before. In America every thing is concealed, whereas in England the operation of government is openly transacted. In England, those subjects which produce impeachments are not opinions.

No man ever thought of impeaching a man for an opinion. It would be impossible to discover whether the error in opinion resulted from a willful mistake of the heart, or an involuntary fault of the head. What are the most common occasions of impeachments? Treaties. Are these previously known? Not till they are presented to the public eye, they are not known.

Those who advised a treaty are not known till then. There ought not to be a publication on the subject of negotiations till they are concluded. So that, when he thinks there is a greater notoriety in this case in England than here, I say he is mistaken. There will be as much notoriety in America as in England. The spirit of the nation occasions the notoriety of their political operations, and not any constitutional requisition. The spirit of liberty will not be less predominant in America, I hope, than there.

With respect to a standing army, I believe there was not a member in the federal Convention, who did not feel indignation at such an institution. What remedy, then, could be provided? Leave the country defenseless?

In order to provide for our defense, and exclude the dangers of a standing army, the general defense is left to those who are the objects of defense, the militia, who will suffer if they become the instruments of tyranny?

The general government must have power to call them forth when the general defense requires it. In order to produce greater security, the state governments are to appoint the officers.

The President, who commands them when in actual service of the Union, is appointed secondarily by the people. This is a further security. Is it not incredible that men who are interested in the happiness of their country - whose friends, relations, and connections, must be involved in the fate of their country - should turn against their country?

I appeal to every man whether, if any of our own officers were called upon to destroy the liberty of their country, believes they would assent to such a thing. If so, he asked if Congress could not inflict the most ignominious punishments on the most worthy citizens of the community. Would freemen submit to such indignant treatment? It might be thought a strained construction, but it was no more than Congress might put upon it.

He thought such severities might be exercised on the militia as would make them wish the use of the militia to be utterly abolished, and assent to the establishment of a standing army.

George Mason Then adverted to the representation, and said it was not sufficiently full to take into consideration the feelings and sentiments of all the citizens. He admitted that the nature of the country rendered a full representation impracticable. But he strongly urged that impracticability as a conclusive reason for granting no powers to the government but such as were absolutely indispensable, and these to be most cautiously guarded. He then recurred to the power of impeachment. On this subject he entertained great suspicions. He apologized for being suspicious. He entered into the world with as few suspicious as any man. Young men, he said, were apt to think well of every one, till time and experience taught them better. After a treaty manifestly repugnant to the interests of the country was made, he asked how they were to be punished. Suppose it had been made by the means of bribery and corruption. Suppose they had received one hundred thousand guineas, or louis d'ors, from a foreign nation, for consenting to a treaty, how was the truth to be come at? Corruption and bribery of that kind had happened in other governments, and might in this. The House of Representatives were to impeach them. The senators were to try themselves. If a majority of them were guilty of the crime, would they pronounce themselves guilty? Yet, says he, this is called responsibility. He wished to know in what court the members of the government were to be tried for the commission of indictable offenses, or injuries to individuals.

He acknowledged himself to be no lawyer; but he thought he could see that they could be tried neither in the state nor federal courts. The only means, therefore, of bringing them to punishment, must be by a court appointed by law; and the law to punish them must also be made by themselves. By whom is it to be made? demanded he. By the very men who are interested in not inflicting punishment. Yet, says he, though they make the law, and fix the punishment to be inflicted on themselves, it is called responsibility.

If the senators do not agree to the law, it will not be made, and thus they will escape altogether. Mr. Mason then animadverted on the ultimate control of Congress over the elections, and was proceeding to prove that it was dangerous, when he was called to order, by Mr. Nicholas, for departing from the clause under consideration

A desultory conversation ensued, and Mr. Mason was permitted to proceed. He was of opinion that the control over elections tended to destroy responsibility. He declared he had endeavored to discover whether this power was really necessary, or what was the necessity of vesting it in the government, but he could find no good reason for giving it; that the reasons suggested were that, in case the states should refuse or neglect to make regulations, or in case they should be prevented from making regulations by rebellion or invasion, then the general government should interpose. Mr. Mason then proceeded thus: If there be any other cases, I should be glad to know them; for I know them not. If there be no other, why not confine them to these cases? But the power here, as in a thousand other instances, is without reason. I have no power which any other person can take from me. I have no right of representation, if they can take it from me.

I say, therefore, that Congress may, by this claim, take away the right of representation, or render it nugatory, despicable, or oppressive. It is at least argumentative, that what may be done will be done, and that a favorite point will be done by those who can.

Suppose the state of Virginia should adopt such regulations as gentlemen say, (and in which I accord with all my heart,) and divide the state into ten districts. Suppose, then, that Congress should order, instead of this, that the elections should be held in the borough of Norfolk. Will any man say that any man in Frederick or Berkeley county would have any share in this representation, if the members were chosen in Norfolk?

Nay, I might go farther, and say that the elections for all the states might be had in New York, and then we should have to go so far that the privilege would be lost altogether; for but few gentlemen could afford to go thither.

Some of the best friends of the Constitution have advocated that the elections should be in one place. This power is not necessary, and is capable of great abuse. It ought to be confined to the particular cases in which they assert it to be necessary. Whatever gentlemen may think of the opposition, I will never agree to give any power which I conceive to be dangerous.

I have doubts on another point. The 5th section of the 1st article provides, "that each house shall keep a journal of its proceedings, and from time to time publish the same, excepting such parts as may, in their judgment, require secrecy. "This enables them to keep the negotiations about treaties secret? Under this veil they may conceal any thing and every thing. Why not insert words that would exclude ambiguity and danger?

The words of the Confederation, that defective system, are, in this respect, more eligible. What are they? In the last clause of the 9th article it is provided, "that Congress shall publish the journal of their proceedings monthly, except such parts thereof, relating to treaties, alliances, or military operations, as, in their judgment, require secrecy." The proceedings, by that system, are to be published monthly, with certain exceptions.

These are proper guards. It is not so here. On the contrary, they may conceal what they please. Instead of giving information, they will produce suspicion. You cannot discover the advocates of their iniquitous acts. This is an additional defect of responsibility.

Neither house can adjourn, without the consent of the other, for more than three days. This is no parliamentary rule. It is untrodden ground, and it appears to me liable to much exception.

The senators are chosen for six years. They are not recallable for those six years, and are re-eligible at the end of the six years. It stands on a very different ground from the Confederation. By that system, they were only elected for one year, might be recalled, and were incapable of reelection. But in the new Constitution, instead of being elected for one, they are chosen for six years. They cannot be recalled, in all that time, for any misconduct, and at the end of that long term may again be elected. What will be the operation of this?

Is it not probable that those gentlemen, who will be elected senators, will fix themselves in the federal town, and become citizens of that town more than of our state? They will purchase a good seat in or near the town, and become inhabitants of that place. Will it not be, then, in the power of the Senate to worry the House of Representatives into any thing? They will be a continually existing body. They will exercise those machinations and contrivances which the many have always to fear from the few. The House of Representatives is the only check on the Senate, with their enormous powers. But by that clause you give them the power of worrying the House of Representatives into compliance with any measure. The senators, living there will feel no inconvenience from long sessions. They will vote themselves handsome pay, without incurring additional expenses. Your representatives are on a different ground, in their short continuance in office. Gentlemen from Georgia are seven hundred miles from home, and wish to go home. The Senate, taking advantage of this, by stopping the other house from adjourning, may worry them into anything. These are my doubts, and I think the provision not consistent with the usual parliamentary modes.

Richard Henry Lee , June 14, 1788

Mr. Chairman, I am anxious to know the truth on this great occasion. I was in hopes of receiving true information, but I have been disappointed. I have heard suspicions against possibility, and not against probability. As to the distinction which lies between the gentlemen for and against the Constitution - in the first place, most of the arguments the latter use pay no regard to the necessity of the Union, which is our object. In the next place, they use contradictory arguments. It may be remembered that we were told there was great danger of an aristocracy governing this country; for their wages would be so low, that the rich alone could serve. And what does another gentleman say? That the price will be so high, that they will fix themselves comfortably in office, and, by their power and extravagant emoluments, ruin us. Ought we to adduce arguments like these, which imply a palpable contradiction?

We ought to use arguments capable of discussion. I beg leave to make some reply to what the honorable gentleman over the way said. (Patrick Henry). He rose with great triumph and exultation, saying that we had conceded that the government was national.

The honorable gentleman is so little used to triumph on the grounds of reasoning, that he suffers himself to be quite captivated by the least appearance of victory. What reason had he to say that we admitted it to be a national government? We agree that the sword and the purse are in the hands of the general government for different designated purposes. What had the honorable member conceded?

That the objects of the government were general, as designated in that system, equally affecting the interests of the people of every state. This was the sole concession, and which by no means warrants his conclusion.

Then why did the honorable gentleman seize it as a victory? Does he mean to object to the Constitution by putting words into our mouths which we never uttered? Did that gentleman say that the happiness of the people depended on the private virtues of the members of the government, and not on its construction? Did any gentleman admit this, as he insinuated? No, sir, we never admitted such a conclusion.

Why, then, take up the time of this house in declaiming on words we never said? We say that it will secure our liberty and happiness, and that it is so constructed and organized, that we need apprehend no danger.

But, says he, the creature destroys the creator. How has he proved it? By his bare assertion. By ascribing infinitude to powers clearly limited and defined, for certain designated purposes.

I shall not repeat the arguments which have fully refuted this idea of the honorable gentleman. But gentlemen say that we must apply to the militia to execute the constitutional laws, without the interposition of civil power, and that a military officer is to be substituted for the sheriff in all cases.

This unwarrantable objection is urged, like many others, to produce the rejection of this government, though contrary to reason.

What is the meaning of the clause under debate? Does not their explanation violate the natural meaning of language? Is it to be inferred that, when the laws are not opposed, judgments must be executed by the militia? Is this the right and liberal way of discussing the general national objects?

I am astonished that gentlemen should attempt to impose so absurd a construction upon the rest of us.

The honorable gentleman last up (George Mason) says, that organizing the militia gives Congress power to punish them when not in the actual Service of the government. The gentleman is mistaken in the meaning of the word organization, to explain which would unnecessarily take up time. Suffice it to say, it does not include the infliction of punishments.

The militia will be subject to the common regulations of war when in actual service; but not in time of peace. But the honorable gentleman said there is danger of an abuse of the power, and attempted to exemplify, that delegated power may be abused.

It would be civil and candid in those gentlemen, who inveigh against this Constitution with such malignity, to show how adequate powers can be given without a possibility of being abased. It appears to me as secured as it can be, and the alterations he proposes would involve many disadvantages. I cannot but conclude that this government will, in my opinion, secure our liberty and happiness, without any alteration.

June 14, 1788

Charles Clay made several remarks; but he spoke too low. He admitted that he might be mistaken with respect to the exclusion of the civil power in executing the laws.

As it was insinuated that he was not under the influence of common sense in making the objection, his error might result from his deficiency in that respect. But he thought that another gentleman was as deficient in common decency as he was in common sense. He was not, however, convinced that the civil power would be employed.

If it was meant that the militia should not be called out to execute the laws in all cases, why were they not satisfied with the words, "repel invasions, suppress insurrections"? He thought the word insurrection included every opposition to the laws; and if so, it would be sufficient to call them forth to suppress insurrections, as a right to execute the laws of the Union.

He added that, although militia officers were appointed by state governments, yet, they were sworn to obey the superior power of Congress, so no checks on security would result from their nomination.

James Madison: Mr. Chairman, I cannot think that the explanation of the gentleman last up is founded in reason. He does not say that the militia shall be called out in all cases, but in certain cases. There are cases in which the execution of laws may require the operation of the militia, which cannot be said to be an invasion or insurrection. There may be a resistance to the laws which cannot be termed an insurrection. My honorable friend over the way has opened a new source of argument. He has introduced the assertions of gentlemen out of doors. If we thus depart from regularity, we shall never be able to come to a decision.

If there be any gentleman who is a friend to the government, and says that the elections may or ought to be held in one place, he is an enemy to it on that ground. With respect to the time, place, and manner of elections,

I cannot think, notwithstanding the apprehensions of the honorable gentleman, that there is any danger, or, if abuse should take place, that there is not sufficient security.

If all the people, of the United States should be directed to go to elect in one place, the members of the government would be execrated for that infamous regulation. Many would go to trample them under foot for their conduct; and they would be succeeded by men who would remove it. They would not dare to meet the universal hatred and detestation of the people, and run the risk of the certain dreadful consequences. We must keep within the compass of human probability. If a possibility be the cause of objection, we must object to every government in America. But the honorable gentleman may say that better guards may be provided. Let us consider the objection. The power of regulating the time, place, and manner of elections, must be vested somewhere. It could not be fixed in the Constitution without involving great inconveniences.

They could then have no authority to adjust the regulation to the changes of circumstances. The question is, whether it ought to be fixed unalterably in the state governments, or be subject to the control of the general government. Is it not obvious that the general government would be destroyed without this control? It has already been demonstrated that it will produce many conveniences. Have we not sufficient security against abuse? Consider fully the principles of the government.

The sum of the powers given up by the people of Virginia is divided into two classes, one to the federal and the other to the state government. Each is subdivided into three branches. These may be kept independent of each other in the one as well as the other. In this system, they are as distinct as is consistent with good policy.

This, in my opinion, instead of diminishing, increases the security of liberty more than any government that ever was; for the powers of government which, in every other country, are given to one body, are here given to two, and are favorable to public liberty. With respect to secrecy, if every thing in which it is necessary could be enumerated, I would have no objection to it being concealed. The British House of Commons can do it. They are in this respect under much less restraint than Congress.

There never was any legislative assembly without a discretionary power of concealing important transactions, the publication of which might be detrimental to the community.

There can be no real danger as long as the government is constructed on such principles. He objects also to the clause respecting adjournment- that neither house shall, without the consent of the other, adjourn for more than three days.

It was before remarked that, if a difference should take place between the houses about the time of adjournment, the President could still determine it; from which no danger could arise, as he is chosen in a secondary degree by the people, and would consequently fix no time which would be repugnant to the sense of the representatives of the people.

Another and more satisfactory answer is this: suppose the Senate wished to chain down the House of Representatives; what is to hinder them from going home? How bring them back again? It would be contrary to the spirit of the Constitution to impede the operations of the government, perhaps at a critical period. I cannot conceive that such difference will often happen. Were the Senate to attempt to prevent an adjournment, it would but serve to irritate the representatives without having the intended effect, as the

President could adjourn them. There will not be occasion for the continual residence of the senators at the seat of government. What business have they more than the House of Representatives? The appointment of officers and treaties. With respect to the appointment of officers, a law may be made to grant it to the President alone. It must be supposed there will be but few and subordinate officers to be appointed, as the principal offices will be filled. It is observed that the President, when vacancies happen during the recess of the Senate, may fill them till it meets. With respect to treaties, the occasions of forming them will not be many, and will make but a small proportion of the time of session.

Charles Clay: Wished to know the instances where an opposition to the laws did not come within the idea of an insurrection.

James Madison: Replied that a riot did not qualify with the legal definition of an insurrection. There might be riots, to oppose the execution of laws, which the civil power might not be sufficient to quell. This was one case. There would be others. He referred to the candor of the committee, whether the militia could be used to destroy themselves.

June 16, 1788, Monday, The convention resolved into a committee to take further consideration the proposed plan of government with Mr. Wythe as chairman.

The 8th section still under consideration: Congressional Power

Patrick Henry: Thought it necessary and proper that they should take a collective view of this section, and revert again to the first clause, which gives Congress the power of raising armies, and proceeded as follows: To me this appears a very alarming power, when unlimited. They can not only raise, but support, armies; to the utmost abilities of the United States.

If Congress shall say that the general welfare requires it, they may keep armies continually on foot. There is no control on Congress in raising or station them. They may billet them on the people at pleasure. This unlimited authority is a most dangerous power: its principles are despotic. If it be unbounded, it must lead to despotism; for the power of a people in a free government is supposed to be paramount to the existing power. Advert to the power thoroughly.

One of our first complaints, under the former government, was the

quartering of troops upon us. **This was one of the principal reasons for dissolving the connection with Great Britain**. Here we may have troops in time of peace. They may be billeted in a manner to tyrannize, oppress, and crush us.

We are told, we are afraid to trust ourselves; that our own Representatives in Congress, will not exercise their powers oppressively; that we shall not enslave ourselves; that the militia cannot enslave themselves, &c. Who has enslaved France, Spain, Germany, Turkey, and other countries which groan under tyranny? They have been enslaved by the hands of their own people. If it will be so in America, it will be only as it has been every where else. I am still persuaded that the power of calling forth the militia, to   execute the laws of the Union, &c., is dangerous.

We requested the gentleman to show the cases where the militia would be wanted to execute the laws. Under the order of Congress, they shall suppress insurrections. Under the order of Congress, they shall be called to execute the laws. It will result, of course, that this is to be a government of force. Look at the part which speaks of excises, and you will recollect that those who are to collect excises and duties are to be aided by military force. They have power to call them out, and to provide for arming, organizing, disciplining, them. Consequently, they are to make militia laws for this state. A law may be made that, if twelve men assemble, if they do not disperse, they may be fired upon. Your men who go to Congress are not restrained by a bill of rights. **They are not restrained from inflicting unusual and severe punishments, though the bill of rights of Virginia forbids it.** What is the consequence? They may inflict cruel and ignominious punishments on the militia, and tell you that it is necessary for their discipline.

James. Madison: June 16, 1788, Mr. Chairman, I will endeavor to follow the rule of the house, but must pay due attention to the observations which fell from the gentleman (Patrick Henry). I should conclude, from abstracted reasoning, that they were ill founded.

I should think that, if there were any object which the general government ought to command, it would be the direction of the national forces. And as the force which lies in militia is most safe, the direction of that part ought to be submitted to, in order to render another force unnecessary.

The power objected to is necessary, because it is to be employed for national purposes. It is necessary to be given to every government. This is not opinion, but fact. The highest authority may be given, that the want of such authority in the government protracted the late war, and prolonged its calamities. True, a standing army was quartered upon us. This was not the whole complaint. We complained because it was done without the local authority of this country without the consent of the people of America. As to the exclusion of standing armies in the states bill of rights, we shall find that though there is something like a prohibition in most of them that provides that no armies shall be kept without legislative authority; without consent of the community.

George Mason, June 16, 1788, asked to what purpose the laws were read. **The objection was, that too much power was given to Congress, power that would finally destroy the state governments more effectually by insidious, underhanded means, than such as could be openly practiced.**

This, said he, is the opinion of many worthy men, not only in this Convention, but in all parts of America, These laws could only show that the legislature of this state could pass such acts. He thought they militated against the session of this power to Congress, because the state governments could call forth the militia when necessary, so as to compel a submission to the laws; and as they were competent to it, Congress ought not to have the power. The meeting of three or four persons might be called an insurrection, and the militia might be called out to disperse them.

He was not satisfied with the explanation of the word organization by the gentleman in the military line, (Mr. Lee.) He thought they were not confined to the technical explanation, but that Congress could inflict severe and ignominious punishments on the militia, as a necessary incident to the power of organizing and disciplining them.

The gentleman had said there was no danger, because the laws respecting the militia were less rigid in other states than this. This was no conclusive argument, His fears, as he had before expressed, were, that grievous punishments would be inflicted, in order to render the service disagreeable to the militia themselves, and induce them to wish its abolition, which would afford a pretense for a standing army.

He was convinced the state governments ought to have the control of the militia, except when they were absolutely necessary for general purposes. The gentleman said that they would be only subject to martial law when in actual service.

He demanded what was to hinder Congress from inflicting it always must finally produce, most infallibly, the annihilation of the state Governments. These were his apprehensions. He prayed God they were groundless.

Mr. Madison: June 16, 1788, replied, that the obvious explanation was, that the states were to appoint the officers, and govern the militia except that part which was called into the service of the United States. He asked if powers were given to the general government, if we must not give executive power to use it. The vice of the old system was, that Congress could not execute the powers nominally vested in them. If the contested clause were expunged, this system would have nearly the same defect.

Patrick Henry: Wished to know what authority the state governments had over the militia.

James Madison: Answered, that the state governments might do what they thought proper with the militia, when they were not in the actual service of the United States. They might make use of them to suppress insurrections, quell riots, &c., and call on the general government for the militia of any other state, to aid them, if necessary.

Patrick Henry: replied that, as the clause expressly vested the general government with power to call them out to suppress insurrections, &c., it appeared to him, decidedly, that the power of suppressing insurrections was exclusively in the hands of Congress. If it remained in the states, it was by implication.

Frances Corbin: After a short address to the chair, in which he expressed extreme reluctance to get up, said, that all contentions on this subject might be ended, by adverting to the 4th section of the 4th article, which provides, "that the United States shall guaranty to every state in the Union a republican form of government, and shall protect each of them against invasion, and, on application of the legislature, or of the executive, (when the legislature cannot be convened,) against domestic violence."

He thought this section gave the states power to use their own militia, and call on Congress for the militia of other states. He observed that our representatives were to return every second year to mingle with their fellow-citizens.

He asked, then, how, in the name of God, they would make laws to destroy themselves.

"The gentleman had told us that nothing could be more humiliating than that the state governments could not control the general government." He thought the gentleman might as well have complained that one county could not control the state at large. Mr. Corbin then said that all confederate governments had the care of the national defense, and that Congress ought to have it. Animadverting on Mr. Henry's observations, that the French had been the instruments of their own slavery, that the Germans had enslaved the Germans, and the Spaniards the Spaniards, &c., he asked if those nations knew any thing of representation. The want of this knowledge was the principal cause of their bondage. He concluded by observing that the general government had no power but such as the state government and that arguments against the one held against the other.

June 16, 1788

William Grayson: In reply to Mr. Corbin, said he was mistaken when he produced the 4th section of the 4th article, to prove that the state governments had a right to intermeddle with the militia.

He was of the opinion that a previous application must be made to the federal head, by the legislature when in session, or otherwise by the executive of any state, before they could interfere with the militia.

In his opinion, no instance could be adduced where the states could employ the militia; for, in all the cases wherein they could be employed, Congress had the exclusive direction and control of them. Disputes, he observed, had happened in many countries, where this power should be lodged. In England, there was a dispute between the Parliament and King Charles who should have power over the militia. Were this government well organized, he would not object to giving it power over the militia. But as it appeared to him to be without checks, and to tend to the formation of an aristocratic body, could not agree to it.

Thus organized, his imagination did not reach so far as to know where this power should be lodged. He conceived the state governments to be at the mercy of the generality. He wished to be open to conviction, but he could see no case where the states could command the militia. He did not believe that it corresponded with the intentions of those who formed it, and it was altogether without equilibrium.

He humbly apprehended that the power of providing for organizing and disciplining the militia, enabled the government to make laws for regulating them, and inflicting punishments for disobedience, neglect, &c. Whether it would be the spirit of the generality to lay unusual punishments, he knew not; but he thought they had the power, if they thought proper to exercise it. He thought that, if there was a constructive implied power left in the states, yet, as the line was not clearly marked between the two governments, it would create differences. He complained of the uncertainty of the expression, and wished it to be so clearly expressed that the people might see where the states could interfere. As the exclusive power of arming, organizing, &c., was given to Congress, they might entirely neglect them; or they might be armed in one part of the Union, and totally neglected in another. This he apprehended to be a probable circumstance. In this he might be thought suspicious; but he was justified by the bad that had happened in other countries. He wished to know what attention had been paid to the militia of Scotland and Ireland since the union, and what laws had been made to regulate them. There is, says Mr. Grayson, an excellent militia law in England, such as I wish to be established by the general government. They have thirty thousand select militia in England. But the militia of Scotland and Ireland are neglected. I see the necessity of the concentration of the forces of the Union. I acknowledge that militia are the best means of quelling insurrections, and that we have an advantage over the English government, for their regular forces answer the purpose. But I object to the want of checks, and a line of discrimination between the state governments and the generality.

June 16, 1788

John Marshall: Asked if gentlemen were serious when they asserted that, if the state governments had power to interfere with the militia, it was by implication. He asked the committee whether the least attention would not show that they were mistaken.

The state governments did not derive their powers from the general government; but each government derived its powers from the people, and each was to act according to the powers given it. Would any gentleman deny this? He demanded if powers not given were retained by implication. Could any man say so? Could any man say that this power was not retained by the states, as they had not given it away? For, says he, does not a power remain till it is given away?

The state legislatures had power to command and govern their militia before, and have it still, undeniably, unless there be something in this Constitution that takes it away. For Continental purposes Congress may call forth the militia, to suppress insurrections and repel invasions. But the power given to the states by the people is not taken away; the Constitution does not say so.

If the Confederation Congress had this power; the state legislatures had it also. The power of legislating given them within the ten miles square is exclusive of the states, because it is expressed to be exclusive. The truth is, that when power is given to the general legislature, if it was in the state legislature before, both shall exercise it; unless there be an incompatibility in the exercise by one to that by the other, or negative words precluding the state governments from it. But there are no negative words here. It rests, therefore, with the states.

To me it appears, then, unquestionable that the state governments can call forth the militia, in case the Constitution should be adopted, in the same manner as they could have done before its adoption. Gentlemen have said that the states cannot defend themselves without an application to Congress, because Congress can interpose!

Does not every man feel a refutation of the argument in his own breast? I will show that there could not be a combination, between those who formed the Constitution, to take away this power. All the restraints intended to be laid on the state governments (besides where an exclusive power is expressly given to Congress) are contained in the 10th section of the first article. This power is not included in the restrictions in that section.

But what excludes every possibility of doubt, is the last part of it that "no state shall engage in war, unless actually invaded, or in such imminent danger as will not admit of delay." When invaded, they can engage in war, as when in imminent danger. This clearly proves that the states can use the militia when they find it necessary.

The worthy member last up objects to the Continental government possessing the power of disciplining the militia, because, though all its branches be derived from the people, he says they will form an aristocratic government, unsafe and unfit to be trusted.

William Grayson: June 16, 1788 answered, that he only said it was so constructed as to form a great aristocratic body.

Author's Comment: This unseemly exchange took place between two men who had formerly been the closest of friends and never would be friends again after the bitter debates in the Virginia Ratifying Convention of 1788.

John Marshall: Replied, that he was not certain whether he understood him; but he thought he had said so. He conceived that, as the government was drawn from the people, the feelings and interests of the people would be attended to, and we should be safe in granting them power to regulate the militia. When the government is drawn from the people, continued Mr. Marshall, and depending on the people for its continuance, oppressive measures will not be attempted, as they will certainly draw on their authors the resentment of those on whom they depend. On this government, thus depending on ourselves for its existence, I will rest my safety, notwithstanding the danger depicted by the honorable gentleman. I cannot help being surprised that the worthy member thought this power so dangerous.

What government is able to protect you in time of war? Will any state depend on its own exertions? The consequence of such dependence, and withholding this power from Congress, will be, that state will fall after state, and be a sacrifice to the want of power in the general government. *United we are strong, divided we fall.*

Will you prevent the general government from drawing the militia of one state to another, when the consequence would be, that every state must depend on itself? The enemy, possessing the water, can quickly go from one state to another. No state will spare to another its militia, which it conceives necessary for itself. It requires a Superintending power, in order to call forth the resources of all to protect all. If this be not done, each state will fill a sacrifice. This system merits the highest applause in this respect. The honorable gentleman (William Grayson) said that a general regulation may be made to inflict punishments. Does he imagine that a militia law is to be ingrafted on the scheme of government, so as to render it incapable of being changed? The idea of the worthy member supposes that men renounce their own interests. This would produce general inconveniences throughout the Union, and would be equally opposed by all the states.

But the worthy member fears, that one part of the Union will be regulated and disciplined, and in another, neglected. This danger is enhanced by leaving this power to each state; for some states may attend to their militia, and others may neglect them.

If Congress neglect our militia, we can arm them ourselves. Cannot Virginia import arms? Cannot she put them into the hands of her militia?

He concluded by observing, that the power of governing the militia was not vested in the states by implication, being possessed of it antecedent to the adoption of the government, and not being divested of it by any grant or restriction in the Constitution, they must necessarily be as fully possessed of it as ever, and it could not be said that the states derived any powers from that system, but retained them, though not acknowledged in any part of it.

William Grayson: June 16, 1788, acknowledged that all power was drawn from the people. But he could see none of those checks which ought to characterize a free government. It had not such checks as even the British government had. **He thought it so organized as to form an aristocratic body.** If we looked at the democratic branch, and the great extent of country, he said, it must be considered, in a great degree, to be an aristocratic representation. As they were elected with craving appetites, wishing for emoluments, they might unite with the other two branches. They might give reciprocally good offices to one another, and mutually protect each other; for he considered them all as united in interest, as but one branch. There was no check to prevent such a combination; nor, in cases of concurrent powers, was there a line drawn to prevent interference between the state governments and the generality.

Patrick Henry: Retained his opinion, that the states had no right to call forth the militia to suppress insurrections, &c. But the right interpretation (and such as the nations of the earth had put upon the concession of power) was that, when power was given, it was given exclusively.

He appealed to the committee, if power was not confined in the hands of a *few* in almost all countries of the world. He referred to their candor, if the construction of conceded power was not an exclusive concession, in nineteen twentieth parts of the world. The nations which retained their liberty were comparatively few. America would add to the number of the oppressed nations, if she depended on constructive rights and argumentative implication. That the powers given to Congress were exclusively given, was very obvious to him. The rights which the states had must be founded on the restrictions on Congress. He asked, if the doctrine which had been so often circulated, that rights not given were retained, was true, why there were negative clauses to restrain Congress.

He told gentlemen that these clauses were sufficient to shake all their implication; for, says he, if Congress had no power but that given to them, why restrict them by negative words? Is not the clear implication that if these restrictions were not inserted, they could have performed what they prohibit? Is it fair to say that you give the power of arming the militia, and at the same time to say you reserve it? This great national government ought not to be left in this condition. If it be, it will terminate in the destruction of our liberties.

James Madison: June 16, 1788, Mr. Chairman, let me ask this committee, and the honorable member last up, what we are to understand from this

reasoning. The power must be vested in Congress, or in the state governments; or there must be a division or concurrence. He is against division. It
is a political monster. He will not give it to Congress for fear of oppression.
Is it to be vested in the state governments? If so, where is the provision for
general defense? If ever America should be attacked, The states would fall
successively. It will prevent them from giving aid to their sister states; for,
as each state will expect to be attacked, and wish to guard against it,

Each will retain its own militia for its own defense. Where is this power
to be deposited, then, unless in the general government, if it be dangerous
to the public safety to give it exclusively to the states? If it must be divided,
Let him show a better manner of doing it than that which is in the Constitution. I cannot agree with the other honorable gentleman, Grayson) that
there is no check. There is a powerful check in that paper. The state
governments are to govern the militia when not called forth for general national purposes; and Congress is to govern such part only as may be in the
actual service of the Union. Nothing can be more certain and positive than
this. It expressly empowers Congress to govern them when in the service
of the United States.

It is then clear that the states govern them when they are not. With respect
to suppressing insurrections, I say that those clauses which were mentioned
by the honorable gentleman are compatible with a concurrence of the
power. By the first, Congress is to call them forth to suppress insurrections,
and repel invasions of foreign powers. A concurrence in the former case is
necessary, because a whole state may be in insurrection against the Union.
What has passed may perhaps justify this apprehension. The safety of the
Union and particular states requires that the general government should
have power to repel foreign invasions. The 4th section of the 4th article is
perfectly consistent with the exercise of the power by the states.
**The words are, The United States shall guaranty to every state in this
Union a republican form of government, and shall protect each of them
against invasion, and on application of the legislature, or of the executive,
(when the legislature cannot be convened,) against domestic violence."**

The word invasion here, after power had been given in the former clause
to repel invasions, may be thought tautologous, but it has a different meaning from the other. This clause speaks of a particular state. It means that it
shall be protected from invasion by other states.

A republican government is to be guaranteed to each state, and they are
to be protected from invasion from other states, as well as from foreign
powers; and, on application by the legislature or executive, as the case may

be, the militia of the other states are to be called to suppress domestic insurrections. Does this bar the states from calling forth their own militia? No; but it gives them a supplementary security to suppress insurrections and domestic violence. The other clause runs in these words: "No state shall, without the consent of Congress. Lay any duty on tonnage, keep troops or ships of war in time of peace, enter into any agreement or compact with another state, or with a foreign power, or engage in war, unless actually invaded, or in such imminent danger as will not admit of delay."

They are restrained from making war, unless invaded, or in imminent danger. When in such danger, they are not restrained. I can perceive no competition in these clauses. They are not be repugnant to a concurrence of the power. If we object to the Constitution in this manner, and consume our time in verbal criticism, we shall never put an end to the business.

George Mason: June 16, 1788, Mr. Chairman, a worthy member has asked who are the militia, if they be not the people of this country, and if we are not to be protected from the fate of the Germans, Prussians, &c., by our representation? I ask, Who are the militia? They consist now of the whole people, except a few public officers. But who will be the militia of the future day. If that paper on the table gets no alteration, the militia of the future day may not consist of all classes, high and low, and rich and poor; they may be confined to the lower and middle classes of the people, granting exclusion to the higher classes of the people. If we should ever see that day, the most ignominious punishments and heavy fines may be expected.

Under the present government, all ranks of people are subject to militia duty. Under such a full and equal representation as ours, there can be no ignominious punishment inflicted, But under this national, or rather consolidated government, the case will be different. The representation being so small and inadequate, they will have no fellow-feeling for the people. They may discriminate people in their own predicament, and exempt from duty all the officers and lowest creatures of the national government.

If there were a particular definition of their powers, and a clause exempting the militia from martial law except when in actual service, and from fines and punishments of an unusual nature, then we might expect that the militia would be what they are.

If this be not the case, we cannot say how long all classes of people will be included in the militia, There will not be the same reason to expect it, because the government will be administered by different people.

We know what they are but not how they may be altered.

George Nicholas: June 16, 1788,

Mr. Chairman, I feel apprehensions lest the subject of our debates should be misunderstood. Every one wishes to know the true meaning of the system; but I fear those who hear us will think we quibble on words.

We have been told, in the course of this business, that the government will operate like a screw. Give me leave to say that the exertions of the opposition are like that instrument. They catch at every thing, and take it into their vortex. The worthy member says that this government is defective, because it comes from the people. Its greatest recommendation, with me, is putting the power in the hands of the people. He disapproves of it because it does not say in what particular instances the militia shall be called out to execute the laws. This is a power of the Constitution, and particular instances must be defined by the legislature. But, says the worthy member, those laws which have been read are arguments against the Constitution, because they show that the states are now in possession of the power, and competent to its execution.

Would you leave this power in the states, and by that means deprive the general government of a power which will be necessary for its existence?

If the state governments find this power necessary, ought not the general government have a similar power? But, sir, there is no state check in this business. The gentleman near me has shown that there is a very important check. Another worthy member says there is no power in the states to quell an insurrection of slaves. Have they it now? Does the Constitution take it away? No part of this Constitution can take away this power, but the argument is drawn, "That no state shall engage in war unless actually invaded, or in such imminent danger as will not admit of delay." The restriction therefore includes only offensive hostility. They are, therefore, not restrained from quelling domestic insurrections, which are totally different from making war with a foreign power. But the great thing is that, during an insurrection, the militia will be called out from the state. This is his argument. Is it possible that, at such a time, the general government would order the militia to be called? It is a groundless objection, to work on gentlemen's apprehensions within these walls. As to the 4th article, it was introduced wholly for the particular aid of the states.

A republican form of government is guaranteed, and protection is secured against invasion and domestic violence on application, Is this not a strong guard? Does it not exclude the unnecessary interference of Congress in business of this sort? The gentleman over the way cannot tell who will be the militia at a future day, and enumerates dangers of select militia. Let me attend to the nature of gentlemen's objections. One objects because there will be select militia; another objects because there will be no select militia; and yet both oppose it on these contradictory principles. If you deny the general government the power of calling out the militia, then we must revert to a standing army. If you are jealous of your liberties, confide in Congress.

George Mason: June 16, 1788, rose, and said that he was totally misunderstood. The contrast between his friend's objection and his was improper.

His friend had mentioned the propriety of having select militia, like those of Great Britain, who should be more thoroughly exercised than the militia at large could possibly be. But he, himself, had not spoken of a selection of militia, but of the exemption of the highest classes of the people from militia service; which would justify apprehensions of severe and ignominious punishments.

George Nicholas: wished to know whether the representatives of the people would consent to such exemptions, as every man who had twenty-five acres of land could vote for a federal representative.

William Grayson: Mr. Chairman, I conceive that the power of providing and maintaining a navy is at present dangerous, however warmly it may be urged by gentlemen that America ought to be a maritime power. If we once give such power, we put it in the hands of men whose interest it will be to oppress us. It will irritate the nations of Europe against us.

Let us consider the situation of the maritime powers of Europe: they are separated from us by the Atlantic Ocean. The riches of all those countries come by sea. Commerce and navigation are the principal sources of their wealth. If we become a maritime power, we shall be able to participate in most beneficial business. Will they suffer us to put ourselves in a condition to rival them? I believe the first step of any consequence, which will be made towards it, will bring war upon us. Their ambition and avarice most powerfully impel them to prevent our becoming a naval nation. We should, on this occasion, consult our ability. Is there any gentleman here who can say that America can support a navy? The riches of America are not sufficient to bear the enormous expense it must certainly occasion. I may be supposed to exaggerate, but I leave it to the committee to judge whether my information be right or not. It is said that shipwrights can be had on better terms in America than in Europe; but necessary materials are so much dearer in America than in Europe, that the aggregate sum would be greater.

A seventy-four gun ship will cost you ninety-eight thousand pounds, including guns, tackle, &c. According to the usual calculation in England, it will cost you the further sum of forty-eight thousand pounds to mail it, furnish provisions, and pay officers and men.

You must pay men more here than in Europe, because, their governments being arbitrary, they can command the services of their subjects without adequate compensation; so in all, the expenses of such a vessel would be one hundred and forty thousand pounds in one year.

Let gentlemen consider, then, the extreme difficulty of supporting a navy, and they will concur with me, that America cannot do it.

I have no objection to such a navy as will not excite the jealousy of the European countries, but I would have the Constitution say, that no greater number of ships should be had than would be sufficient to protect our trade. Such a fleet would not, probably, offend the Europeans.

I am not of a jealous disposition; but when I consider that the welfare and happiness of my country are in danger, I beg to be excused for expressing my apprehensions. Let us consider how this navy shall be raised. What would be the consequence under those general words, "to provide and maintain a navy"? All the vessels of the intended fleet would be built and equipped in the Northern States, where they have every necessary material and convenience for the purpose. Will any gentleman say that any ship of war can be raised to the south of Cape Charles?

The consequence will be that the southern states will be in the power of the northern states.

We should be called upon for our share of the expenses, without having equal emoluments. Can it be supposed, when this question is agitated in Congress, that the Northern States will not take such measures as will throw as much circulating money among them as possible, without any consideration as to the other states? If I know the nature of man, (and I believe I do,) they will have no consideration for us. But, supposing it were not so, America has nothing at all to do with a fleet. Let us remain for some time in obscurity, and rise by degrees. Let us not precipitately provoke the resentment of the maritime powers of Europe. A well-regulated militia ought to be the defense of this country. In some of our constitutions it is said so.

This Constitution should have inculcated the principle, Congress ought to be under some restraint in this respect.

Mr. Grayson then added, that the Northern States would be principally

benefited by having a fleet; that a majority of the states could vote raising a great navy, or enter into any commercial regulation detrimental to the other states.

In the United Netherlands there was much greater security, so the commercial interest of no state could be sacrificed without its own consent. The raising a fleet was the daily and favorite subject of conversation in the Northern States who were in favor of building ships.

He apprehended that, if attempted, it would draw us into a war with Great Britain or France. As the American fleet would not be competent to the defense of all the states, the Southern States would be most exposed. He referred to the experience of the late war, as a proof of what he said. At the period the Southern States were most distressed, the Northern States, he said, were most happy. They had privateers in abundance, whereas we had but few. Upon the whole, he thought we should depend on our troops on shore, and that it was very impolitic to give this power to Congress without any limitation.

George Nicholas: June 16, 1788, remarked that the gentleman last up had made two observations - the one, that we ought not to give Congress power to raise a navy; and the other, that we had not the means of supporting it. Mr. Nicholas thought it a false doctrine. Congress, says he, has a discretionary power to do it when necessary. They are not bound to do it in five or ten years, or at any particular time. It is presumable, therefore, that they will postpone it until it be proper.

William Grayson: had no objection to Congress having the power to raise a fleet to suit the circumstances of the country. But he could not agree to give unlimited power which was delineated in adverting to the clause investing Congress with the power of exclusive legislation in a district not exceeding ten miles square. He said he had expressed his doubts that this district would be the favorite of the generality, and that it would be possible for them to give exclusive privileges of commerce to those residing within. He illustrated by using European examples.

It might be said to be impracticable to exercise this power in this manner. Among the various laws and customs which pervaded Europe, there were exclusive privileges and immunities enjoyed in many places.

He thought this ought to be guarded against; for should such exclusive privileges be granted merchants residing within the ten miles square, it would be highly injurious to the inhabitants of other places.

George Mason: June 16, 1788, Thought that there were few clauses in the Constitution so dangerous as that which gave Congress exclusive power of legislation within ten miles square. Implication, he observed, was capable of any extension, and would probably be extended to augment congressional powers. But here there was no need of implication. This clause gave them unlimited authority, in every possible case, within that district.

This ten miles square, says Mr. Mason, may set at defiance the laws of the surrounding states, and may, like the custom of the superstitious days of our ancestors, become the sanctuary of the blackest crimes. Here the federal courts are to sit. We have heard a good deal said of justice. It has been doubted whether jury trial be secured in civil cases. But I will suppose that we shall have juries in criminal cases. What sort of a jury shall we have within the ten miles square? The immediate creatures of the government.

What chance will poor men get, where Congress have the power of legislating in all cases whatever, and where judges and juries may be under their influence, and bound to support their operations?

Even with juries the chance of justice may here be very small, as Congress has unlimited authority, legislative, executive, and judicial. Lest this power should not be sufficient, they have it in every case. Now, sir, if an attempt should be made to establish tyranny over the people, here are ten miles square where the greatest offender may meet protection. If any of their officers, or creatures, should attempt to oppress the people, or should actually perpetrate the blackest deed, he has nothing to do but get into the ten miles square. Why was this dangerous power given? Felons may receive an asylum there and in their strongholds. Gentlemen have said that it was dangerous to argue against possible abuse, because there could be no power delegated but might be abused. It is an incontrovertible axiom, that, when the dangers that may arise from the abuse are greater than the benefits that may result from the use, the power ought to be withheld.

I do not conceive that this power is at all necessary, though capable of being greatly abused. We are told by the honorable gentleman that Holland has its Hague. I confess I am at a loss to know what inference he could draw from that observation. This is the place where the deputies of the United Provinces meet to transact the public business. But I do not recollect that they have any exclusive jurisdiction whatever in that place, but are subject to the laws of the province in which the Hague is. To what purpose the gentleman mentioned that Holland has its Hague, I cannot see. (Mason wanted to ridicule Grayson). George Mason then observed he would willingly give them exclusive power, as far as the police and good government;

but he would give them no more, because he thought it unnecessary. He was willing to give them those powers which he thought indispensable.

James Madison: Mr. Chairman: I did conceive, sir, that the clause under consideration was one of those parts which would speak its own praise. It is hardly necessary to say any thing concerning it. Strike it out of the system, and let me ask whether there would not be much larger scope for those dangers. I cannot comprehend that the power of legislating over a small district, which cannot exceed ten miles square, and may not be more than one mile, will involve the dangers which he apprehends. If there be any knowledge in my mind of the nature of man, I think it would be the last thing that would enter into the mind of any man to grant exclusive advantages, in a very circumscribed district, to the prejudice of the community at large.

We make suppositions, and afterwards deduce conclusions from them, as if they were established axioms. But, after all, bring home this question to ourselves Is it probable that the members from Georgia, New Hampshire, &c., will concur to sacrifice the privileges of their friends? I believe that, whatever state may become the seat of the general government, it will become the object of the jealousy and envy of the other states.

Let me remark, if not already remarked, that there must be a cession, by particular states, of the district to Congress, and that the states may settle the terms of the cession. The states may make what stipulation they please in it, and, if they apprehend any danger, they may refuse it altogether. How could the general government be guarded from the undue influence of particular states, or from insults, without such exclusive power? If it were at the pleasure of a particular state to control the session and deliberations of Congress, would they be secure from insults, or the influence of such state? If this commonwealth depended, for freedom of deliberation, on the laws of any state where it might be necessary to sit, would it not be liable to attacks of that nature and with more indignity, which have been already offered to Congress? With respect to the government of Holland, I believe the States General have no jurisdiction over the Hague; but I have heard that mentioned as a circumstance which gave undue influence to Holland over the rest. We must limit our apprehensions to certain degrees of probability. The evils which they urge must result from this clause are extremely improbable; nay almost impossible.

William Grayson: It is still June 16, 1788,
Mr. Chairman, one answer which has been given is, the improbability of

the evil that it will never be attempted, and that it would be almost impossible. This will not satisfy us. When we consider the great injury of other states. If we travel all over the world, we shall find that people have aggrandized their capitols. Look at Russia and Prussia. Every step has been taken to aggrandize their capitols. In what light are we to consider the ten miles square? It is not to be a fourteenth state.

The inhabitants will in no respect whatever be amenable to the laws of any state. A clause in the 4th article, highly extolled for its wisdom, will be rendered nugatory by this exclusive legislation.

This clause runs thus: "No person held to service or labor in one state, under the laws thereof, escaping into another, shall, in consequence of any law or regulation therein, be discharged from such service or labor, but shall be delivered up on the claim of the party to whom such labor or service is due." Unless you consider the ten miles square as a state, persons bound to labor, who shall escape thither, will not be given up; for they are only to be delivered up after they shall have escaped into a state. As my honorable friend mentioned, felons, who shall have fled from justice to the ten miles square, cannot be apprehended. The executive of a state is to apply to that of another for the delivery of a felon. He cannot apply to the ten miles square. It was often in contemplation of Congress to have power of regulating the police of the seat of government; but they never had an idea of exclusive legislation in all cases. The power of regulating the police and good government of it will secure Congress against insults.

What originated the idea of the exclusive legislation was, some insurrection in Pennsylvania, whereby Congress was insulted, on account of which, it is supposed, they left the state. It is answered that the consent of the state must be required, or else they cannot have such a district, or places for the erecting of forts, &c. But how much is already given them!

Look at the great country to the north-west of the Ohio, extending to and commanding the lakes. Look at the other end of the Ohio, towards South Carolina, extending to the Mississippi. See what these, in process of time, may amount to. They may grant exclusive privileges to any particular part of which they have the possession. But it may be observed that those extensive countries will be formed into independent states, and that their consent will be necessary. They may grant privileges in that country that are already granted to Congress by the states. The grants of Virginia, South Carolina, and other states, will be subservient to Congress in this respect. Of course, it results from the whole, that requiring the consent of the states will be no guard against this abuse of power.

[A desultory conversation ensued.]

Mr. Nicholas: Insisted that as the state within which the ten miles square might be, could prescribe the terms on which Congress should hold it, no danger could arise, as no state would consent to injure itself; there was the same security with respect to the places purchased for the erection of forts, magazines & C.; and as to the territory of the United States, the power of Congress only extended to make needful rules and regulations concerning it, without prejudicing the claim of any particular state, the right of territory not being given up; that the grant of those lands to the United States was for the general benefit of all the states, and not to be perverted to their prejudice; that, consequently, whether that country were formed into new states or not, the danger apprehended could not take place; that the seat of government was to be still a part of the state and as to general regulations, was to be considered as such.

William Grayson: still June 16, 1788

They were not removed, but rather confirmed, by the remarks of the honorable gentleman, in saying that it was extremely improbable that the members from New Hampshire and Georgia would go and legislate exclusively for the ten miles square.

If it was so improbable, why ask the power? Why demand a power which was not to be exercised? Compare this power, says he, with the next clause, which gives them power to make all laws which shall be necessary to carry their laws into execution. By this they have a right to pass any law that may facilitate the execution of their acts. They have a right, by this clause, to make a law that such a district shall be set apart for any purpose they please, and that any man who shall act contrary to their commands, within a certain ten miles square, or any place they may select, and strongholds, shall be hanged without benefit of clergy.

If they think any law necessary for their personal safety, after perpetrating the most tyrannical and oppressive deeds, cannot they make it by this sweeping clause? If it be necessary to provide, not only for this, but for any department or officer of Congress, does not this clause enable them to make a law for the purpose? And will not these laws, made for those purposes, be paramount to the laws of the states? Will not this clause give them a right to keep a powerful army continually on foot, if they think it necessary to aid the execution of their laws? Is there any act, however atrocious, which they cannot do by virtue of this clause?

Look at the use which has been in all parts of the world, of that human thing called power. Look at the predominant thirst of dominion which had invariably and uniformly prompted rulers to abuse their powers. Can you say that you will be safe when you give such unlimited powers without any real responsibility? Will you be safe when you trust men in Philadelphia with power to make any law that will enable them to carry their acts into execution? Will not the members of Congress have the same passions which other rulers have had? They will not be superior to the frailties of human nature, however cautious you may be in the selection of your representatives, it will be dangerous to trust them with such unbounded powers. Shall we be told, when about to grant such illimitable authority, that it will never be exercised! 1 conjure you once more to remember the admonition of that sage man who told you that, when you give power, you know not what you give. I know the absolute necessity of an energetic government. But is it consistent with any principle of prudence or good policy to grant unlimited, unbounded authority, which is so totally unnecessary that gentlemen say it will never be exercised?

But gentlemen say that we must experiment. A wonderful and unheard-of experiment it will be, to give unlimited power unnecessarily! I admit my inferiority in point of historical knowledge. I believe no man can produce an instance of an unnecessary and unlimited power, given to a body independent of the legislature, within a particular district.

Let any man in this Convention show me an instance of such separate and different powers of legislation in the same country show me an instance where a part of the community is independent of the whole. The people within that place, and the strongholds, may be excused from the burdens imposed on the rest of the society, and may enjoy exclusive emoluments, to the great injury of the rest of the people.

But gentlemen say that the power will not be abused. They ought to show that it is necessary. All their powers may be fully carried into execution, without this exclusive authority in the ten miles square. The sweeping clause will fully enable them to do what they please. What can the most extravagant and boundless imagination ask, but power to do every thing? I have reason to suspect ambitious grasps at power.

The experience of the world teaches me the jeopardy of giving enormous power. Strike this clause out of the government, and how will it stand? Congress will still have power, by the sweeping clause, to make laws within that place and the strongholds, independently of the local authority of the state. I ask you, if this clause be struck out, whether the sweeping clause will not enable them to protect themselves from insult. If you grant them these powers, you destroy every degree of responsibility. They will fully redeem themselves from justice, and preclude the possibility of punishing them.

No instance can be given of such a wanton grasp of power as an exclusive legislation, in all cases whatever.

James Madison: June 16, 1788, Mr. Chairman, I am astonished that the honorable member should launch out into such strong descriptions without any occasion. Was there ever a legislature in existence that held their sessions at a place where they had not jurisdiction? I do not mean such a legislature as they have in Holland; for it deserves not the name. Their powers are such as Congress have now, which we find not reducible to practice.

If you be satisfied with the shadow and form, instead of the substance, you will render them dependent on the local authority.

Suppose the legislature of this country should sit in Richmond, while the exclusive jurisdiction of the place was in some particular county; would this country think it safe that the general good should be subject to the paramount authority of a part of the community?

The honorable member asks, Why ask for this power, and if the subsequent clause be not fully competent for the same purpose? If so, what new terrors can arise from this particular clause? It is only a superfluity. If that latitude of construction which he contends were to take place with respect to the sweeping clause, there would be room for those horrors, but it gives no supplementary power. It only enables them to execute the delegated powers. If the delegation of their powers be safe, no possible inconvenience can arise from this clause. It is at most but explanatory. For when any power is given, its delegation necessarily involves authority to make laws to execute it. Were it possible to delineate on paper all those particular cases and circumstances in which legislation by the general legislature would be necessary, and leave to the states all the other powers, I imagine no gentleman would object to it. But this is not within the limits of human capacity.

The particular powers which are necessary to be given are therefore delegated generally, and particular and minute specification is left to the legislature. [Here Mr. Madison spoke of the distinction between regulation of police and legislation, but he could not be heard.] When the honorable member objects to giving the general government jurisdiction over the place of their session, does he mean that it should be under the control of any particular state, that might, at a critical moment, seize it? I should have thought that this clause would have met with the most cordial approbation. As the consent of the state in which it may be, must be obtained, and as it may stipulate the terms of the grant, should they violate the particular stipulations it would be an usurpation; so that, if the members of Congress were to be guided by the laws of their country, none of those dangers could arise.

[Mr. Madison made several other remarks, which could not be heard] He was obviously grumbling and did not intend to be heard outloud.

Patrick Henry: June 16, 1788, Congress is vested with supreme power of legislation, paramount to the Constitution and laws of the states, the dangers described might happen; for Congress would not be confined to enumerated powers. This construction was warranted, in his opinion, by the addition of the word department, in the clause, and that they could make any laws which they thought necessary in any departments or office in the government.

George Pendleton: Mr. Chairman, this clause does not give Congress power to impede the operation of any part of the Constitution, or to make any regulation that may affect the interests of the citizens of the Union at large. But it gives them power over the local police of the place, so as to be secured from any interruption in their proceedings. Not withstanding the violent attack upon it. I believe, sir, this is the fair construction of the clause. It gives them power of exclusive legislation in any case within that district. What is the meaning of this? What is it opposed to? Is it opposed to the general powers of the federal legislature, or to those of the state legislatures? I understand it as opposed to the legislative power of that state where it shall be. What, then, is the power? It is, that Congress shall exclusively legislate there, in order to preserve the police of the place and their own personal independence, that they may not be overawed or insulted, and of course to preserve them in opposition to any attempt by the state where it shall be. This is the fair construction.

Can we suppose that, in order to effect these salutary ends, Congress will make it an asylum for villains and the vilest characters from all parts of the world? Will it not degrade their own dignity to make it a sanctuary for villains? I hope that no man that will ever compose that Congress will associate with the most profligate characters.

Why oppose this power? Suppose it was contrary to the sense of their constituents to grant exclusive privileges to citizens residing within that place; the effect would be directly in opposition to what he says.

It could have no operation without the limits of that district. Were Congress to make a law granting them an exclusive privilege of trading to the East Indies, it could have no effect the moment it would go without that place; for their exclusive power is confined to that district.

Were they to pass such a law, it would be nugatory; and every member of the community at large could trade to the East Indies as well as the citizens of that district.

This exclusive power is limited to that place solely, for their own preservation, which all gentlemen allow to be necessary. Will you pardon me when I observe that their construction of the preceding clause does not appear to me to be natural, or warranted by the words. They say that the state governments have no power at all over the militia.

The power of the general government to provide for arming and organizing the militia is to introduce a uniform system of discipline to the United States of America. But the power of governing the militia, so far as it is in Congress, extends only to such parts of them as may be employed in the service of the United States. When not in their service, Congress has no power to govern them. The states then have the sole government of them; and though Congress may provide for arming them, and prescribe the mode of discipline, yet the states have the authority of training them, according to the uniform discipline prescribed by Congress, But there is nothing to preclude them from arming and disciplining them, should Congress neglect to, do it. As to calling the militia to execute the laws of the Union, I think the fair construction is directly opposite to what the honorable member says. The 4th section of the 4th article (Republican Government) contains nothing to warrant the supposition that the states cannot call them forth to suppress domestic insurrections. [Here he read the section.] All the restraint here contained is, that Congress may, at their pleasure, on application of the state legislature, or (in vacation) of the executive, protect each of the states against domestic violence. This is a restraint on the general government not to interpose.

The state is in full possession of the power of using its own militia to protect itself against domestic violence; and the power in the general government cannot be exercised, or interposed, without the application of the state a single step beyond the delegated powers. What can it act upon? Some power given by this Constitution. If they should be about to pass a law in consequence of this clause, they must pursue some of the delegated powers, but can by no means depart from them, or arrogate any new powers; for the plain language of the clause is, to give them power to pass laws in order to give effect to the delegated powers.

George Mason: June 16, 1788,
Mr. Chairman, gentlemen say there is no new power given by this clause. Is there any thing in this Constitution which secures to the states the powers which are said to be retained? Will powers remain to the states which are not expressly guarded and reserved?

I will suppose a case. Gentlemen may call it for the general welfare, and under their own construction, say that this was destroying the general peace, encouraging sedition, and poisoning the minds of the people?

And could they not, in order to provide against this, lay a dangerous restriction on the press? Might they not even bring the trial of this restriction within the ten miles square, when there is no prohibition against it? Might they not thus destroy the trial by jury? Would they not extend their implication? It appears to me that they may and will. And shall the support of our rights depend on the bounty of men whose interest it may be to oppress us? That Congress should have power to provide for the general welfare of the Union, I grant. But I wish a clause in the Constitution, with respect to all powers which are not granted, that they are retained by the states. Otherwise, the power of providing for the general welfare may be perverted to its destruction. Many gentlemen, whom I respect, take different sides of this question. We wish this amendment to be introduced, to remove apprehensions. The Confederation reserved for the states every power, jurisdiction, and right, not expressly delegated to the United States.

This clause has never been complained of, but approved by all. Why not, then, have a similar clause in this Constitution, in which it is the more indispensably necessary than in the Confederation, because of the great augmentation of power vested in the former? In my humble apprehension, unless there be some such clear and finite expression, this clause now under consideration will go to any thing our rulers may think proper. Unless there be some express declaration that every thing not given is retained, it will be carried to any power Congress may please.

Patrick Henry: On June 16, 1788, moved to read from the 8th to 13th Articles of the Declaration of Rights.

George Nicholas: In reply to the gentlemen opposed to the clause under debate, went over the same grounds, and developed the same principles, which Mr. Pendleton and Mr. Madison had done. The opposers of the clause, which gave the power of providing for the general welfare, supposed its dangers to result from its connection with, and extension of the powers granted in the other clauses.

He endeavored to show the committee that it only empowered Congress to make such laws as would be necessary to enable them to pay the public debts and provide for the common defense; that this general welfare was united, not to the general power of legislation, but to the particular power of laying and collecting taxes, imposts, and excises, for the purpose of paying the debts and providing for the common defense-that is, that they could raise as much money as would pay the debts and provide for the common defense, in consequence of this power.

The clause which was affectedly called the sweeping clause contained no new grant of power. To illustrate this position, he observed that, if it had been added at the end of every one of the enumerated powers, instead of being inserted at the end of all, it would be obvious to any one that it was no augmentation of power.

If, for instance, at the end of the clause granting power to lay and collect taxes, who could suspect it to be an addition of power? As it would grant no new power if inserted at the end of each clause, it could not when subjoined to the whole. He then proceeded thus: But, says he, who is to determine the extent of such powers? I say, the same power which, in all well-regulated communities, determines the extent of legislative powers. If they exceed these powers, the judiciary will declare it void, or the people will have a right to declare it void. Is this dependent on any man? The gentleman says it may destroy trial by jury; and they may say it is necessary for providing for the general defense.

The power of providing for the general defense only extends to raise any sum of money they may think necessary, by taxes, imposts, &c. But, says he, our only defense against oppressive laws consists in the virtue of our: representatives. This was misrepresented. If I understand it right, no new power can be exercised. As to those which are actually granted, we trust to the fellow-feelings of our representatives; and if we are deceived, we then trust to altering our government. It appears to me, however, that we can confide in their discharging their powers rightly, from the peculiarity of their situation, and connection with us. If, sir, the powers of the former Congress were very inconsiderable, that body did not deserve to have great powers. It was constructed that it would be dangerous to invest it with such.

But why were the articles of the bill of rights read? Let him show us that those rights are given by the Constitution. Let him prove them to be violated. He tells us that the most worthy characters of the country differ as to the necessity of a bill of rights, It is a simple and plain proposition.

It is agreed upon by all that the people have all the power.

If they part with any of it, is it necessary to declare that they hold the rest Liken it to any similar case. If I have one thousand acres of land and I grant five hundred acres of it, must I declare that I retain the other five hundred? Do I grant the whole thousand acres, when I grant five hundred, unless I declare that the five hundred I do not give belong to me still? It is so in this case. After granting some powers, the rest remain with the people.

Gov. Ed. Randolph: June 16, 1788, Had some objections to the clause. He was persuaded that the construction put upon it by gentlemen, on both sides, was erroneous; but thought construction better than anarchy.

Mr. George Mason: still thought that there ought to be some express declaration in the Constitution, asserting that rights not given to the general government were retained by the states.

He apprehended that, if this was not done, many valuable and important rights would be concluded to be given up by implication. All governments were drawn from the people, though many were perverted to their oppression. The government of Virginia, he remarked, was drawn from the people; yet there were certain great and important rights, which the people, by their bill of rights, declared to be paramount to the power of the legislature. He asked, Why should it not be so in this Constitution? Was it because we were more substantially represented in it than in the state government? If, in the state government, where the people were substantially and fully represented, it was necessary that the great rights of human nature should be secure from the encroachments of the legislature, he asked if it was not more necessary in this government, where they were but inadequately represented. He declared that artful sophistry and evasions could not satisfy him. He could see no clear distinction between rights relinquished by a positive grant, and lost by implication. **Unless there were a bill of rights, implication might swallow up all our rights.**

Patrick Henry:
Mr. Chairman, the necessity of a bill of rights appears to me to be greater in this government than ever it was in any government before. I have

observed already, that the sense of the European nations, and particularly Great Britain, is against the construction of rights being retained which are not expressly relinquished.

I repeat, that all nations have adopted this construction, that all rights not expressly and unequivocally reserved to the people are implied and incidentally relinquished to rulers, as necessarily inseparable from the delegated powers. It is so in Great Britain; for every possible right, which is not reserved to the people by some express provision or compact, is within the king's prerogative. In that country which is said to be in such full possession of freedom. It is so in Spain, Germany, and other parts of the world.

Let us consider the sentiments which have been entertained by the people of America on this subject. At the revolution, it must be admitted that it was their sense to set down those great rights which ought, in all countries, to be held indivisible and sacred. Virginia did so, we all remember. She made a compact to expressly reserve, certain rights.

When fortified with full, adequate, and abundant representation, was she satisfied with that representation? No, she most cautiously and guardedly reserved and secured those invaluable, inestimable rights and privileges, which no people, inspired with the least glow of patriotic liberty, ever did, or ever can, abandon.

She is called upon now to abandon them, and dissolve that compact which secured them to her. She is called upon to accede to another compact, which most infallibly supersedes and annihilates her present one. Will she do it? This is the question.

If you intend to reserve your unalienable rights, you must have the most express stipulation; for, if implication be allowed, you are ousted of those rights. If the people do not think it necessary to reserve them, they will be supposed to be given up. How were the congressional rights defined when the people of America united by a confederacy to defend their liberties and rights against the tyrannical attempts of Great Britain? The states were not then contented with implied reservation. No, Mr. Chairman.

It was expressly declared in our Confederation that every right was retained by the states, respectively, which was not given up to the government of the U.S. But there is no such thing here. You, therefore, by a natural and unavoidable implication, give up your rights to the general government. Your own example furnishes an argument against it.

If you give up these powers, without a bill of rights, you will exhibit the most absurd thing that ever the world saw, a government that has abandoned all its powers - the powers of direct taxation, the sword, and the purse. You have disposed of them to Congress, without a bill of rights - without check, limitation, or control. And still you have checks and guards; still you keep barriers pointed where? Pointed against your weakened, prostrated, enervated state government!

You have a bill of rights to defend you against the state government, which is bereaved of all power, and yet you have none against Congress, though in full and exclusive possession of all power!

You arm yourselves against the weak and defenseless, and expose yourselves naked to the armed and powerful.

Is not this a conduct of unexampled absurdity? What barriers do you propose to this most strong, energetic government? To that government you have nothing to oppose. All your defense is given up. This is a real, actual defect. It must strike the mind of every gentleman. When our government was first instituted in Virginia, we declared the common law of England to be in force. That system of law which has been admired, and has protected us and our ancestors, is excluded by that system. **Added to this, we adopted a bill of rights**.

By this Constitution, some of the best barriers of human rights are thrown away. Is there not an additional reason to have a bill of rights? By the ancient common law, the trial of all facts is decided by a jury of impartial men from the immediate vicinage. **This paper speaks of different juries from the common law in criminal cases; and in civil controversies excludes trial by jury altogether**. There is, therefore, more occasion for the supplementary check of a bill of rights now than then. Congress, from their general, powers, may fully go into the business of human legislation. They may legislate, in criminal cases, from treason to the lowest offence-petty larceny. They may define crimes and prescribe punishments. In the definition of crimes, I trust they will be directed by what wise representatives ought to be governed by.

But when we come to punishments, no latitude ought to be left, nor dependence put on the virtue of representatives. What says our bill of rights? "That excessive bail ought not to be required, nor excessive fines imposed, nor cruel and unusual punishments inflicted," Are you not, calling on those gentlemen who are to compose Congress, to prescribe trials and define punishments without this control?

Will they find sentiments here similar to this bill of rights? You let them loose; you do more you depart from the genius of your country.

What paper tells you that the trial of crimes shall be by jury, and held in the state where the crime shall have been committed.

Under this extensive provision, they may proceed in a manner extremely dangerous to liberty: a person accused may be carried from one extremity of the state to another, and be tried, not by an impartial jury of the vicinage, acquainted with his character and the circumstances of the fact, but by a jury unacquainted with both, and who may be biased against him. Is not this sufficient to alarm men?

How different is this from the immemorial practice of your British ancestors, and your own! I need not tell you that, by the common law, a number of hundreds were required on a jury, and that afterwards it was sufficient if the jurors came from the same county. With less than this the people of England have never been satisfied.

That paper ought to have declared the common law in force. In this business of legislation, Congress will loose the restriction of not imposing excessive fines, demanding excessive bail, and inflicting cruel and unusual punishments. These are prohibited by your declaration of rights.

What has distinguished our ancestors? - That they would not admit of tortures, or cruel and barbarous punishment. But Congress may introduce the practice of the civil law, in preference to that of the common law. They may introduce the practice of France, Spain, and Germany of torture. They will say that they might as well draw examples from those countries as from Great Britain, and they will tell you that there is such a necessity of strengthening the arm of government, that they must have a criminal equity, and extort confession by torture, in order to punish with still more relentless severity. We are then lost and undone. And can any man think it troublesome, when we can, by a small interference, prevents our rights from being lost? If you will, like the Virginian government, give them knowledge of the extent of the rights retained by the people, and the powers of themselves, they will, if they be honest men, thank you for it. Will they not wish to go on sure grounds? But if you leave them otherwise, they will not know how to proceed; and, being in a state of uncertainty, they will assume rather than give up powers by implication.

A bill of rights may be summed up in a few words. What do they tell us? That our rights are reserved. Why not say so? Is it because it will consume too much paper? Gentlemen's reasoning against a bill of rights does not satisfy me. Without saying which has the right side, it remains doubtful. A bill of rights is favored by Virginians and the people of the other states.

It may be their prejudice, but the government ought to suit their geniuses;

otherwise, its operation will be unhappy. A bill of rights, even if its necessity be doubtful, will exclude the possibility of dispute; and, with great submission, I think the best way is to have no dispute.

In the present Constitution, they are restrained from issuing general warrants to search suspected places, or seize persons not named, without evidence of the commission of a fact, & c. There was certainly some celestial influence governing those who deliberated on that Constitution; for they have, with the most cautious and enlightened circumspection, guarded those indefeasible rights which ought ever to be held sacred!

The officers of Congress may come upon you now, fortified with all the terrors of paramount federal authority. Excisemen may come in multitudes; for the limitation of their numbers no man knows.

They may, unless the general government be restrained by a bill of rights, or some similar restriction, go into your cellars and rooms, and search, ransack, and measure, every thing you eat, drink, and wear.

They ought to be restrained within proper bounds. With respect to the freedom of the press, I need say nothing; for it is hoped that the gentlemen who shall compose Congress will take care to infringe as little as possible the rights of human nature. This will result from their integrity.

They should, from prudence, abstain from violating the rights of their constituents. They are not, however, expressly restrained. But whether they will intermeddle with that palladium of our liberties or not, I leave you to determine.

As if by pre-decision, Patrick Henry sat down and Grayson stood up.

William Grayson: June 16,1788

Thought it questionable whether rights not given up were reserved. A majority of the states, he observed, had expressly reserved certain important rights by bills of rights, and that in the Confederation there was a clause declaring expressly that every power and right not given up was retained by the states. It was the general sense of America that such a clause was necessary; otherwise, why did they introduce a clause which was totally unnecessary? It had been insisted, he said, in many parts of America, that a bill of rights was only necessary between a prince and his people, and not in such a government as this, which was a compact between the people themselves. This did not satisfy his mind; for so extensive was the power of legislation, in his estimation, that he doubted whether, when it was once given up, anything was retained. He further remarked, that there were some negative clauses in the Constitution, which refuted the doctrine contended for by the other side. For instance; the 2 d clause of the 9th section of the 1st article provided that "the privilege of the writ of habeas corpus shall not be suspended, unless when, in cases of rebellion or invasion, the public safety may require it. "And, by the last clause of the same section, "no title of nobility shall be granted by the United States. "Now, if these restrictions had not been here inserted, he asked whether Congress would not most clearly have had a right to suspend that great and valuable right, and to grant titles of nobility.

When, in addition to these considerations, he saw they had an indefinite power to provide for the general welfare, he thought there were great reasons to apprehend, therefore *that there ought to be a bill of rights.*

George Nicholas: June 16, 1788,

In answer to the two gentlemen last up, observed that, though there was a declaration of rights in the government of Virginia, it was no conclusive reason that there should be one in this Constitution; for, if it was unnecessary in the former, its omission in the latter could be no defect.

They ought, therefore, to prove that it was essentially necessary to be inserted in the Constitution of Virginia. There were five or six states in the Union which had no bill of rights, separately and distinctly as such; but they annexed the substance of a bill of rights to their respective constitutions. These states, he further observed, were as free as this state, and their liberties as secure as ours. If so, gentlemen's arguments from the precedent were not good. In Virginia, all powers were given to the government without any exception. It was different in the general government, to which certain special powers were delegated for certain purposes. He asked which was the more safe. Was it safer to grant general powers than certain limited powers? This much as to the theory.

What is the practice of this invaluable government? Have your citizens been bound by it? They have not, sir. You have violated that maxim, "that no man shall be condemned without a fair trial."

That man who was killed, not secundum artem, was deprived of his life without the benefit of law, and in express violation of this declaration of rights, which they confide in so much.

But, sir, this bill of rights was no security, It is but a paper check. It has been violated in many other instances. Therefore, from theory and practice, it may be concluded that this government, with special powers, without any express exceptions, is better than a government with general powers and special exceptions. But the practice of England is against us. The rights there reserved to the people are to limit and check the king's prerogative. It is easier to enumerate the exceptions to his prerogative, than to mention all the cases to which it extends. Besides, these reservations, being only formed in acts of the legislature, may be altered by the representatives of the people when they think proper. No comparison can be made of this with the other governments he mentioned. There is no stipulation between the king and the people.

The former is possessed of absolute, unlimited authority. But, sir, this Constitution is defective because the common law is not declared to be in force! What would have been the consequence if it had? It would be immutable. But now it can be changed or modified as the legislative body may find necessary for the community.

But the common law is not excluded. There is nothing in that paper to warrant the assertion. As to the exclusion of a jury from the vicinage, he has mistaken the fact. The legislature may direct a jury to come from the vicinage. But the gentleman says that, by this Constitution, they have power to make laws to define crimes and prescribe punishments; and that, consequently, we are not free from torture.

Treason against the United States is defined in the Constitution, and the forfeiture limited to the life of the person attainted. Congress have power to define and punish piracies and felonies committed on the high seas, and offenses against the laws of nations; but they cannot define or prescribe the punishment of any other crime whatever, without violating the Constitution. If we had no security against torture but our declaration of rights, we might be tortured tomorrow; for it has been repeatedly infringed and disregarded. A bill of rights is only an acknowledgment of the preexisting claim to rights of the people. They belong to us as much as if they had been inserted in the Constitution.

But it is said that, if it be doubtful, the possibility of dispute ought to be precluded. Admitting it was proper for the Convention to have inserted a bill of rights, it is not proper here to propose it as the condition of our accession to the Union. Would you reject this government for its omission, dissolve the Union, and bring miseries on yourselves and posterity?

I hope the gentleman does not oppose it on this ground solely. Is there another reason? He said that it is not only the general wish of this state, but all the states, to have a bill of rights. If it be so, where is the difficulty of having this done by way of subsequent amendment? We shall find the states willing to accord with their own favorite wish. The gentleman last up says that the power of legislation includes every thing a general power of legislation does. This is a special power of legislation. Therefore, it does not contain that plenitude of power which he imagines. They cannot legislate in any case but those particularly enumerated. No gentleman, who is a friend to the government, ought to withhold his assent for this reason.

George Mason: June 16, 1788, replied that the worthy gentleman was mistaken in his assertion that the bill of rights did not prohibit torture; for that clause expressly provided that no man can give evidence against himself; and the worthy gentleman must know that, in those countries where torture is used, evidence was extorted from the criminal himself. Another clause of the bill of rights provided that no cruel and unusual punishments shall be inflicted; therefore, torture was included in the prohibition.

George Nicholas: acknowledged the bill of rights to contain that prohibition; that the gentleman was right with respect to the practice of extorting confession from the criminal in those countries where torture is used; but still he saw no security arising from the bill of rights as separate from the Constitution, for that it had been frequently violated with impunity.

There is another provision against the danger, mentioned by the honorable member, of the President receiving emoluments from foreign powers.

If discovered, he may be impeached. If he be not impeached, he may be displaced at the end of the four years. By the 9th section of the 1st article, "no person, holding an office of profit or trust, shall accept any present or emolument whatever, from any foreign power, without the consent of the representatives of the people;" and by the Ist section of the 2d article, his compensation is neither to be increased nor diminished during the time for which he shall have been elected; and he shall not, during that period, receive any emolument from the United States or any of them. I consider, therefore, that he is restrained from receiving any present or emolument whatever. It is impossible to guard better against corruption. The honorable member seems to think that he may hold his office without being re-elected. He cannot hold it over four years, unless he be reelected, any more than if he were prohibited. As to forwarding and transmitting the certificates of the electors, I think the regulation as good as could be provided.

George Mason: June 16, 1788, Mr. Chairman, the Vice President appears to me to be not only an unnecessary but dangerous officer.

He is, contrary to the usual course of parliamentary proceedings, to be president of the Senate. The state from which he comes may have two votes, when the others will have but one. Besides, the legislative and executive are hereby mixed and incorporated together.

I cannot, at this distance of time, foresee the consequences; but I think that, in the course of human affairs, he will be made a tool of in order to bring about his own interest, and aid in overturning the liberties of his country. There is another part which I disapprove of, but which perhaps I do not understand. "In case of removal of the President from office, or of his death, resignation, or inability to discharge the powers and duties of the said office, the same shall devolve on the Vice-President; and the Congress may by law provide for the case of removal, death, resignation, or inability, both of the President and Vice-President, declaring what officer shall then act as President, and such officer shall act accordingly, until the disability be removed, or a President shall be elected."

The power of Congress is right and proper so far as it enables them to provide what officer shall act, in case both the President and Vice-President be dead or disabled. But gentlemen ought to take notice that the election of this officer is only for four years. There is no provision for a speedy election of another President, when the former is dead or removed. The influence of the Vice President may prevent the election of the President. Perhaps I may be mistaken.

James Madison: Mr. Chairman, I think there are some peculiar advantages incident to this office, which recommend it to us. There is, in the first place, a great probability this officer will be taken from one of the largest states; and, if so, the circumstance of his having an eventual vote will be so far favorable. The consideration which recommends it to me is, that he will be the choice of the people at large.

There are to be ninety-one electors, each of whom has two votes: if he have one fourth of the whole number of votes, he is elected V. President. There is much more propriety in giving this office to a person chosen by the people at large, than to one of the Senate, who is only the choice of the legislature of one state. His eventual vote is an advantage too obvious to comment upon. I differ from the honorable member in the case which enables Congress to make a temporary appointment. When the President and Vice President die, the election of another President will immediately take place; and suppose it would not, all that Congress could do would be to make an appointment between the expiration of the four years and the last election, and to continue only to such expiration. This can rarely happen. This power continues the government in motion, and is well guarded.

June 17, 1788, Tuesday
ARTICLE 1, SECTION 9, CLAUSE 1, Limits of Legislative Power in Congress. William Grayson was not present. He was likely ill with gout. Stress did not help his condition and there was plentiful stress.

Testimonies are given in full. The topic is slavery.

George Mason: Mr. Chairman, this is a fatal section, which has created more dangers than any other. The first clause allows the importation of slaves for twenty years. Under the royal government, this evil was looked upon as a great oppression, and many attempts were made to prevent it; but the interest of the African merchants prevented its prohibition.

No sooner did the revolution take place, than it was thought of. It was one of the great causes of our separation from Great Britain. Its exclusion has been a principal object of this state, and most of the states in the Union.

The augmentation of slaves weakens the states; and such a trade is diabolical in itself, and disgraceful to mankind; yet, by this Constitution, it is continued for twenty years. As much as I value a union of all the states, I would not admit the Southern States into the Union unless they agree to the discontinuance of this disgraceful trade, because it would bring weakness, and not strength, to the Union. And, though this infamous traffic be continued, we have no security for the property of that kind which we have already. There is no clause in this Constitution to secure it; for they may lay such a tax as will amount to manumission. And should the government be amended, still this detestable kind of commerce cannot be discontinued till after the expiration of twenty years; for the 5th article, which provides for amendments, expressly excepts this clause. I have ever looked upon this as a most disgraceful thing to America. I cannot express my detestation of it. Yet they have not secured us the property of the slaves we have already. So that "they have done what they ought not to have done, and have left undone what they ought to have done."

James Madison: June 17, 1788,

Mr. Chairman, I should conceive this clause to be impolitic, if it were one of those things which could be excluded without encountering greater evils.

The Southern States would not have entered into the Union of America without the temporary permission of that trade; and if they were excluded from the Union, the consequences might be dreadful to them and to us.

The Union in general is not in a worse situation. That traffic is prohibited by our laws, and we may continue the prohibition.

Under the Articles of Confederation, it might be continued forever; but, by this clause, an end may be put to it after twenty years. There is, therefore, an amelioration of our circumstances.

A tax may be laid in the mean time; but it is limited; otherwise Congress might lay such a tax as would amount to a prohibition.

From the mode of representation and taxation, Congress cannot lay such a tax on slaves as will amount to manumission. Another clause secures us that property which we now possess.

At present, if any slave elopes to any of those states where slaves are free, he becomes emancipated by their laws; for the laws of the states are uncharitable to one another in this respect.

But in this Constitution, "no person held to service or labor in one state, under the laws thereof, escaping into another, shall, in consequence of any law or regulation therein, be discharged from such service or labor; but shall be delivered up in claim of the party to whom such service or labor shall be due." This clause was expressly inserted, to enable owners of slaves to reclaim them. This is a better security than any that now exists. No power is given to the general government to interpose with respect to the property in slaves now held by the states. Taxation is explicit on this subject. Great as the evil is, a dismemberment of the Union would be worse. If those states should disunite from the other states for not indulging them in the temporary continuance of this traffic, they might solicit and obtain aid from foreign powers.

John Tyler: June 17, 1788 (This John Tyler would father a president.)
Warmly enlarged on the impolitic, iniquity, and disgracefulness of the wickedness of slave trafficing. He thought the reasons urged by gentlemen in defense of it were inconclusive and ill founded. It was one cause of the complaints against British tyranny, that this trade was permitted.

The revolution had put a period to it; but now it was to be revived. He thought nothing justify it. This temporary restriction on Congress militant in his opinion, against the arguments of gentlemen on the other side, that what was not given up was retained by the states; for that, if this restriction had not been inserted.

Congress could have prohibited the African trade, The power of prohibiting it was not expressly delegated to them; yet they would have had it by implication, if this restraint had not been provided. This seemed to him to demonstrate most clearly the necessity of restraining them, by a bill of rights, from infringing our unalienable rights.

It was immaterial whether the bill of rights was by itself, or included in the Constitution. But he contended for it one way or the other. It would be justified by our own example and that of England. His earnest desire was, that it should be handed down to posterity that he had opposed this wicked clause. He then adverted to the clauses which enabled Congress to legislate exclusively in the ten miles square, and other places purchased for forts, magazines, &c., to provide for the general welfare, to raise a standing army, and to make any law that may be necessary to carry their laws into execution. From the combined operation of these unlimited powers he dreaded the most fatal consequences. If any acts of violence, should be committed on persons or property, the perpetrators of such acts might take refuge in the sanctuary of the ten miles square and the strongholds. They would thus escape impunity, as the states had no power to punish them. He called to the recollection of the committee the history of the Athenian who, from small beginnings, had enslaved his country. He begged them to remember that Caesar, who prostrated the liberties of his country, did not possess a powerful army at first. Suppose, says he, that a king should be proposed by Congress. Will they not be able, by the sweeping clause, to call in foreign assistance, and raise troops, and do whatever they think proper to carry this proposition into effect? He then concluded that, unless this clause were expunged, he would vote against the Constitution.

ARTICLE 1, SECTION 9, CLAUSES 2 3 & 4,
Presidential Power, State of the Union, Receive ambassadors, Laws Faithfully Executed, Commission Officers, Impeachment

James Madison Was surprised that any gentleman should return to the clauses which had already been discussed. He begged the gentleman to read the clauses which gave the power of exclusive legislation, and he might see that nothing could be done without the consent of the states. With respect to the supposed operation of what was denominated the sweeping clause, the gentleman, he said, was mistaken; for it only extended to the enumerated powers. Should Congress attempt to extend it to any power not enumerated, it would not be warranted by the clause. As to the restriction in the clause under consideration, it was a restraint on the exercise of a power expressly delegated to Congress; namely, that of regulating commerce with foreign nations.

Patrick Henry: Insisted that the insertion of these restrictions on Congress was demonstrative that Congress could exercise powers by implication. The gentleman admitted that Congress could have interdicted the African Trade were it not for this restriction. If so, the power, not having been expressly delegated, must be obtained by implication.

He demanded where, then, was their doctrine of reserved rights. He wished for negative clauses to prevent them from assuming any powers but those expressly given. He asked why it was omitted to secure us that property in slaves which we held now. He feared its omission was done with design. They might lay such heavy taxes on slaves as would amount to emancipation; and then: the Southern States would be the only sufferers.

His opinion was confirmed by the mode of levying money. Congress, he observed, had power to lay and collect taxes, imposts, and excises. Imposts (or duties and excises were to be uniform; but this uniformity did not extend to taxes. This might compel the Southern States to liberate their Negroes. He wished this property, therefore, to be guarded. He considered the clause, which had been adduced by the gentleman as security for this property, as no security at all. It was no more than that a runaway Negro could be taken up in Maryland or New York. This could not prevent Congress from interfering with that property by laying a grievous, enormous tax, to compel owners to emancipate their slaves rather than pay taxes. He apprehended it would be productive of much stock-jobbing, and that they would play into one another's hands in such a manner to lose property for the country.

George Nicholas, June 17, 1788, Wondered that gentlemen who were against slavery should be opposed to this clause; as, after that period, the slave trade would be done away. He asked if gentlemen did not see the inconsistency of their arguments. They object, says he, to the Constitution, because the slave trade is laid open for twenty odd years; and yet they tell you that, by some latent operation of it, the slaves who are so now will be manumitted. At the same moment it is opposed for being primitive and destructive of slavery.

He contended that it was advantageous to Virginia that it should be in the power of Congress to prevent the importation of slaves after twenty years, as it would then put a period to the evil complained of. Because the Southern States would not confederate without this clause, he asked if gentlemen would rather dissolve the confederacy than to suffer this temporary inconvenience, admitting it to be such.

Virginia might continue the prohibition of such importation during the intermediate period, and would be benefited by it, as a tax of ten dollars on each slave might be laid, of which each would receive a share. He endeavored to obviate the objection of gentlemen, that the restriction on Congress was a proof that they would have powers not given them, by remarking, that they would only have had a general superintendency of trade, if the restriction had not been inserted. But the Southern States insisted on this exception to that general superintendency for twenty years. It could not, therefore, have been a power by implication, as the restriction was an exception from a delegated power.

The taxes could not, as had been suggested, be laid so high on Negroes as to amount to emancipation; because taxation and representation were fixed according to the census established in the Constitution. The exception of taxes from the uniformity annexed to duties and excises could not have the operation contended for by the gentleman, because other clauses had clearly and positively fixed the census. Had taxes been uniform, it would have been universally objected to; for no one object could be selected without involving great inconveniences and oppressions. But, says Mr. Nicholas, is it from the government we are to fear emancipation? Gentlemen will recollect what I said in another house, and what other gentlemen have said, that advocated emancipation. Give me leave to say, that clause is a great security for our slave tax.

I can tell the committee that the people of our country are reduced to beggary by the taxes on Negroes. Had this Constitution been adopted, it would not have been the case. The taxes were laid on all Negroes. By this system, two fifths are exempted.

He then added, that he had not imagined gentlemen would support here what they had opposed in another place.

Patrick Henry: June 17, 1788, Replied that, though the proportion of each was to be fixed by the census, and three fifths of slaves were included in the enumeration, yet Virginia's fixed proportion might be laid on blacks only; for the mode of raising the proportion of each state being directed by Congress, making slaves the sole object to raise it. Personalities had nothing to do with the question, which was whether the "paper" was wrong or not.

George Nicholas: Said that Negroes must be considered as persons or property. If as property, the proportion of taxes to be laid on them was fixed in the Constitution. He had apprehended a poll tax on Negroes, but the Constitution prevented it; by the census, where a white man paid ten shillings, a Negro paid but six shillings; for the exemption of two fifths of them reduced it to that proportion.

ARTICLE 1, SECTION 9, CLAUSES 2, 3 & 4.

George Mason: said, that gentlemen might think themselves secured by the restriction, in the 4th clause, that no capitation or other direct tax should be laid but in proportion to the census before directed to be taken; but that, when maturely considered, it would be found to be no security whatsoever. It was nothing but a direct assertion, or mere confirmation of the clause which fixed the ratio of taxes and representation. It only meant that the quantum to be raised of each state should be in proportion to their numbers, in the manner therein directed. But the general government was not precluded from laying the proportion of any particular state on any one species of property they might think proper.

For instance, if five hundred thousand dollars were to be raised, they might lay the whole of the proportion of the Southern States on the blacks, or any one species of property; so that, by laying taxes too heavily on slaves, they might totally annihilate that kind of property. No real security could arise from the clause which provides that persons held to labor in one state, escaping into another, shall be delivered up. This only meant that runaway slaves should not be protected in other states. As to the exclusion of *expost facto* laws, it could not be said to create my security in this case; for laying a tax on slaves would not be *ex post facto.*

James Madison: June 17, 1788,
Replied that even the Southern States, which were most affected, were perfectly satisfied with this provision, and dreaded no danger to the property they now hold. It appeared to him that the general government would not intermeddle with that property for twenty years, but to lay a tax on every slave imported not exceeding ten dollars; and that, after the expiration of that period, they might prohibit the traffic altogether.

The census in the Constitution was intended to introduce equality in the burdens to be laid on the community. No gentleman objected to laying duties, imposts, and excises, uniformly.

But uniformity of taxes would be subversive of the principles of equality; for it was not possible to select an article which would be easy for one state but heavy for another; that, the proportion of each state being ascertained, it would-be raised by the general government in the most convenient manner for the people, and not by the selection of any one particular object; that there must be some degree of confidence put in agents, or else we must reject a state of civil society altogether. Another great security to this property, which he mentioned, was, that five states were greatly interested in that species of property, and there were other states which had some slaves, and had made no attempt, or taken any step, to take them from the people. There were a few slaves in New York, New Jersey, and Connecticut: these states would, probably, oppose any attempt to annihilate this species of property. He concluded by observing that he should be glad to leave the decision to the committee.

George Mason: Apprehended the loose expression of "publication from time to time" was applicable to any time. It was equally applicable to monthly and septennial periods. It might be extended ever so much. The reason urged in favor of this ambiguous expression was, that there might be some matters which require secrecy. In matters relative to military operations and foreign negotiations, secrecy was necessary sometimes; but he did not conceive that the receipts and expenditures of the public money ought ever to be concealed.

The people, he affirmed, had a right to know the expenditures of their money; but that this expression was so loose, it might be concealed forever from them, and might afford opportunities to misapply public money, and shelter those who did it. He concluded it as exceptionable as any clause, in so few words, could be.

Richard Henry Lee (of Westmoreland): Though such trivial argument as that just used by the honorable gentleman would have no weight with the committee. He conceived the expression to be sufficiently explicit and satisfactory. It must be supposed to mean, in the common acceptation of language, short, convenient periods. It was as if it said one year, or a shorter term the Assembly was to meet next week, he hoped they would confine themselves to the investigation of the principal parts of the Constitution.

George Mason: June 17, 1788, Begged to be permitted to use that mode of arguing to which he was accustomed.

However desirous he was of pleasing the worthy gentleman, his duty would not allow that dubious pleasure.

George Nicholas: Said it was better direction and security than in state government. No appropriation shall be made of public money but by law. There can not be misapplication. He thought, instead of censure, it merited applause; being a cautious provision, which few Constitutions adopted.

Francis Corbin: concurred in the sentiments of Mr. Nicholas on this subject and did so succinctly.

James Madison: Thought it better than if a specific period was mentioned; because, if the accounts of the public receipts and expenditures were to be published at stated interludes, to be not so full and connected as would be necessary for a thorough comprehension of them, and a detection of errors.

By giving them an opportunity of publishing them from time to time, as might be found easy and convenient, they would more likely satisfy the public, if published frequently. He thought that this provision went farther than any Constitution of any state in the Union, or perhaps in the world.

George Mason: Replied, that, in the Confederation, the public proceedings were to be published monthly, which was infinitely better than depending on men's virtue to publish them or not, as they might please.

If there was no such provision in the Constitution of Virginia, gentlemen ought to consider the difference between such a full representation, dispersed and mingled with every part of the community, as the state representation was, and such an inadequate representation as this was.

One might be safely trusted, not the other.

James Madison: Replied, that the inconveniences which had been experienced from the Confederation, in that respect, had their weight with him in recommending this in preference for it was impossible, in such short intervals, to adjust the public accounts in any satisfactory manner.

ARTICLE 1, SECTION 9, CLAUSE 7, Limits of Legislative Power

Patrick Henry:
Mr. Chairman, we have now come to the 9th section, and I consider myself at liberty to take a short view of the whole. I wish to do it very briefly. Give me leave to remark that there is a bill of rights in that government.

There are express restrictions, which are in the shape of a bill of rights; but they bear the name of the 9th section. The design of the negative expressions in this section is to prescribe limits beyond which the powers of Congress shall not go. These are the sole bounds intended by the American government. Whereabouts do we stand with respect to a bill of rights? Examine it, and compare it to the idea manifested by the Virginian bill of rights, or that of the other states. The restraints in this congressional bill of rights are so feeble and few, that it would have been infinitely better to have said nothing about it.

The fair implication is, that they can do every thing they are not forbidden to do. What will be the result if Congress, in the course of their legislation, should do a thing not restrained by this 9th section? It will fall as an incidental power to Congress, not being prohibited expressly in the Constitution. The first prohibition is, that the privilege of the writ of habeas corpus shall not be suspended but when, in case of rebellion or invasion, the public safety may require it. It results clearly that, if it had not said so, they could suspend all cases whatsoever. It reverses the position of the friends of this Constitution, that every thing is retained which is not given up; for, instead every thing is given up which is not expressly reserved, It does not speak affirmatively, and say that it shall be suspended in those cases; but that it shall not be suspended but in certain cases; every thing not negatived shall remain with Congress. If the power remains with the people, how can Congress supply the want of an affirmative grant? They cannot do it but by implication, which destroys their doctrine.

The Virginia bill of rights interdicts the relinquishment of the sword and purse without control. That bill of rights secures the great and principal rights of mankind. But this bill of rights extends to but very few cases, and is destructive of the doctrine advanced by the friends of that paper. If **ex post facto** laws had not been interdicted, they might also have been extended by implication at pleasure.

Let us consider whether this restriction be founded in wisdom or good policy. If no *ex post facto* laws be made, what is to become of the old Continental paper dollars? Will not this country be forced to pay in gold and silver, shilling for shilling? Gentlemen may think that this does not deserve an answer. But it is an all-important question, because the property of this country is not commensurate to the enormous demand. Our own government triumphs, with infinite superiority, when put in contrast with that paper. The want of a bill of rights will render all their laws, however oppressive, constitutional.

If the government of Virginia passes a law in contradiction to our bill of rights, it is nugatory. By that paper the national wealth is to be disposed of under the veil of secrecy; for the publication from time to time will amount to nothing, and they may conceal what they may think requires secrecy. How different it is in your own government! Have not the people seen the journals of our legislature every day? Yet gentlemen say that the publication from time to time is a security unknown in our state government! a

How different it is in your own government! Have not the people seen the journals of our legislature every day during every session? Is not the lobby full of people every day? Yet gentlemen say that the publication from time to time is a security unknown in our state government! Such a regulation would be nugatory and vain, or at least needless, as the people see the journals of our legislature, and hear their debates, every day. If this be not more secure than what is in that paper, I will give up that I have totally misconceived the principles of the government. You are told that your rights are secured in this new government. They are guarded in no other part but this 9th section. The few restrictions in that section are your only safeguards. They may control your actions, and your very words, without being repugnant to that paper. The existence of your dearest privileges will depend on the consent of Congress, for they are not within the restrictions of the 9th section. If gentlemen think that searing the slave trade is a capital object; that the privilege of *the habeas corpus* is sufficiently secured; that the exclusion of *ex post facto* laws will produce no inconvenience; that the publication from time to time will secure their property; in one word, that this section alone will sufficiently secure their liberties.

I have spoken in vain. Every word of mine, and of my worthy coadjutor is lost, I trust that gentlemen, on this occasion, will see the great objects of religion, liberty of the press, trial by jury, interdiction of cruel punishments, and every other sacred right, secured, before they agree to that paper.

These most important human rights are not protected by that section, which is the only safeguard in the Constitution.

My mind will not be quieted till I see something substantial come forth in the shape of a bill of rights.

Gov. Edmund Randolph: June 17, 1788, Mr. Chairman, the general review which the gentleman has taken of the 9th is so inconsistent, that in order to answer him, I must, with your permission, who are the custodians of order here, depart from the rule of the house in some degree I declared, some days ago, that I would give my suffrage if the critical situation of our country demanded it. I invite those who think with me to vote for the Constitution. But where things occur in it which I disapprove of, I shall be candid in exposing my objections. Elementary power, only enables them to make laws to execute the delegated powers-or, in other words, that it only involves the powers incidental to those expressly delegated. By incidental powers they mean those which are necessary for the principal thing. That the incident is inseparable from the principal, is a maxim in the construction of laws.

A Constitution differs from a law; a law only, embraces one thing, a constitution embraces a number of things, and has a more liberal construction. I need not recur to the constitutions of Europe for a precedent to direct my explication of this.

The immediate explanation appears to me most rational. The former contend that it gives no supplementary power, but only enables them to make laws to execute the delegated powers or, in other words, that it only involves the powers incidental to those expressly delegated. By incidental powers they mean those which are necessary for the principal thing. That the incident is inseparable from the principal, is a maxim in the construction of laws. Constitution differs from a law; for a law only embraces one thing, but a constitution embraces a number of things, and is to have a more liberal construction. I need not recur to the constitutions of Europe for a precedent to direct my explication of this clause, because, in Europe, there is no constitution wholly in writing. The European constitutions sometimes consist in detached statutes or ordinances, sometimes they are on record, and sometimes they depend on immemorial tradition.

The American constitutions are singular, and their construction ought to be liberal. On this principle, what should be said of the clause under consideration? (The sweeping clause.) If incidental powers be those only which are necessary for the principal thing, the clause would be superfluous.

Let me say that, in my opinion, the adversaries of the Constitution wander equally from the true meaning. If it would not fatigue the house too far, I would go back to the question of reserved rights.

The gentleman supposes that complete and unlimited legislation is vested in the Congress of the United States. This supposition is founded on false reasoning. What is the present situation of this state? She has possession of all rights of sovereignty, except those given to the Confederation. She must delegate powers to the confederate government. It is necessary for her public happiness. Her weakness compels her to confederate with the twelve other governments. She trusts certain powers to the general government, in order to support, protect, and defend the Union.

Now, is there not a demonstrable difference between the principle of the state government and of the general government? There is not a word said, in the state government, of the powers given to it, because they are general. But in the general Constitution, its powers are enumerated.

Is it not, then, fairly deducible, that it has no power but what is expressly given for if its powers were to be general enumeration would be needless. But the insertion of negative restrictions has given cause of triumph, it seems, to gentlemen. They suppose that it demonstrates that Congress are to have powers by implication. I will meet them on that ground. I persuade myself that every exception here mentioned is an exception, not from general powers, but from the particular powers therein vested. To what power in the general government is the exception made respecting the importation of Negroes? Not from a general power, but from a particular power expressly enumerated. This is an exception from the power given them of regulating commerce.

He asks, Where is the power to which the prohibition of suspending the *habeas corpus* is an exception? I contend that, by virtue of the power given to Congress to regulate courts, they could suspend the writ of *habeas corpus*. (Habeas Corpus, which literally means "you have a body." It is a fundamental right under Anglo-American law. Through the writ of *habeas corpus*, a prisoner may challenge the legality of his or her imprisonment, and if the state cannot present adequate evidence to justify the jailing, the court may order the prisoner's release.)

This is therefore an exception to that power. The 3d restriction is, that no bill of attainder, or *ex post facto* law, shall be passed. This is a manifest exception to another power. We know that attainders and *expost facto* laws have been the engines of criminal jurisprudence. This is, therefore, an exception to the criminal jurisdiction vested in that.

The 4th restriction is, that no capitation, or other direct tax, shall be laid, unless in proportion to the census before directed to be taken. Our debates show from what power this is an exception. The restrictions in the 5th clause are an exception to the power of regulating commerce. The restriction in the 6th clause, that no money should be drawn from the treasury but in consequence of appropriations made by law, is an exception to the power of paying the debts of the United States; for the power of drawing money from the treasury is consequential of that of paying the public debts. The next restriction is, that no titles of nobility shall be granted by the United States. If we cast our eyes to the manner in which titles of nobility first originated, we shall find this restriction founded on the same principles. These sprang from military and civil offices. Both are in the hands of the United States, and therefore I presume it to be an exception to that power.

The last restriction restrains any person in office from accepting of any present or emolument, title or office, from any foreign prince or state. It must have been observed before, that, though the Confederation had restricted Congress from exercising any powers not given them, yet they inserted it, not from any apprehension of usurpation, but for greater security. This restriction is provided to prevent corruption. All men have a natural inherent right of receiving emoluments from any one, unless they be restrained by the regulations of the community. An accident which actually happened, operated in producing the restriction.

A box was presented to our ambassador by the king of our allies. It was thought proper, in order to exclude corruption and foreign influence, to prohibit any one in office from receiving or holding any emoluments from foreign states. I believe that if, at that moment, when we were in harmony with the king of France, we had supposed that he was corrupting our ambassador, it might have disturbed that confidence, and diminished that mutual friendship, which contributed to carry us through the war.

The honorable gentlemen observe that Congress might define punishments, from petty larceny to high treason. This is an unfortunate quotation? Or the gentleman, because treason is expressly defined in the 3d section of the 3d article, and they can add no feature to it.

They have not cognizance over any other crime except piracies, felonies committed on the high seas, and against the law of nations.

But the rhetoric of the gentleman has highly colored the dangers of giving the general government an indefinite power of providing for the general welfare. I contend that no such power is given. They have power "to lay and collect taxes," duties, imposts, and excises, to pay the debts and provide for the common defense and general welfare of the United States."

Is this an independent, separate, substantive power, to provide for the general welfare of the United States? No, sir. They can lay and collect taxes, &c. For what? To pay the debts and provide for the general welfare. Were it not this the case, the following part of the clause would be absurd. It would have been treason against common language.

Take it altogether, and let me ask if the plain interpretation be not this - a power infringes our rights, was it not necessary to mention, in our Constitution, those rights which ought to be paramount to the power of the legislature?

Why is the bill of rights distinct from the Constitution? I consider bills of right in this view - that the government should use them, when there is a departure from its fundamental principle admitted in others. In admiralty causes it is not used. Would you have a jury determine the case of a capture?

The Virginia legislature thought proper to make an exception of that case. These depend on the law of nations, and no twelve men that could be picked up could be equal to the decision of such a matter. Then, sir, the freedom of the press is said to be insecure. God forbid that I should give my voice against the freedom of the press.

But I ask, (and with confidence that it cannot be answered,) Where is the page where it is restrained? If there had been any regulation about it, leaving it insecure, then there might have been reason for clamors. But this is not the case. If it be, I again ask for the particular clause which gives liberty to destroy freedom of the press.

He has added religion to the objects endangered, In his conception. Is there any power given over it? Let it be pointed out. Will he not be contented with the answer that has been frequently given to that objection?

The variety of sects which abounds in the United States is the best security for the freedom of religion. No part of the Constitution, even if strictly construed, will justify a conclusion that the general government can take away or impair the freedom of religion.

The gentleman asks, with triumph, Shall we be deprived of these valuable rights? Had there been an exception, or an express infringement of those rights, he might object; but I conceive a very fair reasoner will agree that there is no just cause to suspect that they will be violated. But he objects that the common law is not established by the Constitution.

The wisdom of the Convention is displayed by its omission, because the common law ought not to be immutably fixed. Is it established in our own Constitution, or; the bill of rights, which has been resounded through the house? It is established only by an act of the legislature, and can therefore be changed as circumstances may require it. Let the honorable gentleman consider the destructive consequences of its establishment in the Constitution. Even in England, where the firmest opposition has been made to encroachments upon it, it has been frequently changed. What would have been our dilemma if it had been established?

Virginia has declared that children shall have equal portions of the real estate of their intestate parents, and it is consistent with the principles of a republican government. The immutable establishment of the common law would have been repugnant to that regulation.

It would, in many respects; be destructive to republican principles, and productive of great inconveniences.

I might indulge myself by showing many parts of the common law which would have this effect. I hope I shall not be thought to speak ludicrously, when I say the writ of burning heretics would have been revived by it.

It would tend to throw real property into few hands, and prevent the introduction of many Salutary regulations. Thus, were the common law adopted in that system, it would destroy the principles of republican government. But this is not excluded. It may be established by an act of legislature. Its defective parts may be altered, and it may be changed and modified as the convenience of the public may require it. I said, when I opened my observations, that I thought the friends of the Constitution were mistaken when they supposed the powers granted by the last clause of the 8th section to be merely incidental; and that its enemies were equally mistaken when they put such an extravagant construction upon it.

My objection is, that the clause is ambiguous, and that the ambiguity may injure the states. My fear is, that it will, by gradual accessions, gather to a dangerous length. This is my apprehension, and I disdain to disown it. I will praise it where it deserves it, and censure it where it appears defective. But, sir, are we to reject it, because it is ambiguous in some particular instances? I cast my eyes to the actual situation of America.

I see the dreadful tempest, to which the present calm is a prelude, if disunion takes place. I see the anarchy which must happen if no energetic government be established. In this situation, I would take the Constitution, were it more objectionable than it is; for, if anarchy and confusion follow disunion, an enterprising man may enter into the American throne, I conceive there is no danger. The representatives are chosen by and from among the people; They will have a fellow-feeling for the farmers and planters. The twenty-six senators, representatives of the states, will not be those desperadoes and horrid adventurers, which they are represented to be.

The state legislatures I trust, will not forget the duty they owe to their country so far as to choose such men to manage their federal interests. I trust that the members of Congress themselves will explain the ambiguous parts; and if not, the states can combine in order to insist on amending the ambiguities. I would depend on the present actual feeling of the people of America, to introduce any amendment which may be necessary. I repeat it again, though I do not reverence the Constitution, that its adoption is necessary to avoid the storm which is hanging over America, and that no greater curse can befall her than the dissolution of the political connection between the states.

Whether we propose previous or subsequent amendments, is the only dispute. It is a perogative to repeat the arguments in support of each; but I ask gentlemen whether, as eight states have adopted it, it be not safer to adopt it, and rely on the probability of obtaining amendments, than, by a rejection, to hazard a breach of the Union? I hope to be excused for the breach of order which I have committed.

Patrick Henry: lamented that he could not see with that perspicuity which other gentlemen were blessed with. But the 9th section struck his mind still in an unfavorable light. He hoped, as the gentleman had been indulged in speaking of the Constitution in general, that he should be allowed to answer him before they adopted or rejected it.

ARTICLE 1, SECTION 10 , Powers Prohibited to States

Patrick Henry: June 17, 1788,

Apologized for repeatedly troubling the committee with his fears. But he apprehended the most serious consequences from these restrictions on the states. As they could not emit bills of credit, make any thing but gold and silver coin a tender in payment of debts, pass *ex-post facto* laws, or impair the obligation of contracts, -though these restrictions were founded on good principles, yet he feared they would have this effect; that this state would be obliged to pay for her share of the Continental money, shilling for shilling.

He asked gentlemen who had been in high authority, whether there was not state speculations on this matter. He had been informed that some states had acquired vast quantities of that money, which they would be able to recover in its nominal value of the other states.

James Madison: Admitted there were speculations on the subject. He believed the old Continental money was settled in a disproportionate manner. It appeared to him, however, that it was unnecessary to say any thing on this point, for there was a clause in the Constitution which cleared it up. The first clause of the 6th article provides that "all debts contracted, and engagements entered into, before the adoption of this Constitution, shall be as valid against the United States, under this Constitution, as under the Confederation."

He affirmed that it was meant there should be no change with respect to claims by this political alteration; and that the public would stand, with respect to their creditors, as before. He thought that the validity of claims ought not to diminish by the adoption of the Constitution. But, however, it could not increase the demands on the public.

George Mason: June 17, 1788, Declared he had been informed that some states had speculated most enormously in this matter. Many individuals had speculated so as to make great fortunes on the ruin of their fellow citizens. The clause which has been read, as a sufficient security, seemed to him to be satisfactory as far as it went; that is, that the Continental money ought to stand on the same ground as it did previously, or that the claim should not be impaired.

Under the Confederation, there were means of settling the old paper money, either in Congress or in the state legislatures. The money had at last depreciated to a thousand for one. The intention of state speculation, as well as individual speculation, was to get as much as possible of their money, in order to recover its nominal value.

Where is the power in the new government to settle this money so as to prevent the country from being ruined? When they prohibit the making *ex post facto* laws, they will have no authority to prevent our king being ruined by paying that money at its nominal value.

Without some security against it, we shall be compelled to pay it to the last particle of our property. Shall we ruin our people by taxation, from generation to generation, to pay that money?

Should any **ex post facto** law be made to relieve us from such payments. This enormous mass of worthless money, which has been offered at a thousand for one, must be paid in actual gold and silver at the nominal value.

James Madison: June 17, 1788,

Mr Chairman, it appears to me immaterial who holds those great quantities of paper money which were in circulation before the peace, or at what due they acquired it; for it will not be affected by this Constitution.

What would satisfy gentlemen more than that the new Constitution would place us in the same situation with the old? In this respect, it has done so.

The claims against the United States are declared to be as valid as they were, but not more so. Would they have a particular specification of these matters? Where can there be any danger? Is there any reason to believe that the new rulers, one branch of which will be drawn from the mass of the people, will neglect or violate our interests more than the old? It rests on the obligation of public faith only, in the Articles of Confederation.

It will be so in this Constitution, should it be adopted. If the new rulers should wish to enhance its value, in order to gratify its holders, how can they compel the states to pay it if the letter of the Constitution be observed?

Do gentlemen wish the public creditors should be put in a worse situation? Would the people at large wish to satisfy creditors in such a manner to defraud their creditors. I consider this as well guarded as possible, and rests on plain, honest principles. I cannot conceive how it could be more honorable or safe.

Patrick Henry: Mr. Chairman, I am convinced, and I see clearly, that this paper money must be discharged, shilling for shilling. The honorable gentleman must see better than I can, from his particular situation and judgment; but this has certainly escaped his attention.

The question arising and the clause before you is, whether an act of the legislature of this state, for scaling money, will be of sufficient validity to exonerate you from paying the nominal value, when such a law, called *ex post facto*, and impairing the obligation of contracts, is expressly interdicted by it. Your hands are tied up by this clause, and you must pay shilling for shilling; and, in the last section, there is a clause that prohibits the general legislature from passing any *ex post facto* law; so that the hands of Congress are tied up, as well as the hands of the state legislatures.

How will this thing operate, when ten or twenty millions are demanded as the quota of this state? You will cry out that speculators have got it at one for a thousand, and that they ought to be paid so. Will you then have recourse, for relief, to legislative interference?

They cannot relieve you, because of that clause. America had been more watchful. This state may be sued in the federal court for those enormous demands, and judgment may be obtained, unless *expost facto* laws be passed. To benefit whom are we to run this risk?

I have heard there were vast quantities of that money packed up in barrels: those formidable millions are deposited in the Northern States, and whether in public or private hands makes no odds. They have acquired it for the most inconsiderable trifle. If you accord to this part, you are bound hand and foot. Judgment must be rendered against you for the whole. Throw all pride out of the question, this is a most nefarious business. Your property will be taken from you to satisfy an infamous speculation. It will destroy your public peace, and establish the ruin of your citizens. Only general resistance will remedy. You will shut the door against every ray of hope, if you allow the holders of this money, by this clause, to recover their formidable demands. I hope gentlemen will see the absolute necessity of amending it, by enabling the state legislatures to relieve people from such nefarious oppressions.

George Nicholas: June 17, 1788, Mr. Chairman, I beg gentlemen to consider most attentively the clause under consideration, and the objections against it. He says there exists the most dangerous prospect. Has the legislature of Virginia any right to make a law or regulation to interfere with the Continental debts? Have they a right to make *ex post facto* laws, impairing the obligation of contracts, for that purpose? No, sir. If his fears proceed from this clause, they are without foundation.

This clause does not hinder them from doing-it, because the state never could do it; the jurisdiction of such general objects being exclusively vested in Congress. But, says he, this clause will hinder the general government from preventing the nominal value of those millions from being paid.

On what footing does this business stand, if the Constitution be adopted? By it, all contracts will be as valid, and only as valid, as under the old Confederation. The new government will, give the holders the same power of recovery as the old one.

There is no law under the existing system which gives power to any tribunal to enforce the payment of such claims. On the will of Congress alone the payment depends. The Constitution expressly says that they shall be only as binding as under the present Confederation. Cannot they decide according to real equity? Those who have money must make application to Congress for payment. Some positive regulation must be made to redeem it. It cannot be said that they have power of passing a law to enhance its value. They cannot make a law that money shall no longer be but one for one; for, though they have power to pay the debts of the United States, they can only pay the real debts; and this is no further a debt than it was before.

Application must, therefore, be made by the holders of that money to Congress, who will make a proper regulation to discharge its real and equitable, and not its nominal value.

Gov. Edmund Randolph: Mr. Chairman, this clause, in spite of the invective of the gentleman, is a great favorite of mine, because it is essential to justice. I shall reserve my answer respecting the safety of the people till the objection be urged; but I must make a few observations. He says this clause will be injurious, and that no scale can be made, because there is a prohibition on Congress of passing *ex post facto* laws. If the gentleman did not make such strong objections to logical reasoning, I could prove, by such reasoning, that there is no danger. *Ex post facto* laws, if taken technically, relate solely to criminal cases; and my honorable colleague tells you it was so interpreted in Convention.

George Mason: June 17, 1788, Mr. Chairman the debt is transferred to

Congress, but not the means of paying it. They cannot pay it any other way than according to the nominal value, for they are prohibited from making *ex post facto* laws; and it would be *ex post facto*, to all intents and purposes, to pay off creditors with less than the nominal sum which they were originally promised.

James Madison: I did expect, from the earnestness he has expressed, that he would cast some light on it; but the ingenuity of the honorable member could make nothing of this objection. He argues from a supposition that the state legislatures, individually, might have passed laws to affect the value of the Continental debt. I believe he did not consider this, before he hazarded his observations.

[Another vitriolic exchange]

ARTICLE 11, SECTION 1, June 17, 1788, The Presidency: Election, Installation, Removal

George Mason:
Was still convinced of the rectitude of his former opinion. He thought it might be put on a safer footing by three words. By continuing the restriction of *ex post facto* laws to crimes, it would then stand under the new government as it did under the old.

Gov. Edmund Randolph: Could not coincide with the construction put by the honorable gentlemen on *ex post facto* laws. The technical meaning which confined such laws solely to criminal cases was followed in the interpretation of treaties between nations, and was concurred in by all civilians. The prohibition of bills of attainder he thought proof that *ex-post facto* (retroactive: useage began in 1787), laws related only to criminal cases.

George Mason: June 17, 1788,
Gentlemen who know nothing of the business will make rules concerning it which may be detrimental to our interests. For forty years we have laid duties on tobacco, to defray the expense of the inspection and to raise incidental revenue for the state. Under this clause, that incidental revenue which is calculated to pay for the inspection and contingent charges is to be put into the federal treasury. But if our tobacco-house is burnt, we cannot make up the loss. I conceive this to be unjust and unreasonable. When the

profit rises, it goes into the federal treasury. But when there is a loss or deficiency it cannot be made up. Congress are to make regulations for our tobacco. Are men in the states where no tobacco is made, proper judges of this business? I would concede any power that was essentially necessary for the interests of the Union; but this, instead of being necessary, will be extremely oppressive.

George Nicholas:
I consider this clause a good regulation, agreed to that they will impose duties in the most impartial manner, and not throw the burdens on the community. Every man who is acquainted with our laws must know that the duties on tobacco were as high as sixteen shillings a hogshead. The consequence was, that the tobacco makers have paid upwards of twenty thousand pounds annually, more than the other citizens; because they paid every other kind of tax, as well as the rest of the community. We have every reason to believe that this clause will prevent injustice and partiality. Tobacco makers will be benefited by it. The legislature must defray the expenses and contingent charges by laying a tax for that purpose; for such a tax is not prohibited. The net amounts go into the federal treasury, after expenses

George Mason: replied that state legislatures could make no law but what would come within the general control given to Congress; and that the regulation of the inspection and imposition of duties, must be inseparably blended together.

James Madison: Compared to what other states exported and the taxes and duties. The clause says that "the net produce of all duties and imposts, laid by any state on imports or exports, shall be for the use of the treasury of the United States," which implies that all contingent charges shall have been previously paid.

Gov. Edmund Randolph: Mr. Chairman, the honorable gentleman last up says that I do not mention the parts to which I object. I have hitherto mentioned my objections with freedom and candor. But sir, I considered that our critical situation rendered adoption necessary were it more defective than it is. I observed that if opinions ought to lead the committee on one side, they ought on the other. Every gentleman who has turned his thoughts to the subject of politics, and has considered that the greatest difficulty arises from the executive at the time of his election, the mode of his election, quantum of power, & c. I acknowledge of this business, I had embraced the idea of the honorable gentleman, that the re-eligibility of the President was improper. But, Edmund Randolph admits to having changed his mind with further consideration.

George Mason: June 17, 1788, Mr. Chairman, the Vice President appears to me to be not only an unnecessary but dangerous officer. He is, contrary to the usual course of parliamentary proceeding, to be president of the Senate. I cannot at this distance of time, foresee the consequences; but I think that in the course of human affairs, he will be made a tool of in order to bring about his own interest, and aid in overturning the liberties of his country. There is another part which I disapprove of, but which perhaps I do not understand. "In case of removal of the President from office, or of his death, resignation, or inability to discharge the powers and duties of the President from office, the same shall devolve on the Vice-President and the Congress may declare what officer shall then act as President until the disability be removed or a President shall be elected." But gentlemen ought to take notice that the election of this officer is only for four years. There is no provision for a speedy election of another President. The influence of the Vice Pres. may prevent the election of the President. But perhaps I am mistaken.

James Madison: There are some peculiar advantages incident to this office, which recommend it to us. There is, a great probability this officer will be taken from one of the largest states, and if so, the circumstance of his having an eventual vote will be so far favorable. He thought the man would be the choice of the people at large, than to one of the Senate His eventual vote is an advantage too obvious to comment. He felt that upon the death of the President that the election of another would take place immediately and that Congress would merely appoint an interim man and that occasion would be rare.

June 18, Wednesday,
ARTICLE 11, SECTION 1, Presidential Power

James Monroe, After a brief exordium, in which he insisted that, on the judicious organization of the executive power, the security interest and happiness depended on the construction of this part of the government, we should be cautious to avoid defects in government; and that our circumspection should be commensurate to the extent of powers delegated. He then discussed the entire situation regarding the Presidency, reminding that he would be elected by the electors, not the people; that state governments were responsible for his election. To whom is the President answerable. Who will try him in case he errs. Monroe recommended that the President stay in office for life. He warned about foreign nations owning land in America and how they might approach the President and corrupt him. Monroe felt the Vice-President was useless and a dangerous influence. He succeeds the President and casts a deciding vote in the Senate, which could benefit his state. Monroe disapproved of this clause.

Wlliam Grayson, June 18, 1788

Mr. Chairman, one great objection with this is: If we advert to this democratical, aristocratical, or executive branch, we shall find their powers are perpetually varying and fluctuating throughout the whole. Perhaps the democratic branch would be well constructed, were it not for this defect.

The executive is still worse, in this respect, than the democratic branch. He is to be elected by a number of electors in the country; but the principle is changed when no person has a majority of the whole number of electors appointed, or when more than one have such a majority, and have an equal number of votes; for then, the lower house is to vote by states.

It is thus changing throughout the whole. It seems founded on accident more than any principle of government I ever heard of. We know that there scarcely ever was an election of such an officer without the interposition of foreign powers. Two causes prevail to make them intermeddle in such cases: one is, to preserve the balance of power; the other, to preserve their trade. These causes have produced interference's of foreign powers in the election of the king of Poland. All the great powers of Europe interfered in an election which took place not very long ago, and would not let the people choose for themselves. We know how much the powers of Europe have interfered with Sweden. Since the death of Charles XII, that country has been a republican government.

Some powers were willing it should be so; some were willing her imbecility should continue; others wished the contrary; and at length the Court of France brought about a revolution which converted it into an absolute government and they now wish to make America entirely their own. Great Britain will wish to increase her influence by a still closer connection. It is the interest of Spain, from the contiquity of her possessions in the western hemisphere to the United States, to be in an intimate connection with them, and influence their deliberations, if possible.

I think we have every thing to apprehend from such interferences. It is highly probably the President will be continued in office for life. To gain his favor, they will support him. Consider the means of importance he will have in creating officers. If he has a good understanding with the Senate, they will join to prevent discovery of his misdeeds.

Whence comes this extreme confidence, that we disregard the example of ancient and modern nations. Aristocracies never invested their officers with such immense power. Rome had an aristocratical and a democratical branch, yet consuls were in office for two years. This quadrennial power cannot be justified by ancient history. There is hardly an instance where a republic trusted its executive so long with so much power; nor is it warranted by modern republics. The delegation of power is, in most of them, only for one year.

When you have a strong democratical and a strong aristocratical branch, you may have a strong executive. But, where those are weak, the balance will not be preserved if you give the executive extensive powers for so long a time. As this government is organized, it would be dangerous to trust the President with such powers. How will you punish him if he abuse his power? Will you call him before the Senate? They are his counselors and partners in crime. Where are your checks? We ought to be extremely cautious in this country. If ever the government be changed, it will probably be into a despotism. The first object in England was to destroy the monarchy; but the aristocratic branch restored him, and of course the government **I presume the seven Eastern States will always elect him, as he is invested with the power of making treaties, and as there is a material distinction between the carrying and productive states, the former will be organized on its ancient pinciples.**

But were a revolution to happen here, there would be no means of restoring the government to its former organization. This is a caution not to trust extensive powers. I have extreme objections to the mode of this election. **He disposed to have him to themselves.**

He will accommodate himself to their interests in forming treaties, and they will continue him perpetually in office.

This mutual interest will lead them reciprocally to support one another.

It will be a government of a faction, and this observation will apply to every part of it; for having a majority, they may do what they please.

I have made an estimate which shows with what facility they will be represented. The number of electors is equal to the number of senators and representatives; viz., ninety-one. They are to vote for two persons.

They give, therefore, one hundred and eighty-two votes. Let there be forty-five votes for our four different candidates and two for the President.

He is one of the five highest, if he have but two votes, which he may easily purchase. Let there be forty-five votes for four different candidates. two in this case, by the 3rd clause of the 1st section of the 2nd article, the election is by the representatives, according to states.

Let New Hampshire be for him. Grayson ends with: So that the President may be reelected by the voices of 17 against 139. It may be said that this extravagant case will never happen. In my opinion, it will often happen. A person who is a favorite of Congress, gets two votes of electors, by the subsequent choice of 15 representatives, he may be elected President. Surely he ought not be elected till we offer amendments.

George Mason: Wednesday, **June 18, 1788,** This, in my opinion, is a very considerable defect. The people will, in reality, have no hand in the election. It is a mere ignis factuus on the American people. **It has been wittily observed that the Constitution has married the President & Senate**.

On this great and important subject, I am one of those (and ever shall be) who object to it. There is discussion and much dissent from Madison. The person having the greatest number of votes would not be elected, unless such majority was one of the whole number of electors appointed; that it would rarely happen that any one would have such a majority, and as he was then to be chosen from the five highest on the list, his election was entirely taken from the people.

James Madison: Expressed astonishment and insisted that a number of votes equal to a majority of the electors, which was forty six; for the clause expressly said that the person having the greatest number of votes shall be President, if such number be a majority of the whole number of electors appointed, and suggested that if Mason disapproved, he should point out a proper mode of electing the president.

Discussion ensues between Mason, Lee, Nicholas, Madison, Henry, Grayson, on the Presidency, his election, term of office and the amount of power he held. There are extreme opinions and the debates become loud and the exchanges nasty as tempers flare discussing the Presidency and the manner and place of elections, and more.

William Grayson: After discriminating the difference of what was called the law of nations in different countries, and its different operations, said he was exceedingly alarmed about this clause. His apprehensions increased from what he had seen.

He went over the grounds which had been before developed, of the dangers to which the right of navigating the Mississippi would be exposed, if two thirds of the senators present had a right to make a treaty to bind the Union. Seven states had already discovered a determined resolution of yielding it to Spain.

There was every reason, in his opinion, to believe they would avail themselves of the power as soon as it was given them. The prevention of emigrations to the westward, and consequent superiority of the southern power and influence, would be a powerful motive to impel them to relinquish the river. He warmly expatiated on the utility of that navigation, and the impolicy of surrendering it up. The consent of the President he considered as a trivial check, if, indeed it was any; for the election would be so managed that he would always come from a particular place, and he would pursue the interest of such a place. Gentlemen said that the senators would attend from all the states.

This says he, is impracticable, if they be not nailed to the floor. If the senators of the Southern States be gone but one hour, a treaty may be made by the rest, yielding that inestimable right. This paper will be called the law of nations in America; it will be the Great Charter of America; it will be paramount to every thing. After once consented to it, we cannot recede from it. Such is my repugnance to the alienation of a right which I esteem so important to the happiness of my country, that I would object to this constitution if it contained no other defect.

ARTICLE 11, SECTION 2 Presidential Power.

William Grayson: Thursday, June 19th, 1788, After recapitulating the dangers of losing the Mississippi, if the power of making treaties, as delineated in the Constitution, were granted, insisted, most strenuously, that the clause which the honorable gentleman had cited as a security against a dismemberment of the empire was no real security; because it related solely to the back lands claimed by the United States and different states. This clause was inserted for the purpose of enabling Congress to dispose of, and make all needful rules and regulations respecting, the territory, or other property, belonging to the united States, and to ascertain clearly that the claims of particular states, respecting territory, should not be prejudiced by the alteration of government, but be on the same footing as before; that it could not be construed to be a limitation of the power of making treaties.

Its sole intention was to obviate all the doubts and disputes which existed, under the confederation, concerning the western territory and other places in controversy in the United States. He defended his former position with respect to a particular law of nations. I insist, says he, that the law of nations is founded on particular laws of different nations. I have mentioned some instances: I will mention some more. It is the law of several Oriental nations to receive no ambassadors. It is a particular custom with him, in time of war with Russia, to put the Russian ambassador in the Seven Towers. But the worthy member said that it was odd there should be a particular law of nations. I beg leave to tell him that the Unites States are entering into a particular law of nations now.

I do not deny the existence of a general law of nations; but I contend that, in different nations, there are certain laws or customs regulating their conduct towards other nations, which are as permanently and immutably observed as the general law of nations. Of course there was a law of nations incident to the Confederation. Any person may renounce a right secured to him by any particular law or custom of a nation.

If Congress have no right, by the law of nations, to give away a part of the empire, yet, by this compact, they may give it up. I look on that compact to be a part of the law of nations. The treaty of Munster formed a great part of the law of nations. How is the Scheldt given up? By that treaty, though contrary to the law of nations.

Cannot Congress give the Mississippi also by treaty, though such cession would deprive us of a right to which, by the law of nations, we renounce any particular right. Nations who inhabit on the sources of rivers have a right to navigate them, and go down, as well as the waters themselves.

George Nicholas: Thursday, June 19, 1788, Parallelled the power of the king of England to Congress, saying whatever contracts, treaties, leagues and alliances he enters into, no power in the kingdom can legally delay, resist, or annul.

George Mason: Said that one of the greatest acts of sovereignty ought to be strongly guarded with checks and balances. He found differences between the British government and America; a more favorable situation than perhaps any people ever knew before, that by the Constitution we could secure our liberties on a firm and permanent basis. He felt that consolidating the U.S. into one great government would bring constructive security.

Francis Corbin: June 19, 1788, Insisted that no other clause in the Constitution was more commendable and approved of the power of making treaties be granted to the President and the Senate. He discussed the difference between common treaties and commercial treaties.

Patrick Henry: Suggested that the Constitution lacked responsibility, especially in terms of impeaching a president. He brought up states rights, criminal abuse and was highly discriminating. He compared security of territory to no security for an individual and called for a Declaration of Rights. He ended by saying the amendments which his honorable friend, Grayson had proposed, should be adopted. (refer to Dr. Jon Kukla).

James Madison: Argued that this clause was appropriate and strongly favorable to the security of the country similar to the Confederation.

Francis Corbin: Stood to explain what he meant and discussed the Newfoundland fishery and the treaty controlling its rights.

Edward Pendleton: Discussed the Judiciary and that it be coextensive with legislative power, for all societies.

He wanted some courts to be inferior and one Supreme Court ordained by Congress. Some courts would be appointed by the states, the inferior courts, but Congress would control federal courts and distribute the proper Judges and courts to adjudicate in certain cases, including the Appellate Court for appeals, and the Supreme Court will regulate the greatest cases to exclude dangers.

George Mason: Said he had hoped for those for the Constitution to point out important objections and then **launched into his disappointment that nothing of importance was left to the state courts, feeling that if the state courts were not trusted to administer justice and disputes respecting property, how can they be trusted to legislate?**

His hope was to see political happiness resting on state governments and not on a consolidated, national government. He hinted that he knew many worthy gentlemen who preferred power to rest in the states.

James Madison interrupted him, Demanding to know who these gentlemen were. George Mason: said that many gentlemen in Convention and throughout the U.S. were against consolidation along with most of the delegates from Virginia.

James Madison: Said he was satisfied with the explanation.

George Nicholas: **Made desultory remarks** and said, the last clause was improper, that it was utterly unreasonable to give cognizance to the federal judiciary in disputes between a state and the citizens of that state.

George Nicholas: Outraged, informed Mr. Mason that his interpretation was not warranted by his words and therefore out of place.

George Mason: Argued the law and cases, before which courts they would be heard. And the inequity of such hearings, especially on appeal when a defendant had to travel five hundred miles to seek justice. He then proposed an amendment. (**His alteration was nearly the same as the first part of the 14th amendment. Citizenship rights**) He went on to explain the various Court systems in detail and ended by recalling how the peasants mentioned by Virgil were reduced to ruin and misery, driven from their homes and forced out of their country.
"**Nos patriam fugimus, et dulcia linquimus arva.**"

James Madison: Said that Mason's fears and suppositions are not well founded and explains in candor, his opinion in opposition, saying that the general government will always do what is best for the United States.
The lateness of the hour, caused Madison to further reserve his opinion.

Friday, June 20, 1788
ARTICLE 111, SECTIONS 1 & 2, Judicial Power Vested & 11, Trial by Jury, Original Jurisdiction, Jury Trials

James Madison, Patrick Henry, Mr. Pendleton, George Mason, John Marshall and Governor Edmund Randolph spoke in turn. Grayson was absent, ill with gout, a perennial complaint.

Saturday, June 21, 1788
Mr. Harrison reported for privileges and elections that Richard Morris had

leave to withdraw his name as a delegate.
June 21, 1788

William Grayson: Mr. Chairman, it seems to be a rule with the gentlemen on the other side to argue from the excellency of human nature, in order to induce us to grant away (if I may be allowed the expression) the rights and liberties of our country. I make no doubt the same arguments were used on a variety of occasions. I suppose, sir, that this argument was used when Cromwell was invested with power. The same argument was used to gain our assent to the Stamp Act. I have no doubt it has been invariably argued in all countries, when the concession of power had been in agitation.

But power ought to have such checks and limitation as to prevent bad men from abusing it. It ought to be granted on a supposition that men will be bad; for it may be eventually so.

With respect to the judiciary, my grand objection is, that it will interfere with the state judiciaries, in the same manner as the exercise of the power of direct taxation will interfere with power in the state governments; there being no superintending central power to keep order in these two jurisdictions. This is an objection which is unanswerable in its nature. In England they have great courts, which have great and interfering powers, But the controlling power of Parliament, which is a central focus, corrects them. But here each party is to shift for itself. There is no arbiter or power to correct their interference. Recurrence can be only had to the sword. I shall endeavor to demonstrate the pernicious consequences of this interference. It was mentioned, as one reason why these great powers might harmonize, that the judges of the state courts might be federal judges. **The idea was approbated, in my opinion, with the suggestion that the judges of Virginia be subordinated to the federal judiciary. Our judges in chancery are to be judges in the inferior federal tribunals!**

Something has been said of the independence of the federal judges. I will only observe that this is as corrupt a basis as the art of man can place it. The salaries of the judges may be augmented. Augmentation of salary is the only method that can be taken to corrupt a judge. It has been a thing desired by the people of England for many years, that the judges should be independent. This independence never was obtained till the second or third year of the reign of George III. It was omitted at the revolution by inattention. Their compensation is now fixed, and they hold their offices during good behavior. But I say that our federal judges are placed in a situation as liable to corruption as they could possibly be.

How are judges to operate? By the hopes of reward, and not the fear of a diminution of compensation. Common decency would prevent lessening the salary of a judge.

Throughout the whole page of history, you will find corruption of judges to have arisen from that principle–the hope of reward. This is left open here. The flimsy argument brought by my friend, not as his own but as supported by others, will not hold. It would be hoped that the judges should get too much rather than too little, and that they should be perfectly independent. What if you give six hundred or a thousand pounds annually to a judge? It is but a trifling object, when, by that little money you purchase the most invaluable blessing that any country can enjoy.

There is to be one Supreme Court for chancery, admiralty, common pleas, and exchequer, (which great cases are left in England to four great courts,) to which are added criminal jurisdiction, and all cases depending on the law of nations, a most extensive jurisdiction. **This court has more power than any court under heaven**.

One set of judges ought not to have this power–and judges, in particular, who have temptation always before their eyes. The court thus organized are to execute laws made by thirteen nations, dissimilar in their customs, manners, laws, and interests.

If we advert to the customs of these different sovereignties, we shall find them repugnant and dissimilar. Yet they are all forced to unite and concur in making these laws. They are to form them on one principle, and on one idea, whether the civil law, common law, or law of nations. The gentleman was driven, the other day, to the expedient of acknowledging the necessity of having thirteen different tax laws. This destroys the principle, that he who lays a tax should feel it and bear his proportion of it. This has not been answered; it will involve consequences so absurd, that I presume, they will not attempt to make thirteen different codes. They will be obliged to make one code.

How will they make one code, without being contradictory to some of the laws of the different states? It is said there is to be a court of equity. There is no such thing in Pennsylvania, or in some other states in the Union. A nation in making a law, ought not to make it repugnant to the spirit of the Constitution or the genius of the people. This rule cannot be observed in forming a general code. I wish to know how the people of Connecticut would agree with the lordly pride of your Virginia nobility. They may inflict punishments where the state governments will give rewards. This is not probably; but possible.

It would be a droll sight, to see a man on one side of the street punished for a breach of the federal law, and on the other side another man rewarded by the state legislature for the same act; it would be a droll sight, to see a man laughing on one side of his face and crying on the other.

I wish only to put this matter in a clear point of view; and I think that if thirteen states, different in every thing, shall have to make laws for the government of the whole, they cannot harmonize or suit the genius of the people; there being no such thing as a spirit of laws, or a pervading principle, applying to every state individually.

The only promise, in this respect is, that there shall be a republican government in each state. But it does not say whether it is to be aristocratical or democratical. My next objection to the federal judiciary is, that it is not expressed in a definite manner. The jurisdiction of all cases arising under the Constitution and the laws of the union is of stupendous magnitude.

It is impossible for human nature to trace its extent: It is so vaguely and indefinitely expressed, that its latitude cannot be ascertained. Citizens or subjects of foreign states may sue citizens of the different states in the federal courts. It is extremely impolitic to place foreigners in a better situation than our own citizens. This was never the policy of other nations. It was the policy, in England, to put foreigners on a secure footing. The stature merchant and statute staple were favorable to them. But in no country are the laws more favorable to foreigners than to the citizens. If they be equally so, it is surely sufficient. Our own state merchants would be ruined by it, because they cannot recover debts so soon in the state courts as foreign merchants can recover of them in the federal courts. The consequence would be inevitable ruin to commerce and will induce foreigners to decline becoming citizens. There is no reciprocity in it. How will this apply to British creditors? I have ever been an advocate for paying the British creditors, both in Congress and elsewhere. But here we do injury to our own citizens. It is a maxim in law, that debts should be on the same original foundation they were on when contracted.

I presume, when the contracts were made, the creditors had an idea of the state judiciaries only. The procrastination and delays of our courts were probably in contemplation by both parties. They had no idea how setting new tribunals would affect them.

Trial by jury must have been in contemplation by both parties. And the venue was in favor of the defendant. From these premises it is clearly discernible that it would be wrong to change the nature of the contracts. Whether they will make a law other than the state laws, I cannot determine. But we are told that it is wise, politic, and preventive of controversies with foreign nations. The treaty of peace with Great Britain does not require that creditors should be put in a better situation than they were, but that there should be no hindrance to the collection of debts. It is therefore unwise and impolitic to give those creditors such an advantage over the debtors.

But the citizens of different states are to sue each other in these courts. No reliance is to be put on the state judiciaries. The fear of unjust regulations and decisions in the states is urged as the reason of this jurisdiction. Paper money in Rhode Island has been instanced by gentlemen.

There is one clause in the Constitution which prevents the issuing of paper money. If this clause should pass, (and it is unanimously wished by every one that it should not be objected to), I apprehend an execution in Rhode Island would be as good and effective as in any state in the Union.

A state may sue a foreign state, or a foreign state may sue one of our states. This may form a new, American law of nations. Whence the idea could have originated, I cannot determine, unless from the idea that predominated in the time of Henry IV, and Queen Elizabeth. They took it into their heads to consolidate all the states in the world into one great political body. Many ridiculous projects were imagined to reduce that absurd idea into practice; but they were all given up at last.

My honorable friend, whom I much respect, said that the consent of the parties must be previously obtained. I agree that the consent of foreign nations must be had before they become parties; but it is not so with our states. It is fixed in the Constitution that they shall become parties. This is not reciprocal. If the Congress cannot make a law against the Constitution, I apprehend they cannot make a law to abridge It.. The judges are to defend it. They can neither abridge nor extend it. There is no reciprocity in this, that a foreign state should have a right to sue one of our states, whereas a foreign state cannot be sued without its own consent.

The idea to me is monstrous and extravagant. It cannot be reduced to practice. Suppose one of our states objects to the decision; arms must be recurred to. How can a foreign state be compelled to submit to a decision? Pennsylvania and Connecticut had once, like to have fallen together concerning their contested boundaries. I was convinced that the mode provided in the Confederation, for the decision of such disputes, would not answer. The success which attended it, with respect to settling bounds, has proved to me, in some degree, that it would not answer in any other case whatever. The same difficulty must attend this mode in the execution. This high court has not a very extensive original jurisdiction. It is not material. But its appellate jurisdiction is of immense magnitude; and what has it in view, unless to subvert the state governments?

The honorable gentleman who presides has introduced the high court of appeals. I wish the federal appellate court was on the same foundation. If we investigate the subject, we shall find this jurisdiction perfectly unnecessary. It is said that its object is to prevent subordinate tribunals from making unjust decisions, to defraud creditors. I grant the suspicion is in some degree just. But would not an appeal to the state courts on appeal, or supreme tribunals, correct the decisions of inferior courts? Would not this put every thing right? Then there would be no interference of jurisdiction. But a gentleman (Mr. Marshall) says, we ought to give this power to Congress, because our state courts have more business than they can possible do.

A gentleman was once asked to give up his estate because he had too much; but he did not comply.

Have we not established district courts, which have for their situation; so that there is nothing in this observation.

But the same honorable gentleman says, that trial by jury is preserved by implication. I think this was the idea. I beg leave to consider that, as well as other observations of the honorable gentleman.

After enumerating the subjects of its jurisdiction, and confining its original cognizance to cases affecting ambassadors and other public ministers, and those in which a state shall be a party, it expressly says, that, "In all other cases before mentioned, the Supreme Court shall have appellate jurisdiction, both as to law and fact." I would beg the honorable gentleman to turn his attention to the word appeal, which I think comprehends chancery, admiralty, common law, and every thing. But this is with such exceptions, and under such regulations, as Congress shall make.

This, we are told, will be an ample security. Congress may please to make these exceptions and regulations, but they may not, also.

I lay it down as a principle, that trial by jury is given up to the discretion of Congress. If they take it away, will it be a breach of this Constitution? I apprehend not; for as they have an absolute appellate jurisdiction of facts, they may alter them as they may think proper.

It is possible that Congress may regulate it properly; but still it is at their discretion to do it or not. There has been so much said of the excellency of trial by jury; that I need not enlarge upon it. The want of trial by jury in the Roman republic obliged them to establish the regulation of patron and client. I think this is the case in every country where this trial does not exist.

The poor people were obliged to be defended by their patrons. It may be laid down as a role that, where the governing power possesses an unlimited control over the venue, no man's life is in safety. How is it in this system?

"The trial of all crimes shall be by jury, except in cases of impeachment; and such trial shall be held in the state where the said crimes shall have been committed." He has said that, when the power of a court is given, all its appendages and concomitants are given. Allowing this to be the case by implication, how is it? Does it apply to counties? No, sir. The idea is, that the states are to the general government as counties are to our state legislatures. What sort of a vicinage is given by Congress? The idea which I call a true vicinage. Delaware sends but one member: it would then extend to that whole state. This state sends ten members, and has ten districts; but this is far from the true idea of vicinage. The allusion another gentleman has made to this trial, as practiced in England, is improper. It does not justify this purpose. They might, on particular, extraordinary occasions, suspend the privilege.

The Romans did it on creating a dictator. The British government do it when the habeas corpus is suspended, when the salus populi is affected.

I never will consent to it unless it be properly defined. Another gentleman has said that trial by jury has not been so sacred a thing among our ancestors, and that in England it may be destroyed by an act of Parliament. I believe the gentleman is mistaken. I believe it is secured by Magna Charta and the bill of rights. I believe no act of Parliament can affect it, if this principle be true, that a law is not paramount to the Constitution. I believe, whatever may be said of the mutability of the laws and the defect of a written, fixed Constitution, that it is generally thought, by Englishmen, that it is so sacred that no act of Parliament can affect it. The interference of the federal judiciary and the state courts will involve the most serious and even ludicrous consequences. Both courts are to act on the same persons and things, and cannot possibly avoid interference. As to connection or coalition, it would be incestuous. How could they avoid it, on an execution from each court, either against the body or effects? How will it be with respect to mortgaged property? Suppose the same lands or slaves mortgaged to two different persons, and the mortgages foreclosed, one in the federal and another in the state court; will there be no interference in this case? It will be impossible to avoid interference in a million cases. I wish to know how it can be avoided" for it is an insuperable objection in my mind. I shall no longer fatigue the committee, but shall beg leave to make observations another time.

Governor Edmund Randolph: spoke until closing.

Monday, June 23, 1788 The printer took notes in the absence of the "stenographer," who was indisposed, but would return.

The 1st and 2nd sections of the 3rd article are still under consideration] Judicial Powers Vested & Trial by Jury

George Nicholas: Remarked that the committee knew his sentiments and hoped they were satisfied by the men who last spoke.

Patrick Henry: said that his objections had not been satisfactorily answered, and discussed the federal versus state judiciaries; the dangers to citizens from being forced into the federal court system for land matters or local affairs. He was also upset about the manner of collecting taxes. He suggested they would have an empire of men not of laws. Men, he said without wisdom or integrity would flourish on the ruin of their country.
John Marshall: said that Patrick Henry had misunderstood him, that trial by jury was more secure in the new constitution than in our bill of rights.
 The 8th article of the Bill of Rights (the clerk read them).

Patrick Henry: Was gracious to Mr. Marshall but insisted the trial by jury in the Constitution did not protect the vicinage,(where the party resided), and could see defendants travelling as far as five hundred miles for a court appearance. He felt that British debtors would be dragged to federal courts and ruined. He was also unhappy about the plight of the Indians who had been exploited, made drunk and forced to give up thousands of acres for nothing.

Adam Stephen: (A major military hero who fought with Washington on the frontier prior to the Revolution). Said that Patrick Henry was trying to frighten them with bugbears and hobgoblins and that there were a variety of resources by which people could pay their taxes without losing their property. He described the Mississippi and the western region and suggested that Henry might go there to live if he did not like his government, and offered to teach him several native Indian languages, so he would fare well living among them.

George Nicholas: Was surprised that Henry would accept part of the constitution and suggested that it would be a weird document that the dissenters would create. He referred to the act of Assembly of 1782 that abolished the quitrents, and that those who had bought land from the Indians prior to the opening of the land office under the Virginia Assembly; many had come into large possessions of land, not easily accounted for. (He too had insulted Henry).

Patrick Henry: jumped to his feet saying, if the gentleman means personal insults or to wound my reputation, this is an improper place to do so and said that the gentleman had no right to question how he came to hold property and said that he could explain all of his holdings, then excused himself for injuring any gentleman in the attempt to get information. He was thoroughy insulted by right.

George Nicholas: said he meant nothing personal nor was he resentful, that he was equally offended by contempt. He observed that gentlemen should not be personal but proceed to examine the subject in a peaceful manner. He explained that he had other men in mind and elucidated that certain remarks had been made by the honorable gentleman (Patrick Henry) that should not pass between gentlemen.

James Monroe: was concerned that two separate government entities would have concurrent jurisdiction in the same object (subject in court) and this would cause a certain conflict. His concern was who would have the upper hand, the federal court or the state, and wondered how people would feel, simultaneously oppressed by both.

James Madison: observed that the various county courts performed independently and that federal and states courts would operate on their own, that foreigners would receive justice where none was available before. He said that judges of either federal or state judiciaries would be prevented from holding any other government office or receive emoluments of any kind from anyone.

William Grayson observed, That the federal and state judiciaries could not,

.on the present plan, be kept in perfect harmony. As to the trial by jury being safer here than in England, that I deny. Jury trials are secured there, sir, by Magna Charta, in a clear and decided manner; and that here is not in express and positive terms, as admitted by most gentlemen who now hear me. He concluded with saying, that he did not believe there existed a social compact upon the face of the earth so vague and so indefinite as the one now on the table. (The Constitution).

Patrick Henry: Said that trial by jury had once been safe and now was most certainly not safe at all.

James Madison: Was content that the declaration before them could not diminish the people's security unless a majority of their representatives should concur in a violation.

George Mason: Rose to say that he was troubled with the arguments supporting the clause; that they were totally unsatisfactory because the federal judiciary would be more powerful than the state judiciary and therefore interfere, that there must be reciprocity between the two systems.

He called the Constitution a genius construction for a general government but not for separate states under one central government.

ARTICLE 1V, SECTION 1 was read,The States, Full Faith and Credit between states
George Mason: Confessed that he did not understand, *Full faith and credit shall be given to all acts and he wanted an explanation..*

James Madison: said that the clause was absolutely necessary but that the complaint was tardy.

ARTICLE 1V, SECTION 11 was read, Privileges & Immunities, Extradition, Fugitive Slaves

George Mason: remarked that others had claimed there was security of property under this clause but saw no security at all.

ARTICLE 1V, SECTION 111 was read.
Admission of States

William Grayson: Mr. Chairman, it appears to me, sir, under this section, there never can be a Southern state admitted to the union. There are seven states, which are a majority, and whose interest it is to prevent it. The balance being actually in their possession, they will have the regulation of commerce, and the federal ten miles square wherever they please. It is not supposed, then, that they will admit any southern state into the Union, and lose that majority.

James Madison disagreed. Mason, Monroe and Henry supported Grayson, as they always did.

The remainder of the Constitution was read and the opposition pointed out the mode by which amendments were to be obtained. There was discussion and the Convention adjourned.

James Madison: Said the chance was better for Southern states to be admitted to the Union under the Constitution than the Confederation.

George Mason: looked at the retrospective parts already objected to and tried to show the danger and insecurity of all rights and privileges; that the descriptions were vague, indefinite, ambiguous, and defective. He thought dreadful effects would result and begged gentlemen to pause before involving such awful consequences.

Richard Henry Lee: said, I am so oppressed by the comments of my honorable friend that I cannot suppress my utterance, and am stunned to hear from his own lips, opinions so injurious to our country and so opposed to the dignity of this assembly.

If the dreadful picture which he draws is abhorrent to him, let me ask the honorable gentleman if he has not pursued the very means to bring into action the horrors he so deprecates.

Such speeches within these walls, from a character so venerable and estimable easily progress into overt acts, among less intelligent and base. I pray that all in opposition, remember these impious scenes, should they commence into scenes we abhor and which I execrate, whence and how they began. God of heaven avert from my country the dreadful curse. But if the madness of some, and the vice of other, should risk the awful appeal, I trust that the friends to the paper on your table, conscious of the justice of their cause, conscious of the integrity of their views and recollecting their uniform moderation, will meet the afflicting call with that firmness and fortitude, which become men summoned to defend what they conceive to be the true interest of their Country, and will prove to the world that, although they boast not, in words, of love of country and affection for liberty, still they are not less attached to these invaluable objects than their vaunting opponents, and can, with alacrity and resignation, encounter every difficult and danger in defense of them.

The remainder of the Constitution articles 5, 6 & 7 were read and several objectionable parts noted by the opposition, in particular the mode by which to obtain amendments. Discussion followed and the day ended.

Tuesday, June 24, 1788:

George Wythe, spoke on the necessity of a firm, indissoluble union of the states, and suggested that they ratify the Constitution and then recommend to Congress those amendments deemed necessary. Wythe was a brilliant barrister, who had taught law to many of the patriots.

Patrick Henry: observed that the proposal to ratify was premature and suggested more deliberation. He felt that securing personal rights had not pervaded the minds of men and pointed out other inequities, listing them one by one.

Mr. Henry informed the committee that he had a resolution prepared for a declaration of rights, and amendments to the most exceptional parts of the Constitution, that were intended to go to the other states for their consideration, prior to ratification. The clerk of record then read the resolution, the declaration of rights and amendments, which were the same as those ultimately proposed by the Convention, a fact that was only discovered later.

Gov. Edmund Randolph: said that if only he believed that there was peace and tranquility in the land and no storm gathering, "nothing but the fear of inevitable destruction would lead me to vote for the Constitution with the objections I have of it, **except for what the country faces. He** interpreted Henry as saying that he would secede, (formally withdraw from the majority) believing this was a concession, and that Henry would adopt without previous amendments.

Patrick Henry: denied having said any thing about secession but said he would have no hand in subsequent amendments, that he would stay and vote and then leave, having no other business there.

Edmund Randolph: admitted his mistaken in understanding and said that any members who contemplated seceding from the majority, let me conjure them by all the ties of honor and duty, to consider what they are about to do by refusing to submit to the decision of the majority would be destructive of every republican principle and might kindle a civil war and reduce every thing to anarchy and confusion.

To avoid a calamity so lamentable, I would submit that it contains greater evils than it does. Then he asked, how anyone could go home and say to their constituents, We come to tell you that liberty is in danger and although the majority is in favor of it, you ought not submit.

The governor spoke at great length and then went over every article of Patrick Henry's proposed declaration of rights and tried to prove that all therein was already secured in the provisions of the Constitution and could not be infringed upon by the general government. After going over every amendment Randolph finished by saying, The union of sentiments with the adopting states will render subsequent amendments easy. I rest my happiness with perfect confidence on this subject.

George Mason: Mr. Chairman, with respect to commerce and navigation, he, (Gov. Randolph) has given it as his opinion that their regulation as it now stands, was a sine qua non of the union, and that without it the states in Convention would never concur. I differ from him, It never was, nor in my opinion ever will be a sine qua non of the Union. Mr. Mason went on to explain that for many months commerce and navigation was under scrutiny and that it was decided to require eight states out of twelve in order to pass commercial and navigational laws. This passed with a majority and then a compromise was introduced by the northern states who proposed that the southern states be allowed the temporary importation of slaves if the south would agree in return that navigational and commercial laws remain on the footing on which they now stand. He mentioned that the Newfoundland fisheries require that kind of security. The Eastern States therefore agreed at length that treaties must require the consent of two thirds of the members present in the Senate.

John Dawson: Mr. Chairman, when a nation is about to make a change in its political character, it behooves it to summon the experience of ages which have passed, to collect the wisdom of the present day, to ascertain clearly those great principles of equal liberty which secure the rights, liberties, and properties, of the people. Such is the situation of the United States at the moment we are about to make such a change.

During deliberations in this Convention, several gentlemen of eminent talents having exerted themselves to prove the necessity of the union by presenting to our view the relative situation of Virginia to the other states, the melancholy representation made today, and frequently before, by an honorable gentleman, (Gov. Randolph,) of our state, reduced in his estimation, to the lowest degree of degradation, must now haunt the recollection of many gentleman in this committee.

He questioned the accuracy of the exaggerations and praised the ability of the members gathered, saying if truth be admitted on all sides, then danger of Virginia seceding from the union was always a possibility **and the danger was not yet over.**

Mr. Dawson sensed the deep schism between the factions pro and con the Constitution. I will not say that opponents to the paper on your table are enemies to the union. It may therefore be improper for me to declare that I am a warm friend to a firm, federal energetic government; that I consider a confederation of the states, on republican principles, as a security to their mutual interests, and a disunion as injurious to the whole;

I shall lament exceedingly, when a confederation of independent states shall be converted into a consolidated government; for, when that event shall happen, I shall consider the history of American liberty as short as it has been brilliant, and we shall afford one more proof to the favorite maxim of tyrants, "that mankind cannot govern themselves."

Mr. Dawson said that arguments on merit should not be personal but address only the issues, He held the opinion that had the paper then on the table been presented ten years earlier **when the American spirit shone with a meridian of glory, and rendered the amazement and encomium of the whole world, it would have fallen far beneath the high principles compatible with republican liberty, and doomed to fail.**

Mr. Dawson questioned whether a country so disparate in climates, dispositions and personalities could be ruled under a consolidated government unless by despotic means.

He felt that the friends of the Constitution would deny in vain that every article, section, clause and line, lead to a consolidated government and ventured that historians would undoubtedly say that no government founded on the principles of freedom could rule a nation without consolidation.

Mr. Dawson admitted that his greatest concern was over the power of the President on the concurrence of two thirds of those present in the Senate, may make a treaty by which territory is ceded, or the navigation of any river surrendered, thereby granting five states the power to afflict an act of the highest sovereignty, and not representatives of the entire republic. He brought up the diabolic attempt to give away the rights to the Mississippi river, a cause that should make men tremble and upon which rests the future of the southern states.

He suggested that three fourths of all the Senators were necessary to ratify a treaty respecting the cession of territory, the surrender of navigation rights on rivers or the use of American seas. "Wealth and extent of territory, have a relation to government, and the manners and customs of the people are closely connected with it." He quoted Montesquieu. His vote would go to having amendments before ratification, but he ventured that should the vote go against his wishes that he would first attend to promote happiness and prosperity for the country so dear to his heart.

William Grayson, Mr. Chairman, gentlemen have misrepresented what I said on the subject of Treaties. On this ground let us appeal to the law of nations. How does it stand? Thus, that without the consent of the national legislature, dismemberment cannot be made.

This is a subject in which Virginia is deeply interested, and ought to be well understood. It ought to be expressly provided that no dismemberment should take place without the consent of the legislature. On this occasion, I beg leave to introduce an instance mentioned on the floor of Congress. Francis, king of France, was taken by the Spaniards at the battle of Pavia. He stipulated to give up certain territories, to be liberated. Yet the stipulation was not complied with, because it was alleged that it was not made by the sovereign power. Let us apply this. Congress has a right to dismember the empire. The President may do it, and the legislature may confirm it. Let gentlemen contradict it if they can. This is one of the highest acts of sovereignty, and I think it of the utmost importance that it should be placed on a proper footing. There is an absolute necessity for the existence of the power. It may prevent the annihilation of society by procuring a peace. It must be lodged somewhere.

The opposition wish it to be put in the hands of three fourths of the members of both houses of Congress. It would be then secure. It is not so now.

The dangers of disunion were painted in strong colors.

How is the fact? It is this, that, if Virginia thinks proper to insist on previous amendments, joined by New York and North Carolina, she can procure what amendments she pleases.

What is the geographical position of these states? New York commands the ocean. Virginia and North Carolina, the Spanish dominions. What would be the situation, of the other states? They would be topographically separated, though politically, connected with one another. There would be no communication between the centre and the component parts. While those states were thus separated, of what advantage would commercial regulations be to them? Yet will gentlemen pretend to say that we must adopt first, and then beg for amendments? I see no reason in it. We undervalue our own importance. Consider the vast consequence and importance of Virginia and North Carolina.

What kind of connection would the rest of the states form? They would be carrying states, without having any thing to carry.

They could have no communication with the other Southern States.

I therefore insist that, if you are not satisfied with the paper as it stands, it is as clear to me, as that the sun shines, that, by joining these two states, you may command such amendments as you may think necessary for the happiness of the people. The late Convention was not empowered totally to alter the present Confederation. The idea was to amend. If they lay before us a thing quite different, we are not bound to accept it. There is nothing dictatorial in refusing it: we wish to remove the spirit of party.

In all parts of the world there is a reciprocity in contracts and compacts. If one man makes a proposition to another, is he bound to accept it? Considering the situation of the continent, this is not a time for changing our government. I do not think we stand so secure with respect to other nations as to change our government.

The nations of Europe look with watchful eyes on us, and with reason; for the West India islands depend on our motions. When we have strength, importance and union, they will have reason to tremble for their island. Almost all the governments of the world have been formed by accident. We are not, in time of peace, without any real cause, changing our government. We ought to be cool and temperate, and not act like the people of Denmark, who gave up their liberties, in a transport of passion, to the crown. Let us therefore be cautious, and deliberate before we determine.

What is the situation of Virginia? She is rich when her resources are compared others.

Is it right for a rich nation to consolidate with a poor one? By no means.

It was right for Scotland to unite with England, as experience has shown. Scotland only pays forty–eight thousand pounds, when England pays four shillings to the pound, which amount to two million pounds.

In all unions where a rich state is joined with a poor one, it will be found that the rich one will pay in that disproportion. A union between such nations ought never to take place, except in peculiar circumstances, and on very particular conditions. How is it with Virginia? It is politic for her to unite, but not on any terms. She will pay more than her natural proportion, and the present state of the national debt renders it an object. She will also lose her importance. She is now put in the same situation as a state forty times smaller.

Does she gain any advantage from her central situation, by acceding to that paper? Within ten miles of Alexandria the centre of the states is said to be. It has not been said where the ten miles square will be. In a monarchy, the seat of government must be where the monarch pleases. How ought it to be in a republic like ours? Now in one part, and at another time in another, or where it will best suit the convenience of the people.

I lay it down as a political right that the seat of government ought to be fixed by the Constitution so as to suit the public convenience.

Has Virginia any gain from her riches and commerce? What does she get in return? I can see what she gives up, which is immense.

The little states gain in proportion as we lose. Every disproportion is against us. If she effects of such a contrariety of interests to be happy, it must be extraordinary and wonderful.

From the very nature of the paper, one part, which interest is different from the other, is to govern it. What will be our situation? The Northern States are carrying states. We are considered as productive states. They will consequently carry for us. Are manufactures favorable to us?

If they reciprocate the act of Charles II., and say that no produce of America will be carried in any foreign bottom, what will be the consequences? This, that all the produce of the southern States will be carried by the Northern States on their own terms, which must be very high,

Though this government has the power of taxation, and the most important subject of the legislation, there is no responsibility any where. The members of Delaware do not return to Virginia to give an account of their conduct. Yet they legislate for us. In addition to this, it will be productive of great expenses.

Virginia has assumed an immense weight of private debt, and her imports and exports are taken away. Judge how such an accumulation of expenses will accommodate us. I think that, were it not for one great character (George Washington), so many men would not be for this government. We have one ray of hope.

We do not fear while he lives; but we can only expect his fame to be immortal. We wish to know who, besides him, can concentrate the confidence and affections of all America.

He concluded by expressing hopes that the proposition of his honorable friend (Mr. Wythe) would be acceded to.

James Madison: Mr. Chairman, nothing has excited more admiration in the world than the manner in which free governments have been established in America; for it was the first instance for the creation of the world to the American revolution, that free inhabitants have been seen deliberating on a form of government, and selecting such of their citizens as possessed their confidence, to determine upon and give effect to it. But why has this excited so much wonder and applause?

The United States have, in the middle of war and confusion, formed free systems of government, how much more astonishment, and admiration will be excited, should they be able, peaceable freely and satisfactorily, to establish one general government, where there is such a diversity of opinions and interests, when not cemented or stimulated by any common danger!

How vast is the difficulty of concentrating, on one government, the interests, and conciliating the opinion, of so many heterogeneous bodies. It is a most awful thing that depends on our decision, whether the thirteen states shall unite freely, peaceable, and unanimously, for security of their common happiness and liberty, or whether every thing is to be put in confusion and disorder? Are we to embark in the dangerous enterprise, uniting various opinions to contrary interests, with the vain hope of coming to an amicable concurrence?

Madison then admitted that there had been difficulties impossible to describe in forming the words and ideas of the paper on the table, and said that only flexibility had allowed a concurrence of opinions in forming the paper under dispassionate and calm circumstances, almost impossible without emotion.

Yet even then it was terribly difficult to agree to any system. He went on to warn of the outrageous conditions that would prevail if Virginia failed to ratify and insisted on previous amendments and this was thrown back to the other states. It was a nightmare even to recall

Patrick Henry felt that the arguments given by the opposition were a clear sign that no amendments would be granted after the adoption. He thought the project vain, indecent and improper.

He asked if amendments were not attainable were they then to lay their hands on their hearts and say that they would adopt anyway? He insisted that this kind of theory was not the language of Virginia and asked again for amendments previous to adoption of the Constitution.

He was chilled by the comment that their opposition could exist better without them then they could alone.(were Virginia to secede).

Henry was reduced to agreeing to cooperate if only a security of rights essential to general happiness was granted. (The Bill of Rights).

Lastly, he referred to ethereal beings beyond the horizon that bounds human eyes, watching for their decision and predicted future consequences, future revolutions.

A violent storm erupted and Henry was obliged to conclude.

George Nicholas: Announced the vote for the next day at nine o'clock.

Charles Clay: Clay stood on his feet to oppose.

William Ronald: Opposed the motion and asked for amendments to be prepared by a committee before the vote.

George Nicholas: Contended that the language of the proposed ratification would secure every thing which gentlemen desired and added that the Constitution was derived from the people and would be resumed by them whenever they were injured or oppressed and that powers not specifically granted thereby remained at their will.

William Ronald: Determined that he must know the exact amendments desired before he could make up his mind. Without them he could against every inclination, vote against the adoption as the happiness and security of the people were possibly endangered through omissions.

James Madison: Conceived that defects in the Constitution might be removed by the amendatory process, however he thought them unnecessary and dangerous. He ended by agreeing to accept whatever amendments that were not dangerous.

Wednesday, June 25, 1788, was the last opportunity for debate

Benjamin Harrison: Went into the history that brought them to the current situation, saying that Virginia, finding the power of the Confederation, inadequate, invited other states to a convention to enlarge upon the powers of Congress. He said he felt no danger to the Union until then and warned against rapid changes such as the paper they saw before them. He said any attempt otherwise might be ruinous; that change should come like rivers changing their course gently. He pointed out that no northern states came to help when Virginia was invaded, that General Washington with a contingency of French auxiliarys relieved them. He claimed to be a friend of the Union but thought the adoption of the Constitution was unwarrantable, precipitate and dangerously impolitic and said that it would rush them to perdition and vowed that he would resist as a man. He approved of the amendments but preferred them previous, not after signing.

James Madison: Stood blustering and swore that the gentlemen of the convention would see how easily the amendments would be ratified and included in the Constitution.
He warned of the dreadful effect on the other states if the Constitution were thrown back to them defiled by refusal.

James Monroe: remarked that the last question was amendments, previous or subsequent and that he supported the former. He pointed out that the adopting states should be united with Virginia.
He went on to say that in the worst scenario when states armed against each other, that Virginia would form a proposal consistent with their mutual interests. **Adopt now, and it will never be amended, he said, followed by the recommendation of pursuing amendments with manly fortitude.**

James Innes: explained that his former silence did not stem from neutrality or a supineness of disposition, and would have been desultory.
Feeling that he had now to take part in the most important decision in the councils of America, and grieved to see those brave officers who had gallantly fought and bled for their country and was sadly stunned to be on

a different side then many of them, he prayed for candor and moderation, without which he feared everything with respect to the public would evaporate into nothing.

He had struggled to keep an open mind but was shocked by the threats and horrors summoned by the opposition and deplored the mode of their reasoning, which for him had no effect.

He saw "previous amendments" as a violation of the commission given the people, as no other convention has chosen this route. Making radical changes in the paper on the table would bind the nation to what they knew not at all.

He noted what he called "jealousy" towards our northern brethren and said that not one state had dominion over another, but that America extended from one end of the continent to the other and people loved each other and were unified in 1775. He called for great principles of reciprocal friendship and mutual amity to conciliate the Union, to do otherwise would not only be bad, but madness. Then he warned of Spain and Great Britain and the maritime powers of Europe and cautioned that America must be united and grow strong to offset these dangers. He went on to ridicule the arguments of those opposing adoption. Mr. Innes wanted to approve the paper as there was none better and wanted an end to statements that were imprudent, destructive and calamitous. His speech was magnificent if totally in opposition to the Anti-Federalist view.

John Tyler: wanted his vote against the Constitution explained for posterity. He particularly feared the loose, indefinite construction that meant that those who composed it had not concurred and never would on all matters.

He mocked Innes for saying they had no right to propose amendments, saying they had every right and responsibility. He admitted that their amendments would not be binding on other states and he wished not to be dictated to, that each state would determine their attitude and vote.

He was angry that it was said that the predatory nations of Europe would come and attack them if they failed to adopt this government with all its defects and asked if they were to be frightened into accepting it.

James Innes: Stood to explain how previous amendments would not be binding on those who had not seen or considered them and would cause terrible problems, but that subsequent amendments could be studied and accepted or not; and that Congress would vote on them.

John Tyler: Said that British tyranny would have been more tolerable than this dis-union. He was disturbed by all the warnings and threats to liberty and the inherent dangers and unfairness in the paper on the table.

He said that if they were to be consolidated, let it be on better grounds; declaring that men would never be fully satisfied with their happiness.

He had lost his confidence in the promises of those supporting adoption without previous amendments.

He refuted that any country in Europe had cause to go to war with them and added that **liberty should not to be forfeited without knowing the terms.** He said his conduct throughout the revolution justified him and his opinions. Tyler elaborated on every thing missing from the Constitution and the main dangers. He allowed that his heart would never be at peace until the gross defects were removed. He thought that if the country was divided, politicians would reconcile by introducing alterations as necessary.

He wished for posterity and his family to be proud that his opposition to the paper on the table was based on its danger to the liberties of life and country.

Adam Stephen: Spoke of the absolute necessity of preventing a dismemberment of the confederacy. He suggested that it was genius of the American people that they could reform their government but that the woeful experience had been totally inefficient and knew that the filial duty and affection would impel the genius of Virginia that had formerly resisted British tyranny and in the language of manly intrepidy and fortitude, say to the nation, thus far, and no further shall you proceed.

He mocked the appearance and lack of ability to inspire the others, by appearing mournful, disheveled, distressed with grief and sorrow, supplicating our assistance against gorgons, fiends, and hydras that will devour or spread desolation throughout the country. She bewails the decay of grace, the neglect of agriculture, her farmers, ship builders, carpenters, blacksmiths and tradesmen going unemployed She laments that the profits of her commerce go to foreign states. She bewails the fact that she cannot raise taxes to fit her needs. She sees religion die, public faith prostituted and private confidence lost between men. Expostulations to Congress for the defection of Virginia from the Union. They will wonder what has become of her senses just after she has given an immense tract of country to relieve the general distress and make their country solvent. How can she prove her superiority now and explain to those who tried to save the Union by adopting the Constitution, placing their faith that necessary amendments would be acceded to by their friends in other states He ended by saying that soon Virginians would soon know if they were among the members of the United States or not.

Zechariah Johnson: Spoke of making the greatest decision to effect felicity of himself and posterity. He found no merit in the constraints of the opposition to destroy every word or line and to cause great consternation for no good reason, that the Constitution was a valid piece of true art. That he had listened and been prepared to acquiesce to sound argument but found the paper on the table to be an instrument that protected liberty He was not worried about regulation of the Militia or freedom of religion. He approved of the system of taxation and the manner of electing representatives. My vote for the Constitution lies in its felicity and happiness of my children who are uppermost in my mind. He had read the amendments and disapproved of them, saying they did nothing for personal liberty. He ended by saying that the annuals of mankind had never shown one example of a perfect Constitution.

Patrick Henry: Now knew that previous or subsequent amendments were likely lost and hoped to see changes in the government that would reflect safety, liberty and happiness to the people.

Governor Edmund Randolph: The suffrage which I shall give in favor of the Constitution will be ascribed to motives unknown to my breast. Although for every other act of my life I shall seek refuge in the mercy of God, for Lest, some future analyst in the spirit of party vengeance, deign to mention my name, let him recite these truths –that I went to the federal Convention with the strongest affection for the union' that I acted then in full conformity with this affection; that I refused to subscribe, because I had, and have objections to the Constitution, and wished a free inquiry into its merits; and that the accession of eight states reduced our deliberations to the single question of Union or no union.

George Nicholas said discussions were finished and more talk would be by those who wished to destroy the Constitution.
"We wish it to be ratified and such amendments as may be thought necessary to be subsequently considered by a committee, in order to be

recommended to Congress, to be acted upon according to the amendatory mode presented in itself. He then moved that the clerk should read the resolution proposed by Mr. Wythe, in order that the question might be put upon it." Mr. Tyler moved to read those amendments and the bill of rights by Mr. Henry so they could be voted upon.

WYTHE'S RESOLUTION

"Whereas the powers granted under the proposed Constitution are the gift of the people, and every power not granted thereby remains with them, and at their will, no right, therefore, of any denomination, can be cancelled, abridged, restrained or modified, by the Congress, the Senate or House of Representatives, acting in any capacity, by the President, or any department or officer of the Unites States, except in those instances in which power is given by the Constitution for those purposes; and, among other essential rights, liberty of conscience and of the press cannot be cancelled, abridged, restrained or modified, by any authority of the United States."

"And whereas any imperfections, which may exist in the said Constitution, ought rather to be examined in the mode prescribed therein for obtaining amendments, than by a delay, with a hope of obtaining previous amendments, to bring the Union into danger."

"Resolved, That it is the opinion of this committee, that the said Constitution be ratified, But in order to relieve the apprehension of those who may be solicitous for amendments, "Resolved, that it is the opinion of this committee, that whatsoever amendments may be deemed necessary, be recommended to the consideration of the Congress which shall first assemble under the said Constitution, to be acted upon according to the mode prescribed in the 5th article thereof." The Amendment Process. Wythe's Resolution is voted down by a majority.

The 1st resolution being read a second time, a motion was made, and the question being put, to amend the same by substituting, in lieu of the said resolution and its preamble, the following resolution, "Resolved, that, previous to the ratification of the new constitution of government recommended by the late federal Convention, a declaration of rights, asserting, and securing from encroachment, the great principles of civil and religious liberty, and the unalienable rights of the people, together with amendments to the most exceptionable parts of the said Constitution of government, ought to be referred by this Convention to the other states in the American confederacy for consideration."

On June 24, 1788, The vote to substitute the 1st resolution by substituting Patrick Henry's paper in lieu of the said resolution and it's preamble was voted down, with 80 ayes and 88 noes.

Then, the main vote on ratifying the Constitution was resolved in favor of adopting the Constitution. The vote was: Ayes 89, Noes 79. Ten votes, separated the Anti-Federalists from victory:

A small group of the winning votes were cross-over votes by Anti-Federalists. It was a terrible blow to lose by so small a number as ten votes but the stalwart group of Anti-Federalist behaved like gentlemen as was expected of them. A committee was named to prepare amendments to the Constitution: George Wythe, Benjamin Harrison, Thomas Matthews, Patrick Henry, Gov. Edmund Randolph, George Mason, George Nicholas, William Grayson, James Madison, John Tyler, John Marshall, James Monroe, William Ronald, Paul Carrington, Theodorick Bland, Meriwether Smith, James Innes, Samuel Hopkins, John Blair, Charles Simms. The Virginia Ratifying Convention wrote 20 Amendments. Later when Congress convened, nearly all were rejected, with the exception that along with Virginia, every state insisted on a Bill of Rights, which accounted for the first ten amendments. (68) Regarding the amendments proposed by the committee, Richard Henry Lee said: "We might as well have attempted to move Atlas upon our shoulders." (69)

United in their approach, Richard Henry Lee and William Grayson drafted a letter to the Virginia Legislature, addressed to: Governor, Edmund Randolph, and the speaker of Virginia's House of Delegates Sept. 28, 1789 from New York.

"We have long waited in anxious expectation, of having it in our power to transmit effectual Amendments to the Constitution of the United States, and it is with grief that we now send forward propositions inadequate to the purpose of real and substantial Amendments, and so far short of the wishes of our Country.

By perusing the Journal of the Senate, your Excellency will see, that we did, in vain, bring to view the Amendments proposed by our Convention, and approved by the Legislature.

We shall transmit a complete set of the Journals of both Houses of Congress to your address, which with a letter accompanying them, we entreat your Excellency will have the goodness to lay before the Honorable

Legislature of the ensuing meeting. We have now the honor of enclosing the "Amendments" to the Constitution of the United States that has been finally agreed on by Congress.

We can assure you Sir, that nothing on our part has been omitted, to procure the success of those radical amendments proposed by Convention, and approved by the Legislature of our Country, which as our constituent we shall always deem it our duty with respect and reverence to obey.

The Journal of the Senate herewith transmitted, will at once show exactly how unfortunate we have been in this business.

It is impossible for us not to see the necessary tendency to consolidated empire in the natural operation of the Constitution, if not further amended than as now proposed; and it is especially impossible for us not to be apprehensive for Civil Liberty, when we know of no influence in the records of history, that show a people ruled in freedom when subject to one undivided Government, and inhabiting a territory so extensive as that of the United States; and when, as it seems to us, the nature of man, and of things join to prevent it. The impracticability in such a case, of carrying representation on sufficiently near to the people for procuring their confidence and consequent obedience, compels a resort to fear, resulting from great force and executive power in government.

Confederated republics, where the Federal hand is not possessed of absorbing power, may permit the existence of freedom, whilst it preserves union, strength, and safety. Such amendments therefore as may secure against the annihilation of the state governments we devoutly wish to see adopted.

If a persevering application to Congress from the states that have desired such amendments, should fail of its object, we are disposed to think, reasoning from causes to effects, that unless a dangerous apathy should invade the public mind, it will not be many years before a constitutional number of Legislatures will be found to DEMAND a Convention for that purpose.

"We have sent a complete set of the Journals of each House of Congress, and through the appointed channel will be transmitted the Acts that have passed this session, in those will be seen the nature and extent of the judiciary, the estimated expenses of the government, and the means so far adopted for defraying the latter." Lee and Grayson both signed.

Author's Comment:
This honest and truthful letter was strongly worded but honorable. Still, it was viewed as an inflammatory Broadside. It was printed in italics, and

presented to the Virginia house of Delegates as an example of a piece of Anti-Federalist treachery.

Lee and Grayson were likewise charged by the Federalists with seeming disaffection to the government. (70)

Now that the Anti-Federalists had lost, those in opposition, sensing that the rewards were about to be handed out, the Federalists drew their short daggers and went for the juggler veins of the most prominent Anti-Federalists who gave the slightest provocation.

William Grayson became the prime target and perhaps suffered the most, for he was passed over for any position of merit, even though on intellect alone, he was far more deserving than many. The enemies he made during this struggle, lasted for the rest of his life, but as in crises, so did the friendships and these were the best, most meaningful relationships of his life.

It had to be devastating for William to learn of the success of his enemies who were propelled into powerful positions (rewards) in the new government. Washington overlooked William for any post, but he delayed the final thrust to William's heart, and occasionally spoke in his defense.

However succinct the statement, at least it was sufficient to keep William from utter despair and perhaps political ruin in his peer group. The fact that the public adored William after his noble effort in the Convention and handily voted for him to represent them in the Senate, and not James Madison who had to settle for the Hs. of Representatives, saved him politically and prolonged his life for about a year.

On November 26, 1789, Edmund Randolph sent a copy of Lee and Grayson's letter to George Washington, which he said was his duty, but there was significance in that act along with deceit. His cover letter reeked of treachery, and personal animosity. Clearly Randolph was delighted to inform on his former colleagues; had he not suggested that bitter repercussions would devolve for turning against the majority and becoming opposition leaders especially now that the majority held the highest, most elite positions in America and the accompanying power.

Edmund Randolph had deserted the ranks of the Anti-Federalists when they needed him most and in the most propitious self-serving moment, making it appear to Washington, that he had capitulated because Washington had appealed to him as a matter of honor and righteousness thereby becoming a hand maiden to the chief who rewarded him accordingly, and his reward was so great, how could he care what anyone thought!

There was not an iota of loyalty or extended friendship extant for any of the defeated Anti-Federalists, or for that matter any decency or concern for their welfare or for the fact that they might be politically ruined.

The rewards came quickly as Washington sat at his desk at Mt. Vernon writing letters to those he chose for the highest positions in the land.

Knowing he had won so egregiously, one might think that Randolph would have handled the matter of Lee and Grayson's letter more graciously and found a way to accept the fact that they opposed the Constitution on good grounds, and get on with matters and leave them alone.

He had made it over the bodies of his peers, why stab at dead men?

All rudiments of relationship with Lee and Grayson were finished, but the manner in which Randolph passed that letter on created the final dissemination between them. It was unforgivable. Randolph knew he would go down in history books as a great man, trusted by the president, loved among his peers, but not by those who had witnessed this singular and uncalled for act of revenge.

Edmund Randolph to George Washington, Richmond, Virginia
Dear Sir, Since my last, written about five days ago, the committee of the whole house have been engaged in the amendments from Congress. Mr Henry's motion, introduced about three weeks past, for postponing the consideration of them, was negatived by a great majority. The first ten were easily agreed to. The eleventh and twelfth were rejected by a vote of 64 against 58. Twelve amendments to the Constitution were originally submitted to the states, and two were rejected. The first dealt with the apportionment of seats in the House of Representatives, the other with changing congressional salaries. I confess, that I see no propriety in adopting the two last. But I trust that the refusal to ratify will open the road to such an expression of Federalism, as will efface the violence of the last year, *and the intemperance of the inclosed letter, printed by the enemies to the constitution, without authority*. However our final measures will depend on our strength, which is not yet ascertained. I shall set off on the 15th of January, as I took the liberty of informing you in my last. I am dear sir yr obliged & affectionate friend. Edm. Randolph. (71)

Author's Comment: Edmund Randolph does not sound confident but he moved into the realm of certainty two days later, when he was appointed Attorney General of the United States and his boot came down on Lee and Grayson and anyone who dared oppose his ideologies. George Mason bit terly disillusioned said : "In this important trust, I am truly conscious of having acted from the purest motives of honesty, and love for my country, according to that measure of judgment which God has bestowed on me, and I would not forfeit the approbation of my own mind for the approbation of any man, or all the men upon earth." His words made men weep.

AMENDMENTS PROPOSED BY THE VIRGINIA RATIFYING CONVENTION, JUNE 27, 1788

That there be a Declaration of Bill of Rights asserting and securing from encroachment the essential and unalienable Rights of the People in some manner as the following: (the same as suggested by Patrick Henry.)

First, That there are certain natural rights of which men, when they form a social compact cannot deprive or divest their posterity, among which are the enjoyment of life and liberty, with the means of acquiring, possessing and protecting property, and pursuing and obtaining happiness and safety.

Second, That all power is naturally vested in and consequently derived from the people; that Magistrates, therefore, are their trustees and agents and at all times amenable to them.

Third, That Government ought to be instituted for the common benefit, protection and security of the People; and that the doctrine of non-resistance against arbitrary power and oppression is absurd lavish, and destructive of the good and happiness of mankind.

Fourth, That no man or set of Men are entitled to exclusive or separate [sic] public emoluments or privileges from the community, but in Consideration of public services; which not being descendible, neither ought the offices of Magistrate, Legislator or Judge, or any other public office to be hereditary.

Fifth, That the legislative, executive, and judiciary powers of Government should be separate [sic] and distinct, and that the members of the two first may be restrained from oppression by feeling and participating the public burdens, they should, at fixt periods be reduced to a private station, return into the mass of the people; and the vacancies be supplied by certain and regular elections; in which all or any part of the former members to be eligible or ineligible, as the rules of the Constitution of Government, and the laws shall direct.

Sixth, That elections of representatives in the legislature ought to be free and frequent, and all men having sufficient evidence of permanent common interest with and attachment to the Community ought to have in Virginia "Such amendments therefore as may secure against the right of suffrage: and no aid, charge, tax or fee can be set, rated, or levied upon the people without their own consent, or that of their representatives so elected, nor can they be bound by any law to which they have not in like manner assented for the public good.

Seventh, That all power of suspending laws or the execution of laws by any authority, without the consent of the representatives of the people in the legislature is injurious to their rights, and ought not to be exercised.

Eighth, That in all capital and criminal prosecutions, a man hath a right to demand the cause and nature of his accusation, to be confronted with the accusers and witnesses, to call for evidence and be allowed counsel in his favor, and to a fair and speedy trial by an impartial Jury of his vicinage, without whose unanimous consent he cannot be found guilty, (except in land and naval forces) nor can he be compelled to give evidence against himself.

Ninth. That no freeman ought to be taken, imprisoned, or disseized of his freehold, liberties, privileges or franchises, or outlawed or exiled, or in any manner destroyed or deprived of his life, liberty or property but by the law of the land.

Tenth. That every freeman restrained of his liberty is entitled to a remedy to inquire into the lawfulness thereof, and to remove the same, if unlawful, and that such remedy ought not to be denied nor delayed.

Eleventh. That in controversies respecting property, and in suits between man and man, the ancient trial by Jury is one of the greatest Securities to the rights of the people, and ought to remain sacred and inviolate

Twelfth. That every freeman ought to find a certain remedy by recourse to the laws for all injuries and wrongs he may receive in his person, property or character. He ought to obtain right and justice freely and compleatly without denial, without delay, and that all establishments or regulations contravening these rights, are oppressive and unjust.

Thirteenth, That excessive bail ought not be required, nor excessive fines imposed, nor cruel and unusual punishments inflicted.

Fourteenth, That every freeman has a right to be secure from all unreasonable searches and siezures of his person, his papers and his property; all warrants, therefore, to search suspected places, or sieze any freeman, his papers or property, without information upon Oath (or affirmation of a person religiously scrupulous of taking an oath) of legal and sufficient cause, are grievous and oppressive; and all general warrants to search suspected places, or to apprehend any suspected person, without specially naming or describing the place or person, are dangerous and ought not to be granted.

Fifteenth, That the people have a right peaceably to assemble to consult for the common good, or to instruct their Representatives; and that every freeman has a right to petition or apply to the legislature for redress of grievances.

Sixteenth, That the people have a right to freedom of speech, and of writing and publishing their Sentiments; but the freedom of the press is one of the greatest bulwarks of liberty and ought not to be violated.

Seventeenth, That the people have a right to keep and bear arms; that a well regulated Militia composed of the body of the people trained to arms is the proper, natural and safe defense of a free State. That standing armies in time of peace are dangerous to liberty, and therefore ought to be avoided, as far as the circumstances and protection of the Community will admit; and that in all cases the military should be under strict subordination to and governed by the Civil power.

Eighteenth, That no Soldier in time of peace ought to be quartered in any house without the consent of the owner, and in time of war in such manner only as the laws direct.

Nineteenth, That any person religiously scrupulous of bearing arms ought to be exempted upon payment of an equivalent to employ another to bear arms in his stead.

Twentieth, That religion or the duty which we owe to our Creator, and the manner of discharging it can be directed only by reason and conviction, not

unalienable right to the free exercise of religion according to the dictates of conscience, and that no particular religious sect or society ought to be favored or established by Law in preference to others.

The first ten amendments, collectively known as the Bill of Rights, were ratified simultaneously and adopted between 1789 and 1791. This bill somewhat limited the enormous power of the federal government. This bill was passed due to criticism on its asence from most of the state ratification conventions, and support from Thomas Jefferson.

A sufficient number of states ratified ten of the twelve proposals in the manner proposed in the new constitution, and the Bill of Rights became part of the Constitution.

It was difficult for Patrick Henry, George Mason, Benjamin Harrison, and James Monroe, indeed all of the Anti-Federalists, to accept that their collective ideology regarding the Constitution had injured or destroyed their relationship with Washington, and Thomas Jefferson although Jefferson was not a great fan of the Constitution.

Was it professional or personal jealousy that caused Edmund Randolph to turn so viciously on William Grayson? Obviously Randolph was eager to see William Grayson lose prestige with Washington and his tactics and methods were repulsive; a man is not called a traitor for having a difference of opinion. However, it seems that George Washington had no personal contact with William Grayson or Richard Henry. Lee again. This was heartbreaking for both men who had served Washington most of their lives. It was not out of the realm of possibility that he might recognize the degree of dedication in their commitment, while not totally approving of their ideals and be able to appreciate their high standards.

Certainly Grayson and Lee hoped for a better Constitution than what they finally received.

Perhaps Washington was reluctant to give up this friendship with them entirely, but with rampant jealousy among Grayson's peers, he had no choice. Apparently men whom Washington chose for high office did not want to work with William Grayson, or any of the Anti-Federalists. The fracture that occurred in the convention created permanent scars.

A Frenchman, St. John de Crevocoeur, on the scene to record the events surrounding the new government, related to Thomas Jefferson that Washington said he knew both William Grayson and Richard Henry Lee would be more malleable in the Senate than they had been in the Ratifying convention, and that he had spoken on William Grayson's behalf when people brought him word of Grayson's attitude and speeches while leading the Anti-Federalists. Grayson, true to his word, supported the Constitution once it was ratified. He would continue to try to improve government. Grayson had gained public recognition with his speeches in the Ratifying Convention. No matter how the Federalist's judged him, the public viewed his efforts as noble, the antithesis of someone anti-government.

The public's judgement was to elect Richard Henry Lee and Grayson as Senators from Virginia to the first Federal Congress, under the new Constitution, a consummate honor. It was believed that George Mason was also elected to the Senate, but refused to serve.

Ironically, James Madison also ran for the Senate, and received less votes than either Lee or Grayson, and was forced to run for a seat in the House, a far less prestigious role.

James Madison had once been Grayson's confidant. Now, their relationship was shattered. Where once there was respect there was intolerance. The Constitution has had a total of twenty-seven amendments. Seventeen were based on individual civil rights and political liberties, and were ratified separately. Some amendments addressed changes to the original Constitution of 1787. The 21st amendment superceded the 18th.

More than ten thousand amendments have been introduced to Congress in ensuing years. Most never left congressional committees. Amendments are still pending while others have died through expiration.

INSPIRATION FOR THE CONSTITUTION

1. Frenchman Charles de Secondat, Baron de Montesquieu
2. Republic of the United Provinces (1781)
3. Magna Carta (1215) Article 39: No free man shall be arrested, or imprisoned, or deprived of his property, or outlawed, or exiled, or in any way destroyed, nor shall we go against him or send against him, unless by legal judgement of his peers, or by the law of the land.
4. England's Bill of rights (1689) requires jury trials, prohibits excessive bail and cruel and unusual punishments as well as gives the right to bear arms.
5. The Virginia Declaration of Rights; inspired by the Magna Carta and the English Bill of rights.

CONSEQUENCES FOR THE ANTI-FEDERALISTS

Many looked on William Grayson as an inspirational force and leader of the Anti-Federalist group. Patrick Henry and Richard Henry Lee were better known nationally, Lee, as a brilliant writer, and Henry as brilliant in everything. Anti-Federalists were intelligent, well educated, informed patriots, who wanted a unified country, and never wanted Virginia to lead the south into cessession; " As Virginia went, so went the south." Virginia carried far reaching influence.

Many Anti-Federalists had served in the Continental Army or the Militia. All had supported or worked for the Revolution. They were not the enemy, they were Americans seeking a better government, equality between the north and south, individual liberties and legal rights, and hoping to retain power in the local state governments and judicial system.

John Tyler's son would become President of the United States and James Monroe and James Madison would become Presidents. A descendant of Benjamin Harrison would also be President. John Tyler senior, was a close friend of William Grayson.

The occasion of voting for the Constitution was the beginning of the two party system and would absorb the lessons of compromise.

In 1789 there were few concessions given the Anti-Federalists. George Mason, the most vocal and angriest made his disgust known, and George Washington spoke of Mason as his "quondam friend."

Richard Henry Lee, long an ally of Washington, with a long history of communication between them and a close affinity, was estranged and disillusioned. Perhaps he and Grayson figured their long association with the great man would protect them from the scurrilous events that swirled around them, and they could move through peril to greater things, perhaps even positions in the new government, but Washington never contacted either of them again as far as the record indicates.

Lee, Grayson and Henry retained their integrity, but lost their place with the powerful people who ran the new government tht evolved around Washington. Grayson never asked for anything for himself, but he did write letters asking for positions for good friends, all worthy men.

POST RATIFICATION LETTERS, AFTER 1788, BETWEEN OUTSTANDING MEN

William Grayson to George Wshington, N.Y., 22nd Sept. 1789.

"Sir, I do myself the honor to inform you that the Honble John Tyler & Henry, Judges of the late Court of Admy in Virga have signified their desire of serving in the capacity of district Judge of that State. Mr. Innis Atto Genl of the State of Virga has also expressed his inclination of serving as Attorney

General of the District Court.

I should also presume that the Office of Atto general of the Supreme Court would not be disagreeable. I am with the highest respect Yr Most Obedt & Very Hble Serv. Will'm Grayson." There was no answer. Another calamitous blow.

John Tyler's record of service was commendable. He had been a Judge of the State (Virginia) Admiralty Court from 1785 to 1788.

He was vice president of the Virginia Ratifying Convention and he would be elected a judge in the General Court of Virginia from 1788 to 1808. Afterwards, he became governor of Virginia for three years, and resigned to accept an appointment to the U.S. District Court of Virginia, a post he served until his death at an advanced age.

None of the men recommended by Grayson were propitiously tapped on the shoulder and selected for higher office, neither was William Grayson, who would have been great on the Supreme Court, but his career was changed forever due to his role in opposition to the adoption of the Constitution. To say he was sorry would not be true. Although he must have been disappointed, he never would have forfeited his integrity or principles so he could not have done differently.

Edmund Randolph on the other hand, had shown propitious foresight. Edmund deserted the Anti-Federalists in time to save his career and thereby created a great future for himself. Randolph's vicious denial of his former colleagues, was wholly self-serving. One wonders why he changed sides. Did he acquiesce to promises for advancement, or a personal appeal from Washington, and why couldn't he share his change of attitude with his former compatriots? The Federalists held him in high regard.

Robert Harmon Harrison, lawyer, soldier, statesman, and Grayson's predecessor as Washington's aide de camp, a close friend of Washington and Grayson, did very well as a politician according to the position he was offered in Washington's first administration.

Harrison was extremely critical of the Constitution and risked everything by standing on principle to defend this position when Washington contacted him for his opinion.

On September 28, 1788, Washington was at Mount Vernon going over names for his cabinet. Many were in for big surprises. Perhaps a few already knew what they would be offered.

Washington wrote to Edmund Pendleton who had presided over the Ratifying convention, and offered him the position of Judge of the District Court of Virginia, explaining that, except for Pendleton's health, he would have offered him a seat on the Supreme Court Bench. Pendleton accepted.

Surprisingly, Edmund Randolph was offered the choicest plum of all, a seat on the Supreme Court Bench, which settled any doubt about his motives when he changed sides in the convention. This probably crushed William Grayson. The appointment was one of the highest in the land.

Another dream position was offered to Robert Harmon Harrison. With full intent, Washington offered the position of Attorney General of the United States to his former aide de Camp, to which Harrison politely refused, explaining that the Judicial System as created by the "Constitution" was too flawed in principle for him to accept. We wonder if Grayson would have done the same but we will never know. Grayson never had a chance for any position in Washington's first cabinet and we can only guess why.

Washington let some time pass and wrote to Harrison again: I find that one of the reasons, which induced you to decline the appointment, rests on an idea that the Judicial Act will remain unaltered. But in respect to that circumstance, I may suggest to you, that such a change in the system is contemplated, and deemed expedient by many, in as well as out of congress, and would permit you to pay as much attention to your private affairs as your present station.

As the first Court will not sit until the first Monday in February, I have thought proper to return your commission not for the sake of urging you to accept it contrary to your interest or convenience, but with a view of giving you a farther opportunity of informing yourself of the nature and probability of the changes alluded to.

This you would be able to do with the less risk of mistake. If you should find it convenient to pass some time here, where a considerable number of Members of both Houses of Congress shall have Assembled; and this might be done before it would become indispensable to fill the place offered you.

If, on the other hand, your determination is absolutely fixed, you can, without much trouble, send back the Commission, under cover. Knowing as you do the candid part, which I wish to Act on all occasions; you will, I am persuaded, do me the justice to attribute my conduct in this particular instance to the proper motives, when I assure you, that I would not have written this letter if I had imagined it would produce any new embarrassment on your part. On the contrary you may rest assured, that I shall be perfectly satisfied with whatever determination may be consonant to your best judgment, and most agreeable to yourself. I am, George Washington.

P. S. As you may wish to know the determination of the other Associate Judges of the Supreme Court, 1 have the pleasure to inform you that all of them have accepted their Appointments.

Remarkably, Harrison had the temerity to refuse a second time. James Iredell was not blinded by principle and accepted the appointment. Robert Harmon Harrison followed Grayson to the grave within a few months in 1790. No jobs were offered to the Anti-Federalists. Choice government posts went to those who had supported the Constitution without amendments.

Author's Comment: Even though Richard Henry Lee and William Grayson found inadequacies in the Constitution and wished with all their hearts to see it ratified, once they lost the vote in the Virginia Ratifying Convention, they made a new beginning. Their posture and speeches in the Ratifying convention had made them famous in Virginia.

As Senators, they began to cooperate fully with the new government that was established to support and implement the Constitution. George Washington had predicted accurately regarding Grayson, whose loyalty to the United States became immediately apparent.

Merrill Jensen in "the New Nation," page 424. summed it up rather well: "Politically the dominating fact of the Confederation period was the struggle between two groups of leaders, to shape the character of the state and central governments. The Revolutionary constitutions of the states placed final power in the legislatures and made the Executive and Judicial branches subservient to them. The members of the colonial aristocracy who became patriots, and new men who gained political power during the Revolution, deplored this fact, but they were unable to alter the states constitutions during the 1780's. Meanwhile, they tried persistently to strengthen the central government. These men were the Nationalists of the 1780's." Jensen was speaking on behalf of the Anti-Federalist's. Washington knew that William Grayson would be a fine Senator in the Federal Congress, and said so to Grayson's detractors. The Congress met then in New York, but the arguments continued about the location for a permanent site for the Federal capitol. Much was made about seeking a northern location but nothing was settled. Richard Henry Lee received more votes then Grayson but they went to Congress together. The battle over the Constitution was long and bitter and many relationships were forever doomed.

Samuel A. Otis to Theodore Sedgwick, June 6, 1788, New York

Otis also wrote the following private letter to a "Mr Greenleaf' the following day. As it is addressed only to "Mr Greenleaf," it seems likely that it was hand delivered to a person in New York City, but as Greenleaf was about

hand delivered to a person in New York City, but as Greenleaf was about to leave the city and would be away indefinitely, he was probably not the New York printer Thomas Greenleaf. "My Dear Sir, You need be under no kind of apprehension that your affair with Mr H however public it may become will injure your reputation. Your universally polite modest & obliging demeanour must forever rest the blame upon that rash & unfortunate man; And the spirit & firmness with which you vindicated your honor must endear you to your friends, and encrease the reputation you had before acquired. I had anticipated your intimations in a letter to Mr D, I only regret that my pen cannot do you Justice. As you leave Town before I can have oppy of paying you my personal respects, permit me to wish you an agreeable Journey, not only to Phil. but thro life; And to assure you I esteem it a favor to be inserted in the list of Correspondents Promising the exactest attention upon my part whenever I can communicate any thing that will profit or amuse. With my Complim. Mr & Mrs Ingraham, accept my assurances of much esteem, Your friend & Most Huml Sert, Sam A Otis

James Madison to George Washington, Sept. 14,1788, New York
Dear Sir, The delay in providing for the commencement of the Government was terminated yesterday by an acquiescence of the minor number in the persevering demands of the major.

The time for chusing the electors is the first Wednesday in Jany. and for chusing the President the first Wednesday in Feby. The meeting of the Govt. is to be the first Wednesday in March, and in the City of New York. The times were adjusted to the meetings of the State Legislatures. The place was the result of the dilemma to which the opponents of N. York were reduced to yielding to its advocates or strangling the Government in its birth.

The necessity of yielding, and the impropriety of further delay, has for some time been obvious to me, but others did not view the matter in the same light. Maryland & Delaware were absolutely inflexible.

It has indeed been too apparent that local & state Considerations have very improperly predominated in this question, and that something more is aimed at than merely the first Session of the Govt. at this place.

Every circumstance has shewn that the policy is to keep Congress here till a permanent seat be chosen, and to obtain a permanent seat at farthest not beyond the Susquehannah. N. Jersey, by its Legislature as well as its Delegation in Congress, has clearly discovered her view to be a temporary appointment of New York as affording the best chance of a permanent establishment at Trenton.

I have been made so fully sensible of these views in the course of the business as well as of the impropriety of so excentric a position as N. York that I would have finally concurred in any place more Southward to which the Eastern States wd. have acceded, and previous to the definitive vote, a motion was made tendering a blank for that purpose *At any place South of the Delaware, the Susquehannah at least would have been secured, and a hope given to the Potowmac.*

As the case is, I conceive of being stopped at the Delaware. *Besides this consequence, the decision regarding the* **Susquehannah is the utmost to be hoped for, with no small danger,** *will I fear be regarded at once as proof of the preponderancy of the Eastern strength, and of a disposition to make an unfair use of it. And it cannot but happen that the question will be entailed on the New Governmt. which will have enough of other causes of agitation in its Councils.*

The meeting at Harrisburg is represented by its friends as having been conducted with much harmony & moderation. Its proceedings are said to be in the press, and will of course soon be before the public. I find that all the mischief apprehended from Clinton's circular letter in Virginia will be verified. *The Anti-federalsts. lay hold of it with eagerness as the harbinger of a second Convention; and as the Governor espouses the project it will certainly have the co-operation of our Assembly.* I inclose a sensible little pamphlet which falls within the plan of investigating and comparing the languages of the Aboriginal Americans; the muhhekaneew Indians). With the sincerest attachment I am Dear Sir, Your Obedt. & very hmble. servt., J. Madison Jr.

Paine Wingate to Samuel Lane, June 26, 1788, N.Y.

Dear Sir, By your favor of June 9th I received the first intelligence from the General Court of New Hampshire after their meeting, and am much obliged to you for the trouble you took in giving me that early information. My wife informs me that you took particular pains to convey to me the letter; I am very much gratifyed by knowing how the elections have issued. I have since seen a New Hampshire paper in which there was a list of the court decisions &c. I now Sir with particular satisfaction, congratulate upon the adoption of the new constitution in your State, and which has ensured its taking place. The latest news we have from Virginia is dated the 18 Instant.

By a letter from Govr. Randolph we are told that then there had no question been taken to decide the sense of the Convention, but his calculation was that these were 82 for, 76 against & 10 doubtful.

Another letter which is from an Anti-federalist of, the same date says, that there are reckoned 80 on each side as certain & 8 as doubtful. The event therefore is yet very dubious.

It is supposed that they would come to a determination on Saturday or Wednesday last. Of New-York convention you will have as good an account as I am able to give you by the newspaper which I enclose.

I hope that the spirit of lying & controversy upon this important subject will soon be done away, & that harmony and prosperity will attend the United States. We have no intelligence from Europe than what is seen in the papers. By them we have accounts of very distressing wars & other calamities. It is not unlikely that other nations may be involved. The disturbances in France between the King & his Parliament & other powerful subjects is very considerable. Perhaps it may be a fortunate time for them to regain some of their ancient liberties. The spirit of American liberty which he cherished at a distance seems to have crossed the Atlantic & is not a little troublesome to him. It may perhaps be that wrong to suggest any thing to the reproach of our magnanimous & most Christian ally, but I suppose the truth of the case is that he is a very weak & Scottish prince.

The latter infirmity, if he had not the former, you know will disqualify very soon a man from being active & enterprising, The Dutch are in a much worse condition than when they began their struggle & thousands of them have been obliged to fly their country & are ruined.

It is very probable that those confusions in Europe may be the means of sending emigrants to America. Whether this will conduce to the real comfort & happiness of its present inhabitants I cannot say, but it will hasten on our population & make us a great if not a happy people.

The western country which is yet to people is immense & I do believe it is a country in [which] the inhabitants can subsist themselves as easy as in any part of the world but they have many disadvantages. They are now settled in that country some of them a thousand miles from the sea.

Spaniards are on their West & South & tribes of savages in the midst of them & they will I believe have wars with both of them sooner or later. Congress have agreed to sell large tracts of that country & others are applying. I hope that it will yield some emoluments to the united states. The Congress will I suppose pretty soon take up the new System & prepare to put in motion. I hope that by the latter end of August we shall be able to adjourn.

For my own part I am not for tarrying here any longer than is indespensable. I have my health & find my situation more agreeable than I expected. We have agreed that Kentucky should be independent in a mode conformable to the Confederation, but it cannot take place in the present situation of affairs. I can add no more but my best wishes to attend you & yours and am your obliged friend & humble Servant. Paine Wingate (72)

Nathan Dane to Melancton Smith, July 3, 1788, New York
A commendable letter explaining the situation clearly.

Dear Sir, In my last letter I briefly gave my opinion on the questions you Stated to me; now being more at Leisure & Sensible that the peculiar Situation of our Government at this time is a matter of common concern and highly interesting to us all; and that we have the same object in view, the peaceable establishment of a general Government, on genuine federal and republican principles.

I shall in this be more particular, and submit to your consideration several observations with that candor and frankness it which we have always communicated our sentiments to each other relative on the important subject in question. The Constitution of the United States is now established by the people of ten States, and a day of course must soon be fixed, when all proceedings under the Confederation shall cease.

The line of conduct which shall now be pursued by the three States which have not, as yet ratified is become particularly and deeply interesting to them, and to the whole Confederacy. As things are now circumstanced will it not be clearly for their interest and happiness, as well as for the interest and happiness of all the union to adopt the Constitution proposing such amendments as they may think essential.

The situation of the States is now critical; as the Constitution is already established there can be no previous amendments; and a State which has not ratified, and wishes to be in the union, appears to have but this alternative before her; either to accede with recommending certain alterations, or to make them a condition of her accession: and the probable consequence of either Step must be considered.

I take it for granted that New York and the other two States wish to form a part of an American Confederacy; the readiness with which they Joined in the revolution, and acceded to the articles of Confederation; their open and general professions, and their past exertions to the support of the union Justify this opinion.

In all our late political discussions, a separation of the States, or Separate Confederacies, have scarcely, to my knowledge, been seriously mentioned.

Admitting that Rhode Island, New York, and North Carolina all withhold their assent to the Constitution, and propose similar amendments, their situation is so far removed from each other, and surrounded by ratifying States, that they never can think of confederating among themselves.

Each one of them must be considered as Standing alone; but we have no reason to suppose that any one of those States has a wish to Stand alone, in Case she can Confederate on principles agreeable to her.

If I understand the politics of these three States, they are strongly attached to governments founded in freedom and compact, and possess a Just aversion to those which are the result of force and violence.

They will, therefore, be the last States which will adopt measures tending to foment parties, and give passion an ascendancy over reason, or to hazard steps that may, in the end, lead to a civil war, and consequently to the Government of the prevailing party established by the longest Sword.

It is not to be pretended that the ratifying States will have any Just cause to make war upon any non ratifying State, merely because she does not accede to a national compact, where she has a right to act according to her discretion; nor ought we to presume that hostilities will be commenced by any party without some plausible or Just provocation.

But the ratifying and non-ratifying States will immediately have opposite Interests, which, in the nature of things, they will pursue; the longer they shall remain separate the more their affections and friendship for each other will decrease; and counteracting laws and a disposition for coercive measures will take place; the affairs of the Country will have a propensity to extremities and a thousand accidents may give rise to hostilities.

The question in the ratifying States being settled, it is probable the parties in them will gradually unite.

In the States where the question shall remain unsettled, and the contest continue between the parties in them, as it undoubtedly will, in what manner they shall Join the union, they will grow more hostile to each other; and from what appears to be their present temper and situation, and if we reason from experience and from the character of men we must conclude, it is at least highly probable, that they will have recourse to arms, or to contentions extremely injurious to their common Interest, at no very distant period. And what must be the issue of force, or of such contentions between the parties in any State is not difficult to foresee. If the other States should not interfere, those parties must decide their contest by themselves. If the party called federal Shall prevail, they bring the State into the Union Unconditionally, or establish a State Government of their own, probably, on their own principles. If the other party shall prevail they will keep the State out of the Union, unless the federal Constitution, which can hardly be presumed, shall in the mean time become agreeable to them, and they of necessity add a degree of severity to their laws and measures very incompatible with those principles of freedom they now contend for; this presents a disagreeable Scene in either event.

But should the other States interfere, or a civil war by any accident become general between the advocates and opposers of the Constitution, throughout the United States, which is the probable consequence of any hostile beginnings, what must be the issue? Our people tho enlightened are high Spirited; one party, when both are nearly ruined, may prevail, not in accommodating and fixing a government in freedom and compact, but in force and violence, and may we not expect a more severe high toned partial system established to secure the victorious party, at least a system more despotic than the one we lay aside, or the one we will adopt.

Were there any great number of men heartily attached to the Confederation, their success might establish it; but this in its present form seems to have but few or no advocates.

Were there any great number of men attached to it with certain defined Alterations in it, their success might establish it when so altered; but we have not agreed in those alterations; and if we may Judge from experience, and what appears to be the public opinion, it is more difficult to mold the Confederation to the wishes of the people than the Constitution;

Community in fact consists of two parties, the advocates, who are for establishing the Constitution in its present form, and the opposers, who generally if I understand them consider it as a tolerable basis, but as an imperfect and unguarded system unless amended. Were the advocates attached to the system their success might establish it, but this is not the Case.

We know that many of them and those too, who would have the most influence, from their abilities, address, and activity, in producing a Government, never will agree to a system so favourable to liberty and republicanism even as the one proposed, if by any means they can get one favourable to themselves, and unfavourable to the body of the people.

If the other party, those who wish to have the system but amended, succeed, and they were agreed in the amendments their success might establish the plan so amended; but no set of amendments have been agreed upon, and different ones have been proposed by different Conventions.

You will, therefore, I am confident, agree with me that the friends of liberty and of Governments founded in compact cannot reasonably expect any good consequences from force and violence; the very means are hostile to the end proposed.

Our object is to improve the plan proposed: to Strengthen and secure it's democratic features; to add checks and guards to it; to secure equal liberty by proper Stipulations to prevent an undue exercise of power, and to establish beyond the power of faction to alter, a genuine federal republic. To effect this great desirable object the peace of the Country must be preserved, candor cherished, information extended and the doors of accommodation constantly open.

The votes of the people will avail them much more in establishing a government favourable to them; than any violent or foreseeable proceedings. Consider that five States have adopted the Constitution without proposing any amendments; we have seen the amendments proposed in the Conventions of four States; and it is there appears to be too little in reality proposed to be gained by the amendments to Justify parties in those states carrying matters to extremities; Nor will any one, two or three States expect others to meet them in amendments, but on the principles of accommodation.

Whatever amendments any State may propose, I am persuaded you are too well acquainted with men, not to be sensible that passion, opinion, and self will must have a constant influence in their conduct relative to them, that when terms are rigidly insisted on by one party, they are generally opposed by terms rigidly insisted on by the other.

It cannot be proper for any State positively to say to the others, that unless they precisely agree to the alterations she proposes she will not accede to the Union; this would be rather dictating; a state may take a question upon the Constitution simply as it stands and express its sense of it in it's present form; she may then annex recommended amendments and adopt it with them, or make them the Condition of her accession to the Union. I flatter myself, after a state has expressed her sense upon the simple proposition you will prefer the mode of adopting with recommendatory amendments annexed; the new system must soon go into operation and some of the most important laws be made in the first Congress, and essential amendments be recommended by it; the State that adopts this mode comes into the Union armed with the declared Sentiments of her people, and will immediately have a voice in the federal Councils; she therefore will avail herself of all her influence, and of the advantages of Accommodating principles in bringing the other States to Accord with her sentiments; whereas if she adopts conditionally She will not have a voice in those Councils during the most interesting period;

Party Spirit will, probably, reign in her bosom, and ill will constantly gain ground between her and the other States; and it is in my mind almost an absolute certainty that she must forever remain out of the Union, or relinquish some of her conditions.

It cannot be presumed that any two of the three States will precisely agree in the same Alterations, and should they do it, it is not probable that all the States will agree exactly to them.

There are many and able advocates for valuable amendments, and a good system of laws in every State and may they not prevail should all the States meet in the first Congress but should some of them Stand out, and those in which those amendments and laws have the most friends; *the federal republicans or men who wish to cement the union of the States on republican principles will be divided, and have but a part of their Strength in Congress, where they ought to have the whole.*

When measures of any sort become necessary in a Community, it is generally wise to take part in them, and to bring them as near to our opinions as we can in the first instance, and I have ever thought since a federal Convention was agreed on that Rhode Island and certain individuals, who were appointed to that Convention, missed it exceedingly in not attending it.

They might clearly, had they attended, have engrafted many of the principles and checks they now contend for, into the system; and have given it those features and securities which as it now appears, would meet the approbation of the people in General; they saw a Constitution of some kind was to be made, and before it had taken a fixed direction was the time for exertions. You as well as others know it to be a fact that some parts of the Constitution most complained of, were obtained with much address and after repeated trials, and which never could have been carried had the States and members, I refer to, attended the federal Convention; for any State now to stand out and oppose appears to me to be but a repetition of the same error. I might add many more observations but I think I need not dwell longer on these points. Even when a few states had adopted without any alterations, the ground was materially changed; and now it is totally Shifted.

Tho I retain my opinion respecting the feeble features, the extensive powers, and defective parts of the System, yet circumstanced as we are, I confess, I feel no impropriety in urging the three States to Accede.

Men in all the States who wish to establish a free, equal, and efficient government, to the exclusion of Anarchy, corruption, faction, and oppression ought in my opinion to unite in their exertions in making the best of the Constitution now established; to preserve inviolate the liberties of America, and to promote the happiness of the people by Just and equal laws and an equitable administration; to add constitutional security to those liberties on every proper occasion are still the objects of all good men. This now appears to be the way to disappoint those men who discover a disposition to make a bad use of a Constitution in many parts not well guarded, and to use its powers to corrupt and selfish purposes; a good Constitution is capable of affording much security to the rights of the people, and ought to be aimed at with unremitted attention.

But ought we to expect any Constitution under which the people may safely relax in any considerable degree in their attention to public measures? Can they be secure under any Constitution unless attentive themselves, and unless some of their able leaders are their real friends and their faithful guardians? Tho I think our people have examined the system in question with candor and freedom and discovered a strong attachment to liberty; Yet I would by no means so far rely upon their exertions and vigilance as to lose sight of those Constitutional securities which may be obtained by time and experience; while we view the conduct of rulers with candor, we ought to watch their movements with an Eagle's eye, and guard and secure the temple of freedom with unceasing attention.

To conclude ought we not now to give additional weight to the plea in favor of the Constitution drawn from the peculiarity of our situation, and which when less urgent and pressing appears again and again to have saved the system! And tho the system may be abused by bad men, ought we not to recollect that The road to lasting fame in this Country has generally been Justice, Integrity, prudence and moderation, political information and industry & there is more than an equal chance that this will continue to be the case!

Attempts to palm upon our people vice for virtue, the mere shew of talents for real abilities, and the arts and puffs of party for a well earned reputation have generally failed; and what is wanting but to excite the attention of this intelligent people to render such attempts always unsuccessful?

All these and other considerations help in deciding the Question before Us. With esteem & regard, Your obedt. Hmble servant, Nathan Dane

Author's Comment: Nathaniel Dane and Melancton Smith had been congressional colleagues for nearly three years, the latter's service ended in October 1787. Smith was at the time an Anti-federalist delegate at the New York ratifying convention in Poughkeepsie. Dane replied to Smith's letter.

Samuel A. Otis to John Adams, July 7, 1788, New York

Dear Sir, Permit me tho late to congratulate you & your amiable Lady upon a return to your native Country. The pleasure & delights of which you must relish peculiarly after so long an absence. I have never been much of a traveler, but I can hardly conceive of a Country under all circumstances more eligible; And the prospect of public felicity seems the brighter from the accession of ten states to a System which so far as I comprehend it, promises equal liberty, security of property, & decision.

I do not indeed flatter myself with the return of the Golden Age. If any of our farmers have heard of Arcadia they may not think of rambling in her meadows, or that her rich harvests will spontaneously flow; Ideas like these do very well in the poets imagination. Nor may our commercial people expect Gold & Silver as in Solomon's reign, Yet we may venture to predict that the industrious husbandmen may reap plenteous harvests, & the vigilant, enterprising Merchants may rationally expect his ships full fraught with articles of foreign growth, in exchange for produce of his own Country. At least this is my hope & belief, altho some sensible, & I doubt not well meaning friends, hold up such a doleful picture to the contrary, as if the D; himself had sat for it. At all events the experiment will soon be tried. Ten States have acceded. Congress feeling an obligation to call upon the people to elect their president &c, have chosen a Committee who will in a day or two report the time for operations to commence under the new Government, & which I think will probably be in Jany or Feb 1789. N York are indeed opposed, but the last accounts from their Convention from the leaders in favor of the question "let us hope."

Of North Carolina there can be little doubt; Rhode Island you will be pleased to form your own Judgment upon. They are a kind of Comet. Virginia & N.C. & the New settled regions at the Westward, keep teasing about the Mississippi. You may probably not be informed that Congress have ratified your last loan of 1,000,000 florins, Indeed I know of no other alternative, No resources can at present be brot into operation. You may have heard Congress have resolved "that it is expedient for Kentucky to become a separate State," but this will not take place at present. The Dominion was so sworn, & Kentucky inflamed it was thot prudent to administer this cooling application. The business will not progress under the present Confederation, Vermont must go hand in hand with this business. I should feel myself honored by a communication of your opinion & advice upon any matter of such importance as to claim your attention, And with my compliments to Mrs Adams & all friends I am respectfully, Your Excellencys Most Hum Sert, Sam. A. Otis. John Adams returned from his missions to France, Neth. and Britain, and was received by the Mass. Gen. Court on June 18, 1788.

John Brown to John Smith, July 9, 1788, New York (Abridged)
Dear Smith, Congress on the 3d Instant came to a final determination upon the subject of the Kentucky address; which was to refer the application to the New Government & to recommend it to the State of Virginia & the District to make the Necessary Alterations in their Acts & Resolutions upon that Subject. The great change which has taken place in the Genl. Govt. of the Union in some measure Justified the decision which was contrary to the expectations which I at first entertained; but had it not been for the opposition of the Eastern States Kentucky might have been admitted into the Union before the New Constitution had been adopted by Nine States.

I hope this disappointment will not be productive of any bad consequences to the District; but that unanimity & good Order will still prevail. In my opinion their Interest requires that they should assume their independence, frame a Constitution, & proceed to the exercise of Government & when the New Govt. is in Motion then to make application to be admitted into the Union if it should appear advisable.

I thank you for the Journal of the Virga. Convention containing the Ratification of & proposed Amendments to the New Constitution; the proceedings of that Body were recd. here with every possible mark of Joy.
This State is still in Session, what the result of their deliberations will be is as yet very uncertain. N. Carolina will doubtless adopt it. Congress are now engaged in taking measures for setting it in Motion. The Elections are to be held in Jany. next & the New Congress to meet in Feby; I expect at Philada. I am as yet uncertain which rout I shall take to Kentucky, as I expect to be governed by the State of the River. I propose to leave about the tenth of August & hope to be at Danville the 1st of Septr. in order to attend Court at that term. In the meantime I propose to pay the Eastern States a Visit; & shall set out in company with Genl. Knox for Boston tomorrow morning. I expect to continue my Journey as far as New-Hampshire & to return through Connecticut. I promise myself much pleasure in this excursion as

I shall go part of the way by Sea a mode of travelling new to me. I am happy for the welfare of my fathers family & of my other Relations. I am pleased to find that you still entertain hopes of becoming an Inhabitant of Kentucky together with your fathers family Nothing would add more to my happiness than this Eventuality. Edward & family I expect will remove to that Country this fall. We shall all be there yet. My hopes respecting the future importance of that Country are sanguine.

I have engaged in foreign Negotiations which if Successful will be of great consequence to Kentucky. I am not at present at liberty to inform you of particulars. Remember me most affectionately to all my Relations particularly to your Mama & Cousin Betsy. Tell Capt. Preston that I have not succeeded in procuring a private Teacher for that family agreeable to my expectations express'd in my last letter; but hope shortly to be able to engage with one. I am with great friendship dear Jack, Yours, J Brown (73)

Jeremiah Wadsworth to Mehitable Wadsworth, July 10, 1788

My dear friend, New York , I arrived here last Night at Sun Set. I embarked at New Haven Monday evening; in the same Vessel which we formerly went to Lloyds Neck in & had the same weather as nearly as possible & to add to my troubles I had the sick Head Ache all the way. Jack nursed me and I was benefited by Pickering and am very well. I Lodge at Mrs. Cuylers, and find Mrs. Burr expecting every hour to ly in. My love to sisters and the children. I have hardly got my Head Steady enough to write, it seems yet to be at Sea. I wish You to send my Watch by Brig & desire him to deliver it to Clarke or Beecher to bring to me. I am, Affectionately Yours Jere Wadsworth PS Since Writing the above have seen N & Mrs Lawrence who desire their particular compliments & thanks to You for Your care of Jack.

Peleg Arnold to welcome Arnold, July 11, 1788, New York

Sir, We have this Day Thirteen States on the Floor of Congress which has not been until the present case Since the year 1776. Ten States having Ratified the New Constitution, Congress are now Deliberating on the Time for the States to appoint Electors, to Choose a President and when Proceedings Shall commence under Said Constitution;

In this Important Business from the peculiar Situation of our State the Delegation have Declined to act From the present appearance this is the Last year that Congress will assemble under the old Confederation; The time Reported by the Comtee. to assemble under the New Government is the first Monday in February Next.

the first Monday in February Next.

The Question has not yet been Determined on; but I believe it will not Exceed that Time. The information from this States Convention has generally Been that they would not adopt the New Constitution; But the Last Reports Say that the Federal Party gains Strength and it is generally believed here that it will be adopted. *I presume the amendments by the Virginia Convention have had considerable influence on the minds of the Members of this States Convention* which has occasioned this change.

Î wish to have a Line from you as often as you find it Convenient, and am your assured Friend, Peleg Arnold

Nathan Dane to Caleb Strong July 13, 1788, New York

My Dear Sir, I thank for your obliging letter of the 18 Ulto. It gives me real satisfaction, as I think must you, to see government in Massachusetts so fully restored. The reins by consent of the people themselves have now got into good hands; and I think good men will keep the principal Share in the Government, if they do not govern too much. We now have thirteen states on the floor of Congress; a circumstance which has not happened before for several years past. The Committee appointed to report an Act for putting the Constitution of the United States into operation, reported last week and Congress have spent one day in considering the report.

The States appear to be very unanimous in this business; except as to the place where Congress under the Constitution shall meet. Whether it shall meet at New York or Philadelphia will be a matter much contested. There will not be more than one State majority, I think, for either plan but this you will understand will be a question only in Case N. York shall adopt the Constitution. If she does not there will, I presume, be no question, as it will generally be thought to be improper for Congress to assemble in a non-ratifying state. If she shall adopt, from present appearances, it is probable that a majority of the States will prefer this City (N.Y.) for the meeting of the New Congress. This question will probably be decided in a few days. The Convention of this State is every day now expected to finish its business, and it is hoped it will adopt. I think we shall fix the meeting of the New Government to be about the first Wednesday in February next. The Delegates of Massachusetts and of some other states wish it to be at an earlier period as the States they represent can with ease assemble sooner, but it is said to be impossible for Virginia, North Carolina, &c from their great extent sooner to make their elections and attend. In the enclosed paper you will see the amendments recommended in Virginia. With sentiments of esteem and friendship, I am Dr. Sir, your obedt. Hum.Servant, N.Dane, (74)

Nicholas Gilman to John Langdon, July 15, 1788, New York

Sir **(Private)** I am honored with your Excellency's obliging favor of the 5th instant. Time & place of commencing neighbors. The Honorable Mr. Cochran who is concerned with Lord Dundonald in the tar business has sent me a number of his books. I beg leave to inclose one for your perusal. Mr Wingate desires his Compliments. Excuse haste and believe me to be Most Respectfully, Sir, Your Excellencys Most obedient and Most Humble Servant N. Gilman

Jeremiah Wadsworth to John Chaloner, July 10, New York

Dear Sir, I arrived here last Wednesday, and am yet without your answer to my letter from Hartford. Col. Hamilton being absent, I cannot learn if you have remitted him any Money. But as I have before me a pressing letter from Mr. Church and am otherwise distressed for Money I pray you to let me know immediately what I can depend on and what if any has been sent to Col. Hamilton. I would come to Philadelphia but my duty in Congress will not at present permit me. I beg you will not let me remain without an answer, my love to Mrs. Chaloner & the family. I am dear Sir Your very H.S. Jere Wadsworth. (75)

Jeremiah Wadsworth to Oliver Wolcott, July 15, 1788, N.Y.

Dear Sir, I am sorry to inform you that the Federalists in this State despair of an unconditional adoption of the Constitution; and their is reason to believe this City & its Vicinity will be detached from the upper part of the State.

The convulsions in consequence of this business will certainly reach our State; and too much care can not be taken to prevent any premature Steps. I will write You more particularly in a day or two; and as 1 shall inform you unreservedly on all occurrences You will not suffer any extracts to be published from my letters without particularly marked by me. I am dear sir Yours, J Wadsworth

James Madison to Edmund Randolph, July 16, 1788, New York

My dear friend, The inclosed papers will give you the latest intelligence from Poughkeepsie. It seems by no means certain what the result there will be. Some of the most sanguine calculate on a ratification. The best informed apprehend some clog that will amount to a condition.

The question is made peculiarly interesting in this place, by its connection with the question relative to the place to be recommended for the meeting of the first Congress under the new Government.

Thirteen States are at present represented. A plan for setting this new Machine in motion has been reported some days, but will not be hurried to a conclusion. Having been but a little time here, I am not yet fully in the politics of Congress. I had on the road several returns of a bilious lax which made my journey more tedious & less agreeable than it would otherwise have been. At present I am pretty well again. Hoping this will find you & yours more compleatly so, I remain, Yr. Affete friend, Js. Madison Jr (76)

Nicholas Gilman to John Langdon, July 17, 1788, New York

Sir (Private), This is merely to accompany the papers of the day, by which you will discover the temper of the Poughkeepsie Convention. They are still in session and the heart of their Pharoah is still unrelenting. It is impossible to foresee the issue of this business. The situation is critical. The people of this City are highly federal; they will adhere to the Union at all events and are making preparation for an expensive procession to take place on Wednesday next. With the highest Respect, I have the Honor to be, Sir, Your Excellencys Most Obedient & Most Hmb. Servt, N. Gilman (77)

Samuel A. Otis to George Thatcher, July 17, 1788

Dear Sir, and first I inform you That *we have had Thirteen States frequently upon the floor & have been very industrious; What have you been about? Look at the Journal; One thing seems to be agreed, that a new government is to take place about mid winter.* Next week perhaps the Time will be agreed upon. *The place will be a bone of Contention, Southern people are opposed to N Y, & I think the New Yorkers hang back in such manner.*

I am rather of the opinion it will not be here. For my own part I am in present sentiment for New York but we are all in suspense for the doings of Convention. Probably the question will this day be taken therein. I am of opinion it will not be a favorable decision. Clinton is popular, has a majority at command & is very violent. They may possibly adjourn which is the best expectation I form.

The Yorkers are determined however to have their frolic, & I dont know but we are in danger of running into excess in regard to processions. Perhaps my gravity & aversion to parade may have induced this opinion. *It is an implied triumph over minority which always irritates.* I think the movements of the new Govt. should be mild, discreet & attended with great circumspection. Greenleaf's (the printer) details pretty fairly, To which referring you, I am, With regard & esteem Your Hmble St,

Charles Thomson to George Handley, July 17, 1788

Sir, 1 have the honor to transmit to your Exy herewith enclosed an Act lately passed by the united states in Congress Assembled entitled "

A supplement to an Ordinance entitled An Ordinance for ascertaining the mode of disposing of land in the Western territory," also a report of a Committee which has been agreed to by Congress touching the offer made by the state of Georgia to cede her claim to a certain tract of territory; and an act passed instructing the Superintendt & Comrs. for the southern department to notify, if necessary, to the hostile Indians that should they persist in refusing to enter into a treaty upon reasonable terms the Arms of the United States shall be called forth for the protection of that frontier & the subsequent order passed to give efficacy to this instruction.

I hope this will have the desired effect in restoring peace to your borders & have the honor to be with great respect, Your Excy's. Most Ob. Ser(78) "His Ex. Gov. of Georgia."

Paine Wingate to John Pickering, July 17, 1788, New York

Dear Sir, Heartily fatigued with the business of the day, and with writing I set down to write you a hasty letter. A few days since 1 recd a letter from your Brother. dated June 26, on the day preceding the preceding the night on which he was made prisoner by the insurgents of that country. He was then very well with his family and tho he mentioned that he had been threatened, he said he was under apprehensions of mischief from those villains. He supposed that keeping Franklin confined would be his security, 1 am exceedingly sorry that he found the misfortune of being disappointed. You will see by the enclosed newspaper the measures that have been taken & the intelligence that has been received from your Brother. I do not think that you need be anxious for his safety for I believe they will not venture to use any further violence to his person. I should have informed you sooner of his situation but Major Hodgdon said he had written to Capt. Williams. I thot that the letter, said in the newspaper from your brother, would be an alleviation to your concern & for that reason I write to you at this time.

Should I receive any material intelligence respecting him further I hope soon to have it in my power to give you agreeable intelligence upon that head. We have now a full representation in Congress. The first Wednesday in Dec. is for chusing electors of President, & the last Wednesday of that month for the choice of President. A few days will now determine all those points. We have waited this week to know the determination of New York convention. Our intelligence last evening was not favorable from Pough-keepsie. We expect hourly to hear the final result.

There is too much I suspect of personal animosity among some members of the convention which will be a detriment to that condescension which at this time is very necessary. This city will be exceedingly enraged against the Anti-federal party if they should reject the constitution as it will neces-sitate the removal of Congress which they much fear. Nineteen of twenty are said to be federal in the city. Next Wednesday is the day appointed for the procession in New York celebrating the new Constitution which is to be with extraordinary pomp.

I believe the late principle transactions of Congress will be in your news-papers & needless here to mention. I hope we shall adjourn after a while if not I think I shall return by the beginning of Sept. when I hope I shall have the pleasure of seeing you and all our friends well. I am Dr. Sir your affectionate friend & brother.

Author's Comment: Paine Wingate was married to Pickering's sister Eu-nice. Timothy Pickering, a New Englander, had in 1786 turned his attention to the development of lands he had obtained in northern Pennsylvania, the success of which depended in part upon the settlement of the conflict that had long wracked the Wyoming Valley.

Soon after Pennsylvania created Luzeme County in September 1786, a measure designed to help pacify the region, Pickering was appointed to a number of offices involved in its organization, and for a time appeared to inspire the confidence of both sides in the conflict.

He was increasingly viewed by Connecticut partisans as a captive of Pennsylvania interests and on June 26 a number of dissidents abducted him in a desperate effort to alter events and bring pressure on the state.

William Bingham to Benjamin Rush, July 18, 1788, New York
Dear Sir, I received the letter you inclosed concerning the Effects of the fed-eral Procession on the various Descriptions of Persons that participated in the future Enjoyment, & was much pleased with the Perusal.

I have no occasion for a Stimulus to increase the force of my Exertion to fix the Seat of federal Government at Philadelphia.

I have devoted myself Solely to that Object for a considerable Time past, & have the most flattering Prospect of Succeeding; but it is far from being certain, for the Competition is very great, & there are as many Cities contending for this Advantage, as there were for the Honor of Homers Birth. Our City has So great a start of the others, that many are desirous of depriving us of this Benefit, from the Operation of low minded Jealousy & Envy. You will please to keep this letter secret, as a Strong Expectation of success would rather tend to defeat our Views. I am with much Regard, Dear sir, Your obed. hmble servant, Wm Bingham (79)

Charles Thomson to Thomas Hutchins, July 18, 1788, New York
Sir, I have the honor to transmit to you herewith enclosed a few copies of the Supplement to the land Ordinance, an Act empowering you to appoint Surveyors & fixing the sum to be allowed to the Surveyor, also a Motion which is referred to you to take Order. I am sir your obedt. humble Servt. For this instruction to Hutchins concerning the terms of Virginia's reservation of military bounty lands in its western lands cession, (80). Although Virginia aimed to provide for its bounty claims from lands reserved south of the Ohio River, it had nevertheless stipulated that if insufficient land was available there for this purpose, the deficiency would be "made up to the troops in good lands between the river Scioto and the little Miami on the North west side of the river Ohio." By the enclosed resolve Congress declared invalid any bounty claims surveyed and located prior to ascertaining such an insufficiency. The governor of Virginia was requested "to inform Congress whether there has been any deficiency of good land reserved on the south east side of the Ohio, and if so what is the amount," so that the remaining land could be disposed of "for the general benefit of the Union."

Nathan Dane to Theodore Sedgwick, July 20, 1788, New York
My Dear Sir, I am much obliged to you for Your favor of the 3d instant which I received the 17th instant.

Your account of the character of our General Court for the present year gives me real satisfaction; it is good evidence the people are come to think well on political subjects and to assume a proper temper. The Independence of Kentucky is assigned over to the New Government to do what they may think proper respecting it. The inclosed is the report of the Committee on the subject of putting the Constitution of the United States of America into operation (our reports you know are not made public till acted upon). The report some days ago was agreed to in part, that is Congress have fixed the first Wednesday in Decr. for the appointment of the Electors of the president; and the last Wednesday in the same month for them to assemble and vote for him.

The majority of the states appear to be for fixing the first Wednesday in February for the Govert. to assemble; the Eastern and Middle States could be much more expeditious in this business, but it is Stated by the Southern Delegates, that it is impossible for their States to prepare to elect, sooner than the times mentioned. The principal point in dispute is where Congress will assemble under the Constitution, should this State adopt.From present Appearances a majority of the States will be for this City; those who contended for Philadelphia ten days ago urged vehemently for the decision, but finding Congress not in a disposition to decide until after this State's Convention shall have acted upon the Subject, nothing has been said about it since. As every member, I imagine, has made up his mind on the residue of the report it is, probable, we shall finish it in one day's time after we hear the result of the proceedings of the N. York Convention; you see by the report we make a simple piece of business of it, nor has it caused much debate or delay; having thirteen states on the floor we took up this business sooner than was expected.

We now expect every day to hear this State has decided as to the adoption; but there seems to be no certainty what their decision will be; tho I think the probability, is in favor of their acceding to the New Confederacy. I propose to stay in N. York till the inclosed report shall be acted upon and that I rather expect will be this week. I shall then make a Short tour to Massa.; there is considerable business to be done by the present Congress to clear the files, &c, but none of it very important. It is necessary for me to return to Congress this Summer or early in the fall which I wish to avoid if I could. With sentiments of esteem & regard, I am, Dear Sir, your humble sert. N. Dane (81)

James Madison to Alexander Hamilton, July 20, 1788, N.Y.
My dear Sir, Yours of yesterday this instant came to hand & I have but a few minutes to answer it.

I am sorry that your situation obliges you to listen to propositions of the nature you describe. My opinion is that a reservation of a right to withdraw if amendments be not decided on under the form of the Constitution within a certain time, is a conditional ratification, that it does not make New York a member of the New Union, and consequently that she could not be received on that plan. Compacts must be reciprocal, this principle would not in such a case be preserved.

The Constitution requires an adoption in toto, and forever. It has been so adopted by the other States. An adoption for a limited time would be as defective as an adoption of some of the articles only.

In short any condition whatever must vitiate the ratification. What the New Congress by virtue of the power to admit new States, may be able & disposed to do in such case, I do not enquire as I suppose that is not the material point at present.

I have not a moment to add more than my fervent wishes for your success & happiness. Js. Madison

P.S. This idea of reserving right to withdraw was started at Richmond & considered as a conditional ratification which was itself considered as worse than a rejection. (82)

William Bingham to Tench Coxe, July 21, 1788, New York

Dear Sir, I should have suffered your favor of the 9th instant to have remained so long unreplied to, if I had not been in daily expectation of communicating some pleasing intelligence concerning the subject of that letter. But from various circumstances the question has been delayed. I cannot say with certainty when it will be determined. A competition from different quarters has arisen which divides the suffrages into as many parties; however they may vibrate from one side to the other, they must at last come to rest in the centre, which is in Pennsylvania. Our rising importance in the political scale has caused great jealousy & is one reason for our not uniting all the votes of Congress in our favor, for in every sense, we have the fittest place to assemble the new Congress & that is generally acknowledged. I wish little may be said on this subject for in proportion as we make exertions to establish our pretensions, there are envious characters, that will endeavor to oppose them. The convention of New York is still in session. There are faint hopes entertained of an unconditional ratification, or an Adjournment which will be tantamount. I am with regard, Dear sir, Your Obed. Wm. Bingham (83)

Charles Thomson to Edmund Randolph, July 21, 1788, N.Y.

Sir, Office of Sec. of Congress, I have the honor to transmit to Your Excellency herewith enclosed An Act passed the 17th by the United States in Congress Assembled, touching locations and surveys for the Virginia troops upon continental establishment, between the Scioto & Miami Rivers in the north west side of the Ohio, and requesting the Executive of Virginia to inform them whether there has been any deficiency of good lands reserved by the laws of that State on the southeast side of the Ohio for the said troops, with great respect, 1 have the honor to be, Your Excl. Mst Obed.svt, Charles Thomson

James Madison to George Washington, July 21, 1788, New York
Dear Sir, I have deferred writing since my arrival here in the hourly hope of being enabled to communicate the final news from Poughkeepsie. By a letter from Hamilton dated the day before yesterday I find that it is equally uncertain when the business will be closed, and what will be its definitive form. The inclosed gazettes state the form which the depending proposition bears. It is not a little strange that the Anti-federal party should be reduced to such an expedient, and yet keep their members together in the opposition. Nor is it less strange that the other party, as appears to be the case, should hesitate in deciding that the expedient as effectually keeps the State for the present out of the New Union as the most unqualified rejection.

The intelligent Citizens here see clearly that this would be its operation and are agitated by the double motives of foederalism, and a zeal to give this City a fair chance for the first meeting of the new Government.

Congress have deliberated in part on the arrangements for putting the new Machine into operation, but have concluded on nothing but the times for chusing electors &c. Those who wish to make New York the place of meeting studiously promote delay. Others who are not swayed by this consideration do not urge despatch. They think it would be well to let as many States as possible have an opportunity of deciding on the Constitution: and what is of more consequence, they wish to give opportunities where they can take place for as many elections of State Legislatures as can precede a reasonable time for making the appointments and arrangements referred to them.

If there be too great an interval between the acts of Congr, and the next election or next meeting of a State Legislature, it may afford a pretext for an intermediate summoning of the existing members, who are every where less federal than their successors hereafter to be elected will probably be. This is particularly the case in Maryland, where the Anti-federal temper of the Executive would render an immediate and extraordinary meeting of the Assembly of that State to be called.

On my way thro' Maryland I found such an event to be much feared by the friends and wished by the adversaries of the Constitution. We have no late news from Europe: nor any thing from North Carolina. With every sentiment of esteem & attachment. I remain Dr. Sir Your Obedt. & Affete. servt. Js. Madison Jr (84)

Thomas Tudor Tucker to St. George Tucker, July 22, 1788, N.Y.

My dear St. George, In Congress. I thank you for several kind Favors to the 30th June, the particular Dates of which are not at present before me. Your Poem I received & perused with pleasure. I observe that there are several Alterations made since I formerly read it, which appear to me to be for the better. I am sorry to agree with you that those Sentiments of equal Liberty which make the Ground work as well as Spirit of your whole poem, are getting so much out of Fashion, & at this very early Period after so heavy a Sacrifice to Principle which we are but too much inclined to abandon. The Adoption of the Constitution by your State has given it a firm Foundation, & will be the means of bringing in the State of New York which otherwise would certainly have rejected it; and I suppose N. Carolina would have followed the Example.

The enclosed paper will shew you the present State of the Business in Poughkeepsie. A temporary Adoption, to be conditionally perpetual seems to be likely to take place. In what Light this may be considered, I know not. Some will deem it a valid Adoption; others dear Brother (Nathaniel) will probably think that it is inadmissible & amounts to a Rejection. It gives me infinite pain to find that your Opinion respecting ours corresponds so much with my first Alarms. I could wish to reconcile the Circumstances to a different Explanation. July 28th.

We have receiv'd Accounts of the unconditional Adoption of the Constitution by this State, which has occasioned a great & rather intemperate Joy in the Citizens here. (N.Y. adopted the constitution on July 26.)

We are now upon the Business of the preparatory arrangements, & I will not detain this to make observations on this or any other Subject. From Mr. Madison I had reason to expect you here before this day, which is the reason I have not been anxious to write to you. I directed a Letter to you from the Boys this day. They are well & I hope, going on properly in their Studies. With respect to their Expenses I wish to have more particularly your Sentiments. The Disbursements for them already amount to about 60 & this Curry I cannot add, for we are at this moment on a very interesting point. God bless you. Yrs. most sincerely & affect. Tho. Tucker (85)

James Madison to Thomas Jefferson, July 24, 1788,

Dear Sir, Your two last unacknowledged favors were of Decr. 20 and Feby. 6. They were received in Virginia, and no opportunity till the present precarious one by the way of Holland, has enabled me to thank you for them. I returned here about ten days ago from Richmond which I left a day or two after the dissolution of the Convention. The final question on the new plan of Government was put on the 25th of June. It was twofold whether previous amendments should be made a condition of ratification, directly on the Constitution in the form it bore. On the first the decision was in the negative, 88 being no, 80 only Aye. On the second & definitive question, the ratification was affirmed by 89 Ayes agst. 79 noes. A number of alterations were then recommended to be considered in the mode pointed out in the Constitution itself. The meeting was remarkably full; Two members only being absent and those known to be on the opposite sides of the question. The debates also were conducted on the whole with a very laudable moderation and decorum, and continued until both sides declared themselves ready for the question. And it may be safely concluded that no irregular opposition to the System will follow in that State, at least with the countenance of the leaders on that side. Local eruptions may be occasioned by ill-timed or rigorous executions of the Treaty of peace against British debtors.

I will not pretend to say-altho' the leaders, particularly Henry & Mason will give no countenance to popular violence's it is not to be inferred that they are reconciled to the event, or will give it a positive support.

On the contrary both of them declared they could not go to that length, and an attempt was made under their auspices to induce the minority to sign an address to the people which if it had not been defeated by the general moderation of the party, would probably have done mischief.

Among a variety of expedients employed by the opponents to gain proselytes, Mr. Henry first and after him Col. Mason introduced the opinions expressed in a letter from a correspondent Mr. Donald or Skipwith I believe and endeavored to turn the influence of your name even against parts of which I knew you approved}.

In this situation I thought it due to truth} as well as that it would be most agreeable to yourself and accordingly took the liberty to state some of your opinions on the favorable side}.

I am informed that copies of extracts of a letter from you were handed about at the Maryland convention with a like view of impeding the ratification}. N. Hampshire ratified the Constitution on the 21st. and made the ninth State. The votes stood 57 for and 46 agst. the measure. S. Carolina had previously ratified by a very great majority.

The Convention of N. Carolina is now sitting. At one moment the sense of that State was considered as strongly opposed to the system. It is now said that the tide has been for some time turning, which with the example of other States and particularly, of Virginia prognosticates a ratification there also. The Convention of N. York has been in Session ever since the 17th without having yet arrived at a final vote. Two thirds of the members assembled with a determination to reject the Constitution, and are still opposed in their hearts.

The local situation of New York, the number of ratifying States and the hope of retaining the federal Government in this City afford however powerful arguments to such men as Jay, Hamilton, the Chancellor, Duane and several others; and it is not improbable that some form of ratification will yet be devised by which the dislike of the opposition may be gratified, and the State not withstanding made a member of the new Union.

At Fredericksburg on my way hither I found the box with Cork Acorns, Sulla & peas, addressed to me. I immediately had it forwarded to Orange from whence the Contents will be disposed of according to your order. I fear the advanced season will defeat the experiments. The few seeds taken out here by the President at my request & sown in his garden have not come up. I left directions in Virginia for obtaining acorns of the Willow Oak this fall, which shall be sent you as soon as possible.

Col. Canington tells me your request as to the Philosophical Transactions was complied with in part only, the 1st volume being not to be had. I have enquired of a Delegate here from Rhode Island for further information concerning W. S. Brown, but can learn nothing precise. I shall continue my enquiries, and let you know the result.

We just heard that the Convention of this State have determined by a small majority to exclude from the ratification every thing involving a condition & to content themselves with recommending the alterations wished for. As this goes by way of Holland, I forbear therefore to enter further into our public affairs at this time. I remain with the sincerest affection, Your friend & Servt., James Madison Jr.

James Madison to Tench Coxe, July 30, 1788, New York

Dear Sir, I have been much obliged by your favor of the 23 instant, which I have delayed to answer, in the daily prospect of being able to include the decision of Congress on the place for the first meeting of the New Government. This point continues however unfixt. Perhaps it may be bought to an issue to day. From the result of the first question taken on it, the pretensions of Philada. bade fair for success; and it is very possible may in the end obtain it. Some circumstances which have intervened with the vicissitudes to which such a question in such an assembly as Congress are liable, are notwithstanding very proper grounds for doubtful if not adverse calculations. The observations addressed to your Western inhabitants are in my opinion as well timed as they are judicious. They will be republished here. The conspiracy agst. direct taxes is more extensive & formidable than some gentlemen suspect.

It is clearly seen by the enemies to the Constitution that an abolition of that power will re-establish the supremacy of the State Legislatures, the real object of all their zeal in opposing the system.

From the few enquiries I had an opportunity of making on the subject of Cotton, I found that it enters as far into the culture of the present year in Virginia, as seed could be got for the purpose. I communicated your observations to a friend who patronizes with fervor every plan of public utility, and who will give all the effect he can to your ideas. The very friendly & flattering sentiments with which your letter concludes lay me under fresh obligations to subscribe myself with great sincerity and respect, your obedient friend & servt., Js. Madison Jr

Paine Wingate to John Pickering, July 31, 1788, New York

Dear Sir, I have received no further news from your brother since I wrote last. It is said that he had particularly desired that Franklin may not be released for his sake; that he had rather remain in confinement himself than that event should take place to the dishonor of government, and further that he has not received any personal abuse beside that of confinement.

I think you need not make yourself uneasy, and do not doubt but Mr. Pickering will be set at liberty soon. Congress have agreed that the Executive of Pennsylvania have the direction of ninety Continental troops, if needed, to suppress the rioters, for a limited time. These troops were raised and ready to march to the western country, and I suppose are now going that way. As soon as I shall have any intelligence further from your brother I will send you an account of it.

We have been this week much engaged in the dispute where the new Congress shall meet. The question is not determined and it is so uncertain that I will not give you a conjecture. We have now the fullest Congress that has been since the present Confederation. All the states are present, consisting of thirty-eight members. To accommodate some of the southern states it has been agreed that the Electors of President shall be chosen the first Wednesday of January, and the President be voted for on the first Wednesday of February, and Congress meet on the first Wednesday of March. These periods may be thought by some to be too late, but it was judged necessary, all things considered.

The ratification of New York I think a very favorable event and very unexpected. It was brought about by some persons and circumstances little thought of some time ago. I cannot now give you any further account of our affairs for we are mighty busy. I wrote at this time for the sake of forwarding the enclosed letter which is just come to hand. I am very well, and as soon as Congress shall thin off and some particular matters be over I hope, perhaps within a month, to be on my return home. This I (86) begin to be very desirous of, when I hope you and all our friends well. I am, with much esteem and affection, your friend and brother, Paine Wingate.

Alexander Hamilton to Jeremiah Olney, August 12, 1788, N.Y.
My Dear Sir, We have a of very great importance depending in Congress, which the vote of your state would be decisive. It relates to the place of meeting of the future Congress; Six states and a half prefer New York five and a half Philadelphia. When your delegates were here they voted with us on the intermediate questions; but when the final question came to be put Mr. Hazard's scruples prevailed over his inclination for New York. He however gave me to hope he would return in a short time.

Mr. Arnold would have made no difficulty whatever if his colleague would have gone with him; but he could not be prevailed upon to do it.

This is a matter of such moment not only to this state but to the Northern states in general that I have taken the liberty to address you on the presentation of your state to come forward without loss of time. I am persuaded that the meeting of Congress here or at Philadelphia would make a difference on your politics and would facilitate or impede, as the one or the other place should obtain, the adoption of the Constitution in your state.

The intimate intercourse between us and you makes us look up to you as to a natural ally in this matter. A doubt might perhaps be raised about your right to a vote under the present circumstances. There is not a member of Congress but one who has called your right in question. Tis agreed generally that the power of organizing the government is given by the ratifying states to the United States in Congress assembled, who are mere agents under a special authority and therefore the non-adopting states stand on the same footing with the adopting. Nor can the exercise of that right operate in any manner upon your situation.

If the United States should be considered a foreign power, you might irritate him. What is said respecting him must therefore be received in confidence as indeed must this whole letter. If any difficulty about expense should arise I will with pleasure accept a draft on me. You will excuse this intimation which arises from information that your state has not made provision for its delegates & from a knowledge that individuals have been torn to pieces by your tender laws &.c. With sincere esteem, I remain Yr. Obed Sr, A Hamilton. (87)

Edward Carrington to James Monroe, Sept. 15, 1788, N.Y.

My Dear Friend, I now do myself the pleasure to return the Pamphlet, agreeably to your request. You were kind to favor me with the perusal of your remarks upon the old federal system that perfectly accord with my ideas of that ill concerted Fabric, and display the necessity for a change. I sincerely wish we could associate our opinions of the New Constitution: it is by that comparison which you have done me the honor to propose, that so desirable an object is to be obtained, and whatever may be the difference between us upon this important subject. I acknowledge myself under much obligation for the extensive field you have opened to my view, discovering the quicksands & Rocks to be guarded against, in directing the ship we have launched. You have gone deeply into the subject, and presented many points which engage my serious contemplation.

Upon one or two of your objections I will, however now submit some thoughts which occur to me.

The power of direct Taxation is the first in Magnitude; this, my dear Friend, is, in my estimation the vital principle of the Government; take it away and the Govt. must decline into, nearly, the same contemptible situation which has characterized the old one, or the responsibility of the States must be secured by means such as you have hinted, and seem to rely upon, but which in my opinion, would be utterly inconsistent with every idea of freedom: in the one case we shall have gained nothing by the change in regard to Revenue, but the impost; in the other, Tyranny, which you so much dread will be established, or at least introduced.

You declare this power to be unnecessary, because, when the U.S. possess considerable Revenues, & have at their command a Fleet & Army, with the absolute controul of Trade, you cannot but suppose that their constitutional demands & requisitions, will be complied with. As your reliance seems to rest upon these circumstances of power, it is to be presumed you calculate upon the actual exercise of Military force, or the apprehension of it by the States; in either case the alliances to be effected under military influence.

Now, my dear sir, would this entitle the Constitution to the republican Character? To my Conception of a free Govt. the accomplishment of all its internal purposes by the ordinary operation of Civil authorities, constitutionally created, is essential; and in the levies of Money, in particular, this ought to be the case.

Nor do I agree with those Gentlemen who think that the right of the U.S. to Tax, should be consequent only upon a failure in any State to comply with a requisition, for this would eventually lead to a necessity for the exercise of military force, if the money should be got at all.

Place the business upon this footing, and the federal authority, in whatever shape it might be introduced, would come under the odious character of a minister of punishment; faith could not be placed in Citizens of the same State as agents; resort must be had to those of other States not alike delinquent, & these could not be expected to effect any thing without military aid.

But let the General Government have, at once, the power of direct taxation, such as the Constitution gives, and wise arrangements may be made for the collection, by agents who shall be respectable Citizens of the States in which they are respectively to act, say the Sheriffs or other Collectors of the Counties who act under the authority of the State; one man may be vested with both authorities; the people will scarcely discern a difference between the one & the other power, and a ready obedience will be yielded.

But, perhaps, the impost will be sufficient for all the purposes of the Union! Why then give also a power to collect money by direct Taxation? Should it prove that the impost be sufficient, there can arise no inconvenience from the other power being vested in the Fedl. Govt. because it will never be exercised; But on the other hand should the impost prove deficient public ruin might ensue from a want of the command, constitutionally, of other resources, it is therefore prudent to secure such a provision.

The most certain way to prevent oppressive strides of power, is to make a constitutional provision for every contingency. Your difficulties upon the judiciary appear not to have been brought to any decided objection;

You suggest, however, a dependence upon the State Courts for carrying into effect the greatest part of the Laws of the Genl Govt; you do not say whether they ought in these cases to derive their authority from the Genl. Govt., & therefore I can not combat your opinions upon this point.

My idea, is that all the Courts, upon which the Federal Laws depend for their execution, ought to derive their authorities from, & be amenable to

the Federal Govt. and I think it would be wise to institute, the state courts, where they are well established, as the inferior Federal Courts;

Here I pursue the principle which governed me as to the collection of Taxes; one that will diffuse the federal Authority in full efficiency, and at the same time will scarcely occasion a visible change in the accustomed police of the states I perfectly agree with you that the federal Govt. which we are erecting, can only be successful by preserving a due distinction between the proper objects of it, & those of the State Govts. and it appears to me that the institution of the State Courts, where they are well established, into the inferior fedl. ones, will give us, at least a flattering prospect, that this discrimination will be kept; the Judges will feel an equal obligation & attachment to both, and will be impartial, as well as able, guardians of each; but should the U.S. erect separate Courts the probability is, that bickerings will arise between the two jurisdictions of the Congress, & I trust, that discretion, will be exercised properly. Your remarks upon the Executive pretty fully accord with my ideas.

I have always thought that to assign a Council for the guide of the Chief Magistrate, who is to act by written Laws, is absurd, & that it, in fact, gives him a shelter from the Consequences of the most flagrant abuses. My further remarks upon this subject will be reservd until I have the pleasure to see you in October, when I shall freely confer with you, and doubt not that many of the points upon which we now differ will be placed in different lights in the Minds of each.

You have doubtless been anxious to see the act for giving the Govt. effect, & must have heard something of the cause of the suspension. The southern States thought it incumbent on them to get the meeting more central than N. York; this certainly was a point of great importance, for if it is effected early in the meeting of the New Govt. a warm contest must first be felt, which will destroy the harmony of the Body for perhaps the remainder of the session.

If such removal should not be effected, there will nevertheless have been a warm contest, with the additional mischief of all the great & permanent arrangements being made in the Centre of that part of the Union against where great jealousies already exist in the southern States; and when it is considered with what facility majorities may be made & preserved by calling in absent members &c. this jealousy must be still aggravated.

Upon this question we were deserted by South Carolina, & half of

Georgia, and now old Friend Harry, (Richard Henry Lee) took the same side as he did in the Mississippi business; you must have seen the papers. Most of the votes which passed in the early part of this affair have been published.

We determined to yield to the Majority for N. Y. rather than hazard the consequences of a longer suspension. I shall be with you when the assembly meets of which I learn I am a Member; in the mean time believe me to be, my dr sir, Your Afft. Friend & Serv, Ed. Carrington P.S. The Kortrights are well.

Lyon G. Tyler about Judge John Tyler, 1884

In resisting the tide of Federalism and monarchy, the Legislature of Virginia was ably assisted by the State Judiciary. They had to contend with great odds, having to repel the formidable assaults of the Federal courts, with such men as Elliot and Marshall as Chief Justices, holding their places for life, and Federalists to the heart's core. Nevertheless, the great natural right of expatriation was triumphantly maintained by them, and the compact of the Constitution saved from strangulation by the common law.

No man had a greater hand in effecting this result than Judge Tyler, as will be sufficiently seen as we progress. With stern independence, he and his associate judges of the Admiralty Court, James Henry and Richard Gary, had opposed the Constitution, and the Federalists, in the distribution of the offices, took, of course, especial pains to pass them (As with Grayson)

Instead of appointing Judge Tyler as judge of the district Court of Virginia, President Washington appointed Cyrus Griffin, late pres-ident of the Congress and the Continental Court of Appeals, to preside, "over my old office, because," wrote Tyler to Jefferson, in 1810, "I was not for the new Federal trusted in the British debt cases.

This kind of conduct began the strong distinction which has embittered the cup of life, and in a great measure, produced a spirit of retaliation, when the Republicans prevailed; but the British influence had the best share of the above policy in the beginning, and so it has, at this time, in almost all our measures." (88)

Author's Comment: This was not appropriate treatment for a brilliant man who had literally brought about the Annapolis Convention. Washington and Adams had no compunction regarding exercising the power of removal, but this was not the case with Jefferson. The influence of the British had very little effect on Virginians who were allegiant to their judges of the Admiralty Court. .

William Grayson to Patrick Henry, New York June 12, 1789

Dear sir: I arrived here about three weeks ago in very poor condition indeed. I had a very severe attack of the gout in February and the consequences of it have distressed me extremely ever since. I am now afflicted with a diarrhea, though I hope I am on the mending hand.

Your agreeable favor was handed to me about a week ago. With respect to the unmerited attacks on your character, I think they deserve nothing but contempt on your part.

You have certainly adopted the dignified line of conduct, and I trust and hope you will persevere in it. Nothing would please the author as well as to enter into a literary altercation with you. He would expect to aggrandize himself from the character of his competition. In my opinion, such ill-founded, bad digested calumny ought to give you no manner of uneasiness. Such kind of attacks on characters that are high in the public estimation have been so frequent, and are so well understood, as not to deserve a moment's attention. Envy and detraction, says Mr. Addison, is a tax every man of merit pays for being eminent and conspicuous.

I observe what you say respecting Mr. Martin, and shall pay the most attention thereto. I shall write you further on this subject, perhaps in a post or two.

With respect to the Spaniards, they certainly retain the Natches in their possession, under the supposition of conquest from the British, as also the exclusive right of navigating the river Mississippi. It is also certain they encourage emigration from the United States.

The case of Colonel Morgan and his associates, as also of several other persons to whom they have granted passports on their agreeing to become British subjects, is directly in point. It is true, also, that their descendants, settled on St. Mary's river, encourage the Negroes of Georgia in running away from their masters, and these unhappy wretches they afterward send to the Savannah, where they are sold to a company who put them to work in their mines. This information I had from one of the Senators of Georgia, moreover, told me that there were several complaints of this nature now resting with the Secretary for Foreign Affairs, for the purpose of obtaining redress of Gardoqui. With regard to the navigation of the Mississippi, a gentleman who appears to have the confidence of the President informed me, he was of opinion he would never consent to the surrender of this right to the Spaniards for a moment. I hope and expect this may be the case. However, if this information is thoroughly founded, it is very different from active exertions towards procuring the immediate use of it for the benefit of the citizens of the U. S. It is said that Gardoqui will leave this place in the course of the summer, for old Spain; but this may or may not be true. I presume the event will depend very much on his negotiations with the new government.

With respect to the lands lying on the Mississippi, bounded by 31° north, Georgia claims the whole, and I believe does not mean to surrender a foot to the United States. This I consider as a very great misfortune, for if the government had a greater property in that quarter, and which they might dispose of for the payment of the general debt they would perhaps become more interested in the fate of the Mississippi. The old Congress had their eye on this territory, and threw out several baits for the people of Georgia and North and South Carolina to induce them to make a surrender of lands; the latter were prevailed on to give up a portion, perhaps half as large as the Northern Neck of Virginia.

I am exceedingly sorry it is out of my power to hold out to you any flattering expectations on the score of amendments; it appears to me that both houses are almost wholly composed of Federalists.
Though they call themselves Antis, they are so extremely luke-warm as scarcely to deserve appellation. Some gentlemen here, from motives of policy, have it in contemplation to effect amendments which shall affect personal liberty alone, leaving the great points of the judiciary, direct taxation, etc., to stand as they are; their object is, in my opinion, unquestionably to break the spirit of the party by divisions. I presume many of the most sanguine, after this, expect to go on coolly in; sapping the independence of the State Legislatures. In this system, however, of *divide impera*, they are opposed by a very heavy column from the little States, who, being in possession of rights they had no pretensions to injustice, are afraid of touching a subject which may bring into investigation or controversy their fortunate situation.

Last Monday a string of amendments was presented to the lower House; these altogether respected personal liberty, and I would now enclose you a copy did I not know that Parker had done it already. Even these amendments were opposed by Georgia, New Hampshire, and Connecticut; they were, however, submitted to a Committee of the Whole on the state of the nation, and it is thought will not be taken up again for a while.

I understood that the mover was so embarrassed in the course of the business that he was once or twice on the point of withdrawing the motion, and it was thought by some that the commitment was more owing to personal respect than a love of the subject introduced.

In the Senate, I think that prospects are even less favorable, although no direct proposition has yet been brought forward. I have suggested to my colleague the propriety of bringing forward the amendments of the State before the Senate, but he thinks it will be best to wait till they come from the representatives.

Before my arrival I understood there was a great deal to do about titles. A committee of the Senate reported the propriety of giving the President the title of his Highness and Protector of the Liberties of America, and I have no doubt but this folly would have been committed, if the lower House had not refused their assent to the measure.

Since I came here a question has arisen on application of the clerk for instructions to designate the members in his entries on the journals. On this occasion, I did not fail to express my disapprobation of titles as inapplicable to Republican governments. I believe there are about four other members who think with me on this subject. However the point was carried for the present; that is, it was agreed this was not the time for investigation. The members are therefore known by the names of John, Thomas, and Henry, according to the caprice of their parents. Inclosed you have the bill for the imposts, by which you will see there is a great disposition here for the advancement of commerce and manufactures in preference to agriculture.

I have marked all the amendments made in the Senate that I at present recollect. The bill with the amendments is now before the lower House.

You will easily perceive the ascendency of the Eastern interests by looking at molasses, which is reduced to two-and-a-half cents, while salt continues at six cents, and with an allowance of a drawback to their fish, etc. A bill was reported yesterday for arranging the judiciary, by which all the States are thrown into districts and circuits. I have only heard it read once, and of course know but little about it ; but as it is very important, as soon as it is printed I will send you a copy.

Another bill is before the Senate for discriminating between American shipping and foreign shipping, and between foreign shipping in alliance with those not in alliance. I shall be extremely obliged to you for your sentiments on the doctrine of discrimination. There is a bill now depending before the lower House for the collection of the revenue. The ports already agreed on, particularly in the Eastern States, will swallow up a great part of the revenue, and have no other good effect except that of creating dependence on the new government. The raising of money by impost has been thought favorable throughout America. I am, however, of opinion, that considering the extent of our coasts, and the impossibility of preventing smuggling, that it will be found on experiment to be the most expensive mode of raising money that could be devised. Satisfied I am it will be particularly injurious to the Southern States, who do not and cannot manufacture, and must therefore pay duties on everything they consume.

The cry here is raise everything this way; and to be sure this is good policy with the States east of Maryland; some of the other States, join in the cry, not because it is in their interest, but because they are afraid of trying any other mode of taxation. An excise is talked of, also a stamp duty, and I believe seriously aimed at by a good many; but whether there will be found a majority in both Houses for this sort of business, is more than I can pretend to determine. If the Antis have their uneasy sensations, in my opinion the Federalists are not altogether on a bed of roses. The creditors of the domestic debt (the great supporters of the new government) are now looking steadfastly on their friends for a permanent provision for their interest. But how is this to be accomplished?

The impost, after deductions for smuggling, cutters, tide-waiters, searchers, naval officers, collectors, and controllers, etc., will not yield, after supporting the expenses of government, more than will pay the French and Dutch interest, if so much. What is then to be done? Ah! There is the question. There are an infinity of people here waiting for offices-many of them have gone home for want of money. This accounts for the great number of patriots who were so very sanguine for the new government. It is certain a hundredth part cannot be gratified with places; of course ninety-nine will be dissatisfied.

There has been a most severe attack upon Governor Clinton. He has been slandered and abused in all the public newspapers for these five months by men of the first weight and abilities in the State. Almost all the gentlemen, as well as all the professional men in the State-as well as all the merchants and mechanics-combine together to turn him out of his office; he has had nothing to depend on but his own integrity and the integrity of an honest yeomanry, who supported him against all his enemies. He did me the honor of a visit yesterday, and gave me such an account of his business as shocked me. As this gentleman is the great palladium of Republicanism in this State, you may guess at the situation of Anti-ism here, as he did not carry the election by more than five hundred or six hundred.

Many gentlemen here are of opinion say that the Federalists aim at a limited monarchy, to take effect in a short time. This, however, I doubt extremely, except in the Eastern States, who, I believe, if the question was left to them, would decide in favor of one tomorrow. They say, they have no surety in their fisheries, or in the carrying business, or in any privileges without a strong government. Is it strange that monarchy should issue from the east ? Is it not still stranger that John Adams, the son of a tinker, and the creature of the people, should be for titles and dignities and pre-eminencies, and should despise the herd and the ill-born? It is said he was the *primum nobile* in the Senate for the titles of President, in hopes that in the scramble he might get a slice for himself.

The, committee of the lower House have reported five thousand dollars for his salary, at which he is much offended, and I am in great hopes the House will still offend him more by reducing it.

June 13th - Since writing the above, I have been informed that Col. Connelly has been in the district of Kentucky, and made offers (in case of their effecting independence of the Union) of the assistance of the British to procure the navigation of the Mississippi. I am not at liberty to tell you my authority, but I believe it to be true. Perhaps, you have heard. I have also procured a copy of Col. Morgan's handbill inviting a settlement, under the authority of Spain, at New Madrid, near the mouth of the Ohio, on the Spanish side. A copy of this document I shall send you in my next, unless I should have time to copy it before this goes off. One article, at all events, it may be not improper to send you at this time, to-wit:

"All persons who settle with me at New Madrid, and their posterity, will have the free navigation of the Mississippi, and a market at New Orleans free from duties for all the produce of their lands, where they may receive payment in Mexican dollars for their flour, tobacco, etc."

I am sure I have fatigued you by this time. I shall therefore conclude, with one request, which is, that, as I shall write you frequently, and in all probability make free with men, measures, characters, and parties, that our correspondence may be perfectly confidential and forever confined to ourselves. This letter will go safe by a private hand.

When I write by post, it will be on general subjects. I remain, with the most sincere regard, your affectionate friend, William Grayson.

Statement from the First Congress under the Constitution: 1789
"There are an infinity of people waiting for offices. Many of them have gone home for want of money. This accounts for the great number of

patriots who were so sanguine for the new government.: William Grayson

Author's Comment: The first consideration of the First Federal Congress in 1789 was to place the permanent seat of government on the Susquehannah, in Pennsylvania, by majority vote. This choice, so different from that of the House made the question moot.

William Grayson to Patrick Henry, New York Sept. 29, 1789

I have received your favor, for which I am exceedingly thankful ; indeed I was very uneasy at not hearing from you, apprehending some indisposition might have prevented you.

I remain still in a low state of health, but hope to get better from a cessation of business and from exercise. (Undoubtedly he would like to be on his horse again riding freely about the countryside.)

The session is this moment closed, and the members would have parted in tolerable temper if the disagreeable altercations on the score of the seat of government had not left very strong impressions on the minds of the Southern gentlemen. They suppose with too much reason that the same kind of bargaining which took effect with respect to the Susquehannah may also take effect in other great National matters which may be very oppressive to a defenseless naked Minority, the bill has been ultimately defeated in the Senate & the point remains open. Gentlemen now begin to feel the observations of the Antis, when they inform them of the different interests in the Union & the probable consequences that would result therefrom for the Southern States, who would be the milch cow out of whom the substance would be extracted.

If I am not mistaken, they will e'er long have abundant cause to conclude that the idea of a difference between carrying States & producing States & manufacturing States & slave States is not a mere phantom of the imagination. If they reflect at all on the meaning of protecting duties-by way of encouragement to manufactures & apply the consequences to their own constituents. I think they would now agree that we were not totally beside ourselves in the [Virginia ratifying] Convention. In my opinion whenever the impost will come into action the freedom of the South will be let into some secrets that they do not or will not at present apprehend.

You would be astonished at the progress of manufactures in the seven Easternmost States if they go on in the same proportion for seven years they will pay very little on imports: while the South will continue to labor under the pressure: This added to the advantage of carrying for the productive States will place them in the most desirable situation whatever.

With respect to amendments matters have turned out exactly as I appre-
hended from the extraordinary doctrine of playing the after game: the lower
house sent up amendments which held out a safeguard to personal liberty
in a great many instances, but this disgusted the Senate and though we
made every exertion to save them, they are so mutilated scarified & gutted
that in fact they are good for nothing, & I believe as many others do, that
they will do more harm than benefit: The Virginia amendments were all
brought into view, and regularly rejected

Perhaps they may think differently on the subject the next session, as Rhode Island has refused for the present acceding to the constitution; her reasons you will see in the printed papers. There are a set of gentlemen in both houses who during this session have been for pushing matters to an extraordinary length; this has appeared in their attachment to titles, in their desire of investing the President with the power of removal from Office & lately by their exertion to make the writs run in his name; their maxim seems to make up by construction what the constitution wants in energy.

The Judicial bill has passed but wears so monstrous an appearance that I think it will be felo- de- Se (suicide) in the execution; these amendment of Virginia respecting this matter has more friends in both houses than any other, & I still think it probable that this alteration may be ultimately procured. Whenever the Federal Judiciary comes into operation I think the pride of the States will take the alarm, which added to the difficulty of attendance from the extent of the district in many cases, the ridiculous situation of the Venue, & a thousand other circumstances, will in the end procure it's destruction.

The salaries I think are rather high or the temper or circumstances of the Union, & furnish another cause of discontent to those who are dissatisfied with the government. I have made every exertion in favor of Mr. [Joseph] Martin, but there have been such representations against him, that I fear he will derive no benefit from any thing in my power to effect. With respect to the lands at the Natches, they are unquestionably according to prevailing ideas the property of Georgia, but the Spaniards are in possession and hold it by force: Georgia some time since ordered or offered to cede a great part of their state including this territory to Congress, but the cession was so loaded as they conceived with unreasonable conditions that they rejected it: it is highly probable that the present treaty will produce peace with the Creeks, & that excellent lands may be procured reasonably on the Altamaha.

If I can be of any service to you in this or any other matter your commands will be a pleasure.(89) I remain with the highest respect, Your

commands will be a pleasure.(89)   I remain with the highest respect, Your affectionate friend and most obedient servant, Will'am Grayson. This is the last letter of record from William to Patrick Henry.

WILLIAM GRAYSON SAID AT THE VA. RATIFYING CONVENTION:

"Were it not for one great character (George Washington) in America, so many men would not be for this government. We have one ray of hope. We do not fear while he lives; but we can only expect his fame to be immortal. We wish to know who besides him can concentrate the confidence and affection of all America other than him."

CONCERNING PATRICK HENRY AT THE END OF HIS LIFE:

There was controversy regarding Patrick Henry's political philosophy as the "Illustrious" Henry had turned down the post of Chief Justice, offered by president and commander in chief, George Washington.

Maybe Henry regretted doing so towards the end of his life. For whatever reason, the great man suddenly came out in defense of the Alien and Sedition Laws, making him instantly popular with his former detractors. This caused many of his oldest friends to turn away in stunned silence, except for Judge John Tyler who with sincere affection for Henry, looked on this supposed "change of heart and attitude" as one of the normal political shifts that occur in a man's life.

JUDGE JOHN TYLER WRITING ABOUT PATRICK HENRY:

"It seems that the close of his life was clouded by the opinion of many of his friends, that he was attached to the aristocratic party; but however much he might have erred in his opinions in his aged and infirm state I felt it impossible he could be an aristocrat.

His conceptions were too well fixed; his love of liberty grew always tenfold stronger. I lament that I could not see him before he died. He asked to see me and sent me a message expressing his desire to satisfy me as to how much he had been misrepresented."

"Men might differ in ways and means, and yet not in principles."(90) Judge Tyler when questioned about which man had more difficulty dealing with problems that effected his friends and ideals, and staying loyal, Patrick Henry or George Washington.

Tyler's comment was that he would always stand by Patrick Henry as a man of impeccable ideals who dealt fairly with everything and everyone.

Merrill Jensen in his book, "The New Nation," called Grayson a true

Federalist, because the greatest thing a Federalist could do would be to unite the nation under sound government.

Undoubtedly William missed the camaraderie with Washington. No record remains if these two men reconciled and in place of the former warmth, perhaps there was a cursory note at William's death.

Unknown to William who was in New York attending the first session of the Federal Congress, his beloved wife Eleanor had died at their home in Fredericksburg, on September 22, 1789 Word had not yet reached William by September 29th, the last day of Congress. There had not been time for a courier to arrive by horseback, the fastest mode of travel.

William had been closeted for days, writing letters, one was written to his mentor and commander George Washington recommending his close compatriots for offices in the new government. Grayson wrote a long letter to his friend Patrick Henry, bringing him current on the events in Congress.

Unaware of the personal tragedy that would drastically alter his life and bring him the ultimate sadness of his life, William left New York the following morning for the two to three week carriage ride to Fredericksburg, Virginia. If the weather held they could make the trip in two weeks.

Perhaps William did not learn of Eleanor's death until he walked into the house in Fredericksburg and was greeted by weeping children.

Undoubtedly the courier sent to intercept him and deliver the terrible news, has passed by William in the night. He and Punch had to stop at night if the moon was not bright enough to see the road.

William walked into his new home in Fredericksburg looking to embrace Eleanor, but his beloved Eleanor was gone and not a trace of her was left. She had been buried at Belle Aire for almost a month. The only reminder of her was a closet of sweet smelling dresses. The shock was simply too great to sustain. Heartbroken and ill, William succumbed and was put to bed where he remained for months, desperately ill.

Members of the family were summoned and friends appeared but William was barely cognizant of the outside world.

William had put his all into the Ratifying Convention; losing by ten votes was devastating, followed by being passed over for every great position in Washington's first cabinet even though he was in many cases the most qualified man. That was a terrible blow.

Losing Eleanor had at last crushed him.

Six months later, William was still weak and not fully recovered. He had scarcely been out of bed. Painfully he pulled himself up, determined to attend the second session of Congress. A strong sense of duty filled him with hope of accomplishing something meaningful.

Dragging himself from bed, he summoned Punch. It was March 9th, 1790, fast approaching the Ides of March.

Wan and pale and desperately ill, but determined to represent Virginia in Congress, William Grayson, Punch helped settle William in the carriage an they set out from Fredericksburg for NewYork. They had gone only six miles, when William asked Punch to stop at Belle Aire.

THE END OF WILLIAM GRAYSON'S LIFE

Hearing a carriage, Spence ran out. Seeing William's condition, he carried William to his old room and summoned the doctor. Word was also sent by courier to Congress and many along the way were informed that the great man was close to dying.

Letters arrived along with carriages, bringing family and close friends. William remained weakly responsive to those who came to show their love. He truly was dying and the doctors could not prolong his life by any means although everything known and practiced remedy of that era was applied.

In pain and suffering, William drifted in and out of consciousness, his , life hanging in the balance. The third day a hush filled Belle Aire as the word that death could come at any moment was circulated through the house and filtered out to the dwellings of the field slaves.

William Grayson's life hung by the narrowest thread. More people arrived to pay their last respects and massive amounts of food were brought by friends to feed the large number of guests who came to show their respect and catch a last glimpse of the man they loved and admired.

Spence adored his brother and had always been his greatest advocate along with their dutiful and loving cousin James Monroe. Neither left William's side. Both were at hand once William drew his last breath, a sigh of great magnitude, as he lay down his earthly burden and hurried to the heavenly embrace of his beloved Eleanor.

Gently, Spence placed his fingers on William's eyes to close them for the last time while his tears fell copiously on the counter pane.

William's end had been sad but peaceful. The large company in the room heard a few prayers from the lips of those who felt compelled to say something to add to the solemnity of the moment; a great life passing, and to comfort his children who wept uncontrollably. Punch, his face smeared with tears stood hat in hand beside the bed, wondering what to do with the rest of his life. Punch was yet to learn that William's last request was to free all his slaves. The Fredericksburg newspaper, The Advertiser, published this obituary on the second page:

"Dumfries, Virginia. On Friday the 12th of March
Died at this place on his way to Congress,
The Hon. Col. WILLIAM GRAYSON,
     Senator of the United States.
His remains were this Day, attended by
A numerous Circle of his Acquaintance,
Deposited in the Family vault, at the
Rev. Mr. Spence Grayson's, (Belle Air)

By the Death of this Gentleman the public,
As well as his own family, have sustained
An irreparable Loss. His abilities were
Equaled by few; his integrity surpassed by none."

Copies of this newspaper are available at the main Fredericksburg library. Finding out where the Grayson family had lived in Fredericksburg is still a mystery although I went there and tried hard to find out more about the years the Grayson's lived in the area after their home in Dumfries was destroyed by fire. Nearing the end of William Grayson's life one tragedy after another was heaped upon him.

A large sheaf of Grayson's papers were found in an attic in Dumfries years ago in the 20th century and turned over to the authorities, but were not located at the time of this writing. I would love to see them.

Grayson's sense of justice and vigilance over state sovereignty versus the power of the Federal government was well served after his death, in a Law Suit filed by The Old Indiana Land Company, (one of Grayson's investments) where his name was first on the list of investors, against the state of Virginia in the Supreme Court. Constituents from every state, aware of the implications, banded together to present an amendment to Congress to end the assaults on sovereign states and end the onerous situation of Federal jurisdiction over state constitutions.

William Grayson's will was destroyed during the battle of Manassas Junction in the Civil War, but a copy was located in the land office of Maryland. William appointed his close friend Robert Hanson Harrison, Benjamin Grayson Orr his sister'son, and his children as his Executers. His will was signed March 11, 1790.

This paper was found with his will: The representatives of William Grayson are entitled to the additional proportion of land allowed as a Colonel of the Continental line for 10 months service more than six years.

It was signed, John Tyler, Governor Council Chamber, September 12, 1809 Warrent #5854 for 926 acres issued 26 July, 1810 to representative of William Grayson deceased and delivered to Samuel Coleman (8T120)

Eight years after William Grayson's death, George Washington walked the swampy land on the Maryland side of the Potomac, across from Virginia, and chose eight acres for the ten mile square site of the nation's capitol. It was one of the wisest decisions Washington ever made and one that would have made William Grayson very happy.

For William's entire political career he had witnessed vast differences between the north and the south proliferate. It was true that whatever small advantage it was to have the capitol in a southern location was to be grasped as a factor to alleviate the imbalance that few believed would ever be settled.

Others, like Grayson believed it would be settled by a massive blow up, even war. A year after choosig the capitol Washington would be dead. He had outlived William by nine years. Patrick Henry was to die the same year as Washington.

Sixty- two years later the infamous Civil war would ensue to the shame of America. By far the most infamous moment in America's history.

The Constitution that had been feared and despised by so many as a new, untried document, survived and eventually became loved and leaned upon as the greatest governing document in America even though many attempted to defile or change it. Two hundred and twenty-one years after its inception, it is still the ruling document of the United States confirming once and for all time, the genius of the Founding Fathers.

Never since the era of our early patriots have as many great men gathered to meet the greatest challenges of an era and succeeded so well. We most revere their memory and be grateful for their sacrifices and brilliance.

In later years William Grayson's family appealed to Congress for more land claiming it was due to them to honor Grayson'service of six years, ten months in the Continental Army, ending with the rank of colonel. The request was granted. The judge hearing this appeal was none other than the John Tyler, the son of Grayson's great friend.

The End

FOOTNOTES

1   RC (DLC: Washington Papers.
2   Sections and Politics in Virginia. 1781-1787 by Jackson T. Main, Prof. Of History at San Jose State College CA.
3   Washington Papers (Abbot) Confederation Series, 2:280-8
4   Grigsby, "Virginia Convention of 1788."
5   Vestry Minutes, Truro Parish, Virginia, 1 732-1785, Pg. 108
6   "The Grayson Family" by John Breckinridge Grayson Jr. 1877, Contributed by Margaret L.E. Edwards
7   Papers of G.Mason, 1:482. Grayson to Wash. Dec. 27, 1774
8   April 6, 1776, John Page letter to Jefferson
9   "William Grayson, A Study in VA. Biog. of the 18th Century." Bristow. Pg. 80
10 Washington's Diaries
11 Papers of Lund Washington
12 Frederick County Deed Bk 19, pg.378, abstract by Amelia Gilreath.
13 Prince William Reliquary
14 Exe. V/P of the Patrick Henry Nat'l Mem.1250 Red Hill Road, Brookneal, Virginia, author of "A Wilderness so Immense."
15 "Phil Richard Fras."
16 "The History of the Virginia Federal Convention of 1788" by Hugh Blair Grigsby, Vol. 1, pg.196.
17 Weston Bristow, "William Grayson, A study in Virginia Biography of the Eighteenth Century.
18 Grayson to General Horatio Gates, the board of War Letters
19 Virginia Mag. of Hist. & Biog. Vol 13, Pg. 417, April 1925
20 National Archives Experience - Bill of Rights
21 Papers of Madison 8:509-510
22 Hugh Blair Grisby's History of the Virginia Federal Convention of 1788. Vol.II, pg. 234
23 Maclay's Diaries
24 Justice Story's Commentaries
25 MacClay's Diaries
26 "Washington and His Colleagues," Chapter, Great Decisions,
27 "Letters of Delegates to Congress, Volume 24 James Madison to George Washington, Nov. 18, 1787
28 Jackson Turner Main. 'The Anti-Federalists: Critics of the Constitution, 1787
29 Payson J. Treat, The Nat'l Land system, N.Y. 1910 pg.40
30 Document Library, Founding Era
31 Washington's Correspondence & Letters
32 Letter of Delegates, American Memory
33 Grayson's sister Susanna at 16, married Mr. Orr who had a successful 440 acre plantation overlooking the Tappahannock River.

34 Washington married Martha Dandridge Custis in 1759, when she was a widow with two children. Martha was born in 1731

35 See JCC, 26:82; and Schlenther, Charles Thomson, pp. 178, 278n.26.

36 Boyd S. Schlenther, Charles Thomson, A Patriot's Pursuit (Newark: University of DelawarePress,1990),pp.8-79

37 JCC, 28:26n, 103-5, 173-78, 211-14; & PCC, item 31,fols.275.80

38 Jonn L. Fitzpatrick's, Writings of George Washington

39 RC (DLC: Madison Papers)

40 RC (MHi: Pickering Papers)

41 RC (DLC: Madison Papers

42 RC (DLC: Washington Papers

43 Margaret M. O'Dwyer, "Louis; Guillaume Otto in America"

44 JCC, 16:344; 45,29:625n, 650, 662

45 RC (DLC: Madison Papers)

46 RC (Vi: Continental Congress Papers)

47 Shakespeare's Merry Wives of Windsor, act 3, sc. 5, line 9

48 Madison Papers (Hutchison) 8:59-61,426n.3,454

49 RC VIU: Lee Family Papers

50 RC (DLC: Madison Papers).See Lee to Madison, October 19.

51 Weston Bristow's William Grayson, A Study in Va. Biography, Pg. 109

52 DLC: Monroe Papers.

53 Archer B. Hulbert, "Andrew Craigie and the Scioto Assoc

54 Papers of Richard Henry Lee

55 George C. Groce, William Samuel Johnson: A Maker of the Constitution New York: Columbia University Press, 1937), pp. 172

56 Archer B. Hulbert, "Andrew Craigie and the Scioto Assoc."

57 RC (DLC: Washington Papers)

58 Jr. RC (DLC: Madison Papers). (Rutland), 10: 199; 200

59 Madison, Papers (Rutland), 10:204.

60 Life of R.H. Lee,2vls.(Phil.H. C. Carey,I. Lea, 1825), 2:78--;81.

61 RC (DLC: Washington Papers). Madison, Papers (Rutland), 10:196; 97. See ibid, pp. 189; 90. (62) See JCC, 33:690.692;93

63 Ibid., pp. 34 1,43.

64 TC (DLC: William Short Papers

65 Gulliver 's Travels by Jonathan Swift, Part III, Chapter 5

66 RC (MHi: Sedgwick Papers.

67 The Pictorial Field book of the Revolution by Benson J.Lousing, Vol II, 1972, Charles E. Tuttle Co., Rutland Vermont

68 "The Birth of the Bill of rights, 1776-91" Robert A. Rutland U N.C. Press 1955

69 "The Bill of Rights" by Brant 1966

70 ALS, DLC: George Washington

71 ALS, DLC, George Washington

72 RC MH 1: Sedgwick Papers

73 RC cty: John Mason Brown Papers

FOOTNOTES CONTINUED

74. RC MNF: Strong Collection
75. RC PHI-Chaloner and White Collection
76. Papers of James Madison
77. RC Capt. J.G.M. Stone, Annapolis, Md. 1973
78. LB (DNA: PCC item 18B)
79. Tr DLC: Burnett Collection of Mr. C.E.L. Wingate
80. RC PHI Alexander Biddle Collection
81. JCC, 34:332-34
82. RC MHi: Sedgwick Papers
83. DCL Hamilton Papers, Madison Papers, Rutlad 11-198
84. C PHI; Coxe Papers
85. RC VjW: Tucker: Coleman Papers
86. Rprinted from Wingate, Lige and Letters. 1:240-241
87. RC DLC Hamilton Papers, Rutland 11-198
88. The Letters and Times of the Tylers, Vol. 1, pg. 165
89. Letters and Times of the Tylers, Vol. 1. pg/169
90. From a faded manuscript of Judge Tyler to william Wirt Henry: Life and Times of the Tylers
91. George Washington to William Grayson, June 22, 1785

Eleanor Smallwood was born in Charles County Maryland in 1742. Her brother, William was rich in land holdings in Baltimore, Maryland and became governor of the state. During the American Revolution he was a General. Their father Bayne Smallwood was a Court justice and a delegate to the Maryland Assembly. Eleanor met William Grayson socially. They corresponded during his years of study in London and married immediately upon his return to the states.

INDEX

INDEX   (CONT.)

INDEX (CONT.)

INDEX (CONT.)

BELLE AIRE PLANTATION MANSION, artistic representation according to written description, drawn by Lucy Baker

BIBLIOGRAPHY

1. Prince William, the Story of It's People and It's Places, Wm. & Mary Quarterly
2. Landmarks of Old Prince William by Fairfax Harrison
3. This Was Prince William by R.J. Ratcliffe
4. Dr. Joseph Esposito, a phamphlet
5. A Political Biography of Virginia's First United States Senator By James E. DuPriest, Jr.
6. William Grayson, An Overview of the Life of One of Virginia's First U.S. Senator 's, by Marilyn Nehring
7. The States Rights Debate: Anti-Federalists & The Constitution, by Englewood Cliffs, N.J. 1964-1985
8. A Wilderness so Immense, Dr. Jon Kukla
9. The New Nation, Merrill Jensen
10. American Constitution, Paul Goodman
11. The Federal Constitution in Virgnia, 1787-1788 Worthington C. Ford
12. What Would The Founding Fathers Do? Richard Brookhiser
13. The Papers of John Marshall, 1974 Houghton Mifflin

14. Univ. of VA., Alderman Library, Special Collections:

   a. Richard Henry Lee Papers, Am. Philosophical Society
   b. Letters to Nathaniel Dane, William Grayson Ms
   c. Letter of Edmund Randolph to James Madison, Ms
   d. Papers of Va.Members of the Continental Congress,Ms
   e. The Political Career of Col. William Grayson, Harry Edgar Baylor
   f. Papers of James Madison
   g. Papers of James Monroe
   h. Papers of Patrick Henry
   i. Papers of the Gordon Family
   j. Papers of George Mason
   k. Papers, Diaries of George Washington
   L. William Grayson's Notes on the U.S. Constitution, Jon Kukla, Virginia Phoenix 7, No 1, 1974
15. Library of Virginia, Richmond, Virginia, Manuscripts
16. Documentary History of the Ratification of the Constitution, 1976, Merrill Jensen, et als, eds.
17. Journals of the Council of State of Virginia, 5 Vols. 1931
18. Journals of the Senate of Virginia
19. Journal of the Virginia House of Delegates

20. Letters & Papers of Edmund Pendleton, 2 Vols. 1967,David Mays, Ed.
21. The Memoir of James Monroe, Esq., James Monroe, 1828 1788, American Memory, L.O. C.
22. The Papers of George Mason, 3 Vols. 1970 Robert Rutland, et als, Eds.
23. The Anti-Federalist Papers, 1 through 85, from Nov. 26, 1787 to March 6, 1788, American Memory, LOC.
24. The Anti-Federalists, Jackson Turner Main, Chapel Hill, N.C. 1961
25. Creation of the American Republic, 1776-1787, Gordon S. Wood, Chapel Hill, N.C., 1969
26. A Study in Virginia Biography of the 18th Century, Weston Bristow, Richmond College, Dictionary of Am. Biog.
27. James Monroe Papers, Univ. of Mary Wash. Fred. Va., Daniel Preston
28. Letters of Richard Henry Lee, Ed. James Ballagh, 2Vols.1914
29. Letters of Members of the Continental Congress, Edmund C. Burnett, Ed., 1921-1936
30. Writings of Thomas Paine, Moncure D. Conway, 3 Vols. 1894
31. Writings of George Washington, John C. Fitzpatrick, Ed. 39 Vols. 1931-1944
32. Writings of James Monroe, Stanislaus Hamilton, Ed. 7 Vols. 1898-1903
33. Patrick Henry, Life, Correspondence & Speeches, Wm. W. Henry, et al
34. Writings of James Madison, Gaillard Hunt, Ed. 9 Vols. 1908
35. Infamous Scribblers, Eric Burns
36. The Debates in the Several State Conventions on the Adoption of the Federal Constitution as Recommended by the General Convention at Philadelphia in 1787, 5 Vols. Jonathan Elliot Ed. 1888, reprint N.Y.: Burt Franklin, N.D.
37. Encyclopedia of Political Economy & Political History of the U.S. by the Best American & European Writers, Ed. John T. Lelor, Maynard, Menit, Pub 1881
38. The Pictorial Field Book of the Revolution, Benson Lousing, Vol II, 1972, Charles E. Tuttle Co, Rutland, VT.
39. History of the Virginia Federal Convention 1788, Hugh Blair Grigsby, Ed. R.A. Brock, 2 Vols, Richmond, 1890/91
40. Encyclopedia of Virginia Biography, Lyon Gardiner Tyler, 5 Vols. N.Y., 1915
41. The Diaries of George Washington, Henry Cabot Lodge
42. The Life of General Washington, Mason L. Weems

43. The Letters & Times of the Tylers, Lyon G. Tyler, Vol.1 & II
44. History of the formation of the Constitution of the United States of America, George Bancroft
45. Alexander Hamilton, Ron Chernow
46. Liberty & Freedom, David Hackett Fischer
47. History of the Rise, Progress & Termination of the American Revolution, 1805 Mercy Otis Warren
48. Letters of the Federal Farmer to the Republican, L.O.C.
49. Authorship of the Federal Farmer, Wm & Mary Quarterly, 3rd Series XXX1 1974 299-308, Gordon S. Wood
50. Eliott Debates III, LOC
51. Men of Little Faith, Cecilia Kenyon
52. Election of President, Bryan Family Papers, special Corresp.
53. Omitted Chapters of History Disclosed in the Life and Papers of Edmund Randolph, New York 1889.96
54. The Power of the Purse: A History of American Public Finance, 1776- 1790, Chapel Hill, N.C. 1961
55. The Constitution of England, John de La Lolme
56. Domestic History of the American Revilution by Mrs. Ellet, Philadelphia, J.B. Lippincott & Co., 1876
57. Unimpeached Integrity, Potomac News, Dec. 1955, Eileen Mead
58. Virginia Magazine of History & Biography, Oct. 1984, Vol. 92, New Light on William Grayson, His Guardian's Account, edited by Joseph Horrell.

1774 parchment with the signature of William Grayson, from the archives of the Treasure Room at the University of Virginia, at Charlottesville.

ANTI FEDERALISTS AT THE VIRGINIA RATIFYING CONVENTION

Edmund Custis,
John Pride III
Edmund Brooker,
William Cabell,
Samuel Jordan
John Johns Trigg,
Charles Clay III,
Parker Goodall,
Henry Lee of Bourbon
John Jones,
Charles Patterson,
David Bell,
Robert Alexander,
Thomas Reed
Stephen Pankey,
Thomas H. Drew,
Joel Early,
Joseph Jones,
William Watkins
Meriwether Smith,
Alexander Robertson,
William Grayson
Henry Dickenson
George Mason
Thomas Edmunds
James Montgomer
John Carter Littlepage
Thomas Cooper
John Marr
Thomas Roane
Holt Richeson
Benjamin Temple
Stephens T. Mason
William White
Jonathan Patteson
Christopher Robertson
John Logan
Henry Pawling

John Dawson
Thomas Carter
Theodorick Bland
Robert Lawson
Patrick Henry
Thomas Turpin
James Wilson from PA
Robert Williams
John Steele
Matthew Walton
Abraham Trigg
Walter Crocket
John Evans
George Carrington
Isaac Coles
William Sampson
John Guerrant
Thomas Arthurs
John Early
Joseph Haden
Samuel Richardson
John Fowler
James Upshaw
Richard Cary
Andrew Buchanan
James Monroe
Cuthbert Bullitt
Edmund Ruffin
Thomas Alien
Richard Kennon
Samuel Hopkins
Green Clay
French Strother
Joshua Michaux
John Tyler
Edmund Winston
John Miller

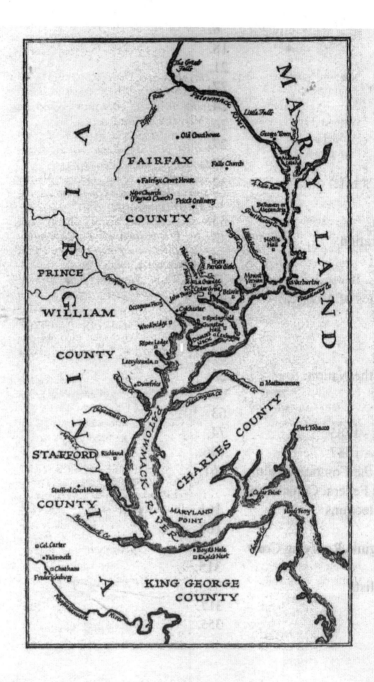

The region of the upper Potomac as it was in William Grayson's time. Placenames and spelling conform to the Fry-Jefferson map of 1755. Plantations, town sites, ferries and public buildings are approximated.
prepared by Richard J. Stinely of Colonial Williamsgurg, Inc.

The deplorable condition of the Grayson Burial Vault where William and Spence are buried along with all their family members, dating back to the 1700's. At Belle Air, Woodbridge, Virginia, June, 2007

Only five acres remain of the immense thousands of acres of Grayson's Belle Aire in Woodbridge, Virginia. The property, including the Grayson Burial Vault is presently owned by The Good Shepherd Housing Foundation, at P O Box 4428, 3166 Golanski Blvd. suite 102, Woodbridge, Virginia, an affliate of the Lutheran Church of the Good Shepherd. The nineteenth c. farm house is currently used to house mentally ill homeless men. The Grayson tomb is in dire need of restoration and if not repaired will be lost in time. Many Graysons are buried there and graves lie on the hillside over the vault. This is the tomb of Virginia's first senator, William Grayson.

BOOKS BY LUCY BAKER

1. William Grayson and the Constitution, 1788, Hardcover: $24.95
I.S.B.N. 978-1-929440-13-9. A full account of how the Constitution
 was written and ratified and the speeches of William Grayson and
the members of the Virginia Ratifying Convention. Learn the role of
the Anti-Federalist's, who they were and compare their sacrifices.
Read of Grayson's dedication to Virginia and the nation as a Patriot
and Founding Father.   384 pages

2. The Life of William Grayson, A Screenplay, I.S.B.N. $20.00
978-1- 929440-14-6, Meet William Grayson as a young man in
 Woodbridge, Virginia and journey through his life amid rural
 scenes and learn about his political career and service in the
 Continental Army. Attend battlefields and manor houses on the
 James River in Grayson's beloved Virginia.   70 pages

3. Poppelsdorfer Allee I.S.B.N. 978-1-929440-11-5 $24.95
A history of Germany from 800 c.e. and Charlemagne to the
 present as witnessed by a German family's stormy lives.
 Experience the daily world of Lucia Tellenbrock and her
 daughter 's, their joys and betrayal by a well loved and trusted
 relative who owed everything to the Tellenbrocks.   384 pages

4. Miracles, I.S.B.N. 978-1-929440-00-9 $15.00 Senta, a San $14.95
Francisco lawyer, takes her dying father and brother to an
 extraordinary island to encounter a spiritual awakening of
 enormous magnitude. The mysteries that confound and frighten
 Senta and her family lead to the most important discovery of their
lives once the island gives up its fabulous secrets.   338 pages

5 In Six Months You Get Bananas, I.S.B.N. 978-976-8056-85-6 $14.95
Two women relocate in the Caribbean looking for adventure and
 challenge and discover pirates, and crooks. Beset by physical danger,
 corruption and unbridled moral decay on a gorgeous island, they live
 with insecurity and fear where there is no respect for human life on a lawless island and justice is a joke yet one heroine finds love.   384 pages

6. Heart of Stone, I.S.B.N. 978-976-9501-64-5 $14.95
5000 people live on the volcanic island of Saba where a disillusioned
lawyer comes to drink himself to death and meets a wonderful woman and falls
in love. Amidst startling events, highjacking, a fire-fight and massive island poisoning witness the simple life of the good people of Saba's paradise ...setting .
355 pages

8.In God's Hands, ISBN: 978-929440-07-8 $19.95

Over 200 original watercolor paintings combine with a metaphysical
text, the need to recognize theHigher Consciousness or "True Self"
to bring spiritual reality into daily life. Understand your purpose
and meaning in life through studying esoteric truths and actual
spiritual experience in a lifetime of study and experience. Follow
the joyous path that ultimately leads to the Light of all Creation,
the source and home of our God created, living soul.   384 pages

10. Poisonous Plants of the Caribbean, ISBN 978-1-929440-03-0 $14.95

150 pages of text and 150 original watercolor paintings of the
flowers and plants that are dangerous to humans and animals.

11. Fish of the Caribbean, ISBN 978-1-929440-04-7 $14.95

138 pages of text and color paintings of Caribbean fish. Introduction, de scriptions, habitats, marine terms and fish groups.

12, **Secrets of Lost River** I.S.B.N. 978-1-929440-01-6 $15.00

Life for a young family in Arizona becomes bizaare when they
move into a haunted house. Trauma causes the marriage to
collapse, but the young wife bravely holds her family close and
solves the mystery of the haunting by connecting with her
native American roots.   .   315 pages

13.**Dark Before Dawn**, ISBN 978-1-929440-10-8 $22.00

117 adventurous British citizens arrive on Roanoke Island to begin
a colony in a dangerous life and death scenario. Daily life becomes
grim and starvation a reality as the ships fail to return. Meet the real
colonists in their struggle to survive and create a life sustaining
reality as Powhatan plans an evil revenge and few colonists escape the
massacre. The Croatoan Indians are the pilgrims only friends and perhaps are the only ones to witness the fate of the Lost Colony.   384 pages

14. **Heart of Stone, Screenplay,** ISBN 978-1-929440-09-2 $25.00

15. **Miracles, Screenplay**, ISBN 978-1-929440-08-5 $25.00

Being Written: Forgotten Patriot, Letters and Papers of William Grayson,
founding Father & Patriot, by Lucy Baker .

William Grayson at Sixteen

by Lucy Baker

William Grayson was 54 when he died, on March 12, 1790

by Lucy Baker

William Grayson's Great granddaughter Nancy Farmer
Grayson married my great grandfather, Henry Bascom Baker.

LUCY BAKER'S BIOGRAPHY

Lucy Baker was born in Berkeley, CA. She has American Indian and Teutonic warriors on her father's side. Her mother, Lucia Amelia was a German heiress who met Walter Baker, an American soldier serving in the occupation in Germany following WWI. They married in Brussels, before moving to California where Lucy and Claire were born.

The girls visited Germany every year until the death of their beloved Grossfater in 1938.

Heir to the Tellenbrock fortune, the girls were cheated from inheriting by their Uncle Hugo who had been a schemer since his marriage to Lucia's sister Cecilia.

After her parents divorced, a new marriage brought a brilliantly achieving step-father who served in high positions with the Am. government. On their way to sojourn in Europe in 1938, the family was stopped by a German submarine and finally released only to find themselves trapped in war torn Germany. While waiting two years for exit visas the girls went to school in Wurzburg.

Finally back in Bethesda, Maryland, Lucy began Ballet classes at the Washington School of Ballet in 1939/40. Quickly advancing to premier danseuse (soloist) with the Washington Concert Ballet, Lucy perormed with the National Symphony Orchestra at the National Theatre and Constitution Hall.

Lucy has been designing, painting and writing her whole life. Her favorite media is water color. She has had many art shows and written 12 books and three screenplays.

At 17 she entered Abbott Art School in Washington D.C. to major in Costume Design. She returned after marriage to study Interior Design. She did work in both fields before and after marrige.

Lucy sang opera and especially loved operettas. Several operatic companies asked her to join. Lucy eloped with David Harfield with whom she had two wonderful daughters. In her second marriage she had four more children. They are today a very close family.

Involved in the Arts all her life, Lucy will tell you how blessed her life has been. She still writes and paints everyday and keeps engaged in artistic projects, and her flower and vegetable garden.

Discovering her relative William Grayson, she became his biographer with the screenplay, "The Life of William Grayson," then William Grayson and the Constitution, 1788, and is working on "Letters and Speeches of William Grayson"

Lucy has lived in europe and travelled extensively. She owned Morning Glory Guest House in St.Maarten and now resides in Boynton Beach, Florida.